Early Modern Literature in History

General Editor: **Cedric C. Brown**
Professor of English and Head of Department, University of Reading

Within the period 1520–1740 this series discusses many kinds of writing, both within and outside the established canon. The volumes may employ different theoretical perspectives, but they share an historical awareness and an interest in seeing their texts in lively negotiation with their own and successive cultures.

Arthur F. Marotti (*editor*)
CATHOLICISM AND ANTI-CATHOLICISM IN EARLY MODERN
ENGLISH TEXTS

Mark Thornton Burnett
MASTERS AND SERVANTS IN ENGLISH RENAISSANCE DRAMA AND CULTURE
Authority and Obedience

The series Early Modern Literature in History is published in association with
the Renaissance Texts Research Centre at the University of Reading.

Early Modern Literature in History
Series Standing Order ISBN 0-333-71472-5
(*outside North America only*)

You can receive future titles in this series as they are published by placing a standing order.
Please contact your bookseller or, in case of difficulty, write to us at the address below with
your name and address, the title of the series and the ISBN quoted above.

Customer Services Department, Macmillan Distribution Ltd, Houndmills, Basingstoke,
Hampshire RG21 6XS, England

'This Double Voice'

Gendered Writing in Early Modern England

Edited by

Danielle Clarke

and

Elizabeth Clarke

First published in Great Britain 2000 by
MACMILLAN PRESS LTD
Houndmills, Basingstoke, Hampshire RG21 6XS and London
Companies and representatives throughout the world

A catalogue record for this book is available from the British Library.

ISBN 0–333–67745–5 hardcover
ISBN 0–333–67746–3 paperback

First published in the United States of America 2000 by
ST. MARTIN'S PRESS, INC.,
Scholarly and Reference Division,
175 Fifth Avenue, New York, N.Y. 10010

ISBN 0–312–23220–9

Library of Congress Cataloging-in-Publication Data
"This double voice" : gendered writing in early modern England / edited by
Danielle Clarke and Elizabeth Clarke
p.   cm. — (Early modern literature in history)
Includes bibliographical references and index.
ISBN 0–312–23220–9
1. English literature—Early modern, 1500–1700—History and criticism. 2.
Women and literature—England—History—16th century. 3. Women and litera-
ture—England—History—17th century. 4. English literature—Women authors—
History and criticism. 5. English literature—Male authors—History and criticism.
6. Literature and history—Great Britain. 7. Gender identity in literature. 8. Sex
role in literature. 9. Men in literature. I. Clarke, Danielle, 1966– II. Clarke,
Elizabeth, 1954– III. Series.
PR113 .D68   2000
820.9'9287'09031—dc21
                                                                99–088692

This book is printed on paper suitable for recycling and made from fully managed and sustained
forest sources.

10   9   8   7   6   5   4   3   2   1
09   08   07   06   05   04   03   02   01   00

Printed and bound in Great Britain by
Antony Rowe Ltd, Chippenham, Wiltshire

Contents

Notes on the Contributors

Amy Boesky is Associate Professor of English at Boston College. She is the author of *Founding Fictions: Utopias in Early Modern England* (1996) and of various articles in *English Literary History*, *Journal of Modern Philology*, and *Milton Studies*. She is currently writing a book on early modern constructions of time, identity and desire.

Danielle Clarke is Lecturer in English at University College Dublin. She has published articles on gender and writing in the early modern period, and is the editor of *Three Renaissance Women Poets*, (forthcoming). She is currently working on a book on the politics of early modern women's writing.

Elizabeth Clarke is Research Lecturer at Nottingham Trent University, where she is director of the A.H.R.B.-funded Perdita Project for early modern women's manuscript compilations. Her book, *Theory and Theology in George Herbert's Poetry,* was published in 1997. She is the author of several articles on women's manuscript writing and is working on a book for Macmillan on the forms and significations of devotional rhetoric in the seventeenth century.

Lorna Hutson is Professor of English Literature at the University of Hull. She is the author of *Thomas Nashe in Context* (1989) and *The Usurer's Daughter* (1994) and of various articles on Renaissance literature and culture.

James Loxley is Lecturer in the Department of English at the University of Edinburgh. He is the author of articles on Marvell, and a book, *Royalism and Poetry in the English Civil Wars: the Drawn Sword*, (Macmillan, 1997). He is currently working on problems in poetics in the early modern period.

Diane Purkiss is Professor of English at the University of Exeter. She is the author of *The Witch in History* (1996) and editor of *Three Tragedies by Renaissance Women* (1998). She has completed a book entitled *Broken Men: Masculinity and the Irrational in the English Civil War* (forthcoming), and is working on a book on fairies, *Darkness Visible*.

Rosalind Smith is a lecturer in the Department of English at the University of Newcastle, Australia. She recently completed a DPhil at the University of Oxford on sonnet sequences attributed to women in the English Renaissance, and has an article on Lady Mary Wroth's 'Pamphilia to Amphilanthus' forthcoming in *English Literary Renaissance*.

Jane Stevenson is co-editor of the forthcoming *Oxford Book of Early Modern Women Poets,* and is also writing a monograph on women poets writing in Latin, *Poetissae: Women and the Language of Authority*. Recent publications include 'Women and Classical Education in the Early Modern Period', in *Pedagogy and Power*, ed. Y-L. Too and N. Livingstone (1998), and a collection of fiction, *Several Deceptions* (1999).

Alan Stewart is Lecturer in English at Birkbeck College, University of London. He is the author of *Close Readers: Humanism and Sodomy in Early Modern England* (1997) and, in co-authorship with Lisa Jardine, of *Hostage to Fortune: The Troubled Life of Francis Bacon 1561–1626* (1998). An editor of the Oxford Francis Bacon, he is currently preparing volume 5 (Writings 1608–1612).

Frances Teague is Professor of English at the University of Georgia. Her books include *Bathsua Makin: Woman of Learning* (1998), *Shakespeare's Speaking Properties* (1991) and *The Curious History of 'Bartholomew Fair'* (1985).

Helen Wilcox is Professor of English Literature at the University of Groningen, The Netherlands. Her research interests include early modern devotional and autobiographical texts, women's writing and Shakespeare. Among her recent publications is *Women and Literature in Britain, 1500–1700* (1996). Her annotated edition of Herbert's poems is forthcoming, and she is currently preparing, with Elizabeth Clarke, an anthology of seventeenth-century English women's devotional verse.

Marion Wynne-Davies is Senior Lecturer at the University of Dundee. She has published widely in the field of early modern literature including *Women Poets of the Renaissance* (1999) and, with S.P. Cerasano, *Renaissance Drama by Women: Texts and Documents* (2nd edition, 1999) and *Readings in Renaissance Women's Drama: Criticism, History, and Performance 1594–1698* (1998).

Acknowledgements

There comes a point in the production of any collaborative volume when you think that your chosen title is a prophecy rather than a description. This book has been 'doubled' in all sorts of ways, not least by the fact of its being edited in two different countries, and in multiple computer formats. Volumes of essays are nothing without their contributors, and we would like to thank ours for their enthusiasm, patience and commitment: many of these essays were researched and written in specific response to the project. The intimate acquaintance with the writing of so many gifted people necessitated by the editing process has been one of the pleasures and privileges of putting together this volume. Elizabeth Clarke's work has been made possible by a Research Lectureship from Nottingham Trent University: Danielle Clarke is grateful for the granting of a President's Research Grant from University College Dublin, offering welcome financial assistance in travel costs and index production. Several people have facilitated the production of this volume: the series editor, Cedric Brown, who was enthusiastic about the project from the very beginning, and moved with flattering speed to sign us up: Charmian Hearne, who worked very hard to secure this volume, and whose patience and encouragement has made it a pleasure to work with Macmillan. Several of the essays were tried out in the supportive and stimulating environment of the Women, Text and History seminar at Oxford University. We have been glad of the friendship and advice of Ros Ballaster, Lorna Hutson, Sarah Poynting, Diane Purkiss and David Norbrook.

Danielle Clarke would like to thank, first and foremost, Elizabeth, who has been a supportive, incisive and sympathetic co-editor. Colleagues and friends have played their part in providing advice and diversion: particular debts are owed to Andrew Carpenter, Janet Clare, Róisín Collins, Susan McNulty and Maria Stuart. Elizabeth Macfarlane has been unfailing in her support, not only reading my work, but providing hospitality and criticism of the highest quality.

Elizabeth Clarke would like to thank Nigel Smith, Jeremy Maule and David Norbrook who provided encouragement at various stages of the project, and in particular Danielle, whose intelligence and stylishness made the process of editing a mind-expanding experience, and who wrote a marvellous introduction to the volume. I am very grateful to my family, especially Matthew who provided welcome computer advice at various points, to my mother, who is an emergency baby-sitter whenever a deadline looms, and to Emily and Lucy whose unfailing affection and cheerfulness maintain morale.

During the production of this book, four people closely associated with it did their bit to increase its readership: Lucy, Miranda, Robbie and Ellie are happily welcomed to the new future which we have tried to gesture towards.

Introduction

Danielle Clarke

I see a voice

(*Midsummer Night's Dream*, V.i.190)

Are there sound mirages? When you hear a voice, do you ever really know who is speaking?

(Janette Turner Hospital, *Oyster*, p. 7)

The title for this volume comes from Shakespeare's 'A Lovers Complaint' where many of the concerns of these essays are fore-shadowed. It belongs to the amorphous but influential Renaissance sub-genre of complaint, variously turned to address social, economic and political issues, as well as providing a pretext for the recreation of a vernacular English history and a repeated examination of the proper place of the articulate woman within Elizabethan and Jacobean society.[1] Not a canonical form *per se*, the complaint took up residence in a variety of forms, both popular and élite, straddling the divide between print and manuscript cultures, between the reinvigoration of classical literature and the durability of the ballad tradition. Whilst the contexts for the complaint impinge upon and are influenced by the interpellation of gender into most aspects of Renaissance culture, even by negation, the main interest of complaint poems for the issues addressed in this volume lies in their explicit focus on the poetic voice and their interest in this voice as somehow 'sexed'. It is not at all remarkable that a writer described by a particular sexual category should depart from that taxonomy for the purposes of literary writing – without such imaginative fluidity, Western literature could scarcely exist. But we believe that an investigation of the terms of such an exchange, and of the meanings attached to voices designated as 'male'

1

and 'female' within textual artifacts, is long overdue. This entails a rigorous scrutiny of the process whereby such constructions are referred back to the sex of the author. The gynocritical tendency to attribute certain qualities to the text on the basis of the writer's sex has proved a valuable critical and political tactic, but it now looks simplistic as a methodology, and it disables any attempt to examine the ways in which texts themselves contribute to the networks of meanings hovering around the gendering of authorship.[2] Furthermore, the category of sex can no longer be assumed to be an unproblematic biological given; nor can it be taken to be ontologically stable; nor, in this period, can the author be situated outside the text as a biographical entity who can oversee or guarantee the meanings of the text.[3] The sex of the author is neither a reliable nor an authentic indication of the speaker's gender, and this is as true for women's writing as for that by men. There is much to be learned, we suggest, from an investigation of the representation of women's speech by men (subject matter, syntax, style, form, as well as conventional wisdom on this matter), and from the recognition that women writers too produce culturally determined *representations* of their own speech, rather than acting (or speaking) purely as autonomous agents in their own right.[4] In short, the essays in *'This Double Voice'* mark a shift away from the essentialization of women's voices in this period, choosing to situate them in the context of the gendered constructedness of all literary voices. In line with recent developments spearheaded by the encounter of queer theory with deconstructive criticism, our attention is directed to gender as a discursive and unstable field.[5] Within an extended feminist framework there is still much work to do, both bibliographical and critical, but it is our contention that we need to rethink our basic categories of analysis.

The germane aspect of Shakespeare's poem is the degree to which the male poet represents the female voice simultaneously as being multiply mediated, and as subject to the poet's control, by the self-conscious display of rhetorical tropes and figures, puns and word-play. Rather than being an autonomous utterance in its own right, the woman's voice is revealed to the reader through the framework of an overtly artificial discourse. Whilst this is arguably true of male literary speech in this period, it remains true, by and large, that the *conditions* of utterance betray notions of linguistic difference, traceable to the posited sex of the speaker. The articulate woman speaks upon different terms from the eloquent man; frequently, her articulation amounts to saying that she cannot, or will not, speak (this may have a bearing on the particular use made by women writers in this period of the humility *topos*). The narrative of Shakespeare's lamenting woman is self-consciously placed within the distorting and disembodied precedent of the myth of Echo, and further distanced from the 'original' utterance by Shakespeare's poetic record of a voice marked by its secondariness:

> From off a hill whose concave womb reworded
> A plaintful story from a sist'ring vale,
> My spirits t'attend this double voice accorded,
> And down I laid to list the sad-tuned tale.[6]

Kerrigan comments upon the architectonic doublings at work here, and notes that the poem as a whole draws attention not only to a structural doubleness 'because the Danielesque maiden recounts, within her complaint, the plaint which has wrought her downfall' (p. 16), but to the duplicity of the male lover himself. Hence, the 'lover' of the title might refer to either the maiden or to the young man. But Kerrigan misses the careful distinction between speakers made in the poem. Although the young man's verbal deception is immoral, he is presented as (mis)using language in the process of conscious persuasion. His narrative is introduced in terms which anticipate Donne's use of the image of the lover as besieged city and recall the devices of the Ovidian narrator in the *Amores*:

> And long upon these terms I held my city,
> Till thus he 'gan besiege me.

> (ll.176–7)

This echo allies the speaker with Ovid's aggressive lover, who uses words as tokens of sex, and therefore highlights the lover's act of imaginative imitation, his rhetorical control and his deliberate deception. However destabilized his speech might have been by the opening frame, his duplicity is a moral and rhetorical quality. It is immoral precisely because it is calculated to deceive: 'This is moral Doublespeak of the worst, most complacent kind' (Kerrigan, p. 16). The doubleness of his speech is an effect, something motivated and made possible by the fact that male speech is understood to signify on its own terms; indeed, this self-sufficiency is what makes the maiden's deception possible in the first place. Her deception, on the other hand, proceeds from her lack of linguistic scepticism, her failure to perceive the instability of the relationship between language and meaning, an irony which is under-scored by her own unwitting repetition of the Ovidian trope.

By contrast, the maiden's narrative, whilst it forms the subject of the poem, is constantly being wrenched away from her, displaced into other voices and other sources. From the opening lines, it is voiced by her but is not her own, refracted and fragmented, the cryptic trace of the (absent) originary utterance. Her grief is represented in terms of a textualized physicality, loosely recalling the conventions of Ovid's *Heroides*: 'Tearing of papers, breaking rings a-twain' (1.6); her handker-chief has on it 'conceited characters' (1.16). Her 'often reading what contents it bears' (1.19) implies a fissure between what she reads and what she says; in neither case does the narrative clearly 'belong to' or originate with her. The indirect invocation of the figure of Echo in the opening lines situates the problematic plurality of this poem in relation to a conventional Renaissance figure which foregrounds, as Hollander suggests, 'such matters as the inherence of voice in source, and the relative presences of either'.[7] Concerns such as these – namely: Who is speaking when a woman speaks? Is a masculine subject position a necessary precondition to writing? Is it possible to discern the trace of gender in the voice? – are central to the intelligent exploration of the connections between narrative and gender, untrammelled by prior assumptions derived from the identification of the author's sex.

In Shakespeare's poem, the absent presence of Echo alerts the reader to the Ovidian precedent of the bereft and disembodied mourner, whose speech not only asserts its derivative status, but displays the constructedness of discourse itself. It is also an instructive example of the complexity of the connections between voice, gender, imitation and culture. According to John Hollander, Echo is not merely a 'musical or linguistic repetition', but 'in some way a qualified version' (p. 3). Just as Shakespeare posits an imaginary narrative and then derives an echoic variation from it, echo is not simply repetitive, but powerfully transformative. Ovid's Echo can only repeat the last words of what has been uttered, but in her pursuit of Narcissus seeks to turn this to her own rhetorical advantage:

> How often she wished to make flattering overtures to him, to approach him with tender pleas! But her handicap prevented this, and would not allow her to speak first; she was ready to do what it would allow, to wait for sounds which she might re-echo with her own voice.[8]

As the story proceeds, it is clear that through the device of echoing Narcissus' anxious questions are turned into powerful assertions by Echo, trangression registered by diminished copying: 'he called out: "Is anybody here?" Echo answered: "Here"!' (p. 84). His terrified 'I would die before I would have you touch me' becomes the sexually overt 'I would have you touch me!' (p. 84). As Hollander suggests, such fragmented repetition frequently has a destabilizing effect upon the originating discourse, a process of linguistic subversion easily identified in an inherently comparative form such as echo (pp. 7–12). Her punishment is to lose her body, to become nothing but voice, incapable of enacting the demands her voice had made upon Narcissus, exposing the absence at the heart of language. Within this powerful myth we can see that a process of retrospective substitution is at work: Echo is punished by Juno for her garrulity and thus her betrayal of the moral task of unmasking Jove's infidelity, making her a type of trangressive femininity. She loses her body for her subversion of speech to erotic ends, and finally her disembodied voice is troped as feminine because of its emptiness, its belatedness and its inability to signify except in relation to an already established discourse.

Hollander's suggestive book stresses the transformative power of echo (and its rhetorical cognates), but consistently assumes the gender neutrality of what he calls 'the presence of disembodied voice' (p. 6). Yet as his own examples conclusively reveal, the business of echo is thoroughly grounded in the gendered dynamics of literary production; she may be disembodied, but Echo's voice is always somehow female. This is not a matter of a sexed identification, but rather of the positioning of the figure in relation to inherited texts, its reorientation towards a new set of contemporary readers and the masculine rivalry which underwrites the act of imitation.[9] Seemingly, it is the very echo of Echo that renders the repetition of autonomous utterance a particularly feminine property, the unspoken invocation of Ovid within the act of revocalization itself. If, as Hollander argues, echo is a trope, then it is a trope that is understood to signify as feminine. But it is also largely deployed by male writers in the attempt to situate themselves in relation to literary tradition, in a double gesture of invocation and diminution 'melting by degrees, and every reflection more weak and shady than the former'.[10] The 'femininity' of Echo is evoked in order to voice anxieties regarding literary dependency and (in)fidelity to the poetic heritage; arguably, Echo serves as a feminine figure onto which such worries can be displaced, a means of self-conscious but distanced reflexiveness about the poetic enterprise.

The classical precedent of Echo often provides an occasion for reflection upon imitation, confronting the fear of diminution, and presents a male version of the female voice. It supplies a troubling connection between the failed encounter with literary forebears, displacing the threat of subjugation to a source or antecedent on to a tragic female and playing upon the disjunction of speaker and text. Sandys' translation of Ausonius demonstrates this quite clearly:

> Daughter of aire and tongue: of judgment blind
> The mother I; a voice without a mind.
> I only with anothers language sport:
> And but the last of dying speech retort.

> (quoted in Hollander, p. 9)

The force of Ausonius' epigram is heightened by the meta-commentary supplied by Sandys' own engagement in translation, which has uncanny parallels with the workings of echo in its repetition of another's language, and its own perpetuation of 'dying speech'.

What this amounts to is the seemingly uncontroversial assertion that authorial sex and textual gender are not at all the same thing: neither, apparently, is the creation of a female voice purely and simply a matter of the representation of that voice. The field of Renaissance criticism seems quite comfortable with this notion, viewing a variety of female utterances, from Britomart to Mistress Quickly, as complex inscriptions of writerly anxieties about sexuality, power and writing. Yet such readings work precisely because the masculinity of the writer has been taken as the norm against which all variations must be judged and measured: the particular investments and aims of feminist criticism are such that there is little interest in assuming the reversibility or flexibility of this paradigm. Hence, although post-structuralism and its cognate fields of critical theory have forced us to scrutinize the investments of the male literary voice much more closely, it has failed to upend the idea that female-scripted voices are always and unproblematically female. Not only is it naive in the extreme to preclude or wilfully ignore the fact that women writers use the male voice, or to assume that doing so can necessarily be attributed to the pressures bequeathed by a monolithic patriarchalism: such a reading strategy tends to reproduce the very power dynamic that it purports to disrupt and displace. This model leaves us in the position where the field of discourse is primarily occupied by the male voice, marked by its visibility and flexibility, its rhetorical power to invent and imagine, whereas the female voice always proceeds from the body, from the interior spaces of experience, maternity and privacy. Whilst moves are being made to rhetoricize the female-authored voice in work on the early modern period, we still find texts being treated as autobiographical or private documents, when the point would seem to be that the self-construction of the female voice in particular generic forms is only partly the product of exclusionism; it is also, to some extent, a motivated choice. It is crucial to distinguish between material conditions and their effect upon the contours and texture of a piece of writing, and to identify a retrospective appropriation of those texts to serve the interests of a belated and beleaguered feminism. We need to start to shift the ground, or at least open it up for debate if the study of gender in the early modern period is not to fall into anachronism and misreading, as Margaret Ezell's critiques have demonstrated.[11] This is not only central to an understanding of how women inscribe themselves within texts, but the models they work with, within and against, as Grosz suggests:

> It is crucial that feminists ... now turn to the question of the status and nature of textuality, if feminism is to understand not only what a feminist text is but, as significantly, what constitutes a patriarchal text, what the possible (and actual) relations between them are, as well as what the political investments feminism itself has in trying to set up a clear-cut and definitive separation between its products and those of the patriarchal orthodoxy it seeks to undermine.[12]

One might argue that in relation to the Renaissance, this needs to be taken a step further still: not only are most of the texts in question not feminist in any legible sense, they are also subject to a series of conditions and regulations which we do not always recognize. If these texts refuse to yield up feminism, it may also be the case that feminism, as it has been applied, does not yield up the texts.

It has become a commonplace of literary criticism that a difference can be asserted, if not analysed and clearly discerned, between male representations of women and female-authored representations of women. This paradigm of literary difference has been adopted almost wholesale as part of a wider feminist strategy to place writings by women within the confines of the canon in the face of objections relating to quality, quantity and significance. Yet difference itself is a problematic premise, particularly when it is understood in terms of a

series of binarisms or polarities. Difference is not a qualitative distinction, and whilst we can recognize that social structures will often
organize difference(s) hierarchically, such differences are often the
symbolic means by which a hierarchy is expressed: they are not constitutive of it, however invisible or naturalized they are made to seem.
In the face of economic and institutional imperatives to justify the
validity of one project over another, difference has been variously
mobilized in relation to women's writing to mean 'inferior' (for its
detractors) or 'superior' (for its advocates). Difference cannot be
reduced to a simple or single trajectory: difference is a nexus of
elements, a cluster of forces social, economic and ideological. A further
difficulty regarding the notion of difference, as used gynocritically as
opposed to deconstructively, is that it leaves the very binarism it is
designed to displace or unsettle wholly intact. It is our undertaking
here to rethink difference, and to render it more thoroughly plural,
precisely by reading texts in context, and resisting their reduction to
the single frame of gender.

The project of *'This Double Voice'* is not primarily to continue or
repeat the arguments for attending to women's writings in this period:
such arguments are by now quite well rehearsed, even if practice lags
behind the theory. Rather, it is to engage critically with the assumptions underlying feminist readings of the Renaissance, sometimes to
critique those assumptions, sometimes to modify them, sometimes to
undermine them. Inevitably, in the best tradition of Echo, this pre-
supposes an unease or disquiet, as well as a homage, in relation to
what has preceded us. Feminist scholarship has bequeathed us a
contradictory and paradoxical legacy in the early modern period. On
the one hand, the literary-historical map has been, and is being,
redrawn in far-reaching ways, from the rediscovery of manuscript
miscellanies compiled by women, to the integration of women's
writing in the classical languages, and the uncovering of archive
evidence relating to female gossip networks and the organization of
female social space.[13] New editions of texts by Renaissance women, in
all their plurality, are appearing with great frequency. On the other
hand, the basic paradigms have yet to shift: as Ezell suggests, this is
partly attributable to the fact that the critical methodologies for the
discovery and interpretation of texts by women were established
through readings of nineteenth- and twentieth-century Anglo-
American texts and gradually inched their way backwards chronologic-
ally.[14] Thus, such models are derived from notions of authorship,
publication and literary value which cannot be applied without serious

modification to a period where such notions were at least in flux, if not in the infancy of their formulation.[15]

It is not our intention to undermine the painstaking work involved in the 'recovery' of Renaissance women writers: without it, little of our work would be possible. But there are ways in which the very methodologies which restored this material to us stand in the way of interpretation. This is a crucial difficulty, because the feminist frame which led to the discovery of these writers is the very same frame which has led us to misread them: we are all working within a bizarre form of 'double-think', where what the material tells us is fundamentally at odds with what drew us towards them in the first place. Inevitably, the excavation of 'forgotten' texts and traces by women was based upon the unproblematic inscription of a an ontologically stable female subject, defined primarily in terms of sex, and only secondarily by class, religion or political allegiance. This is fine and necessary up to a point, but it does fundamentally skew what we think we find, if at some level the category of sex, and as a consequence, that of gender, is somehow fixed in advance. Also, once the first stage has been completed, the reinstatement of known, usually noble women for whom documentation exists, the female subject and the textual traces she leaves behind, become more problematic.[16] What is female agency, and how might we identify it? If, as Frances Dolan has recently suggested, we privilege literacy as the sign of agency and subjecthood, where else might we look, and how do we 'read' what we find there?[17] Perhaps most importantly of all, how might we answer Jonathan Goldberg's searching question about 'the gendered difference between a man's hand and a woman's'?[18] The conflicts that we confront in this peculiarly doubled activity of reading texts by early modern women (and indeed those by men) are multiple.

Such multiplicity should be embraced and not shirked. There is no place for the imposition of a critical orthodoxy on this diverse body of material: one might argue that this has precisely been the problem. The need to 'rescue' women from the margins has replicated the model that it aimed to displace, by rendering women's constructedness visible, whilst often assuming a stable construction for men. Hence women remain 'other', on the outside of Renaissance culture. Neither does the strategy of incorporating women as ready formed subjects particularly help: it leads us to impose anachronistic expectations and norms about self-expression, autonomy and independence upon women who did define their roles partly in relation to men, a situation deeply embedded in social and institutional structures, from land distribution to seating in churches. These two dynamics, the assumption of female subjectivity as given and distinct on the one hand, and the notion that the discourse of gender is just that on the other, leaves us with two apparently irreconcilable positions. *Either* women can be situated as historical subjects, *or* we interrogate gender in such a way as to negate not only the specificity of the female subject, but its very possibility.

We wish to suggest in this volume, by looking at a number of gendered texts, from a variety of critical positions, that there might be a way of drawing together these disparate strands. Furthermore, that it is actually necessary to do so. Plurality and contestation in the field of early modern feminist studies is a vital sign; it indicates that we are moving beyond a ghettoization of female-authored texts, and that they are no longer in thrall to our late twentieth-century narratives of how women are inscribed and how they behave. The essays gathered here reflect this multiplicity in all its complexity, by attending to narratives of gender across the divide of sex, by unsettling the fixity of gendered positions inherent in a comparative approach, and pulling in new areas of inquiry which dispense with clear disciplinary boundaries. The range of approaches that the project elicited elucidates the difficulties attendant upon the investigation of gender in the early modern period, and the unlikelihood of reaching clear, epistemic conclusions.

The aim, at all points, has been to investigate the assumptions behind feminist criticism on the period: hence the volume opens with a clear challenge to the oft-repeated axiom that women were excluded from the dynamics of Latin humanist discourse and hence precluded from the prevalent constructions of authorship. Jane Stevenson situates neo-Latin women writers within an ongoing and exemplary tradition, thereby challenging the notion that the republic of letters had no room for women. The theme of the availability of the classical literary tradition is continued in those essays which deal centrally with the use of Ovid's *Heroides*, a paradigmatic text for the investigation of the inscription of the female-gendered voice within male rhetorical culture. Despite the *Heroides'* central place as a founding text for the literary construction of gender in the early modern period, few studies have placed this aspect centrally.[19] Lorna Hutson's essay unpicks the assumptions underlying notions of credible character, demonstrating that not only are interpretations of Renaissance texts conditioned by modern expectations, but that the *Heroides* have frequently been read in terms of the morality of the woman speaker, rather than in relation to legal ideas of breach of promise and equity. Danielle Clarke's essay echoes these arguments, in its suggestion that the constructed women of the *Heroides* are re-presented by male writers in contextual and ideological ways in order to contain or offset the potential threat enshrined by the model of the vengeful articulate woman. She demonstrates that whilst women did utilize the precedent of Ovid's speaking heroines, they do not do so straightforwardly, but are forced to reproduce the conditions of utterance on their own terms, and within quite different forms of textual circulation.

One of the greatest strengths of feminist criticism, buttressed by new historicism's attention to textual artifacts rather than *belles-lettres* literature, has been its willingness to look beyond mainstream genres and forms. Two of the essays here build upon this impulse, and take it a stage further by investigating the gendered underpinnings of two quite different discourses. Diane Purkiss reads a number of diverse texts against one another – the empowering myth of the fairy queen is set against reformulations of fictions of maternal power in popular literature, suggesting that the particular ways in which gender is configured is contingent upon a complex network of influences: class, region, religion. Amy Boesky explores one of the master discourses, that of time, through a careful examination of material culture, in particular, the differing meanings attached to male and female ownership of time-pieces. She illustrates how the ideas of sexual difference articulated in the giving of watches can be discerned in sixteenth-century writing, tracing an integral and mutually informing connection between material culture and literary practice.

Given the preponderance of devotional writing in the period as a whole and within women's writings in particular, it is not surprising to find many of our contributors looking at the differences between male and female participation in religious literature. Again, in this field, it has too often been taken for granted that women were merely rehearsing, without reflection, either what male culture prescribed, or their personal and spiritual concerns. Questions of voice, subjectivity and authority are particularly vexed in this area, whatever the gender of the speaker, for there is a sense in which his/her voice is always not his/her own, as Mary Sidney's dedicatory poem to the Psalm metaphrases clearly indicates: 'hee did warpe, I weav'd this webb to end; / the stuffe not ours, our worke no curious thing'.[20] Not only is the Countess of Pembroke engaged in the collocation of multiple inter-texts, her 'original' itself is written in a number of voices, her work is collaborative in a personal and a textual sense, and the 'voice' at work in the Psalms is ultimately that of God. Helen Wilcox's essay addresses the differences at work in male and female attempts to hybridize the secular lyric with religious content, illustrating a recurrent theme in these essays, namely that women writers' search for adequate authorization often bequeaths them models of marginality, or at least a highly contested relationship to the discourses in which they write. The area of spirituality is an overtly contestatory one, where the gendered body of the author can be seen to interact most forcefully with an already gendered sacred rhetoric in the construction of a subjectivity for poet and God, and where the ownership of the text is particularly vexed. The issue of attribution is addressed in Rosalind Smith's essay, where she asserts that the desire for reclamation of women's texts has sometimes blinded us to their complexities, in particular, the degree to which they depend upon male literary networks.[21] Smith argues, and the editors would concur, that if these texts are to be read as historically as possible, then it is vital that they are seen as a part of such networks, rather than as separate from them. Only in this way will it be possible to redistribute the focus from the private and domestic to the public and political. However, as Elizabeth Clarke's essay shows, this is easier said than done, especially when we consider the very real (and gendered) differences found in the metaphors used by writers themselves to describe literary production. She deals with a particular problem: the presentation of women's lyrics as 'babes' or 'offspring', whilst male poets prefer the title 'ejaculations', and shows, through an examination of the lyrics of the 1650s, that questions of religious and political affiliation have to be considered if gender is to be fully understood.

Clarke's and Smith's essays suggest the importance, long remarked by the New Bibliographers, of assessing the role played by paratexts and contexts in the reception of Renaissance texts.[22] It is often here that we find established *topoi* being manoeuvred and rewritten in powerfully gendered ways. Two of the essays here deal explicitly with the functions of paratexts in constructing authorial images. James Loxley uncovers the connections between Katherine Philip's use of voice and the gendered constructions found in contemporary Cavalier poetry. He also foregrounds the problematics attached to inferring the gender of the text from the sex of the author, by demonstrating how such a strategy was used to deflect attention from what had been written onto the fascinating and compelling femininity of the author. Alan Stewart too draws attention to the ways in which paratextual features direct interpretation, by pinpointing the fact that Anne Cooke

Bacon's voice cannot be heard separately from its mediations, textual and familial. In particular, he suggests that her voice is heard through the already established roles of wife, noblewoman, pious believer and widow, buttressed and at times contradicted by her particular politico-religious allegiance.

The essays in this volume show, in various ways, the problematics of taking gender as a given, of isolating it as a category unrelated to others, and the difficulty of locating gender unequivocally within specific discourses. Rather than seeking to separate women's writings on the grounds that they are exceptional, these essays stress the degree to which they are necessarily implicated in the culture of which they are a part: this often means that a belated feminism risks either disappointment or distortion unless a more historically rigorous approach is taken. It is becoming increasingly obvious that women writers were in *dialogue* with their male contemporaries, and that often the reverse is also true. Marion Wynne-Davies' essay on the echoes and exchanges between members of the Sidney circle illustrates the fallaciousness of assuming a model of single authorship, and outlines the complex gender negotiations at work in the adaptation and imitation of texts. Frances Teague adopts a fruitfully comparative approach in her exploration of later seventeenth-century writers on education, demonstrating how the dynamics of allusion, indebtedness and departure reflect gendered readings of educational theory and practice.

With their differing approaches to the problematics of gender in the early modern period, these essays can be seen as a representative cross-section of work in this field. Each of them reflects the attempt to situate gender in context and to integrate the frame of gender with other powerful discourses, such as politics, religion and social class. However, they also represent a change of methodological direction, signposts for the way forward.

Notes

1. For a useful, if flawed, account, see John Kerrigan, ed., *Motives of Woe, Shakespeare and the 'Female Complaint': A Critical Anthology* (Oxford: Clarendon Press, 1991).
2. See Elizabeth Grosz, 'Sexual Signatures: Feminism after the Death of the Author', in her *Space, Time and Perversion: Essays on the Politics of Bodies* (New York and London: Routledge, 1995), pp. 9–24.
3. See, for example, Judith Butler, *Bodies That Matter: On the Discursive Limits of 'Sex'* (New York and London: Routledge, 1993). On the anachronism of the notion of the author, see Michel Foucault, 'What is an Author?', in David

Lodge, ed., *Modern Criticism and Theory: A Reader* (London: Longman, 1988), pp. 197–210. The implications of Foucault's essay have been pursued recently by, amongst others, Jeff Masten's *Textual Intercourse: Collaboration, Authorship, and Sexualities in Renaissance Drama* (Cambridge: Cambridge University Press, 1997).

4. Useful beginnings have been made in this area by Douglas Bruster, '"In a Woman's Key": Women's Speech and Women's Language in Renaissance Drama', *Exemplaria* 4 (1992), pp. 235–66, and Juliet Fleming, 'Dictionary English and the Female Tongue', in Jean R. Brink, ed., *Privileging Gender in Early Modern England, Sixteenth Century Essays and Studies XXIII* (Kirksville, 1993), pp. 175–204.

5. The tension between political agendas requiring an identifiable 'subject' and attempts to resituate the formation-process of that 'subject' is marked within queer studies as well as in women's studies. Relevant work in queer theory would include Judith Butler, *Bodies that Matter*, Eve Kosofsky Sedgwick, *Between Men: English Literature and Male Homosocial Desire* (New York: Columbia University Press, 1985), and Elizabeth Grosz, *Space, Time and Perversion*.

6. *The Sonnets and A Lover's Complaint*, ed. John Kerrigan (Harmondsworth: Penguin, 1986), ll. 1–4.

7. John Hollander, *The Figure of Echo: A Mode of Allusion in Milton and After* (Berkeley: University of California Press, 1981), p. 5.

8. Ovid, *Metamorphoses*, trans. Mary Innes (Harmondsworth: Penguin, 1955), p. 84.

9. See George Pigman III, 'Versions of Imitation in the Renaissance', *RQ* 33 (1980): 1–32.

10. George Sandys, trans. Ovid, quoted in Hollander, p. 11.

11. See Margaret J.M. Ezell, *Writing Women's Literary History* (Baltimore: Johns Hopkins University Press, 1993).

12. 'Sexual Signatures', p. 10.

13. See, for example, Arthur F. Marotti, *Manuscript, Print, and the English Renaissance Lyric* (Ithaca, NY: Cornell UP, 1995), pp. 48–61; Brenda M. Hosington, 'England's First Female-Authored Encomium: The Seymour Sisters' *Hecatodistichon* (1550) to Marguerite de Navarre. Text, Translation, Notes, and Commentary', *SP* XCIII (1996), pp. 117–63; Laura Gowing, *Domestic Dangers: Women, Words, and Sex in Early Modern London* (Oxford: Clarendon Press, 1996); and Bernard Capp, 'Separate Domains? Women and Authority in Early Modern England', in *The Experience of Authority in Early Modern England*, ed. Paul Griffiths, Adam Fox and Steve Hindle (Basingstoke: Macmillan, 1996), pp. 117–45.

14. Ezell, p. 4.

15. See Masten, p. 4.

16. It is notable, however, that questions of attribution have not really been intelligently debated within this field. See Rosalind Smith's essay in this volume for a full discussion of these issues.

17. 'Reading, Writing, and Other Crimes', in *Feminist Readings of Early Modern Culture: Emerging Subjects*, ed. Valerie Traub, M. Lindsay Kaplan and Dympna Callaghan (Cambridge: Cambridge University Press, 1996), pp. 142–67, 158–61.

18. In *Sodometries: Renaissance Texts, Modern Sexualities* (Stanford: Stanford University Press, 1992), p. 86.
19. See for example, Jonathan Bate, *Shakespeare and Ovid* (Oxford: Clarendon Press, 1993) and Howard Jacobson, *Ovid's Heroides* (Princeton, NJ: Princeton University Press, 1974).
20. 'Even now that care', in *The Penguin Book of Renaissance Verse 1509–1659*, sel. and introduced by David Norbrook, ed. H.R. Woudhuysen (Harmondsworth: Penguin, 1992), no. 31, ll. 27–8.
21. Jonathan Goldberg provides a provocative account of the problematics of gender and attribution in *Sodometries*, pp. 81–101.
22. For an application of this, see Wendy Wall, *The Imprint of Gender: Authorship and Publication in the English Renaissance* (Ithaca, NY: Cornell University Press, 1993).

1

Female Authority and Authorization Strategies in Early Modern Europe

Jane Stevenson

This essay looks principally at a distinctive group of élite European women: those who write poetry in Latin, the language of authority. Since the world of the humanists was an international one, national boundaries are of less significance to women Latinists than to women writing in vernacular languages. The composition of Latin poetry (particularly in classical metres) is a learned, highly specialized skill, entirely independent of the ability to comprehend or translate Latin texts. Any woman who has left an *oeuvre* of Latin verse is by definition occupying a space normally regarded by men as entirely their own which is far harder to assess than more familiar 'feminine' texts such as letters or translations. These women occupy the same authorial space as educated men, and it is extremely interesting to see the effect of this. Constanza Varano, for example, writes a poem of praise to her fellow woman scholar, Isotta Nogarola of Verona (the birthplace of Catullus), which includes the lines,

> O Verona, city most abundant in your fruits,
> This girl already attracts more praise than the poet Catullus![1]

How could a woman write such a thing about another woman in mid-fifteenth-century Italy? How dared she speak as if Isotta were potentially, herself, an authority?

I want to begin with the problem of finding precedents, or, as pre-modern writers tended to put it, 'authorities'.[2] The identification and citation of authorities is in fact not classical in origin, but Christian. In order to demonstrate the orthodoxy of their own arguments, Christian writers from the fourth century onwards buttress their work with catenae of citations from earlier writers whose orthodoxy is not in doubt. But if author/authorities are by definition male, how can the female subject become an author – is authorship, or is it not, like becoming a father? Could the experience of maternity offer an appropriate paradigm for creation?

Joan Kelly posed a now famous question, 'Did women have a Renaissance?', and was inclined to give it the answer 'no'.[3] It is a question crucial to authority and authorization; and in order to answer it, we must first come to a definition of 'renaissance'. The Renaissance is not, except indirectly, about vernacular literature (which was already thriving in most of the countries of Europe by the late Middle Ages). It began as a scholarly movement, focused on Latin and Greek, and the central humanist project was the joyous, sometimes faintly piratical, extraction of classical texts from their long sleep of ignorance in monastic libraries (as the humanists saw it), and their triumphant relaunching in *editiones principes* from the great humanist publishing houses.[4]

However, viewed from this perspective, women *did* have a Renaissance: a minute one, compared to the mass of writing by men that was flowing from the presses of Europe, but perfectly genuine, which gave women a small and precious group of *auctrices* of their own.[5] And with respect to women's intellectual history, the distinction between 'some' and 'none' has been of far greater significance to the aspirations of later generations than the distinction between 'some' and 'many'. Not, of course, that this is something peculiar about women. We might remember that very few country lads ever found the streets of the city paved with gold; but a tiny number of glittering successes lured thousands to follow in their footsteps. The idea that it can be done at all is the crucial factor, one that arises again and again in women's history.

A symbolically important event in the history of Renaissance rediscovery and reappropriation focuses directly on a woman's body. During the pontificate of Pope Paul III (1534–49), a tomb was opened on the Appian Way, the occupant of which was identified as Cicero's daughter, Tullia.[6] This caused immense excitement among both poets and scholars, not least because it was said to contain a light which was still burning when it was discovered:

> Now as in Tullia's tombe, one lampe burnt cleare
> Unchang'd for fifteen hundred yeare.[7]

This was a truly magical symbol of continuity with the Roman past. It may or may not be fortuitous that the link is through a woman. Thomas More, in an epigram, focuses on this same Tullia, and suggests that she must have been highly educated to earn the love for her which Cicero's letters reveal him to have felt. At the very least, it brought into focus a Roman antiquity populated by women as well as men.

When we look at the print-history of classical women poets, we find that they are far from being an afterthought – it is worth remembering that printing reached Italy only in 1465. A mere seven years later, three editions of Tibullus printed *c.* 1472 compete for the title of *editio principes*, not only of Tibullus, but of his contemporary Sulpicia, some of whose poems are preserved in the so-called *appendix Tibulliana*.[8] A long poem from perhaps the fifth century AD, a satire attributed to a later Sulpicia attested by Martial, was discovered at Bobbio in 1493, believed genuine, and printed twice before the end of the century, in Venice in 1498, and Parma in 1499.[9] Letters attributed to the Virgin Mary circulated in many late medieval manuscripts, and also appeared in the *editio princeps* of St Ignatius' letters, printed in Paris in 1495. The *Cento* of Faltonia Betitia Proba, the 'only woman placed among the Fathers of the Church' (a Mother of the Church?), according to Isidore, was an important schooltext throughout Late Antiquity and the Middle Ages, and into the Renaissance itself.[10] The *editio princeps* of the *Cento* is by Bartolomeo Girardini, Venice, 1472, and there were two sixteenth-century editions (1588 and 1597): in addition, a number of manuscripts still circulated in the fifteenth century.

Similarly, the first printing of the texts of classical Greek women poets goes back to 1494, when Janus Lascaris printed the first edition of the so-called *Greek Anthology* (a huge collection of epigrams and short poems which preserves a number of poems by and about women), based on Planudes' 1301 manuscript edition.[11] Henri Estienne, the scholar-printer of Paris, printed another edition, based on a bigger version of the *Anthology*, in 1566.[12] Somewhat earlier, he had printed Sappho's 'Hymn to Aphrodite', both in his edition of Dionysius of Halicarnassus (1546) and also in his great edition of Anacreon in 1554. The other poem of Sappho's to survive in a near-complete form ('he seems to me equal to the gods ...') was also published in the same year, at Basle, in Francesco Robortello's edition of Longinus. In 1560, Estienne also published a Greek-Latin edition of nine Greek lyric poets, including all the fragments of Sappho's writing then available: the second edition of 1566 printed still more. Significantly, the 1566 edition also includes Ovid's 'Sappho to Phaon', an ominous sign that this was being treated as an authoritative account of Sappho's biography (this text's importance for humanist women will be discussed at length later in this essay).[13] Humanist access to Greek women poets was further extended by Fulvius Ursinus's edition of the works of nine classical Greek *women* poets, published at Antwerp in 1568.[14] Nor was this editorial work ignored. For example, Jean Dorat, French scholar and poet (1508–88), attracted huge audiences, both of future scholars and of contemporary poets, to his lectures on Greek literature: one of his subjects was the Lascaris edition of the *Greek Anthology*.[15]

If we turn now to the most significant women writers of the Latin Middle Ages, Conrad Celtes found the primary manuscript of the tenth-century canoness Hrotsvitha of Gandersheim in 1494 and published it in a lavish folio at Nuremberg in 1501. Some of the epigrams from members of Celtes' literary circle at Nuremberg hail her as a proto-humanist, because of her close study of the classical Latin playwright, Terence.[16] In 1513, Henri Estienne published a *Liber trium virorum et trium spiritalium virginum*, bringing to light mystical writings from High Medieval women visionaries, Hildegard of Bingen, Elizabeth of Schönau and Mechthild of Hackeborn (the latter two translated into Latin). Among more recent writers, St Catherine of Siena (1347–80), one of only two women to be named a Doctor of the Church, was first published in 1472, and many editions followed, including a Spanish translation, printed in 1511, and an English one in 1519. There were, of course, editions of other medieval women writers: I name only a few of the most important.

This rediscovery of women's writing is demonstrably of genuine significance to Renaissance women. Women writers, or would-be writers, who moved in international humanist circles did not necessarily do so in depressed and self-conscious isolation: they often knew about 'the Ancients' (not just Sappho), and they also tended to know about their female contemporaries and immediate predecessors. It sometimes suited the patrons of women scholars to stress their uniqueness, of course, but the rhetoric of Phoenixes, Tenth Muses, and so forth must not be confused with social realities: it conceals much unobtrusive interchange of letters and poems between women themselves.[17] Isotta Nogarola has been much discussed, mostly as a woman whose relationship to the academy was problematic.[18] But she was certainly aware that she and her contemporaries were not breaking absolutely new ground. In a letter of 1436/7, Giorgio Bevilacqua wrote to Isotta and her sister Ginevra, recommending Proba to their attention: since the *editio princeps* of the *Cento* was still 35 years in the future, he must have had one of the many manuscripts. In the same year, Isotta wrote a begging letter to her maternal uncle Antonio Borromeo, asking for money to buy some decades of Livy, and invoking the name of Proba in order to underline that women in the past had gained distinction as scholars.[19] Apart from Proba, she advances the Muses ('the Muses themselves were women'), four Greek women philosophers (Laschenia, Mantinea, Axiothea and Philonia), and Cornelia, mother and educator of the Gracchi. Isotta was writing before the humanist publishing enterprise really got under way. By the end of the fifteenth century, a woman who wished to match herself against a tradition of feminine writing was in a far better position to do so.

Two poems written to Elizabeth Jane Weston in the late sixteenth century are of interest in this connection. Paulus Stransky's poem to her invokes a Latin poetess of antiquity as well as Sappho:

> I tell you, Perilla, living in Ovid's verse, to yield:
> And yield, O Sappho, with your Lesbian lyre.[20]

Humanist Latin verse by men, irrespective of the gender of the addressee, frequently displays a mania for ranking; part, perhaps, of their general fascination with list-making and categorization, to say nothing of their extreme competitiveness. In the case of poems addressed to learned women, the poet is frequently placed in a pecking-order above her contemporaries, and either above or immediately below Sappho. A poem by Wenceslas Ripa, addressed to Weston in the *Parthenicon*, opens with an 'authority', the great French textual scholar, Joseph Justus Scaliger (1450–1509).

> As the great Scaliger tells us, when the great Caesar Domitian was ruling the world
> and the Ausonian [Italian] powers,
> a virgin poetess arose from the family Sulpicius,
> a girl who was called by her family name.
> He thinks this Sulpicia surpasses the Latin poets,
> and the satires of Ausonius to be hers.
> This learned virago was the first who taught young Roman women
> to contend with the Greeks in divine song ...
> Applaud, Muses: if Sappho is your tenth, Sulpicia follows,
> and learned Elizabeth comes as a companion to her.

This can be directly related to the 'Women's Renaissance'. The satire attributed to 'Sulpicia' was printed at Parma in 1499 together with the works of Ausonius. The repeated (punning) use of 'Ausonian' ('Italian' or, 'connected with the fourth-century poet, Decimus Magnus Ausonius') implies that the 1499 edition *and* Scaliger's lecture, essay or letter thereon, were known to both to this Bohemian nobleman and to Weston herself, for otherwise, she would not have been able to make sense of this poem. Scaliger himself was in touch with Weston, who had been brought to his attention by Martin à Baldhoven on the latter's visit to the Netherlands.[21]

Early modern women who moved in advanced humanist circles could appeal, successfully, to the existence of a tradition of *auctrices*, women writers in Latin and Greek. This is the strategy most consistently favoured by women themselves. They argue, or imply, that women have always written, and thus that the tradition of authority either includes women or that a parallel, female tradition has always existed. This strategy does not involve jumping from Sappho to 'the second Sappho'; it is more likely either to invoke a succession of women writers across time (as Isotta Nogarola did in the letter quoted above), or an appeal to the existence and activities of well-known contemporaries. It is usually assumed that the 'litany' of learned women often produced by women writers and their male defenders is drawn from the *defensiones mulierum*: this is sometimes the case (as with Stransky's evocation of Perilla, whose poems have long since been lost), but not always.[22] I hope to demonstrate that, while the *defensiones* may be cited for additional support, the women advanced as models for contemporary woman Latinists were often those whose works were actually available. In either case, this approach refuses to see women's writing as a problem. It simply adds Latin verse composition to the list of élite activities, such as, for example, making music or hunting, practised by both sexes. Here Weston illustrates both of the primary ways in which the tradition of women writers are invoked in the early modern period:

> I should not be said to be able to conquer Praxilla, Sappho
> and learned Corinna with my songs.
> I do not seek to be set in front of you, learned Fulvia;
> since my tiny genius flows from a dried-up fountain.
> O, if my Muse were comparable with the skilful Morellae,
> a praise which was worthy of me would arise from my Muses ...

This poem demonstrates that she knew of *three* ancient Greek poetesses, Praxilla, Corinna and Sappho, suggesting that she knew Ursinus or Estienne's editions of Greek women poets, or some version

of the *Greek Anthology*. It also shows that she was aware of several contemporary women writing in Latin; the recently deceased Olympia
Fulvia Morata (1526–51), and the three learned daughters of Jean de
Morel in Paris, Camille, Lucrèce and Diane. She is quite likely, again, to
have accessed some of their work (which was in print), through
personal connections: one possible route is through Charles Utenhove,
who translated some of Olympia Morata's poetry, taught Camille de
Morel, and arranged the publication of some of her verse.[23] Utenhove
was a good friend of Paul Melissus, Librarian of the Palatine Library at
Heidelberg, who was in turn a friend of Elizabeth Jane Weston's. One
salient feature of the lives of women Latinists in early modern Europe
is that they maintained a lively and active grapevine: they did get to
hear of one another.[24]

In the remainder of this essay, I want to consider other strategies by
which women's writing in the language of authority can be accounted
for, and also to consider which of these strategies were useful to
women, and which were not. First, I want to explore types of Latin
verse which could be seen as responsive to the demands of higher
authority (hence, within the bounds of feminine behaviour), then to
look at some possible role-models. A substantial category of writing
involving the direct encounter with male authority is answer-poetry.
Its importance may be a comment not so much on women writers, but
on the transmission of women's texts. For example, a Polish Latinist,
Philippa Lazea, wrote a collection of poems in Latin (subjects
unknown), which was probably never printed and does not appear in
any manuscript collection. But Jean-Jacques Boissard printed a poem of
hers among his own works, because it explains and contextualizes two
poems of his own, the one which evoked it, and his reply: thus we
know she existed. She is not the only such case. One Anna Suys is said
to have played an active part in the intellectual life of her home city
(Dordrecht), but only a witty verse exchange with another poet is
preserved, printed with his works.[25]

Answer-poetry is important to humanism, since the development of
international links of scholarly *amicitia* is crucial to both to the
humanist enterprise and to humanists' view of themselves as civilized,
'classical' people.[26] Before deducing that all answer-poetry perpetuates
female subordination, we should note that the terms of poetic
exchange are power- rather than gender-based: Boissard, an established
poet, outranked Lazea, a young aspirant, regardless of gender. On the
other hand, Mildred Cecil, Lady Burghley (née Cooke), immensely
powerful and wealthy, dominates a poetic correspondence with the

Scottish poet George Buchanan who, though one of the best Latin poets of the century, was a beneficiary not a dispenser of patronage. Buchanan's poems are evidence for Mildred's position of power as a patron. The first of his four poems collected under the title 'To Mildred, wife of William Cecil, a matron outstanding for her virtue and learning' is a new year *xenium*, apparently sent speculatively, and hinting that the author might benefit from her interest. Her poetic reply accompanied substantial gifts, and the tone of his reply locates him as a client, a position which he is happy to accept.[27] However, the early editors of Buchanan saw no point in including Mildred's poem(s), even if Buchanan himself had kept them, which of course he may not have done. And, while William Cecil appears to have kept practically every word he ever wrote, his wife did not; and since she kept her papers private from him, they were not lumped in with the collection as a whole.[28]

Another kind of verse which ran little risk of evoking male wrath is that in which the subject takes precedence over the author. In the early modern period, *tumuli* (verse necrologies) were a common form of response to the death of an important individual.[29] The woman's necrology on John Dryden, *The Nine Muses*, is a well-known English example.[30] Camille de Morel's first appearance in print, at the tender age of twelve or so, was a contribution to a *tumulus* for the French king Henri II created by her tutor and mentor, Charles Utenhove.[31] It is particularly notable that the death of the French poet-princess Marguerite d'Angoulême called forth tributes from several women, in both Latin and French, including Latin distichs from the three youngest daughters of the Lord Protector of England.[32] Similarly, the impulse to memorialize a loved spouse came upon many widows, as well as upon grieving husbands, and importantly, was socially permissible in the sixteenth century.[33]

The Bible also provided contradictory models for writing women. The Old Testament puts a number of female figures in positions where their words are authoritative, but the most important to early modern women is the personification of *chochma*, Holy Wisdom, the Beloved of God. As an image of supernatural female creativity and power, she is potentially a fertile model for women.[34] The description of Wisdom in Ecclesiasticus overlaps with that of the Bride in the Song of Solomon, identified both with the Church and with the Virgin Mary, creating a single, polysemic, feminine, image of creativity.[35] To some medieval commentators, the Seven Liberal Arts were the daughters or hand-maidens of Wisdom, and hence, the study of the *auctores* was justified because they were a means towards Her: this formulation gives a feminine personification a status beyond that of male authorities. But the principal reason why Holy Wisdom is important is that she was also identified with Minerva, famously in Mantegna's great painting, *The Expulsion of the Vices from the Garden of the Virtues*, a classicization of the old Christian theme of *psychomachia*.[36]

There is a strong element of syncretism in humanist classicism. While most Renaissance scholars were profoundly Christian, they did not look to the Bible for guidance in secular affairs: for humanist women, far and away the most useful role model for women writers was Minerva. Giordano Bruno speaks for many humanists in creating a richly syncretistic figure, a many-layered 'Wisdom', containing the ideas or forms by which God created all things, who is at once a Cabalistic *sephiroth* ('emanation'), a neo-Platonic Idea, a classical goddess, and Ecclesiasticus' *Chochma*:[37]

> In the first grade, the Divine Mind is called and denoted through the *Sephiroth*, *'chochmah'* by the Cabalists. In the second, by Orphic theologians, it is called *Pallas*, or *Minerva*. In the third, it is generally designated by the name *Sophia*.

Other Renaissance neo-Platonists and Cabalists make similar parallel schemes: the Cabalists' three highest *sephiroth* are identified either with the Christian Father, Son (as the *Logos*) and Holy Spirit, or with the neo-Platonists' Zeus, Athena, and Aphrodite.[38] Giovanni Boccaccio, followed by Marsilio Ficino and others, also makes use of the myth of Athena's motherless birth from the head of Zeus, which he understands allegorically: all wisdom has its origin in God.[39] Minerva also replaces Mary in a neo-Platonic Trinity devised by Conrad Celtes: Jupiter, Apollo and Pegasus stand for the three Persons, supported by Minerva, replacing Mary, and Hermes (the messenger) replacing John the Baptist.[40]

So central a figure as Minerva/Wisdom, at once pagan and Christian, was of course invoked by men as well as women. In the Greek tradition she classically favoured men over women: she is Odysseus's constant guardian in the *Odyssey*, and at the end of Aeschylus's *Oresteia*, she specifically argues for the primacy of male rights over female. In the Renaissance she has a special relationship with Leiden University, and many Renaissance academies were similarly under her aegis, but she also had a special meaning for humanist women.[41] For example, when a French writer, Claude de Taillemont, attempted to argue for a just relation between the sexes in 1551, he presented it as a dream delivered to him by Athena.[42] The fact that the Goddess of Wisdom was female (though of a very male-identified kind) and also, unlike Sappho, virginal, made the imitation or invocation of Minerva a possible strategy for a woman anxious to claim classical precedent but nervous of Sappho's mixed reputation. Minerva's strong image as a man's woman made her potentially useful to any woman wishing to present a woman scholar (herself or another) as a splendid anomaly, but also to anyone who wished to associate herself with a nexus of wisdom, learning *and chastity*. Minerva is used, for example, by Philippa Lazea:[43]

> It is enough, if the girls who cultivate Minerva in sweet study reread
>   me;
> It is enough, if Jean-Jacques reads me with his friend Alardus.

This poem is in response to one by Jean-Jacques Boissard which ends,

> Rightly you deserve the additional name of 'The Illyrian Sappho' for
>   your work:
> No girl has ever been more worthy of it.[44]

Notably, this wary refusal of the status of 'Illyrian Sappho' is couched in Sapphic metre. Lazea's use of the figure of Minerva, not Sappho, is also interesting in that she rejects the potentially isolating strategy of Boissard, who wants her to claim primacy over other women poets. Her preference is to see herself as part of a group, something which we see again and again. While she rejects the special claims made for her, she actually asks for something potentially much more upsetting: equality, since 'Alardus', in the above verse, was another friend of Boissard's, Alardus Quintulus of Narni. She is thus asking to be fairly considered by a male contemporary, to be admitted explicitly into a rank-order of poets, not 'poetesses'. Boissard's reply fails to acknowledge this wish.

Another English woman Latinist, Bathsua Rainolds (later Makin) appeals to Minerva in her poem to Anne of Denmark, presented in 1616, which opens:

> Pandora ('all-gifted') is imagined by the Ancients to have had the wit
>   of Minerva,
> the face of Venus, and, O Apollo, your gifts:

if we might think that the doctrines of Pythagoras were true,
O Goddess, it is her soul which has sought your breast.[45]

Although this poem mentions the Queen's beauty, it focuses on her
intelligence and intellectual gifts. James's strong patriarchal principles
led him to deny his wife the place in governance which she felt
entitled to.[46] In the first masque she organized, she chose the part of
Pallas, an identification which stresses masculine, political virtues.[47]
Aemilia Lanyer similarly celebrates Anne as Minerva, supporting and
extending the Queen's valuation of herself, while Johanna Othonia's
epithalamion for Anne's daughter Elizabeth's marriage to Frederick,
Count Palatine has Pallas as the main speaker, and similarly stresses
her public virtues.[48] Anna Maria van Schurman uses Minerva to
articulate her graceful poem in praise of Marie de Gournay, 40 years
her senior, who wrote, lived alone and never married, and who was to
van Schurman a near-fabulous survivor from what in retrospect looked
like a golden age:

> You bear the arms of Pallas, virago undaunted by war;
> That you may wear the laurels, you bear the arms of Pallas.
> Thus it is right to call you a defender of [our] innocent sex,
> to make men harmless with the proper weapon.[49]

Schurman herself is often compared to Minerva. Similarly, when
another Low Countries Latinist, of an earlier generation, Petronia
Lansenberg, contributes a poem to the *album amicorum* of Emmanuel
van Meteren, she refers delicately to herself as well as to the image of
an armed Minerva sketched on the opposite page.

The 'sodality of Minerva' is so central to Latinate women as a form
of validation that it is allowed to create problems of its own. The
works of Elizabeth Jane Weston, for example, are most familiar under
the title *Parthenicon*. The title clearly associates her with the archetypic
Παρθενος, Athena/Minerva. But Weston married in 1603. Though à
Baldhoven's first attempt at editing her work came out in 1602, it was
called *Poemata*: *Parthenicon*, his second edition, post-dates her
marriage (it seems to have appeared in 1605 or 1606). A poem on
Weston by Johannes Matthaeus à Wackenfels printed in Weston's
necrology is titled 'On the same, compared with other *Virgins*' and
addresses this mother of seven in the course of the poem itself as
'*O Virgo!*' – though in the title to the whole pamphlet, she is correctly
identified as the wife of Johann Leon.[50] In privileging Minerva, and

the association of poetry with chastity, women committed themselves to a form of self-censorship. One of the things which became unsayable, even more unsayable than romantic passion (which I shall discuss later, in the context of the figure of Sappho), was their experience of motherhood.

In *Parthenicon*, we know that Weston has a brother, who predeceased her. There are also poems to her husband (by name: the relationship between them is not foregrounded). But her many children are absent: as a subject, they seem to have been impossible. A hint that this constitutes active suppression is offered by Weston's long memorial poem to her own mother. The alert insight which she shows into her mother's desperate position as a young widow with two children under three suggests transference from her own experience as a not wealthy young mother, which apparently could not be directly articulated or expressed within the constraints of her medium. Similarly, Lady Burghley and her sister Anne Bacon were devoted mothers, as we learn from family letters: an experience which apparently could not be directly articulated within the constraints of her medium.[51] Humanist men were often loving fathers, and there are poems by men about their children, but even if a married woman Latinist did not feel constrained to assume a persona of fictive virginity, a mother could not use male models to write about her children, since her relationship to them, and her experience of them, was very different.

The limitations of Minerva as a model brings me to a consideration of classical role models who, in practice, turn out to be even less useful to women, or who are sometimes used by men in ways which are divisive or entrapping. The first of these is the Muse, or the Nine Muses. A woman who did write could be identified as an avatar of the Muses: the number of women hailed as the Tenth Muse, from Sappho herself to Anne Bradstreet, is legion. But the Tenth Muse is a difficult figure, from a woman's point of view: the main problem is that she is singular. It is notable that, while a number of poems survive written by one woman Latinist to congratulate another, they do *not* use this trope. The majority of women Latinists who say anything on the subject at all show an active concern for the existence of a female tradition and try to place themselves within it; they accordingly resist this flattering but entrapping title, which promises them uniqueness and actually offers them monstrosity.

There is another way in which the invocation of the Muses, and especially, of a Muse, is potentially problematic for women: many writers understood the relationship between poet and Muse as sexual.

Anyone considering women's creativity from this point of view is forced to problematize it, as Ben Jonson does in an epigram on Cecelea Bulstrode:

> What though with Tribade lust she force a muse
> And in an Epicoene fury can write newes.

Cecelea's offence, in Jonson's eyes, was to have taken part in a court game, the writing of occasional poetry, or 'News': his reaction is violent, considering the low level of provocation, since he presents even the writing of trivial *vers d'occasion* as homosexual rape of one woman by another.[52]

Having raised the topics both of Muses and of female homosexuality, another figure inevitably presents herself for consideration. In theory, the woman poet or her defenders could appeal to the example of Sappho. The fact that for classical antiquity, while 'the poet' was Homer, 'the poetess' was Sappho, meant that it was impossible for anyone actually to deny that women could write poetry.[53] And thus, one might assume that Sappho would be much used as a role-model. In fact, after the publication of 'Sappho to Phaon', and perhaps before, Sappho's reputation was for reckless passion. This made her a difficult model for women to claim, even though her homo- or bisexuality is almost entirely edited out of the text.[54] The notably obscene Martial, complimenting two women poets of his acquaintance, declares in both cases that the woman is as talented as Sappho, *but chaster*.[55] 'Second Sappho' is a title given to women poets by male supporters.

It is of course highly relevant to ask if there is such a thing as a feminine voice in Latin. There is one: but it is Ovid's. While the *Heroides* all represent women ruled by the primary passion of romantic love, 'Sappho to Phaon', the only one in the voice of a woman *writer*, is distinguished even within the group as a whole for its heroine's abandon, and also for her sexual explicitness. Two recent commentators were both drawn to use the word 'grotesque'.[56] To Renaissance women writers, Ovid's crazy, ageing erotomaniac was considerably worse than useless, she was positively damaging; and if they used her diction or subject-matter (i.e. romantic love) they could not get away from her. For all the good intentions of Renaissance scholars, Latin was a great deal more important in humanist studies than Greek. With only the rarest exceptions, while they were excited by the idea of the Greek Sappho, humanists approached Greek through Latin, which they learned first, and almost always more thoroughly. Since Ovid, an author absolutely central to the medieval canon, held his central significance into the Renaissance, Sappho was inevitably approached through 'Sappho to Phaon'.[57] The fifteenth-century commentaries support Ovid's text: they create an environment in which Ovid seems to be retailing the end of the story told by the *Suda*, the *Greek Anthology*, and Sappho's own poems. 'Sappho to Phaon' is read as authoritative biography.[58]

Thus Sappho becomes a serious problem, in addition to the fact that proverbial wisdom associated chastity so strongly with silence. Renaissance men interested in the education of women suggest again and again that women are chaster when better instructed; but folk wisdom continued obstinately to make a metonymic association between the open, publicly uttering mouth and the opening of other female orifices which should remain closed.[59] There is almost no Latin love-poetry by Renaissance women to set against the vast mass of Renaissance love poetry by men, some of which is extremely sexually explicit. A very little emerges directly out of marriage, and is published either by the husband or not at all. It is probable that the women who might have written it consider it strategically dangerous – or perhaps, that they found the voice in which they might have written pre-empted by Ovid in unacceptable ways. The mood of the *Heroides* is of coloratura emotional display: this is *the diction which men expect women to use*. Actually, it is impossible to find unequivocal examples of women Latinists who actually do so: if anything, women Latinists are so anxious to distance themselves from Ovid's idea of the heroinic that they express themselves with the crisp propriety of Jane Austen heroines.

Heroical epistles are written by humanist men. Such poems might be seen as exercises in classical rhetoric, the *progymnasmata* of the classical schoolrooms, and they proliferate in the sixteenth century.[60] Francesco Maria Molza's *Ad Henricum Britanniae Regem*, in the person of Catherine of Aragon, is a characteristic example.[61] Molza of course was a Catholic, so *Ad Henricum* is a tirade of justified indignation: the extreme self-restraint, dignity and propriety of Catherine's own occasional remarks about her husband and their relationship suggests strongly that that remarkable woman would have been horrified by the words thus put in her mouth. This is in itself a good illustration of the gap between women's own writing and that of men writing in a female persona. A more ambiguous case is the verse epistle addressed by Hippolyta Taurella to her husband Baldassare Castiglione, or more probably, written by him in her name. Its combination of dignity and self-restraint with wifely affection would make it an unusual heroical epistle, but perhaps tells us something of Castiglione's perception of his young wife, and suggests the possibility that he is indirectly educating her in what it is proper for her to feel and express, rather than giving us an insight into Taurella herself.[62]

Probably the most interesting and remarkable heroical epistle of the Renaissance is the witty and psychologically penetrating *Urania Titani*, 'Urania (the Muse of Astronomy) to Titan (the Sun)' by Tycho Brahe, which is written in the person of his sister Sophie. Sophie, considerably the younger, was the only member of the intensely aristocratic Brahe family to value the astronomy to which Tycho had devoted his life and fortune.[63] She worked alongside Tycho on his astronomical and medical experiments, and she could probably write a little Latin, since Latin was the language of record for the work they shared.[64] A brief poetic *jeu d'esprit* in that language, headed 'Tycho Brahe played this with his sister Sophie on Andreas Schelius' estate', suggests as much.[65] Sophie was also the only Brahe to recognize Tycho's marriage to a non-noble. The attachment between them was powerful.[66] Sophie married a suitable nobleman in 1579, but after his early death (1588), she paid four or five visits a year to Tycho, and while visiting, met and fell in love with his friend Erik Lange, who, though noble, was an alchemist by vocation, and consequently penniless. The family inevitably objected (though as a widow, she was not directly controllable by them); but Tycho reciprocated her own support for his marriage by fostering her relationship with Lange, who unfortunately was forced to flee from his Danish creditors in 1591, and went to ground in Prague. In 1594, Tycho wrote an intensely sympathetic poem in which he impersonates his own sister, close friend and coadjutor as a mature woman in love, frank about her physical longing for the absent Lange.[67] No ordinary literary exercise, the poem appears to have been intended as an actively helpful intervention by Tycho in his sister's affairs, since the surviving manuscript implies that the poem was meant to have been signed by Sophie herself, and sent to Erik Lange as a real letter: the first four lines which contain the name of the addressee appear as a colophon, with the heading 'This will be the superscription of this letter, when it has been composed, and signed by Urania'.[68]

Urania Titani is profoundly Ovidian. It is modelled very closely on *Heroides* I 'Penelope to Ulysses', though he also makes use of *Heroides* II, 'Phyllis to Demophoon', the frantic letter of a wife deserted by a deceiving man. He picks up, with considerable insight and sympathy, the fear about the passing of time which is a feature of *Heroides* I. But while Ovid's Penelope worries, generally, that Ulysses will come back to find an old woman, Urania speaks of her longing to bear Erik's child. When it was written, she was already 35, and must have been acutely aware of the years slipping by (in fact, they were not to marry until she was 43). Tycho's awareness of his sister's emotions transcends cliché, even Ovidian cliché: *Urania Titani* is far more committed to the woman's point of view than are the *Heroides* themselves, in which Ovid, though he allows his *grandes amoureuses* to speak for themselves, forbids the reader to find their piteous wailings genuinely pathetic. Tycho's genuine sympathy is clear throughout the poem, and also in another brief poem which was sent to Lange in Sophie's name.[69]

The *Heroides* in effect pre-empted women Latinists: Ovid did not so much provide a model for women's writing in Latin, as create a no-go area – an effect very different from his impact on women's writing in various European vernaculars. One of the few Latin women writers of this period to make overt use of Ovid as a model, Elizabeth Jane Weston, has no use whatsoever for the *Heroides*, but turns instead to his *Tristiae*: thus, she is explicitly presenting herself as a poet of exile, rather than as a woman. The poem is written as a series of parallels: you, on the one hand, suffer this; I, on the other hand, suffer that, concluding with the sentiment, 'ah, how much better your fate was than mine!' The poem has nothing to say about gender; it stresses similarity between herself and another poet, on the common human ground of finding oneself reluctantly and unavoidably in the wrong place.

The last few pages have sought to outline ways in which early modern men responded to women's writing as a problem, and in some cases, sought, by implicitly divisive or belittling strategies, both to praise and to explain away women's achievements. But there are contexts in which writing is simply seen as one of the things which women do, and are admired for doing: '[Lovers] like sometimes to recite their poems to their ladies, sometimes to hear their ladies do the same'.[70] Thomas More writes eloquently (in a poem first published in 1516) of the benefits of marrying a learned woman, arguing that only an educated woman is a true friend and companion.[71] In such a marriage, in which the wife's instructed, thoughtful speech is prized by her husband, poetry is one of the things which can emerge out of the interplay of a genuine conversation; as it does, clearly, in the case of Aemilia 'Rosina' Jordan and her husband Paul Melissus. Melissus' *Schediasmata* includes no fewer than thirteen poems addressed to his wife, profoundly affectionate in tone. Two Latin poems in the

Schediasmata are addressed by Rosina to Melissus, and like his own verses, are very warm in tone, suggesting a genuinely companionate marriage of the kind advocated by More.[72]

There are many contexts in which it was considered appropriate for early modern women to create; to produce lyrics, *vers d'occasion*, or meditations on God. Much of the Latin poetry which I discuss here survives in contexts which do *not* represent the seizing of the press, or the deliberate circulation of copies: they are poems printed in *tumuli* or in the works of other, male poets, carved on gravestones, or written in *alba amicorum*. Relatively few women – among them Bathsua Rainolds, Johanna Otho, Anna Maria van Schurman – launched into print on their own account with a whole book, or books, of their own. Their motives were various, though they often include a healthy interest in personal solvency. But it should be noted that a great number of humanist women who make it into print do so with a man as midwife. Olympia Morata, dying in Heidelberg, ends her last letter, to Coelio Secundo Curione:

> I send you such of the poems as I have been able to write out from memory since the destruction at Schweinfurt – all my other writings have perished. I request that you will be my Aristarchus and polish them. Again, farewell![73]

The most interesting example of male editorial intervention, since we can see more than one side to it, is that of Elizabeth Jane Weston's *Parthenicon*, published by the Silesian nobleman, Martin à Baldhoven. Weston herself was far from delighted: a poem in her own hand in the copy in the British Library (dated 16 August, 1610) expresses her feelings.[74] She was not trying to avoid publication on principle: she seems, in fact, to be stating that she has every intention of publishing a book herself in future, and doing so properly. Her grievance seems to be that à Baldhoven's editorial work left her own writings randomly mixed up with those of others.

> Reader, everything you see in the little book before you
> is published under my name.
> I do not conceal that I have written, but there is another reason
> why I did not want to see these things committed to type:
> Everything is incredibly jumbled together, in no order,
> and joined, 'to the Parthenicon which I gave out when newly
> married'

here, there and everywhere they are full of printers' errors
(and I fear that indolent malice will attribute them to me)
An un-friend, trusting I know not who,
has filled my pages without justification
In this book is superadded a series of learned poets,
which, while they are extra, are at the same time, an unwelcome
kindness:
You must realise that many of my own compositions are missing,
while you will see others' poems mixed with mine.
I ask, do you want a book of the days of Weston,
you, who scarcely allow a place TO Weston?
It would have been better to earn proper praises for an intact book,
Which we could both have worthily rejoiced in.
Since you have linked these poems with a woman; minor works,
Great things are diminished by contact with lesser
I will not delay the Reader, if he takes the negative away from me,
and reads the positive with an open mind.
There will be a time when without you (if the Fates permit)
the page itself fills up its space with Westonian poems.

Weston is an unusually dissatisfied editee. *Parthenicon* contains many poems and letters to à Baldhoven, who was her patron, and who obviously felt himself augmented by having such a remarkable person under his wing: as we have already seen, he went about the Low Countries telling some of the greatest contemporary humanist scholars, such as Scaliger, about her and her poetry. The poems and letter addressed to him in *Parthenicon* express, prettily and wittily, her gratitude. This explosive poem gives a quite different side of the patron/client relationship: it seems to convey Weston's conviction that in thus publishing her work, à Baldhoven was feeding his own vanity, rather than her interest.

This poem of Weston's is unique in its stance. But even leaving aside editions of 'the Classics' (such as Sulpicia, Proba, Hrotsvitha), many other examples of male editors could be produced (especially if we looked at vernacular as well as Latin poets), and we should ask ourselves why this is the case. One reason, probably, is that this was an age of *wunderkamer*, of curiosities, as well as of curiosity; women writers, whatever their individual merits, were also curiosities, which in itself was a reason for allowing them some public space. When Bathsua Rainolds launches herself upon the attention of the world at the age of sixteen, she is doing so as a prodigy (and hoping, we may reasonably assume, to gain the attention of a patron, and an appropriate reward for so doing). Because of their rarity, women humanists had a certain cachet, which is one of the reasons why some men appointed themselves protectors and champions: à Baldhoven is perhaps one such. Denisot, in publicizing the work of the Seymour girls, almost certainly had publicizing himself as his primary motive, since he had been their tutor; and his career is hardly distinguished by its disinterestedness.[75] Others of these men were of a different stamp. A man such as Coelio Secundo Curione, who had been friend, mentor and supporter to Olympia Morata from her teens, published her work out of motives which included interest, respect and affection. Some men educated their daughters in pursuit of a private theory about education, or deliberately to produce a wonder for the sake of advancement of the family unit as a whole (either might be the case with Bathsua Rainolds, who is careful to put her *father's* qualifications – Schoolmaster and Language-Lover – on her title-page); others, of whom St Thomas More is the most famous example, enjoyed the company of educated women, and believed that sound sense was often to be found in female heads.

We end with a paradox. There is a 'feminine voice' in Latin, regularly used by ventriloquizing men, but, ironically, avoided by women since it transgresses the social rules by which actual women had to live. Women's writing in Latin is self-limited, in that it fails to establish discourses for areas of female experience that would go beyond available models. The only area in which women Latinists can really be seen as having constructed a different discourse is, perhaps inevitably, on the subject of being a woman Latinist, where their preferred rhetorical strategies and role-models are distinctly different from those applied to them by men. Women Latinists saw themselves as members of a group; the group of learned women, daughters of Minerva, fully members of their immediate literary and social milieu. Learned women, on the basis of their own writings, clearly perceived other learned women as assets, and potential allies. Conversely, men in contact with women Latinists prefer to see them as unique – Sappho, a Tenth Muse, a phoenix – and often use this rhetoric of uniqueness to situate them outside the sodality of poets in general. Furthermore, when men concede the existence of a number of women poets, they almost always rank them, and suggest that the others are negligible compare to their particular 'second Sappho'. Since she could not be excluded on grounds of ignorance, as most of her sex could be, efforts were often made to shunt her onto a parallel track. In mastering the ability to write Latin elegiac couplets, a woman did not necessarily fall heir to the language of authority.

Notes

1. ''Constantia Varaneia ad dominam Isotam Nogarolam', *Isotae Nogarolae Veronensis Opera quae supersunt omnia*, ed. E. Abel, 2 vols (Vienna: Gerold & Cie, 1886), II, pp. 7–8.
2. *Troilus and Criseyde*, II.49, 'myn auctour shal I folwen, if I konne', *The Works of Geoffrey Chaucer*, ed. F.N. Robinson, 2nd edn (London: Oxford University Press, 1966), p. 402: see also I. 393–4, II.18.
3. Joan Kelly, 'Did Women have a Renaissance?', in *Becoming Visible: Women in European History*, ed. Renate Bridenthal and Claudia Koonz (Boston: Houghton Mifflin, 1977), pp. 137–64.
4. See, for example, Rudolf Pfeiffer, *A History of Classical Scholarship from 1300 to 1850* (Oxford: Oxford University Press, 1976); and Ann Moss, *Ovid in Renaissance France: A Survey of the Latin editions of Ovid and Commentaries Printed in France before 1600*, Warburg Institute Surveys 8 (London: Warburg Institute 1982), p. 1: 'the humanists of the Renaissance regarded themselves first and foremost as rediscoverers, restorers and interpreters of ancient culture'.
5. Latin *auctor*, pl. *auctores*, permits a parallel formation, *auctrix*, pl. *auctrices*, a female creator – rare, but attested.
6. Stuart Piggott, *Ruins in a Landscape: Essays in Antiquarianism* (Edinburgh: Edinburgh University Press, 1976), pp. 87–8.
7. John Donne, *Epithalamion* (1613).
8. Reynolds, L.D. *et al.*, 1983, *Texts and Transmission: A Survey of the Latin Classics* (Oxford: Clarendon Press, 1983), p. 424.
9. It is edited with a German translation by H. Fuchs, 'Das Klagelied der Sulpicia', *Discordia Concors, Festgabe für Edgar Bonjour*, 2 vols (Stuttgart: Helbing & Lichtenhahn, 1968), I, pp. 32–47.
10. *De viris illustribus* I.18, 'femina iccirco inter viros ecclesiasticos posita sola', *Opera Omnia*, ed. Faustino Arévalo, 7 vols (Rome, 1797–1803), VII, p. 149. Note that some subliminal unease has caused Isidore to use the phrase *viri ecclesiastici* rather than *patres*: I have had to use 'fathers' in my English version, since 'men of the church' suggests far too loose a significance. Patrica Wilson-Kastner *et al.*, *A Lost Tradition: Women Writers of the Early Church* (Washington DC: University Press of America, 1981), p. 37.
11. There is a text and translation of the complete *Greek Anthology* in Loeb Classics, trans. W.R. Paton, Harvard University Press, in five volumes. Some of its poems on women were translated by G.R. Woodward, *Epigrams on Sappho and Other Famous Greek Lyric Poetesses* (privately printed, London, 1931). Greek women poets themselves are translated in Diane Rayor, *Sappho's Lyre: Archaic Lyric and Women Poets of Ancient Greece* (Berkeley: University of California Press, 1991).
12. Alan Cameron, *The Greek Anthology: From Meleager to Planudes* (Oxford: Clarendon Press, 1993), pp. 164, 178.
13. For the early print-history of Sappho's poems and fragments, see François Rigolot, 'Louise Labé et la Redécouverte de Sappho', *Nouvelle Revue du Seizième Siècle* 1 (1983), pp. 19–31. See also Mary Morrison, 'Henry Estienne and Sappho', *Bibliothèque d'Humanisme et Renaissance* 24 (1962), pp. 388–91.
14. *Carmina Novem Illustrium Feminarum.*

15. Pfeiffer, *A History*, p. 104. Joan DeJean has demonstrated conclusively that a number of male writers in sixteenth-century France were excited by this rediscovery of Sappho and made use of her work in a variety of ways. Joan DeJean, *Fictions of Sappho, 1546–1937* (Chicago: University of Chicago Press, 1989), pp. 30–41.

16. *Hrosvite Illustris Virginis et Monialis Germano Gente Saxonica Orte Opera Nuper à Conrado Celte Inventa*. Celtes wrote a poem on Hrotsvitha, which compares her to both Sappho and Proba: *Fünf Bücher Epigramme von Konrad Celtes*, II.69, ed. K. Hartfelder, S. Calvary (Berlin, 1881), p. 42.

17. Cassandra Fedele of Venice (1465–1558), for example, corresponded with Alessandra Scala, and Constanza Varano wrote a poem to Isotta Nogarola: in the sixteenth century, Jeanne Otho and Camille de Morel corresponded, and in the seventeenth, Anna Maria van Schurman exchanged letters with most of the learned women of Europe.

18. Margaret King, 'Thwarted Ambitions: Six Learned Women of the Italian Renaissance', *Soundings* 59 (1976), pp. 276–304; 'The Religious Retreat of Isotta Nogarola', *Signs* 3 (1978), pp. 807–22; 'Book-Lined Cells: Women and Humanism in the Early Italian Renaissance', in *Beyond their Sex: Learned Women of the European Past*, ed. P.H. Labalme (New York: New York University Press, 1980), pp. 66–90.

19. D.M. Robathon, 'A Fifteenth Century Bluestocking', *Medievalia et Humanistica* 2 (1944), pp. 106–11, p. 109. The text is in *Isotae Nogarolae Veronensis Opera*, I, pp. 42–45.

20. Perilla was a young woman poet praised by Ovid in *Tristia* III.7. He urges her not to give up writing on account of his exile (and their consequent separation), but to persevere, since if she does, she will be surpassed only by Sappho.

21. *Parthenicon* III A.4. There is also a letter from Weston to Scaliger, in Munich, Bayerische Staatsbibliothek Clm Lat. 1084, f. 277. Scaliger was also the recipient of a poem by Margarita Bockin van Gutmansdorf, preserved in Munich, Bayerische Staatsbibliothek, Collectio Camerariana 33, s. xvii, f. 275.

22. For catalogues of illustrious women, see Ruth Kelso, *Doctrine for the Lady of the Renaissance* (Urbana: University of Illinois Press, 1956), pp. 327–424, which lists 891, and for critical discussion, Glenda MacLeod, *Virtue and Venom: Catalogs of Women from Antiquity to the Renaissance* (Ann Arbor: University of Michigan Press, 1991), and Pamela Joseph Benson, *The Invention of the Renaissance Woman: The Challenge of Female Independence in the Literature and Thought of Italy and England* (Pennsylvania: Pennsylvania State University Press, 1992).

23. *Olympiae Fulviae Moratae mulieris omnium erudissime Latina et Graeca, quae haberi potuerunt, monumenta*, ed. Coelio Secundo Curio (Basel, 1558), pp. 87–92, 95–6. (He was translating from Greek originals into Latin.) S.F. Will, 'Camille de Morel: a Prodigy of the Renaissance', *PMLA* 51 (1936), pp. 83–119, sketches de Morel's relationship with Utenhove.

24. See R.L. Hawkins, 'A Letter from One Maiden of the Renaissance to Another', *Modern Language Notes* 22.8 (1907), pp. 243–5. For Weston's relationship with Melissus, see J.W. Binns, *Intellectual Culture in Elizabethan and Jacobean England: The Latin writings of the Age* (Leeds: Francis Cairns, 1990), p. 111, and the poems scattered through *Parthenicon*.

25. Nicolas Grudius, *Epigrammata*, in Ranutius Gherus *Delitiae Poetarum Belgicorum, huius superiorisque aevi illustrius*, 3 vols (Frankfurt, 1614), II, p. 586.

26. Pfeiffer, *A History*, p. 10, and *passim*.

27. *Georgii Buchanani Scoti Poemata quae extent* (Amsterdam 1687), pp. 381–2. See also Ian Macfarlane, *Buchanan* (London: Duckworth, 1981), p. 329.

28. Cecil wrote a memorandum on his wife's death: 'since her death [it] is manifestly known to me and confessed by sundry good men (whose names and ministries she secretly used) that she did charge them most strictly that while she lived they should never declare the same to me nor to any other.' Conyers Read, *Lord Burghley and Queen Elizabeth* (London: Jonathan Cape, 1960), pp. 446–7.

29. See for example, Ijsewijn, J., Tourney, G., and de Schepper, M, 1985 'Jean Dorat and his Tumulus Iani Bryononis', in *Neo-Latin and the Vernacular in Renaissance France*, ed. Grahame Castor and Terence Cave (Oxford: Clarendon, 1984), pp. 129–55.

30. Mary Delariviere Manley (ed.), *The Nine Muses, or, Poems written by nine Severall Ladies upon the Death of the Late Famous John Dryden, esq.* (London, 1700).

31. Charles Utenhove, *Epitaphium in Mortem Henrici Gallorum Regis Christianissimi* (Paris 1560).

32. *Annae, Margaritae, Janae, sororum virginum, heroidum Anglarum, in Mortem Margaritae Valesiae, Navarrorum Reginae, Hecatadistichon*, ed. N. Denisot (Paris, 1550).

33. See, for example, John Harington, *Orlando Furioso in English Heroical Verse* (London, 1591), p. 314.

34. Ecclesiasticus 24.9, and generally 24 and 25. 'Wisdom' was not inevitably a feminine figure: to St Paul, St Augustine Wisdom was Christ (as the *Logos*: 'Word'). Eugene F. Rice, Jr., *The Renaissance Idea of Wisdom* (Cambridge, Mass.: Harvard University Press, 1958), p. 21.

35. Caroline Walker Bynum, *Jesus as Mother: Studies in the Spirituality of the High Middle Ages* (Berkeley: University of California Press, 1982), pp. 234, 244.

36. See Philippa Berry, *Of Chastity and Power: Elizabethan Literature and the Unmarried Queen* (London: Routledge, 1989), pp. 9–37, p. 10. The picture is now in the Louvre, but originally painted for Isabella d'Este, Duchess of Mantua, in 1502.

37. Giordano Bruno, *Opera Latina*, ed F. Fiorentino, 8 vols (Stuttgart-Bad Cannstatt: Friedrich Frommann Verlag, 1962), 1.1, p. 13.

38. Joseph L. Blau, *The Christian Interpretation of the Cabala in the Renaissance* (Port Washington, NY: Kennikat Press Inc., 1965), pp. 15, 46. See also Du Perron's neo-Platonic 'discours spirituel': Frances A. Yates, *The French Academies of the Sixteenth Century* (London: Routledge, 1988), p. 179.

39. Giovanni Boccaccio, *Genealogie deorum gentilium libri*, ed. Vincenzo Romano, 2 vols (Bari: Giuseppe Laterza & figli, 1951), I, pp. 72–3, and Rice, *The Renaissance Idea of Wisdom*, p. 67.

40. Edgar Wind, *Pagan Mysteries in the Renaissance*, 2nd edn (Oxford: Oxford University Press, 1980), p. 252.

41. Yates, *The French Academies*, p. 179.

42. Claude de Taillemont, *Le Discours des champs faez, à l'honneur, et exaltation de l'amour et des dames. Contenant plusieurs chansons, quatrains, dialogues,*

complaintes, & *autre joyeusetez d'amours,* (Paris, 1557), discussed in Constance Jordan, *Renaissance Feminism: Literary Texts and Political Models* (Ithaca: Cornell University Press, 1990), p. 189.

43. 'Ad I.I. Boissardum Philippa Lazea', Jean-Jacques Boissard, *Poemata* (Metz, 1589), pp. 317–18.

44. *Ibid.,* p. 317.

45. *Musa Virginea Graeco-Latino-Gallica* (London, 1616), sig. A3.

46. Lewalski has explored Anne's construction of resistance. Barbara Lewalski, *Writing Women in Jacobean England,* (Cambridge, MA: Harvard University Press, 1993), pp. 15–43, p. 21. On James, see Jonathan Goldberg, *James I and the Politics of Literature* (Baltimore: Johns Hopkins University Press, 1983).

47. Lewalski, *Writing Women,* pp. 29–30.

48. Aemilia Lanyer, *The Poems of Aemilia Lanyer* ed. Susanne Woods (New York and Oxford: Oxford University Press, 1993), 'Potentissimi Principis Friderici Comitis Palatini Rheni, S. Rom. Imp. Electoris Ducis Bavariae &c., et Elizabethae Jacobi, Regis magnae Britanniae, Filiae Epithalamion', *Carminum diversorum libri duo* (Strasbourg, 1616), I., sigs. b4r–c2v.

49. *Magni ac generosi animi Heroinae Gornacensi, causam sexus nostri fortiter defendenti gratulatur, Nobiliss. Virginis Annae Mariae à Schurman Opuscula Hebraea, Graeca, Latina, Gallica: prosaica et metrica* (Leiden, 1648), p. 303; this is with reference to Marie De Gournay's *L'egalité des hommes et des femmes* (Paris, 1622).

50. *In Beatissimum decessum faeminae nobilissimae, Poëtriae celebratissimae, Dn. Elisabethae Iohannae Leonis, ex nobilissima anglorum familia Westoniae* (Prague, 1612), sig. A1v.

51. For a discussion of this poem, see Susan Bassnett, 'Revising a Bibliography: A New Interpretation of the Life of Elizabeth Jane Weston (Westonia) Based on her Autobiographical Poem on the Occasion of the Death of her Mother', *Cahiers Elizabethains* 37 (1990), pp. 1–9. The only exception to this silence which is known to me is Lady Russell's verses on the deaths of her daughters composed for their tomb in her family chapel at Bisham, Berks., collected by Elias Ashmole in *The Antiquities of Berkshire,* 2 vols (London, 1719), II, pp. 470–1.

52. Lewalski, *Writing Women,* p. 109.

53. Galen, *Quod animi mores corporis temperamenta sequantur,* IV.771.18

54. In 'Sappho to Phaon', Ovid's heroine makes one elliptical mention of her earlier relationships with women, which have become meaningless since she is now 'really' in love with Phaon (ll.18–19).

55. This trope resurfaces in the Renaissance: the impure Sappho is compared with the pure Catherine des Roches in 1582. See Ann Rosalind Jones, 'Contentious Readings: Urban Humanism and Gender Differences in *La Puce de Madame des-Roches* (1582)', *Renaissance Quarterly* 48 (1995), pp. 109–28. In the next century, Madeleine de Scudéry, who was referred to as 'Sapho' by contemporaries, has that name with the rider that she 'eclipsed [Sappho] with her virtue': DeJean, *Fictions of Sappho,* p. 105.

56. Howard Jacobson, *Ovid's Heroides* (Princeton, NJ: Princeton University Press, 1974), p. 297. Florence Verducci, *Ovid's Toyshop of the Heart: Epistulae Heroidum* (Princeton: Princeton University Press, 1985), p. 137.

57. Caroline Jameson, 'Ovid in the Sixteenth Century', *Ovid*, ed. J.W. Binns (London: Routledge & Kegan Paul, 1973), pp. 210–42, esp. pp. 213–14; Moss, *Ovid in Renaissance France*, p. 1.

58. There were many editions of Ovid printed before 1500. The text does not vary greatly (humanist manuscripts of 'Sappho to Phaon' derived from a single common source), but there were two principal commentaries, that of Domitius Calderinus and that of Georgius Merula, which went from edition to edition. Calderinus' commentary depends heavily on the medieval Greek dictionary known as the *Suda*. From it he derives a list of Greek poetesses (Erinna, incidentally, with the note 'who was Sappho's *concubina* [bedmate]'), and the names of Sappho's disciples. He represents Sappho as a sort of finishing-school mistress for Lesbian young ladies, teaching poetry and the use of the *cithara*. The Merula commentary lifts information from that of Calderinus, but lays more stress on her sexual reputation: in addition to the three disciples mentioned by Calderinus, he also names three girlfriends (*amicae*), and states that tradition records that she did unspeakable (*turpissima*) things with them.

59. An attack on Isotta Nogarola includes this appeal to common knowledge: '[the saying] of many wise men I hold to be true: that an eloquent woman is never chaste,' in (Margaret L. King and Albert Rabil, Jr, *Her Immaculate Hand: Selected Works by and about the Woman Humanists of the Quattrocento* (Binghampton, NY: Center for Medieval and Early Renaissance Studies, 1983), p. 18.

60. H.I. Marrou, *A History of Education in Antiquity* (London: Sheed & Ward, 1956), pp. 286–7, 342.

61. In *Renaissance Latin*, ed. Perosa and Sparrow (London: Duckworth, 1979), pp. 261–4, from the Milan, 1563 and Paris, 1576 editions of Molza's verse.

62. 'Hippolytae Taurellae Mantuanae Epistola ad maritum suum Balthasarem Castilionem apud Leonem X Pontific. Rom. Oratorem', in *Olympiae Fulviae Moratae foeminae doctissimae ac plane diuinae orationes, dialogi, epistolae, carmina, tam Latina quam Graeca* (Basel, 1562), pp. 274–8.

63. Victor Thoren, *The Lord of Uraniborg: A Biography of Tycho Brahe* (Cambridge: Cambridge University Press, 1990), p. 150.

64. Thoren, *Lord of Uraniborg*, pp. 208, 213, and F.R. Friis, *Sofie Brahe Ottesdatter: En biografisk Skildring* (Copenhagen: E.C. Gad's Universiteitsboghandel, 1905), pp. 57–9.

65. [Anonymous], 'Esterretning om den Iaerde Fru Sophia Brahe, Tyges Søster', *Danske Magazin* 3 (1747), pp. 12–32, 43–52, p. 18

66. Thoren, *Lord of Uraniborg*, p. 424.

67. Peter Zeeberg, 'Alchemy, Astrology and Ovid: A Love Poem by Tycho Brahe', *Acta Conventus Neo-Latini Hafniensis*, International Association for Neo-Latin Studies VIII, Medieval and Renaissance Texts and Studies 120, pp. 997–1007. The poem survives in manuscript (discussed below), and was also printed, by Petrus Johannis Resenius, *Inscriptiones Hafniensis Latinae Danicae et Germanicae* (Hven, 1668), pp. 410–29.

68. Zeeberg, 'Alchemy, Astrology and Ovid', p. 1007, n. 24.

69. 'Erici Langii nomine Sorori Sophiae Tycho Brahe', in 'Esterretning', pp. 18–19.

70. Pietro Bembo, *Gli Asolani*, trans. with intro. Rudolf B. Gottfried (Bloomington: Indiana University Press, 1954), p. 122. This was written *c.* 1500.

71. Benson, *Invention*, pp. 158–9. See also Lee Cullen Khanna, 'Images of Women in Thomas More's Poetry', *Quincentennial Essays on St Thomas More*, ed. Michael J. Moore (Boone, NC: Albion, 1978), pp. 78–8. The text is printed in *Dominici Baudii Amores*, ed. Petrus Scriverius (Amsterdam, 1638), pp. 281–88, together with other works on the sort of wife best suited to a man of letters: the anonymous *Dissertatio de literati matrimonio* speaks warmly in favour of marrying educated women (pp. 371–2).
72. *Melissi Schediasmata Poetica* (Frankfurt, 1574), p. 392. See also pp. 19, 392, 393, 394, 394, 394, 397, 398, 399, 646, 654, 654–5, 656 for Melissus' poems to his wife, and pp. 631–2, 672, for 'Rosina''s poems to him.
73. [A.G. Smith], *Olympia Morata: Her Times, Life, and Writings*, 2nd edn (New York, 1834), p. 241.
74. Elizabeth Jane Weston, British Library copy of *Parthenicon* [British Library C 61 d 2], second flysheet r & v.
75. *Catalogue of the State Papers (Foreign Section) of the Reign of Mary, 1553–1558*, HMSO, London 1861, p. 549.

2

'In a mirrour clere': Protestantism and Politics in Anne Lok's *Miserere mei Deus*

Rosalind Smith

In 1560, Anne Lok published a translation of four of Calvin's sermons on Isaiah 38, prefaced by a dedicatory epistle to Catherine Brandon and followed by a sonnet sequence in two parts – five sonnets 'expressing the passioned minde of the penitent sinner', followed by a longer sequence paraphrasing the 51st psalm.[1] It is an unsettling text in a number of ways. Generically anomalous, it contains the first sonnet sequence not only to be written in English, but to combine the Petrarchan genre of the sonnet sequence with that of psalm paraphrase. Compiled by a middle-class woman from the community of Protestant exiles in Geneva, it emerges from beyond the English court, in contrast to the texts of aristocratic women surrounding Catherine Parr which form the major precedent for women's publication in England before 1560. The text's strangeness disturbs the practice which underpins criticism on early modern women's writing of this period: characterizing women's textual activity in terms of a restricted class of aristocratic authors, in a secondary or derivative relationship to male-authored texts, and confined to religious genres and topoi. Lok's text draws upon largely male-authored French Calvinist and Anglo-Genevan traditions of psalm paraphrase to construct a text in which textual virtuosity works to out-trope the sonnets and psalm paraphrases of Thomas Wyatt, Lok's main poetic predecessor in England.

The text's recent critical reception has been characterized by a reluctance to analyse its anomalous position, its rhetorical ambition, or to engage with its problems of attribution.[2] Attention to the text's disruptions provides a way of repositioning it within the divergent male-authored traditions with which it engages, as well as suggesting a context for its radicalism in the deployment of Petrarchism in the pursuit of a specific political purpose: the promotion of Calvinist religious policy in the early Elizabethan state. Contrary to its recent reception as an obscure or private 'feminized' text, the sequence engages in genres, traditions and political projects closely aligned with canonical male-authored Protestant texts, and questions an unproblematic separation of men and women's writing in this period. The entry of a female voice into these male-authored traditions is neither straight-forward nor a direct assumption of an established subject position, and it demands different discursive strategies which rewrite the fields in which the text circulates. The apparent anomalies of Lok's text, rather than characterizing the text itself, challenge the categories by which a gendered voice might be understood, and suggest that a broader, more flexible, and historically specific construction of gendered voice in this period is required to accommodate its diversity.

The attribution problems attached to Lok's sonnet sequence mean that it already occupies an unstable position as a gendered text. Not only is the text as a whole published under Lok's initials, which meant that it was not automatically read in gendered terms by an early modern audience, but its concluding sequences are preceded in the text by a disclaimer of authorship:

> I have added this meditation folowyng unto the ende of this boke, not as a parcell of maister Calvines worke, but for that it well agreeth with the same argument, and was delivered me by my frend with whom I knew I might be so bolde to use & publishe it as pleased me. (Aa1v)

The disclaimer raises interpretive problems of its own, attracting two consistent responses. The first takes the statement at face value and identifies the 'frend' who delivered the text as John Knox; the second expediently ignores the statement in making an uncomplicated attribu-tion of the sequence to Lok. Both readings are destabilized by the textual practices of the overlapping manuscript and print cultures in the sixteenth-century court. A literal reading fails to register its rhetorical status, and its place within the culture of the court, where the circulation of a text in print carried class implications that a writer might wish to disguise. Theories of the 'stigma of print' argue that participation in coteries of manuscript exchange in the late sixteenth century upheld the boundaries of aristocratic culture against a rising middle class.[3] However, contemporary textual disclaimers generally differ from Lok's assertion that the sonnets were supplied by a friend; Tottel justifies publication in terms of a nationalistic promotion of the vernacular, associating manuscript circulation with 'ungentle horders,' while early writers such as Barnabe Googe and Nicholas Grimald assert that they published through the urgings or actions of friends.[4] Unlike Lok, they claim authorship of their texts, but minimize their responsibility for circulating them in print. The presence of a disclaimer at all in the text written from the emergent middle class against whom the mechanisms of aristocratic manuscript circulation were a protection might, of course, be related to gendered fears of social censure attached to the unmediated writing and publication of poetry by a woman. Little precedent exists within the English tradition at this point for Lok's publication of poetry: Catherine Parr's two volumes of meditations, the lost text of psalms and proverbs by Lady Elizabeth Fane, and Elizabeth's meditation on psalm 13 following her translation of *A Godly Meditation of the Soul*.[5] All carry regal or aristocratic authority. However, Margaret Ezell's work issues a caveat against the construction of disclaimers in women's texts, arguing that they were less motivated by specifically gendered fears of social censure than by their participation in a rhetoric of modesty shared by writers of both sexes.[6] Lok's text is such an early example of a middle-class woman's publication of poetry that it increases the possibility that a disclaimer might have operated as a protective mechanism, but this argument would be more convincing if the text were circulated under Lok's name rather than her initials. Whether a reflection of anxieties related to gender, class or their intersection, the disclaimer remains a sufficiently problematic statement that it cannot be ignored in considering the question of the text's attribution.

Equally problematic are the literal readings of the disclaimer identifying the friend who delivered the text to Lok as John Knox. These are based on the personal relationship of Lok and Knox, and Lok's role in supplying some of Knox's work to the publisher John Field in 1583.[7] These speculative foundations for the attribution to Knox are even less likely given that his only poetic publication was the psalms in *The Book of Common Prayer*, which correspond so closely to the Sternhold and Hopkins *Psalter* that they are not considered to be Knox's work. Knox's *Psalms and Liturgy* also contains 41 psalms specific to the Scottish edition, but these were written by William Kethe, William Whittingham, John Pulleyn, Robert Pont and I.C. (probably the Edinburgh minister John Craig).[8] Lok's text was prepared during her time in Geneva, between mid-1557 and 1559, yet the detailed and consistent correspondence form Knox to Lok in this period makes no mention of the text or the sonnets. The only other argument suggested by critics in support of the attribution to Lok rests with her later publishing history. Lok's 1590 translation of Jean Taffin's *Des Marques des Enfans de Dieu*, dedicated to the Countess of Warwick, is also concluded by a long poem which is not in the copytext, Taffin's revised third edition published in 1588.[9] Further, the copytext contains some of Taffin's own poetry which could have been used by Lok to conclude her translation, but instead was replaced by the poem 'The necessitie and benefite of affliction.' The 1560 sonnet sequence and the 1590 long poem share some thematic and structural similarities, dramatizing the affliction of the sinner through the Old Testament figures of David and Job, but the similarities between the two pieces stop there. The contrast between the dramatized and internalized exploration of the speaker's experience of sin through David's voice in the sonnets, and the flat, third-person exemplary use of Job in the later poem, make the pieces seem closer to models of authorship by writers within a Protestant tradition than to individualized authorship. The later poem, itself of uncertain attribution, provides little support for the attribution of the sonnet sequences to Lok; however, a Latin lyric in the Bartholo Sylva manuscript attributed to Lok and supporting the radical religious politics of her second husband, Edward Dering, provides more secure proof of her facility with poetic composition.[10]

More significant support for the attribution, however, can be located in overlooked connections within the different sections of the 1560 text itself: between Lok's dedicatory epistle to Catherine Brandon, her translation of the sermons and the sonnet sequence. Calvin's sermons on Isaiah 38 focus upon the figure of Hezekiah, his physical affliction and divine cure, and the ramifications for the political state of the godly king. In the epistle, Lok specifically links Hezekiah and David, the focus of the sonnet sequence, as complementary examples of the same principle:

> And that you maye be assured, that this kinde of medicine is not hurtfull: two moste excellent kinges, Ezechias and David, beside an infinite numbre haue tasted the lyke before you, and haue founde health therin. (A4r)

Hezekiah and David are offered as the models through which the text's medicine is administered, and by whom the reader should be assured of its efficacy. Their linking in the epistle, in a text which goes on to offer Hezekiah in the sermons and David in the psalm paraphrase as examples of those suffering affliction redeemed and cured by God's mercy, is a strong indication that the concluding sonnet sequences were included by Lok as a complement to her translation of the sermons on Hezekiah. This connection is not necessarily evidence for authorship of the sequence, but may be a gloss on her editorial method, reinforcing her line in the disclaimer that she has added the meditation 'for that it well agreeth with the same argument.' The connection is supplemented by a similar use of Petrarchan imagery in both the epistle and sequences. Calvin's account of Hezekiah's suffering and restoration to health in the sermons works largely metaphorically in presenting a model of right and godly government. Lok's text, on the other hand, expands upon the Calvinist text in both the dedication and sonnet sequence in stressing the physicality of that affliction, its effects upon the body of the king. Calvin's recreation of Hezekiah's suffering is given this gloss in Lok's dedicatory epistle:

> So here this good soules Physicia[n] hath brought you where you maye se lyinge before youre face the good king Ezechias, somtime chillinge and chattering with colde, somtime languishing & meltyng away with heate, nowe fresing, now fryeng, nowe spechelesse, nowe crying out ... You se him sometyme yeldyngly stretch oute, sometyme struglinglye throwe his weakned legges not able to sustein his feble body: sometime he casteth abrode, or holdeth up his white & blodless hand toward the place where his soule longeth. (A7v–A8r)

This anatomizing of Hezekiah's body in illness offers a particularly Petrarchan blason: his sick body is dismembered in the second section of the quoted passage, following the use of Petrarchan tropes of freezing and burning, repeated to the point of ubiquity in the Renaissance. But in 1560 in the Elizabethan court, such tropes would have had a freshness which they later lost, and their appearance in Lok's epistle suggests an interest in Petrarchism consistent with her composition of a Petrarchan sonnet sequence at the end of the text. The sonnets construct David's sinful body in the same terms of a physically detailed account of disease: 'leprous bodie and defiled face', 'splat my ripped hert' (Aa4r–v). Lok's emphasis on the reconstruction of the diseased body, its material rather than metaphoric aspect, in a text seeking to present the figures of Hezekiah and David as admonitory models of princeliness, constructs an anxiety around the body of the ruler that exceeds Calvin and reinforces a sense of instability at the beginning of Elizabeth's reign. Following the early deaths of Edward VI and Mary Tudor, the illness of the sovereign carried with it potential for political and religious change deeply disturbing to a Protestant community still in exile following Mary's reign. The Calvinist model of godly kingship is therefore invested with an anxious materialism in both the marginal sections of the text, expressed through an idiosyncratic use of Petrarchan discourse which suggests a common authorship of both sections.

The use of the sonnet form for the meditations concluding Lok's text has no precedent in the English tradition of psalm paraphrase, and this very anomaly may also be recruited as some support for Lok's authorship of the sequences. The major sonneteers in the English tradition up to 1560 were Surrey, and more particularly Wyatt, who also translated the psalms, including a paraphrase of Psalm 51. Although Wyatt and Surrey wrote in the earlier half of the sixteenth century, the delay in their publication gives an originality to the form for a reader such as Lok, whose middle-class upbringing may have excluded her from access to or knowledge of the manuscript versions of these poems circulating in the court. Wyatt's *Penitential Psalms* were first printed in 1549, but more significantly, the first edition of *Tottel's Miscellany* was published in 1557. This context makes the choice of the sonnet form for Lok's meditation seem less unfashionable. Six editions of Tottel were published by the end of 1559; its influence on the sequence in Lok's text is indicated by the sequence's adoption of the specifically 'English' rhyme scheme invented and used by Wyatt and Surrey. Lok's position in the Genevan community would also have provided her with access to the French and Anglo-Genevan traditions of sonnet and psalm paraphrase. The publication of Louise Lab's *Oeuvres* in 1556 offered the only gendered precedent of published and accessible woman-authored sonnets.[11] Lok also would have had available to her the published poems of Margaret of Navarre, who, like Catherine Parr, published a series of pious meditations. These meditations adopted a variety of lyric forms, although none is a sonnet, displaying a level of formal experimentation which exceeds the Parr texts; a parallel can be drawn with the male-authored tradition of psalm paraphrase in France and England, where Sternhold's counterpart in the French court was Clément Marot, whose metrical psalm paraphrases used a wide variety of lyric forms and rhyme schemes and a less literal interpretive compass than those of Sternhold.[12] Unlike Sternhold, Marot paraphrased the 51st psalm, and the method of aggregation of the 1560 sonnets, each linked to and expanding on a line from the psalm, follows a pattern used in Marot's quatrains on the text. Although this impulse towards a more experimental tradition of psalm paraphrase may have been drawn upon by Lok if she wrote the 1560 sequences, scarcely more precedent exists within the French and Anglo-Genevan traditions than the English for the packaging of psalm meditations as sonnets. Bordier's collection of Huguenot songs contains only one sonnet: 'Angoisse de l'âme' by Malingre, first published in *Chansons spirituelles a l'honneur et louange de Dieu* in 1555.[13] As in England, the increased popularity of the sonnet form in the late sixteenth century in France gave rise to some devotional sequences, but it was far from a standard generic combination in 1560.[14] Nevertheless, the more interpretive cast of the 1560 sequence and its lyrical experimentation may indicate that Marot's influence combined with the suggestive examples of sonnets in *Tottel's Miscellany* to produce sonnet meditation. A translator such as Lok, with links to the gospelling tradition of the court of Edward VI and the Calvinist psalm para-phrases of Marot and Beza during her time in the Genevan exile community, seems perfectly positioned to produce a sequence that seems strangely anomalous in its use of the sonnet genre if viewed in terms of an English tradition of psalm paraphrase alone.

Although there is a reasonable amount of evidence supporting Lok's authorship of the sonnets, Lok's disclaimer should not be expediently erased: some of the uncertainties surrounding the question of attribution may illuminate the nature of a gendered text. The critical responses to the disclaimer privilege authorship as the sole ground for determining what a gendered text might be, and exclude other forms of textual agency – such as editing – in a way that not only simplifies authorship in the sixteenth century, but also unnecessarily restricts the relationship of text and gender. How important is the determination of attribution to reading the sequences as gendered texts? Attribution has an important place in establishing the existence of a body of early modern women writers, a political function essential to the feminist gynocritical project begun in the 1970s. However, the politics of recovering early modern women writers has resulted in a suppression of the problems of attribution which surround many of these texts, and has restricted the definition of the gendered text to reductive identifications between author, text and textual subject. Ignoring the problematics raised by Barthes and Foucault surrounding the reduction of meaning in a text to the single interpretive frame of authorial intention, gynocritical models of the gendered text assume that the gender of the author unproblematically informs the gender of the text, without allowing for the ambiguities and slippages of meaning inherent in every act of reading and interpretation. The sense that gynocritical feminism is out of step with a wider critical context has been the subject of many critiques, and a set of feminist critical alternatives has been offered in response – defining a gendered text in terms of its content, its style and the gender of its audience. But these definitions also have their problems. The construction of the gender of a text's content identifies either a set of feminine preoccupations, or a feminine sensibility, both of which depend upon homogenizing 'women' as a group. They are defined solely in terms of their relationship to an oppressive patriarchy, rather than in terms of their specific position in a complex intersection of cultural discourses including, for example, race or class. The identification of a particularly gendered 'style' meets similar problems, assuming a consistently feminine writing position or relation to language which again writes out local difference, and tends to pre-empt the political investments of such texts. The strategy of relating the gender of the text to the gender of its reader appears at first to sidestep the essentialism inherent in both gynocritical and revisionary models, but, as Elizabeth Grosz argues, it still depends upon the idea of a con-tinuous, intentional subject, reducing the meaning of a text to a single destination.[15] If there is no way of defining a gendered text without recourse to a problematic attribution, simplistic models of reading or essentialist models of the feminine, must the question of gender be erased in speaking about texts such as Lok's sonnet sequences?

I would suggest that there is a sense in which Lok's text, edited by a woman writer and dedicated to Catherine Brandon, is gendered at a specific moment in its circulation history – that is, it may be read as gendered in terms of a contingent and local circulation which need not be extended to encompass a universal identification of its gender nor to imply a single, unified reading subject. The text is gendered in two ways, through its activation of a particular, feminized line of political pressure directed towards the sovereign, and through the textual negotiations necessitated by the entry of a middle-class gendered voice into the political sphere at this moment in history. The dedication to Brandon mobilizes her status within the court and as a popular figure for a wider Protestant readership for Lok's project of disseminating God's word through Calvin: it also has a more specific political focus in addressing a second gendered reader, Elizabeth I.

The Elizabethan state in 1559 and 1560 was characterized by anxiety over Elizabeth's religious allegiances, especially among the exiled Protestant communities. The perceived fragility of Elizabeth's commit-ment to Protestantism and her need for correction is articulated in Calvin's letter to William Cecil, 1559:

But since it is scarcely possible that in so disturbed and confused a state of affairs, she should not, in the beginning of her reign, be distracted, held in suspense by perplexities, and often forced to hold a vacillating course, I have taken the liberty of advising her that having once entered upon the right path, she should unflinchingly persevere therein.[16]

It has been argued that Elizabeth was a committed Protestant, who in 1559 achieved her preferred religious settlement in the face of con-servative Catholic opposition.[17] Recent revisions of that position argue that the religious settlement was made by a queen under constraint, manipulated within the court, and that a document seen to register her early Protestantism, such as her translation of *A Godly Meditation of the Soul*, was a conservative piece hijacked by John Bale for the Protestant cause. In contrast, her religious conservatism, which has been dismissed by those arguing for her commitment to Protestantism as expedient public policy, was so consistently manifested that Patrick Collinson argues for it as a reflection of Elizabeth's own position.[18] A point of focus for this personal conservatism was Elizabeth's reinstatement of the cross and candlesticks in the royal chapel in October 1559 for the marriage of one of her ladies, in the face of official injunctions of the same year calling for the removal of 'things superstitious' from churches, a designation interpreted by Protestants to include the cross. The reaction of Protestant bishops to Elizabeth's retention of the cross and candlesticks in the royal chapel indicates the anxiety that her action provoked in Protestant circles, and the uncertainty attaching to her religious alliances during this early period of her reign.[19]

Catherine Brandon specifically writes to William Cecil in the early months of 1559 expressing a parallel concern to that expressed by Calvin and the wider Protestant community as to the extent of Elizabeth's commitment to Protestantism in the light of her engagement with the outward forms of Catholicism:

Wherefore I am forced to say with the Prophet Elie, 'How long halt ye between two opinions?' If the mass be good, tarry not to follow it, nor take from it no part of that honour which the last Queen in her notable stoutness brought it to and left it in, wherein she deserved immortal praise, seeing she was so persuaded that it was good. But if you be not so persuaded, alas, who should move the Queen to honour it with her presence, or any of her councillors. Well, it is so reported here that Her Majesty tarried but the Gospel, and so departed. I pray God that no part of the report were true, but that you know there is no part of it good after that sort as they use it.[20]

This focus on the mass in Brandon's letter indicates a Protestant political activism which makes her choice as the object of Lok's dedication for her translation of sermons on Hezekiah particularly pointed. The biblical model repeatedly recruited to Protestant iconoclasm was Hezekiah. His rule was characterized by an active support for the purge of idolatry during his reign and his history, as Margaret Aston has shown, was closely associated with the typology and symbolism of the cross.[21] Hezekiah's purge of idolatry was centred on the destruction of 'the brasen serpent that Moses had made.'[22] This serpent, made by Moses at God's command, was set upon a pole as a sign of God's granting of eternal life to the faithful, and in the Old Testament prefigured the body of Christ upon the cross as a sign of God's salvation. But to early Elizabethan Protestants, the brazen serpent and the cross were linked as images which had become idols, irredeemably abused by false worship. Hezekiah's destruction of the serpent became a model directed by Protestants towards their sovereigns, promoting the destruction of the idol of the cross. Calvin's dedicatory epistle in the Geneva bible specifically cites Hezekiah to Elizabeth as a warning for rapid reform of the state to avoid God's punishment.[23] Nicholas Udall's play *Ezechias*, written under Henry VIII, was performed for Elizabeth when she visited Cambridge in 1564, and contemporary accounts describe its opening with Hezekiah's destruction of idols and restoration of the true religion. These contexts reposition Lok's translation of the sermons on Hezekiah as an admonitory text directed towards Elizabethan policy during 1559. The translation makes reference to Hezekiah's purge of idolatry in the first sermon as an example of 'howe he framed all hys lyfe to the law of God' and established the 'trewe and pure religyon' in the state. Lok's translation places no special gloss on this passage; it conforms almost exactly to the French edition of Calvin's sermons on Hezekiah published by François Estienne in 1562.[24] The text's intervention comes not as a gendered rewriting of Calvin's sermons, but through the dissemination of Calvin's text in English at an historical moment where the policies of Hezekiah could be seen as a comment upon Elizabeth's religious actions.

Any admonitory instruction of Elizabeth from a figure such as Lok, writing from beyond the court, must be couched in less direct terms than the attempted interventions by letter from Calvin or Catherine Brandon. Consequently, her admonition to Elizabeth is inferred indirectly through the models of Old Testament kingship and constructed as an instruction in duty to Catherine Brandon rather than as a direct address to the queen. Brandon, the object of God's healing medicine, enters into a relationship of 'receipt,' of bondage to the physician and messenger:

> But we se dayly, when skilfull men by arte, or honest neyghbours havyng gathered vnderstandyng of some specyall dysease & the healing therof by theyr owne experiment, do applie their knowledge to the restoring of health of any mans body in any corporall sicknesse, howe thankfully it is taken, howe muche the releved patient accompteth him selfe bo[u]nd to him by meane of whose aide and ministration he findeth himself holpen or eased. What then deserveth he, that teacheth such a receipt ...? This receipte God the heavenly Physitian hath taught, his most excelle[n]t Apothecarie master Iohn Calvine hath compounded, & I your graces most bounden & humble have put into an Englishe box, & do present unto you. (A3r)

It is the receipt, the concept of duty, rather than the message, which is packaged for Brandon here; the text invokes the relationship as much as the teaching, and in this move Lok seeks to mobilize Brandon's demonstrated political interests and agency within the court in the service of her text's project. The duty owed slips from physician to messenger in the looseness of the phrase 'him by meane of whose aide and ministration he findeth himself holpen or eased,' allowing Lok to invoke the bonds of personal patronage as well as a wider duty to the promotion of Calvinism in the figure of Brandon. This relationship of duty is extended from Brandon to Elizabeth through the text's mediation of its message through the affliction visited on the bodies of King David and King Hezekiah. While it does not attempt to teach Elizabeth her duty directly, the text concerns itself with invoking and defining the relationship and extent of duty between author and ideally Protestant patron in the epistle, and between subjects and an ideally Protestant sovereign in the sermons.

What makes the text particularly interesting is that it mobilizes a female patron to put political pressure upon the sovereign through a persuasive rhetoric of service and duty, which is analogous to that practised in male patronage relationships. Moreover, the message packaged for the sovereign is one which diverges little from its male-authored copytext. It offers few grounds for the location of an essentially 'feminine' sensibility within the text, and its engagement with the public sphere contests received notions of early modern women's confinement to the private sphere of the household. Gender does not preclude the possibility of political engagement in this context, but it defines the ways in which that political pressure is exerted – the patronage circles and subject positions open to a particular middle class woman editor such as Anne Lok. These are avenues exploited by Lok again in 1572, in a manuscript produced by two of the Cooke sisters, Elizabeth Hoby and Mildred Cecil, dedicated to Leicester, and aimed again at Queen Elizabeth. Lok's Latin poem is a Protestant humanist attempt to conciliate Elizabeth and direct her towards a more radical position, in line with the politics of Lok's second husband, Edward Dering.[25] It is again a political text, but one which is circulated in ways which might be defined as gendered only through a particular, local circulation history; in this instance, through a mobilization of a particular patronage network, and the pursuit of Dering's, rather than Calvin's political agenda. Both texts resist generalized definitions of 'the gendered text' and act as caveats against the limitations which such definitions impose upon writing by early modern women; they suggest that a more open, less essentialist model of the gendered text might allow these texts to be seen to work in new and surprising ways in the period.

The limitations of conventional models of the early modern gendered text do not only extend to a text's political engagements in the period, but also to its literary position. It is a critical commonplace in discussions of the Petrarchan sonnet sequence to characterize the genre in terms of its strictly defined gender codes, in which the male Petrarchan subject constructs his erotic subjectivity against the body of his silenced female beloved, his desiring gaze reflected back upon himself to create, according to John Freccero's analysis, a self-enclosed, idolatrous trinity.[26] The entry of the woman subject into these configurations is clearly more complex than direct appropriation, but a text such as Lok's challenges the received critical view that the female Petrarchan subject wrote texts confined to the private sphere, if she were able to assume that subject position at all. Gender shapes the engagement with the genre and its political function, but does not preclude the possibility of that engagement. In an English tradition and to an English audience, the taking up of both the sonnet and psalm paraphrase seems to be an out-troping of Wyatt, whose sonnets were circulating in print from 1557 and whose psalms were published in 1549. An emphasis on the place of the sequence in terms of the gendered precedent in the tradition of penitential meditation obscures their generic innovation as sonnet sequences, and the text's rhetorical ambition.

What might this impulse to out-trope signify? In Tottel, Wyatt was praised by Surrey as a psalmist, whose depiction of David provided an admonitory model for rulers: 'Where rulers may se in a mirrour clere / The bitter frute of false concupiscence'.[27] I suggest that the text's engagement with Wyatt's poetry presents not only formal parallels, signalling a Petrarchan textual over-reaching, but also parallels his use of David as a mirror to the sovereign in an admonitory project which matches her deployment of the figure of Hezekiah in the sermons. The 1560 text positions itself with Wyatt's paraphrase on the 51st psalm by adopting Wyatt's innovative structure of prefacing the psalm paraphrase with a short, original sequence. Wyatt presents David 'wearied,' at rear and alone, overcome with grief and deprived of sense: 'Down from his eyes a storm of tears descends, / Without feeling, that trickle on the ground.'[28] Lok's penitent sinner is similarly confronted and confounded by sin, and represented in the opening sonnet of the preface through the same tropes of blood and tears: 'dimmed and fordulled eyen / Full fraught with teares' (Aa2r). The reworking of Wyatt in this section shifts from his third-person, descriptive observation of David, to a first-person expansion on the now genderless penitent sinner's subjective experience of sin. This shift stresses the individual's interaction with God in line with Calvinist theology, and provides by default or omission a subject position available to readers of both genders. But the text does more than rework Wyatt's formal strategies for a gendered reader. As Carl Rasmussen has argued, the poetry of Petrarchism, with its intense focus upon the construction of the speaking subject and that subject's psychological shifts, provides the Protestant subject with a model for the construction of subjectivity at a point where spiritual doctrine placed a new emphasis on the subjective state of the individual through the psychologizing of its major tenets.[29] The 1560 reworking of Wyatt's prologue to the 51st Psalm in terms of the penitent sinner's subjective experience of despair extends a nascent shift in Wyatt from the divine to the secular, through a shift in the Petrarchan subject's access to lines of sight. Wyatt's David has one refuge in despair, the sight of God – 'he can none other thing / And look up still unto the heaven's king'. However, Lok's newly genderless penitent sinner is blind, a blindness elaborated on in detail in the second sonnet of the preface.[30] The 1560 text picks up on a movement at the conclusion of

Wyatt's prefatory sequence of four poems, where the gaze is averted from God to self and leads into the release of the desiring voice in psalm paraphrase:

> Like as he whom his own thought affrays
> He turns his look. Him seemeth that the shade
> Of his offence again his force assays
> By violence despair on him to lade.
> Starting like him whom sudden fear dismays,
> His voice he strains and from his heart outbrings
> This song that I not whether he cries or sings.[31]

The focus of the 1560 text on Wyatt's internal direction of the gaze of the penitent subject shifts the emphasis of the sequence from God to self, privileging the subjective apprehension of God over his objective presence, in a movement which is typically Petrarchan both in its emphasis on the textual subject and its anxiety of influence. Its innovative generic combination of sonnet and psalm paraphrase expands a connection offered, but not exploited, by Wyatt's psalm paraphrase and its generic history.

The text's formal out-troping of Wyatt is supplemented in the longer psalm paraphrase by a similar Petrarchan dynamic of poetic competition transferred to the role of admonitory psalmist to sovereigns. The 'mirrour clere', identified by Surrey in Wyatt's work, is taken up in Lok's text to supplement the example of the iconoclast Hezekiah as a model for Elizabeth. Sonnet 5 uses the blason again to present a self-motivated display of the sinful body of the speaker, David:

> My cruell conscience with sharpned knife
> Doth splat my ripped hert, and layes abrode
> The lothsome secretes of my filthy life,
> And spredes them forth before the face of God.

> (Aa4v)

The body is dismembered and displayed in order that it might become a vehicle for the redemption of the church through the body of its king, thus reinforcing and dilating the male speaker's subjectivity in a movement parallel to Petrarch's construction of his subjective self as laureate over the fragmented body of Laura. The sequence parallels David's broken body with that of Christ on the cross, recruiting even his objectification to a neo-Platonic project where the speaker, like God, offers a part of himself as a sacrifice to redeem the world:

> But thy swete forme alone,
> With one sufficing sacrifice for all
> Appeaseth thee, and maketh the at one
> With sinfull man, and hath repaird our fll.
> That sacred hoste is ever in thine eyes.
> The praise of that I yeld for sacrifice.
>
> (Aa7v)

The redemption which this sacrifice effects is for the political and religious state of David's realm:

> Shew mercie, Lord, not unto me alone:
> But stretch thy favor and thy pleased will,
> To sprede thy bountie and thy grace upon
> Sion, for Sion is thy holly hyll:
> That thy Hierusalem with mighty wall
> May be enclosed under thy defense,
> And bylded so that it may neuer fall
> By myning fraude or mighty violence.
> Defend thy chirch, Lord, and advaunce it soe,
> So in despite of tyrannie to stand,
> That tre[m]bling at thy power the world may know
> It is upholden by thy mighty hand:
> That Sion and Hierusalem may be
> A safe abode for them that honor thee.
>
> (Aa7v–Aa8r)

The reference to 'thy chirch' represents a departure from the words of the psalm, and the available paraphrases before 1560, where religion is couched in more general terms.[32] The paraphrase dramatizes David's spiritual and physical abasement in order to construct a parallel to Christ's sacrifice by God to repair the fall of the members of the Christian Church. David's song is rewritten in the 1560 sequence as a sacrifice through which God's grace will redeem not only the city of Jerusalem, but the Church. The inclusion of a reference to Christ's sacrifice on the cross – 'But thy swete forme alone, / With one sufficing sacrifice for all' – which allows David's despair to become redemptive of Church as well as state, is, of course, an anachronism, projecting David's voice forward to describe an event in the future: this substantial deviation from the words of the psalm is made obvious by the practice of juxtaposing paraphrase and psalm text. The prolepsis moves the sequence forwards to the origins of Christianity and beyond to the author's own period, and the exemplary figure of David, Elizabeth. The text works as a prosopopoeia for Elizabeth's voice as a New Testament David.

Hezekiah is offered in the sermons as an exemplary king in his destruction of the brasen serpent, Old Testament type of the cross; the voice of David in the sonnets offers the sinner's redeemed heart as an equivalent to Christ's death on the cross, as an appropriate sacrifice to God, and a means of redeeming state and Church. Both Marot and Wyatt place a typically Protestant gloss on David's rejection of sacrifice in the 51st Psalm by suggesting that the sacrifice which God desires is internal and individual: 'sprite contrite; low heart in humble wise'; 'une Ame dolente / Un coeur submis, une Ame penitente.'[33] Both, however, maintain that these reformed hearts allow and authorize the 'outward deeds' of sacrifice in a paraphrase of the final lines of the psalm. In the 1560 sequence, however, the external deeds of the sacrifice become the yielding of the heart. The detailed inventory of 'sacrifice of righteousness' in the psalm – 'burnt offringes and oblations ... young bullockes' – which is maintained in Marot's version of the psalm as 'Oblations telles que tu demandes: / Adonc les Boeufz,' is changed in the 1560 paraphrase to a metaphorical sacrifice of the reformed heart:

> Then on thy hill, and in thy walled towne,
> Thou shalt receave the pleasing sacrifice.
> The brute shall of thy praised name resoune
> In thankfull mouthes, and then with gentle eyes
> Thou shalt behold upon thine altar lye
> Many a yelden host of humbled hart,
> And round about then shall thy people crye:
> We praise thee, God our God: thou onely are
> The God of might, of mercie, and of grace.
> That I then, Lorde, may also honor thee,
> Releve my sorow, and my sinnes deface:
> Be, Lord of mercie, mercifull to me:
> Restore my feling of thy grace againe:
> Assure my soule, I crave it not in vaine.

(As8r)

The paraphrase retains some points of reference to the psalm – the term 'brute' and the reference to God's 'gentle eyes' recall imagery that might be associated with sacrificial bullocks – but the literal sacrifice is made through the 'yelden host.' The host is represented in terms of sight or knowledge of God – 'That sacred host is ever in thine eyes' – rather than a physical sacrifice, and the sequence concludes with a more ambiguous reading of the righteousness of physical sacrifice and outward deeds in favour of a sustained emphasis on the sacrifice implicit in the reformed and humbled heart. David's internal reformation has led to the parallel reformation of his subjects; but this restored church is contingent upon his personal restoration to grace. The sequence again departs from the paraphrase and from earlier versions of the psalm in its conclusion in uncertainty. It ends not with the imagery of right sacrifice but with the speaker's individual desire for mercy and grace, which, if granted, will restore his state and Church. If Lok's linking of the figures of Hezekiah and David in the epistle suggests that both elements of the text seek to direct the sovereign as complementary examples of ideal Protestant sovereignty, then the message to Elizabeth in the sonnets is clear. The reformed heart of the monarch will lead to a similar reformation in the hearts of the people and a restoration of the Church and state, but it involves a humility, a yielding to God and a pursuit of the godly path on the part of the ruler, which is seen as by no means assured.

The sequence finishes by reinforcing the model of godly government and the iconoclastic message associated with Hezekiah by the Protestant community and outlined by the sermons. The sonnets function as a carefully constructed gloss on the sermons. As if the veiled association of Elizabeth with Hezekiah were not enough, the figure of David is recruited as a subjective restatement of the monarch's frailty and the consequences of his sin for the religious and political state. The 'bitter frutes of false concupiscence' which Wyatt sought to reveal through David's voice become not the results of carnal desire that disturbed the Henrician state, but the results of a nascent Elizabethan adherence to 'things of the world' in religion, the material trappings of Catholicism, over the cultivation of a subjective godliness preferred by radical Protestants. The text as a whole, edited by Lok and directed initially towards a specifically feminized readership as a way of exerting political pressure upon the sovereign, shows a gendered voice operating in surprisingly ambitious and uncircumscribed ways in the political and literary spheres of the early Elizabethan state. Surprising, however, only in terms of models of gender which rely upon essentialist constructions of the feminine located either in the body of the author and reader, or in the style of the text. A more flexible and contingent model of gender opens up the possibilities and limitations of the gendered voice speaking in the same contexts as the male voice, in ways which reflect the complex specificity of each historical moment of a text's production and circulation.

Notes

1. A[nne] L[ok], *Sermons of John Caluin, vpon the songe that Ezechias made after he had bene sicke, and afflicted by the hand of God, conteyned in the 38. Chapiter of Esay* (London, 1560).
2. See Elaine Beilin, *Redeeming Eve: Women Writers of the English Renaissance* (Princeton: Princeton University Press, 1987), pp. 61–3; Margaret P. Hannay, '"Strengthening the walles of ... Ierusalem": Anne Vaughan Lok's Dedication to the Countess of Warwick', *ANO* 5 (1992), 71–5, and '"Unlock my lippes": the Miserere mei Deus of Anne Vaughan Lok and Mary Sidney Herbert, Countess of Pembroke,' in *Privileging Gender in Early Modern England*, ed. Jean R. Brink (Kirksville, Mo.: Sixteenth Century Journal Publishers, 1993), pp. 18–36; Susanne Woods, 'The Body Penitent: A 1560 Calvinist Sonnet Sequence,' *ANO* 5 (1992), 137–40. Of these texts, only Margaret Hannay's 1993 essay considers the attribution problems raised by the disclaimer, but she finds 'internal evidence' to link the sonnets and the dedication in a similarity of theme and in Lok's own parallel of the songs of Hezekiah and David, and makes the attribution in the face of a lack of external evidence to the contrary. Hannay (1993), pp. 21–2.
3. J.W. Saunders, *The Profession of English Letters* (London: Routledge and Kegan Paul, 1964), p. 44; Wendy Wall, *The Imprint of Gender: Authorship and Publication in the English Renaissance* (Ithaca, NY: Cornell University Press, 1993), p. 13.
4. Hyder Rollins, ed., *Tottel's Miscellany* 2 vols. (Cambridge, Mass.: Harvard University Press, 1965) 1:2; Barnabe Googe, *Eclogues, Epitaphs and Sonnets*, ed. Judith M. Kennedy (Toronto: University of Toronto Press, 1989); Le Roy Merill, ed., *The Life and Poems of Nicholas Grimald* (New Haven, Conn.: Yale University Press, 1925), pp. 100–2.
5. Catherine Parr, *Prayers and Meditations* (London, 1545) and *The Lamentacion of a Sinner* (London, 1547); Lady Elizabeth Fane, *The Lady Elizabeth Fane's 21 Psalms and 102 Proverbs* (London, 1550); Elizabeth I, *A Godly Meditation of the Soul* (London, 1548). Although Elizabeth Fane's text is now lost, it was described by George Ballard as 'several psalms and pious meditations, and proverbs, in the English Tongue,' George Ballard, *Memoirs of Several Ladies of Great Britain* (London, 1752), p. 119.
6. Margaret J.M. Ezell, *The Patriarch's Wife: Literary Evidence and the History of the Family* (Chapel Hill: University of North Carolina Press, 1987), pp. 62–100.

7. Patrick Collinson makes the attribution tentatively, as 'perhaps Knox's work', in 'The Role of Women in the English Reformation Illustrated by the Life and Friendships of Anne Lok,' *Studies in Church History* 2 (1965), p. 265; the notes to *Mrs Lok's Little Book* (London: Olive Tree, 1973), a reprint of the British Museum text of the sermons, makes the attribution more definitely: 'No doubt the second item in Mrs Lok's little book, "A meditation of a penitent sinner," a metrical paraphrase of Psalm 51, was sent to her by Knox at the same time as the first' (p. 127). W. Stanford Reid's biography of Knox follows Collinson's more tentative position: *Trumpeter of God: A Biography of John Knox* (New York: Charles Scribner's Sons, 1974), p. 141.

8. Laing glosses the psalms published in Knox's texts as 'although sanctioned by Knox, they cannot be considered as forming any part of the Reformer's works.' David Laing. ed., *The Works of John Knox*, 6 vols. (Edinburgh: Bannatyne Society, 1846–64), 6: 284–5.

9. Jean Taffin, *Des Marques des Enfans de Dieu* (Harlem, 1588).

10. Cambridge University Library MS. li.5.37, fol. 5r. I would like to thank Jane Stevenson for bringing this manuscript to my attention.

11. Pernette Du Guillet's *Rymes* of 1546 contains no sonnets, although it provides a precedent for the publication of women's lyric poetry; the first edition of the *Oeuvres* of Catherine Des Roches, which does contain sonnets, appeared in 1578.

12. For a discussion of Marot's formal innovation, see Michel Jeanneret, *Poésie et Tradition Biblique au XVIe Siecle* (Paris: J. Corti, 1969).

13. Henri-Léonard Bordier, *Le Chansonnier Huguenot du XVIe Siècle* (Paris: Libraire Tross, 1870), p. 367.

14. Terence Cave, *Devotional Poetry in France, c. 1570–1613* (Cambridge: Cambridge University Press, 1969), pp. 97–9, pp. 135–45.

15. For a full and clear critique of definitions of a feminine text, see Elizabeth Grosz, 'Sexual Signatures: Feminism after the Death of the Author,' in *Space, Time and Perversion: The Politics of Bodies* (London and New York: Routledge, 1995), pp. 9–24.

16. John Calvin, *Letters of John Calvin Selected from the Bonnet Edition* (Edinburgh, Pa.: Banner of Truth Trust, 1980), pp. 207–8.

17. Wallace T. MacCaffrey, *Elizabeth I* (London: Edward Arnold, 1993), pp. 49–51: Norman L. Jones, *Faith by Statute: Parliament and the Settlement of Religion, 1559* (London: Royal Historical Society, 1982), p. 9; Winthrop S. Hudson, *The Cambridge Connection and the Elizabethan Settlement of 1559* (Durham, NC: Duke University Press, 1980), pp. 90–9, pp. 131–7.

18. Patrick Collinson, 'Windows in a Woman's Soul: Questions about the Religion of Queen Elizabeth I,' in *Elizabethan Essays* (London: Hambledon Press, 1994), pp. 87–110.

19. Ibid., p. 112.

20. 'Catherine, duchess of Suffolk, to Cecil,' 4 March 1559. *CSP* I (1558–1559), pp. 160–1.

21. Margaret Aston, *The King's Bedpost: Reformation and Iconography in a Tudor Group Portrait* (Cambridge: Cambridge University Press, 1993), pp. 113–27.

22. 'And he did uprightly in the sight of the Lord, according to all that Dauid his father had done. He toke away the hie places, and brake the images, and

cut down the groves, & brake in pieces the brasen serpent that Moses had made': *The Geneva Bible: A Facsimile of the 1560 Edition*, intr. Lloyd E. Berry (Madison and London: University of Wisconsin Press, 1969), 2 Kings 18:4. All subsequent biblical references are from this edition.

23. 'Moreover the marvelous diligence and zeale of Iehoshaphat, Iosiah, and Hezekiah are by the singuler providence of God left as an example to all godly rulers to reforme their countreys and to establish the worde of God with all spede, lest the wrath of the Lord fall upon them for the neglecting thereof.' Ibid., iiv.

24. Jean Calvin, *Sermons de Jehan Caluin Sur le Cantique que fait le bon Roy Ezechias apres qu'il eut este malade & afflige la main de Dieu* (Geneva, 1562), p. 20.

25. Edward Dering was suspended from preaching after he delivered a sermon at court before Elizabeth in February 1570 indicting the clergy and criticizing Elizabeth for inaction in the face of their corruption. By 1572, however, he was appointed divinity reader at St Paul's, a position which he used to renew his attacks upon the clergy, criticizing their ignorance and internal disputes in *A briefe and necessarie Catechism* (London, 1572).

26. John Freccero, 'The Fig Tree and the Laurel: Petrarch's Poetics', *Diacritics* 5 (1975), pp. 34–40.

27. *Tottel's Miscellany*, 2:27.

28. R.A. Rebholz, *Sir Thomas Wyatt: The Complete Poems* (New Haven, Conn.: Yale University Press, 1978), pp. 206–9.

29. See Carl J. Rasmussen, '"Quietnesse of Minde": *A Theatre for Worldlings* as Protestant Poetics', *Spenser Studies* 1 (1980), pp. 3–27.

30. 'So I blinde wretch, whome Gods inflamed ire / With pearcing stroke that throwne unto the grou[n]d, / Amidde my sinnes still groveling in the myre, / Finde not the way that other oft have found, / Whome cherefull glimse of gods abounding grace / Hath oft releved and oft with shyning light/Hath brought to ioy out of the ugglye place' (Aa2r).

31. Rebholz (1978), pp. 206–7.

32. The copytext for the psalm paraphrased and included in part at the margin of each sonnet corresponds most closely to the 1557 Genevan psalter published by Jean Crespin, although at points the text in the margins diverges from the 1557 version and corresponds to the 51st psalm printed in the Genevan Bible of 1560. In the final four sonnets, however, where the paraphrase deviates from the words of the psalm and previous paraphrases most significantly, the text of the psalm is a close translation of the 1557 Genevan psalter.

33. Rebholz (1976), p. 209; Clement Marot, *Oeuvres* (Paris, 1551), p. 357r.

3

'Formd into words by your divided lips': Women, Rhetoric and the Ovidian Tradition

Danielle Clarke

> But sure he would not be guilty of such an oversight, to call his work by the names of *Heroines*, when there are divers men, or heroes, as namely Paris, Leander, and Acontius, joined in it.[1]

Dryden's complaint about the 'feminization' of Ovid's *Heroides*, as the text's Latin title, *Epistolae Heroidum*, is translated as *Letters of the Heroines*, is symptomatic of the problematics of gender as they relate to the text which is the subject of this essay. Dryden draws attention to a fact of fundamental importance: that the *Heroides* is in no sense a straightforwardly 'feminine' text, despite its almost exclusive concentration upon the modulations of the female voice. Its transmission demonstrates the *Heroides* to be a text written, translated and adapted by men for the consumption of men, and that its meanings are thoroughly grounded in the masculine dynamics of rhetorical culture.[2] This raises problematic questions about the functions of the female voice for the male poet, and about the inequalities of value attached to women's appropriations of *male* voices. When the male poet speaks in a female voice, seemingly, he demonstrates his linguistic and inventive power; when the female poet uses a male voice, she is deemed to be locked into mere reproduction and circulation, with little hint of the 'subversive mimesis' that Luce Irigaray has attributed to women's words.[3] A masculine verbal economy, however constituted or theorized, would seem to be the precondition of female utterance, whatever the biological sex of the speaker.

The *Heroides* is frequently cited in the writings of early modern women, and used as a problematic authorization for the articulation and circulation of their voices, perhaps because Ovid's epistles uniquely enable speech as a form of virtue and redress within a framework which is simultaneously public and private.[4] The *Heroides* seem to provide a model of how the female voice might be scripted at a textual level. This essay is concerned with the effects and meanings of the creation of a female voice, and how it might operate differently for the male and female writer and reader. Furthermore, I am interested in how it might be (im)possible to identify the gender of a textual voice, suggesting that feminist accounts of Renaissance women writers have assumed too quickly the ontological stability of the female speaking subject: I am thus concerned not with the identification of the female voice, but with an understanding of its constructedness within early modern culture.

It has long been recognized that the adaptation and imitation of Ovid was central to literary expression and generic innovation in the English Renaissance, and that engagement with this particular Latin forebear was fundamental to a system of rhetorical education which had eloquence as its primary goal. Yet it was not only as a stylistic exemplar that Ovid occupied a central place in the literary and mythological lexicon of the lettered early modern, but as a poet fundamentally concerned with the dynamics of the self. This might fairly be assumed to be a primarily masculine self, whose values would be imbibed along with his style and explicitly articulated in opposition to a female 'other', whose stance of grief and lament contingent upon the absence and treachery of the male lover/husband serves finally to reinforce her dependence upon the male term. In other words, despite the apparent 'femininity' of Ovid's text, its ultimate function is to reinforce and underline patriarchal power through the assertion that what is at stake in women's abandonment by men is not only loss of status and virtue, but the loss of self. The Heroidean tradition also recognizes the necessity of male mediation if women's words are to be heard, acknowledging the erasure of both voice and self which is contingent upon the act of lamenting.[5]

The *Heroides* have been viewed as a generic mess, defying clear classification, and difficult to track across the various and varied uses which are made of them. I am concerned here with three varieties of appropriation: translations from Ovid, imitations which specifically invoke Ovidian heroines and the looser form of the complaint or female-voiced epistle. The first group, because they rely so heavily upon a knowledge of Latin, are exclusively male-authored; the latter two include texts by women as well as men. This is a telling reversal of the usual paradigm relating to the gendering of literary production in the Renaissance, where women frequently translate, but more rarely engage in 'original' writing. Both categories raise questions about identification and the uses to which such female-voiced narratives are put – audience and readership would seem to be crucial factors in determining the precise meaning for a male author of using a female voice, and asking what is at stake for a female writer when she 'inserts' herself into such an overdetermined literary tradition. The issue that is raised goes to the heart of the concerns of this volume: when a woman speaks in the early modern period, can she speak as herself? Is the constructedness of her voice any different from the rhetorical self-projection of a male poet? What is the relationship between woman as textual trope and woman as a historically situated speaking subject? Why is it that male-scripted female voices often seem to sit more easily with modern sensibilities?[6] The *Heroides* are fundamental to such questions, as they self-consciously create female voices out of the gaps and silences of classical tradition, but in so doing serve to displace actual women's voices, resorting to a collocation of myth, tradition and convention. Ovid's text might be seen as the ultimate homosocial text, mediating textual power and ideology through the female body, but originating from and directed towards the reinforcement of masculine discourse.

I

The feminized nature of the *Heroides'* content is sharply at odds with the uses to which it was put within rhetorical education. For most commentators the form of the text is paramount, an ideal way to instruct pupils in the conventions of letter writing and the use of *prosopopoeia*. Despite the objections of writers like William Prynne, the *Heroides* formed a central part of the lower school curriculum:[7]

> From 'moral matter' [boys of the fourth form] proceeded gently into unmoral or immoral matter as represented by the *De Tristibus*, *Metamorphoses*, and *Epistles* of Ovid. These were to 'induce' the boys to poetry, and had long been standard works for that process.[8]

This notion of the *Heroides* providing helpful poetic initiation was a commonplace, and testifies that form was at least as important as content, for it was Ovid's processes of invention from Latin and Greek sources that were to serve as the model:

> your Scholars may be brought to the reading of Terence his Adelphi ... and then to some verses, as Psalmi Buchanini, Epistolae

Ovidii, or Ode Horatii, where both the matter and the metre is to be observed; and will be great help afterward to the making of verse, which will not be hard, if he then join that piece of Grammar rules withall, to know the quantity of syllables and kind of verse, after he hath been exercised in making examples of every figure of Grammar.[9]

As well as providing a useful poetic spawning ground, the *Heroides* were advanced as stylistic models of some utility. Despite his scruples about the *Heroides'* status as letters, Erasmus nevertheless places them centrally as models of good epistolary practice, but in such a way as to require a kind of textual 'taming'. The themes of letters, he argues, should be

novel, or amusing, or otherwise congenial to boys' minds. One should seek them out in the stories of the poets or the historians ... In the first category are the love letters of Ovid, which perhaps are not to be recommended as classroom exercises for those of tender years. On the other hand they are comparatively innocent, and there is nothing to prevent a chaste and seemly treatment even of this kind of letter – for instance, a suitor seeking a girl in marriage with cajoling letters, or Helen restraining Paris from an illicit love.[10]

This entails a careful and selective rewriting of the texts, as they are marshalled to a larger stylistic purpose, and Erasmus's concern is clearly with the moral good of *boys*, not the representations set forth by Ovid. The 'femininity' of Ovid's heroines is brought into conformity with Erasmus's own version of female virtue. This rather cavalier attitude to the content of the *Heroides* is important, for their pedagogical function is self-consciously stylistic and poetic as well as grammatical and rhetorical, which may account for the apparent looseness of connection between the text *qua* text and the series of rather wayward sub-genres that it produces in the Renaissance. The *Heroides* function differently for men and for women, not only in terms of the differential and unequal functions of gender, and the public/private divide, but in terms of a central/marginal relationship to the entire humanistic republic of letters.

In order to understand what is at stake ideologically in these texts, it is necessary to address the central and crucial question of how the voice is scripted as feminine. In the Latin texts (and the school exercises produced by them) this is at base a relatively simple matter of grammatical gender, signalled by inflected endings, but in their later English manifestations such identifications have to be indicated by a wider set of ideological and cultural moves. In this positing of the speaking voice as feminine, what is at issue is not only the display of the female body (as wronged, lamenting, grieving) but (male) rhetorical mastery of this body and the language which inscribes and describes it. The Renaissance translations of the *Heroides* are not simply concerned with the transmission of a particular text, but with the reinscription of women's voices to answer to new concerns and new conditions, specifically that of print and the emergence of a female readership, apparently eager to put Ovid's texts to their own uses.

The earliest English translation of the *Heroides* exemplifies the humanist orientation of Ovid's text in the Renaissance. George Turberville's *Heroycall Epistles of the learned poet Publius Ovidius Naso, in Englishe Verse* carries the hallmarks of the poet making his reputation as a versifier via the translation of an authoritative and revered writer.[11] The conventional modesty *topoi* are in place, together with the search for patronage from the text's dedicatee, Lord Thomas Howard. The paratexts give no hint of its 'feminine' material; indeed, the presentational strategies seem, like Erasmus's interpretation of the *Heroides*, to distance themselves from this association. The prefatory materials place heavy emphasis upon the difficulty of the task, the ambitions of the poet, and on the implicit connections of the form with the heroic: 'The very name, *Heroycal* ... deserved an Honorable & Heroycall Personage to be their garde' (sig. A4r). Whilst Turberville does not draw attention to the fact, his translation is also an extended exercise in English versification, linking this enterprise with the reinvigoration of English poetry via a marriage of the classical and the native.

However, Turberville's translation of Epistle V ('Oenone to Paris') demonstrates an abiding concern with questions of gender in its attempt to render the inflected female voice into English.[12] Turberville introduces a much more emphatic language of guilt and blame for his heroine, frequently rendering her utterance into the passive voice, where it has been active in the original, making her the antithesis of the assertive, angry heroine identified in Ovid by Jacobson.[13] Instead, she becomes a wheedling petitioner uncertain of the validity of her own position: 'May not thy novell wife endure / that thou my Pistle

reade?' (26), replacing the urgent imperatives of Ovid's Latin ('Perlege –
non est / ista Mycenaea littera facta manu!' V.1–2). These changes are
often subtle, but telling. Turberville translates the Latin verb *opposuit*
not as 'stands in the way of', but as 'deservde':

> Or by what guilt have I deservde
> that *Paris* should decline?
> Take paciently deserved wo
> and never grutch at all:
> But undeserved wrongs will greeve
> a woman at the gall. (26)

This contrasts with the literal meaning of the Latin, 'What guilt stands
in my way, that I may not remain your own?' (Loeb).[14] Not only does
Turberville introduce the idea of Oenone's culpability here, but he does
so by producing a translation which in addition to reversing Oenone's
rejection of her lot, suggests that the state of vengeance is a specifically
female one. This feminization of Oenone's position is compounded by
Turberville's tendency to flatten out the class aspect of her complaint;
Ovid's text insists upon the irony of her abandoned position given
Paris's transformation from shepherd to prince, but the English text
frequently glosses over this, focusing upon sexual morality and eliding
the powerful language of insult that Ovid provides for his heroine. The
increased stress upon sexual morality cuts both ways, however, being
applied by Turberville both to Oenone's self-presentation *and* to Paris
through the medium of her voice:

> At parture saltish teares were shed
> thou canst but say the same:
> In fayth this latter love of thine
> deserves the greater shame. (28)

Oenone's directness is elided by circumlocution, and the focus is
shifted from Paris's treachery to the immorality of Helen – the final
couplet quoted above is not found in Ovid's text. Throughout,
Turberville tends to select much more pejorative terms with which to
describe Helen, which serves to divert attention from Oenone's anger
with Paris towards a cat-fight between two women over him:

> (Alas) of all my traveling toyle
> a harlot hath the fruite. (28)

Here 'harlot' translates *paelice*, meaning 'mistress' or 'concubine'. Ovid's text reveals a preoccupation with legal categories and terminology, which Turberville generally converts into purely moral positions:

> Now hast thou brought them [treacherous women] home by seas
>> and over wandred waves
> That have their loyall husbands fled
>> and left as lothsome slaves. (29)

'Loyall' here translates the Latin *legitimos*, meaning legally married, and serves to deprive Oenone of the authority that derives from her legal position, which denies her the possibility of redress and relegates her to impotent revenge.[15] Turberville's translation, then, reveals very little interest in the female voice *per se*, concentrating instead upon sexual morality, and undermining, however subtly, the forceful language of justice and retribution that Ovid allots to his heroine. Oenone is to some extent de-rhetoricized and removed from the legal context which enables her to speak, and allied with the position of revenge and emotion which permits the relegation of women's speech to the margins. This is the archetype of an appropriative translation, both in terms of Turberville's reorientation of Ovid's text to answer to the demands of an emergent English poetic culture, and in relation to the rewriting of the heroine's voice as marked not by specific elements of articulation, but by the moral position of the speaker.[16]

This partial erasure of the speaker's gender and the rendering of Oenone as the trace of a masculine rhetorical economy is in stark contrast, at first glance, to Wye Saltonstall's feminization of the *Heroides*. Saltonstall's translation participates in many of the same linguistic manoeuvres, but within an altered perception of the function and audience of the *Heroides*. *Ovid's Heroicall Epistles* (1636) declares its orientation from the start, being dedicated to 'The Vertuous Ladies and Gentlewomen of England', clearly indicating both its intended readership and its moral tenor.[17] In contrast to Turberville's interest in rhetorical and poetic form, Saltonstall is concerned with the *Heroides'* exemplary status, their ability to communicate both precepts and precedents to his audience:

> Your beauties (Ladies and Gentlewomen) are but types and shaddowes of the beauty of your vertuous mind, which is discerned by Noble and Courteous actions. I may therefore presume that *Ovid's* Heroicall

> Epistles, chiefly translated for your sakes, shall find a gentle accep-
> tance, sutable to your Heroicall dispositions, for Curtesie and
> Ingenuity, are the companions of Gentility. (sig. A3r–v)

Where Turberville erases or ignores the gender of the voice in his text
because the primary relationship for him is that between (male)
author/translator and (male) reader, Saltonstall foregrounds it,
presenting it to his readership in terms of a two-way reflection of
textual heroines and readers. The close identification of body and text
serves to erase any potential for independent selfhood or subjectivity
for women and reduces it to a question of biology rather than discursive construction: the female voice consists only of the absorption
of the woman reader into the rhetoric and ideologies of the male-
authored text. This notion is a commonplace in this period and it
serves to distance the woman reader from the humanist model of
reading for utility and public action, a distance carefully underlined
by Saltonstall's insistence upon the necessity of an English text for his
female readers: 'for your sakes come forth in English' (sig. A4r). It is
not surprising, then, to find the translator carefully rewriting the text,
both through presentation and translation, to suit the gender
ideologies of his own period.

Ovid's Heroicall Epistles in Saltonstall's version are not designed to function primarily as a display of the translator's abilities, but as a model for
women to emulate in relation to their own behaviour and speech. In
effect, rather than drawing attention to the constructedness of the voices
in the text, Saltonstall presents them as unproblematically feminine,
based upon the ontological stability of the connection between the body
and speech – and expects that his readership will do so. This strategy of
identification, however, requires some judicious juggling of the messages
of the text, as Saltonstall attempts to direct the readers' interpretation
away from the legitimacy of the women's complaint towards a position
of steadfast virtue and suffering:

> Besides, these Epistles, in regard of their subject have just relation to
> you, Ladies and Gentlewomen, being the complaint of Ladies and
> Gentlewomen, for the absence of their Lovers. (sig. A3v–A4r)

The multiplicity of Ovidian complaint is collapsed into a single idea,
which serves to reinforce the dependence of women upon their 'others'
for identity, 'others' provided by Saltonstall/Ovid in the absence of the
real thing.

Saltonstall apparently grants an authoritative form of expression to his audience. Yet it is clear that the conflation of body and voice in the readerly dynamic set up here is actually for the consumption and pleasure of the text's male readership (or for Saltonstall himself). The encounter of reader and text is figured in courtly and erotic terms and serves as a way of circumscribing the liberatory potential of the text (if such there be), because the female reading subject is seen as a body which offers pleasure to the male reader/author as he observes the objectified and eroticized scene he has constructed.[18] She is a passive participant observed by the controlling male gaze, unable to assert her own agency, and subject to the text's/author's/translator's power. Saltonstall's dedication outlines a textual erotics at work in the three-way relationship between text, reader and author/translator:

> Ladies and Gentlewomen, since this book of *Ovids*, which most Gentlemen could read before in Latine, is for your sakes come forth in English, it doth at first addresse it selfe as a Suiter, to wooe your acceptance, that it may kisse your hands, and afterward have the lines thereof in reading sweetned by the odour of your breath, while the dead letters formd into words by your divided lips, may receive new life by your passionate expression, and the words marryed in that Ruby coloured temple, may thus happily united, multiply your contentment. (sig. A4r)

Aside from the bifurcation of the readership on gender (and educational) lines, Saltonstall uses the common figure of the translation as an ambassador to develop gender difference into a form of courtship which figures the relationship of text and reader as an eroticized one.[18] The Petrarchan idiom is strategically deployed, but with the expectation that, unlike the chaste mistress of the sonnet sequence, these readers will capitulate to the erotic advances of the 'Suiter', an acquiescence they will signal by their *repetition* of the text's words, 'Let English Gentlewomen as kind appeare / To Ovid, as the Roman Ladies were' (sig. A5v).[19] This comment additionally suggests that the scenario that Saltonstall constructs here is actually concerned with a *lack* of self-knowledge on the part of his female readership, as his reference conjures the comically titillating spectacle of English women being seduced by Ovid, just as Roman women were, the daughter of Augustus in particular. The difference is that his readers are to *think* that they are encountering exemplary models of virtue, whilst the male reader takes a voyeuristic delight in the sight of them repeating the words of an 'obscene' and unsuitable poet.[20] Under the guise of benign encouragement, Saltonstall slips in a school-boy joke for the entertainment of his male contemporaries.

The woman reader's role is not to adapt the text for her own purposes, but to embellish it, to decorate it and to give it living form: 'the dead letters formed into words by your divided lips, may receive new life by your passionate expression'. Just as Ovid's heroines are spoken for rather than speaking, constructed rather than self-constructing, Saltonstall's reader is to ventriloquize his text, literally em-bodying it in a double sense. This is almost the opposite of Ovid's strategy, where the constructed female voice absents the body except as an instrument for the expression of grief. For Saltonstall, the body erases the voice except as a physically produced presence:

> He doth so mournfully expresse their passion
> In such a loving, and a lively fashion,
> That reading them grefe will not let you speake,
> Until imprison'd teares from your eyes breake.

> (sig. A5r-v)

The interpretive turn envisaged here in the name of giving the text to women readers involves placing any notion of an authentic female voice at a further remove (under the guise of grounding and essentializing its meanings by conflating it with the material body), and paradoxically opening the gap between women's discourse and what they are given to speak by the attempt to close that rupture. They are intended to express normative male constructions of femininity as their own, without recognizing their constructedness, whilst at the same time asserting their virtue and chastity in the face of the overt eroticism of the text.

It is this contradiction – that the female body and the male-authored feminine text must be asserted as both the same and as different – which necessitates the careful rewriting of Ovid's text in translation. The translation tends to condense Ovid's lines – like Turberville's version, the use of the couplet often leads to the compression of meanings, and an overall reduction of nuance and subtlety. Despite the considerable differences in the two translators' perception of the purposes of the text, the effect at the level of surface is remarkably similar. Once again, active assertions are rendered into the passive mood, and accusatory interrogatives become straightforward statements:

> I shew'd thee both, what Lawnes and Forests were
> Likely to yeeld much store of game. (27)[21]

This diminishes the all-important connection between speaker and imagined interlocutor, locking Oenone into a cycle of repetition and echo, rather than enabling her to exercise her rhetorical power to some effect. Saltonstall frequently omits figures of speech which presuppose a listener who will respond, in particular Ovid's habitual deployment of apostrophe:

> And as the body of the tree doth, so
> The letters of my name do greater grow. (27)

This is in stark contrast to the desire for inscription and display insisted upon by Ovid's Oenone ('crescite et in titulos surgite recta meos!' V. 26) and her use of the imperative. The cumulative effect of these omissions is the de-rhetoricization of the speaker, the loss of the effectiveness of her defence of her innocence. Saltonstall's speaker is a lot less certain of her position, much less judgemental of both her lover and his rival, and significantly less vengeful – Ovid's powerful *gremio turpis* (V. 70) becomes merely 'Thy Sweet Heart'. In line with this pacification of Oenone, presumably with the intent of taming his 'Ladies and Gentlewomen', Saltonstall expands the Latin original in such as way as to shift the focus towards female chastity. Following the passage where Oenone wishes that Paris will suffer the same misery as Menelaus, the translator rewrites Ovid's text:

> So wilt thou then confess, no Art, or cost,
> Can purchase honesty, that once is lost.
> She that is bad once, will in bad persever,
> And being bad once, will be bad for ever. (30)

Not only is Oenone's curse on Paris neutralized, but a gender-neutral statement about chastity (*pudicitia*) is turned into a sex-specific attack on female chastity, with the usual conflation of one woman with all women.

II

If, as I have suggested, translations of the *Heroides* in this period, whether their intended audience is primarily male or female, serve to reinscribe assumptions about gender under the guise of the authentic female voice, using sex to legitimate ideological constructions, then we might expect imitations of the same text to do the same thing on a larger scale. This appears to be the case in the many versions and appropriations of Ovid's epistolary model by male poets circulating in the early modern period, where what is at stake is the display of poetic skill within a framework of complex relationships between voice, gender and power. This is usually at the expense of the historical female subject, who finds herself in a position where male-scripted versions of her voice provide the only authority for her to speak, whether this entails the translation, imitation or ventriloquization of the *Heroides*, the rewriting of the Psalms mediated through the projected but authorizing voice of Sir Philip Sidney, or a complex self-inscription of the the female voice through familial discourse. I would argue that there is properly no such thing as an unequivocally 'female' voice (just as there may not be an unequivocally 'male' one) – texts simply do not circulate in ways which refer inter-pretation back solely to the sex of their 'author'. Rather, they are criss-crossed by a series of discourses and are subject to a variety of conditions which render the gendering of the text – not to mention that of the author – highly problematic.[22]

Thomas Heywood's *Oenone and Paris* (1594) signals its debt to Ovid in its title – something that none of Ovid's female appropriators do. Their stake in the text would appear to be more closely tied to the status of the speaking heroines than to the authority of the Latin poet. Aside from Heywood's titular evocation of Ovid, the rest of the text bears only a passing similarity to Epistle V – Heywood varies and modulates rather than expresses any specific indebtedness to Ovid. This appropriation has only a minimal interest in the construction of the female voice: the epistle is effectively reformulated to conform much more closely to the model of paired epistles found at the end of the *Heroides*. Paris takes control of the narrative, and his presence as an audience serves to curtail, and ultimately to silence, Oenone's utterance. Heywood's complaint is symptomatic of the usage of this form as a literary apprenticeship, including the overt deployment of rhetorical tropes and figures, frequent use of classical allusion, and a degree of generic experimentation.[23] *Oenone and Paris* splices together several generic models through the medium of the exchange between lovers: pastoral, complaint and the fashionable form of the epyllion. The voice here is multiply framed, by the narrator and by Paris, placing Oenone's utterance at a series of removes, rather than the more direct encounter with the constructed voice that we find in Ovid. Heywood orients his narrative poem towards the conventions of complaint, rather than depending directly upon Ovid: the use of a rural setting, the bereft (and as yet unidentified) lover weeping on the banks of a river, and the melancholic observer. Through the use of style and detail, Heywood's poem allies itself with his con-temporaries.[24] The words apportioned to Oenone function to marginalize her within the poem and to render her moral position untenable. The poem becomes a meditation upon male anxieties and desires, rather than upon the legitimacy of the woman's position, as Oenone is finally over-powered by Paris's self-aggrandizing rhetoric and abandoned to grief, lament and loss of position, expressed in terms of her rootlessness, her literal lack of place:

> So wanders poore Oenone through the thickets,
> Uncertaine where to stay, or where to rest her,
> Nowe sittes she still, now doeth she chace the prickets,
> Heaven helpe (poore soule) her new searcht wound doth fester.

> (st. 134)

The fundamental difference between Heywood's approach to the female voice and that of Ovid is that Heywood is more concerned with the grounds on which a woman may speak, rather than with what she says. It is not that either voice is more or less constructed, simply that they are being put to different ends; Ovid plays out the rhetorical category of *ethopoeia* to its logical conclusion; Heywood uses the deficiencies and excesses (moral and linguistic) of the female voice to reassert the author-ity of masculine poetic discourse in the face of the textual challenge prof-fered by Oenone. The ways in which he does so illustrate that the female voice functions as a response to absence, as a form of expression closely linked to the body, and in its corporeality, teeters dangerously on the brink of female sexual passion. The anxiety about vocalization is, in Heywood's poem, specifically a matter of gender. Paris is presented as the melancholic Renaissance lover, giving him a degree of cultural validity and currency. His initial silence is quite different from that of the absent addressees of Ovid's *Heroides*, for in his presence Oenone speaks with an expectation of return, reply, retribution. He is placed in a position of authority, able to judge:

> And art thou come to prosequute the cause?
> Of well or woe, my loosing or my winning?
> > Say gentle Trojan, wordes that may delight me,
> > And for thy former lust I will acquite thee.
>
> > > (st. 10)

Paris has the power to grant or deny Oenone's suit, and the poem attests to the fact that what is at stake in the suit is her selfhood, 'But finding thee, loe, I have lost my selfe' (st. 93).[25]

Oenone puts her case first, in the hope of persuading Paris to accept her once again. Ironically, this is an acceptance that she hopes to find in his speech, which is already characterized by its deception: 'Thy flattering tongue thy falshood did conceale' (st. 20). In contrast to the pleading terms of Oenone's suit, Paris's voice is constructed in terms of power and authority: 'In flowting tearmes he thought to reprehend her' (st. 26). There is none of the faltering that marks out Oenone as a speaker:

> A source of teares (præamble to a passion)
> Hath stopt the passage of her further mone:
>
> > (st 8)

> Pausing a while (for passions made her pause),
> Shee thus beganne, (that hardly found beginning).
>
> > (st. 10)

In each case speech is directly linked with passion. Paris, by contrast, struggles only to make his rhetoric overcome his guilt – it becomes an instrument from which his 'self' remains distinct: 'But when hee knewe she was his quondam wife, / The white and redde were in his face at strife' (st. 26). His speech opens confidently, conforming to rhetorical precepts and employing poetic conventions and classical *topoi*:

> Oenone fayrer then the dame of Troy,
> Staine to the Nimphes of fountaines, flowres, and trees,
> A blot to those that woone in Castalye,
> Fayre Cinthiaes overmatch, in bewty, (more then these)
> When Arte to nature had thy face resigned,
> The Rose, and Lilly, shee in the same combined.
>
> > (st. 28)

Although Paris argues from flawed premises (namely, that it isn't his fault, he was beguiled by Cupid and he wouldn't have married her if he'd known he was a prince) he marshalls his rhetoric effectively, precisely by the destruction of Oenone's character on the grounds of the unduly passionate nature of her sex through an *ad feminam* attack:

> Thy selfe no lesse oe'r-heated with this flame:
> Well I remember thou diddest often tell mee
> That Phebus hath requested even the same
> Which I obtained.

> (st. 116)

By contrast, despite the truth and moral validity of her argument, Oenone loses because her speech is discredited before she utters a word. In Heywood's version, much of the narration which is Oenone's in *Heroides* V is reattributed to Paris – he wins literally by appropriating her speech as rhetorically fashioned and constructed by Ovid, and he does so by viewing it as authoritative rhetoric, not as feminine speech. In Heywood's version, unlike Ovid's, however problematic the conjunction, rhetorical power and femininity are antitheses.

Paris's speech conforms to what we would expect from the rhetorically trained courtier: urbane, smooth, authoritative. What is it, then, about Oenone's utterance in Heywood's version that exiles her to further loss, misery and loss of self? How does she become the marginal Other against which Paris defines his new identity? Part of the answer lies in the alteration of Heywood's title, *Oenone and Paris*, from Ovid's unidirectional 'Oenone to Paris'. The substitution of the copula realigns the power hierarchy that obtains between the speakers. What Oenone says is continually governed by her desire, thus undermining the power of moral argument because it is subjugated to physical passion:

> Then cleave sweete Paris, to thy first election,
> Kisse, and imbrace me in these verdaunt meddowes.
>> If these (as earst they did) can not content thee,
>> Yet voutch thou safe at leasure to frequent me.

> (st. 17)

Without Paris, Oenone only becomes the lack of him, and it is this lack, rather than her self which she vocalizes: 'Thus she laments, for that hee went without her' (st. 121). At the same time, it is grief which disables Oenone's speech, permitting the display of her body as the source and origin of meaning: 'sad sorrow hath her language choked', relegating her to the paradoxical in-between of 'dull extasie' (st. 25). When Paris claims that his own ignorance of his origins had misled him into marrying Oenone, she is once more reduced to her body:

> Oh at that worde, a sudden trembling,
> And uncouthe feare possessed every member,
> Replye she would once more without dissembling,
> But sighes and sorrowes did her language hinder.
>> As doe the windy stormes drive haile and rayne,
>> So sighes drive teares from forth her troubled brayne.

> (st. 53)

Within this economy of language as presence, loss of speech amounts to a loss of self, and the remainder of the poem draws attention to the fact that as a rhetorical construction or projection, Oenone can only remake herself in Paris's image, and to do otherwise is to be exiled to placelessness and lack of identity, except as the mourner of the loss of the other. Oenone presents her self as entirely defined by Paris:

> If thou catch blowes, I shall nor breathe, nor blowe,
> My life is pawned, if thou lackest gages,
> My heart is scorched, if thy anger glowe.

> (st. 71)

In order to regain Paris, she offers to fashion herself to his liking, to remake herself according to the image he desires, so that female self-hood becomes the collapse of difference into sameness: 'Bee what thou wilt, and I will be the same' (st. 76). Her voice is to be erased even as it is heard, as she asks the river to take her cares '[u]nto the strond, where sinnefull soules doe languish' (st. 125); in other words, into nothing-ness, non-differentiation. Her voice, in lament, is no longer her own (if it ever was), as the task of complaint is projected onto the natural world:

> Yee ragged cliffes of never touched rockes,
> Helpe to recount my sorrowes and my crosses,
> You huntresses tricked up in tucked frockes,

Helpe to lament yours, theirs, mine, all their losses.
> Howle, & lament, you cliffes, rockes, clowdy mountains,
> Clear-chrystal streams, wels, brooks, & lovely fountains.

(st. 128)

Finally, Oenone can no longer express her grief as hers, but takes refuge in silence ('Her late lost love she inwardly bewayles', st. 131) and an inner discourse which is based upon simile, the ultimate form of displacement, 'Like to a shippe ... ', 'Or likest to a new strooke bleeding hart' (sts. 132, 133).

III

If, as the evidence presented so far suggests, 'women' in complaint are not women at all, and the posited unwieldiness of women's speech is erased by the rhetorical schematization imposed upon it by men, how is it possible to read or understand women's voices which are scripted by historically real actors? How can the female speaker position herself in relation to a literary form which represented her as a trope, as a linguistic trick?[26] We have seen how women's speech is negated by means of a close association with the body, to which meaning might be referred, and I want to suggest here that one way of negotiating the difficulty of inheriting an already scripted voice, an already inhabited tradition, is precisely by effecting a series of subversions of the patriarchal paradigm of the relationship between speech/text and the body. To a large extent, this is a matter of the strategies of display and self-display found within women's texts which use and adapt the Heroidean model, and a question of the material conditions envisaged or set up by them in their own texts. The entry of women into the form of complaint provides a useful example of the way in which female authorship has to be negotiated: it is not a simple matter of inverting the established textual models, but a question of subverting them from within, because the space of the feminine is already constructed, already occupied by male projections of the 'female' voice. Despite her exploitation of the superficial analogy between complaint poem and female voice, when a woman writes the form, the trope is defigured, literalized and made actual. This is not to say that female-authored complaint is 'true', but that the intervention of an author whose sex is continuous with that of the constructed speaker serves to reconceptualize the trope which underwrites this form. Perhaps most importantly of all, the self which 'speaks' in the poems of Isabella Whitney and Lady Mary Wroth is also a construction, but it is a masquerade of the self, the self made Other. This images women's relation to discourse as a whole, at least as we have come to understand it, such that women have to speak, not as themselves, but as projected images of themselves, articulated in relation to the normative constructions of speech and writing laid down for them.

For Whitney and Wroth, the appropriation of the complaint form constitutes a rewriting and a rereading of inherited forms and structures, where relationships between writer, text and reader are altered. Instead of the female voice functioning purely as a rhetorical performance or construct, the linkage between voice and author is changed. Or put another way, the voice here is a construct, but it is one which does not simply bear an oppositional relation to the speaker: it is marked by sameness *and* by difference. Whereas male-authored female complaint flaunts its performative nature, women writers are placed in a position where they 'perform' speech which is simultaneously their own and wrested from them – hence both Wroth and Whitney construct a (fictional) relationship between teller and tale, and between author and narrator. The process is thus one of *re*-appropriation, as they ventriloquize their own subjectivity as refracted through male representations of female speech. It is necessary for the woman writer to disrupt the dynamics of the male–female relationship troped in the complaint if she is not herself to be troped out of existence.

Isabella Whitney's *The Copy of a Letter* differs from male-authored female complaint in several ways. In the first instance, its generic models are different from those adopted by male poets, owing far more to a popular tradition of complaint poem than to more culturally central discourses of courtliness and Petrarchanism.[27] Secondly, read in conjunction with *A Sweet Nosgay* (1573), it is implicated in the concerns of that volume, namely lack of position, loss of a living, the dynamics of publication and circulation, in short, the material.[28] *The Copy of a Letter* is asserted as an epistolary form, allying it with one aspect of the Ovidian tradition, but one which uses absence as a pretext for writing with the hope of material or financial gain rather than the hopeless articulation of loss.[29] What is at stake here is absolutely not the loss of self, or a sense of sexual shame, but rather material consequences and the socially useful function of giving advice, a careful reversal of the loss of position recounted in the volume as a whole. Thirdly, unlike many of the heroines of complaint, Whitney makes no apology for her utterance, however much the printer tries to unsettle the relation between the fictional voice and its actual counterpart:

> Perchaunce my wordes be thought,
>   uncredible to you:
> Because I say this Treatise is,
>   both false and also true.
>
> The matter of it selfe,
>   is true as many know:
> And in the same, some fained tales,
>   the Auctor doth bestow.
>
> ('The Printer to the Reader', A2v)

The attention paid to the material form of the letter destabilizes the power relations of the *Heroides* and their Renaissance reworkings, by literalizing the epistolary form, so that the text becomes grounded in the written, rather than the performative. This alteration of the conditions of utterance is compounded by the fact that Whitney's addressee remains anonymous, unnamed, whereas in the *Heroides* the interlocutor is always partially identified (and fashioned) by her (often more famous) addressee. She is thus always in a position of secondariness, derivation. Where Ovid's heroines speak within the framework of privacy, Whitney's narrator speaks both publicly and privately – it is her lover who is being displayed here, not her self, as she wittily inverts the female blazon and applies it to her lover's moral conduct.[30] Whitney's addressing of her text to a double audience, 'her unconstant lover' and 'to al yong Gentilwomen, and to all other Mayds in general' posits her text as one which is to be circulated primarily amongst women (much of the 'private' message of the text is directed to the lover's new wife-to-be), rather than as a feminized text/body to be circulated amongst men, as she proposes a counter-paradigm of male behaviour which is defined by its deviation from the female norm: 'Example take by many a one / Whose falshood now is playne' (sig. A2v). The masculine voice is written out of the narrative and made subject to the controlling female voice, itself constructed out of the traditions of the *Heroides* and complaint.

The text is not only invested in the display of male treachery, but in refuting the notion that loss of the female self is contingent upon it – Whitney's speaker is clearly not consigned to silence in the same way as Heywood's Oenone. This turnaround is brought about, to some extent, not only by inverting the inherited roles and traditions, but by re-reading the texts which construct these roles. In the light of the way in which male writers script female voices to make them voice their own marginalization, this can be seen to be a radical move, as the version of the 'self' that Whitney finds in the *Heroides* is carefully repositioned as definitively 'Other':

> For they, for their unfaithfulnes,
> did get perpetuall fame:
> Fame? wherfore dyd I terme it so?
> I should have cald it shame.
>
> (A3v)

Her re-reading of the *Heroides* reproduces many of the conflations present there, but deflects them back upon men, viewing her lover in relation to men in general, just as women have been read in terms of type, and using the language of shame and display to make her moral point clear:

> Example take by many a one
> Whose falshood now is playne.
>
> (A2v)

This is compounded by her revision of the *Heroides*, which concentrates wholeheartedly upon the treachery of men, rather than the complicity of women. 'The Admonition' continues this assault by deconstructing the terms within which male betrayal of women is permitted, in particular locating duality and deception as a quality of male speech:

> Beware of fayre and painted talke
> beware of flattering tonges.
>
> (A6r)

This is reinforced once again by reference to the *Heroides*, in a way which constitutes a rereading of that text:

> Or if such falshood had ben once
> unto Oenone knowe:
> About the fieldes of Ida wood,
> Paris had walkt alone.
>
> (A7r)

The male in this poem is only residually addressed, and the traditions of the form are reoriented so that rather than lamenting for his return, she functions as a test for his loyalty and fidelity, and he is constructed textually as an example for other women to view. He is thus a male who is exchanged between women (reader/writer; narrator/wife).

Lady Mary Wroth's *Urania* (1621) contains several poems which conform to the complaint model, but that authored by Dorolina provides the most direct engagement with the Ovidian model.[31] In this instance too, the conditions in which the text is circulated are vitally important to the construction of the female voice. Like Whitney's text, Dorolina's narrative is presented as a poem which circulates examples of male treachery for the consumption of women, within a highly coded discourse of secrecy and discretion which enables a readership of women to read, speak and interpret within a framework of sexual constancy, rather than display and sexual misdemeanour. At one level, these texts are private texts, to be circulated amongst a community of readers familiar with their codes, where clear demarcations are made between insiders and outsiders. In this way, reading is asserted both as a female space and as a form of virtue. Yet this point can only be made if women's narratives in the *Urania* are also public texts, something which is asserted by Wroth's use of the medium of print and her enclosure of the dynamics of manuscript circulation within the confines of the book. In effect, the *Urania* is a printed text which continually uses the modes of manuscript circulation, producing a doubleness which can be exploited to the end of giving the female voice a location and a purpose which is not predicated upon the assumed meanings of the sexed body.[32]

Wroth's poem conforms quite closely to the model of verse epistle bequeathed by Ovid, and it is the only text authored by a woman that I am aware of that directly appropriates both the form and content of the *Heroides* to the end of asserting female constancy. Like Whitney's poem, Dorolina's narrative is directed towards a female audience, so that the text displays examples of male infidelity to be circulated amongst women for their censure. The poem reverses the dynamic of Ovidian epistle by moving from the general to the particular, rather than vice versa, so that the Heroidean tradition is read quite explicitly in terms of the self, not as an erasure of the female self, where it is subordinated to the rhetorical tradition which produces it. The narrative explains that Dorolina wrote this poem on 'the subject of many unhappy Women, but bringing them all to my sadd estate', thereby asserting inconstancy as a definition of masculinity, as it is traced across individual experience and classical tradition.[33] The poem opens with the epistolary address, as laid down by commentators such as Erasmus:

> Deare, though unconstant, these I send to you
> As witnesses, that still my Love is true.

(U35, ll.1–2)

The anonymity of the recipient is important here, for it means that the text is conceived very much as the property of the speaker and that it is possible to make the subject of the poem male inconstancy *in general*. The notion of her lines as 'witnesses' immediately establishes the female voice in terms of presence, rather than absence, and substitutes speech for the body. Her personification of 'Love' places a crucial distance between her subject and her self, enabling her to maintain a position of virtue and to place her self outside or upon the margins of patriarchal discourse. Her lines express her constancy, not her desire for the lover.

Even here, where it appears that we might be able to find a secure female voice, the poem is overlaid with contradictions and difficulties which make it difficult to claim that this female voice is uttered on its own terms. In the first instance, precisely because Wroth follows the model of the *Heroides*, there is a sense in which Dorolina's words are not her own. This can be seen in the way in which the poem constantly gestures towards its own erasure, 'Receive these Lines as Images of Death' (U35, l.3), and the repeated preoccupation with the suicides of abandoned women. The examples that Wroth has Dorolina choose from the *Heroides* are significant: Dido and Phyllis both kill themselves; Medea vows revenge, making her into a powerful threat to masculinity; and Ariadne draws attention to her loss of security and position. Whilst these models provide a means of articulation for Dorolina, they also raise the insistent spectre of her own annihilation:

> Come, and give life, or in your stay send death
> To her that lives in you, else drawes no breath.

(U35, 99–100)

This gesture is also a threat, as she envisages their lives being intertwined. This ending also matches the models of closure found in Ovid's *Heroides*. The repeated use of paradox provides a different perspective upon the struggle to find a female voice, as it is constructed here in terms of oppositions and contradictions, irreconcilable positions which indicate that the female voice is in process, to be found in the gaps in discourse, rather than within discourse itself.

This need to read the silences is enacted by Dorolina herself, just as we need to undertake it as readers of her narrative. Under the guise of representing her own experience, Dorolina is forced to renegotiate the male-authored examples which seek to describe that experience *for her*: a problematic but productive interpretive gap is opened upon between what she feels and what she reads. These precedents both articulate and undermine her position: 'my ending is the lesse, / When I Examples see of my distresse' (7–8). She reads herself through Ovid's examples, and distances herself from them. As she works through her chosen precedents, she overwrites them and counterposes a female poetics of constancy, which is asserted against the male desire for change. She also points to the inadequacy of these models, showing how they fail to describe the position of the abandoned women: Dorolina thus strikes a blow to the notion of the male-authored female voice as being the dominant cultural form of female articulation. Her employment of these literary examples is less in the spirit of identification than authorization, as they are marshalled to the support of her cause, which is an argument both general and specific. As she evokes each heroine, the particulars of their Ovidian contexts are invoked too; in the case of Ariadne, the stress upon status and violated honour:

> I *Ariadne* am alike oppress'd,
> Alike deserving, and alike distress'd.
>
> (27–8)

Her identification with the Ovidian heroines is used rhetorically to advance her argument, and there is none of the conflation of self and literary example that Saltonstall advocates for women readers of this text. When she turns her attention to Phyllis, her fate is used *metaphorically* to describe Dorolina's suffering:

> While *Phillis* selfe, her lovely selfe did kill,
> Making a Tree her Throne, a Cord the end
> Of her affections, which his shame did send.
> I strangled am, with your unkindnes choak'd
> While cruelty is with occasions cloak'd.
>
> (38–42)

Medea's withcraft is presented as less dangerous than Jason's deception and abandonment (45–8).

Rather than turning the arguments upon herself, Dorolina draws attention not only to her lover's infidelity, but to his lack of coherence, juxtaposing different versions of his self for his, and the reader's, scrutiny:

> Turne backe the eyes of your chang'd heart, and see
> How much you sought, how fondly once sought me,
> What travell did you take to win my love?
> How did you sue that I as kind would prove?
> This is forgot as yesterdayes like sport,
> Love winning lasting long, once won proves short.
>
> (53–8)

This is balanced by her adoption of Penelope as a model, foregrounding the notion of female constancy and asserting it, rather than merely assuming it, as male writers of complaint frequently do. Constancy as an abstract state is presented as defining femininity:

> I like *Penelope* have all this time
> Of your absenting, let no thought to clime
> In me of change, though courted, and pursu'd
> By love, perswasions, and even fashions rude
> Almost to force extending, yet still she
> Continued constant, and as I am free.
>
> (59–64)

There is of course nothing particularly feminist about the adoption of constancy as an ideal, but it is here a self-defined ideal, the delineation of a space which enables a degree of freedom. It may be a response to male constructions of femininity, but it can be used in the service of female desires: in particular, the inscription of constancy enables Dorolina to speak without undermining what she says, because her words are not constantly referred back to her body, and they do not circulate as sexed markers amongst her envisaged audience of women. Rather than repeating what the male writer projects as her concerns, Dorolina, by the very act of utterance, disrupts the normative construction of the woman who is abandoned by her lover, yet cannot find an unmediated space outside of this construction, and therefore has to speak through a series of echoes, repetitions, and disruptions. It is the speaker here who offers to redeem her lover's reputation, to save him from the opprobrium heaped on the treacherous men that she herself has re-read:

> ... all passd falts shall in my breast be hid,
> Try me againe, and you shall truely find,
> Where fairness wanteth, clearenes of a minde.

> (78–80)

Whilst Dorolina's voice cannot be asserted as unproblematically 'feminine' it is the case that she works within the gaps of inherited tradition to unsettle the normative construction of the female voice which leaves her speechless on the margins.

IV

It is clear from the ways in which male and female writers utilize the Ovidian heritage that it is possible to identify textual differences which can be mapped onto gendered positions. However, the evidence presented here warns us against assuming too close a fit between a falsely monolithic notion of gender and the voice of the text; rather we need to inspect the terms and conditions of utterance more closely. It is much easier to provide pointers than to reach solid conclusions, and the recuperation of internally coherent 'women's' voices, tied straightforwardly to biological sex and cultural prescriptions, is as much a misreading as the omission or suppression of those same voices. This essay has tried to point to a more self-reflexive and historically grounded way of reading gendered voices in the Renaissance: it is time for a thoroughly feminist criticism, alert to complexity, difficulty, and historical difference.

Notes

1. John Dryden, 'Preface to Ovid's Epistles' (1680), in *Essays of John Dryden*, ed. W.P. Ker (Oxford: Clarendon Press, 1926), I:236.
2. See Nancy K. Miller '"I's" in Drag: The Sex of Recollection', *Eighteenth Century* 22 (1981): 47–57, and Elizabeth D. Harvey, *Ventriloquized Voices: Feminist Theory and English Renaissance Texts* (London: Routledge, 1992).
3. See Harvey, p. 32, and Luce Irigaray, 'The Power of Discourse' in *This Sex Which is Not One*, trans. Catherine Porter (Ithaca, NY: Cornell University Press, 1985), pp. 68–85, esp. p. 76.
4. See Gillian Beer, '"Our unnatural No-voice": The Heroic Epistle, Pope, and Women's Gothic', *YES* 12 (1982): 125–51, especially p. 134, where she

suggests that these texts envisage a dual readership, the addressee and the audience.

5. Ovid's heroines repeatedly acknowledge the impotence of their language, and the threatened erasure of both artifact and actor. Phyllis threatens suicide; Phaedra imagines that her letter will not be read (*Ep.* IV.3), and finds herself unable to speak (IV.7–8). All citations and translation from the Loeb edition, trans. Grant Showerman (London: Heinemann, 1977).

6. I am indebted to Lorna Hutson for raising this crucial question, discussed also in her essay in this volume.

7. See *Histrio-Mastix* (1633), p. 916.

8. T.W. Baldwin, *William Shakspere's Small Latine & Lesse Greeke* (Urbana: University of Illinois Press, 1944), 2 vols, I: 120.

9. Quoted in Baldwin, I: 348.

10. *De conscribendis epistolis*, tran. Charles Fantazzi in *The Collected Works of Erasmus: Literary and Educational Writings 3*, vol. 25 (Toronto: University of Toronto Press, 1985), ed. J.K. Sowards, p. 24.

11. First published in 1567. Editions in 1569, 1570 and 1600 indicate the text's popularity.

12. For sources, see Howard Jacobson, *Ovid's Heroides* (Princeton: Princeton University Press, 1974), ch. X. For ease of comparison, my discussion will concentrate upon this epistle, not least because it is frequently used and alluded to by women writers.

13. See pp. 180, 189.

14. See also 'yet needlesse is that *Priam* should / of such a daughter shame' (29), where 'shame' translates *recusere*, literally 'to protest against, refuse'.

15. On the legal contexts of complaint, see Lorna Hutson, in this volume, and John Kerrigan, ed. *Motives of Woe, Shakespeare and 'Female Complaint': A Critical Anthology* (Oxford: Clarendon Press, 1991), p. 28.

16. I do not mean to imply that Ovid's text is somehow more 'genuine' in its representation of gender, merely that constructions of gender are ideological and historical and need to be read as such.

17. Subsequent editions were published in 1639, 1663, 1671, 1686 and 1695.

18. On the 'sexualization' of the woman reader, see Mary Ellen Lamb, 'Women Readers in Wroth's *Urania*', in *Reading Mary Wroth: Representing Alternatives in Early Modern England* (Knoxville: University of Tennessee Press, 1991), pp. 210–27.

19. On female repetition, see Juliet Fleming, '*The French Garden*: An Introduction to Women's French', *ELH* 56 (1989): 19–51, and Patricia Parker, *Shakespeare from the Margins: Language, Culture, Context* (Chicago: Chicago University Press, 1996), pp. 116–48.

20. I am grateful to Jane Stevenson for this point. Fleming's article, '*The French Garden*' considers the dynamics of this kind of situation.

21. For *quis tibi monstrabat saltus venatibus aptos, / et tegeret catulos qua fera rupe suos?*, V.17–18.

22. See Loxley's essay in this volume, and the introduction.

23. See M.C. Bradbrook, *Shakespeare and Elizabethan Poetry* (London: Chatto and Windus, 1951), p. 54.

24. See 'Introduction', in *Elizabethan Minor Epics*, ed. Elizabeth Story Donno (London: Routledge & Kegan Paul, 1963), p. 11. All quotations will be taken from this edition.

25. Heywood's use of legal language links the poem to Shakespeare's *Lover's Complaint* and to 'The Lay of Clorinda': 'Ay me, to whom shall I my *case* complaine' (l.1, my emphasis), in *The Yale Edition of the Shorter Poems of Edmund Spenser*, ed. William A. Oram *et al.* (New Haven, Conn.: Yale University Press, 1989). It is also an allusion to the legal framework of complaint, namely the pursuit of a grievance through the law; in the case of women, usually a defence of character from sexual slander. See Laura Gowing, *Domestic Dangers: Women, Words, and Sex in Early Modern London* (Oxford: Clarendon Press, 1996), chs. 2 and 3.

26. See Wendy Wall's question: 'How could a woman become an author if she was the "other" against whom "authors" differentiated themselves?', *The Imprint of Gender: Authorship and Publication in the English Renaissance* (Ithaca, NY: Cornell University Press, 1993), p. 82.

27. Wall, pp. 296–310 uses Petrarchism as a frame to interpret Whitney's *Nosgay*. For popular sources, see Paul A. Marquis, 'Oppositional Ideologies of Gender in Isabella Whitney's *Copy of a Letter*', *MLR* 90 (1995): 314–24, and Lawrence Manley, *Literature and Culture in Early Modern London* (Cambridge: Cambridge University Press, 1995), chs. 2 and 3.

28. See Lorna Hutson, *The Usurer's Daughter: Male Friendship and Fictions of Woman in Sixteenth-Century England* (London: Routledge, 1994), pp. 122–28.

29. See Hutson, pp. 125, 128.

30. See Wall, pp. 96–310 on Whitney's *Wyll*, where she makes a similar argument.

31. All quotations are from *The Poems of Lady Mary Wroth*, ed. Josephine A. Roberts (Baton Rouge: Louisiana State University Press, 1983).

32. See Danielle Clarke, 'Translation, Interpretation and Gender: Women's Writing ca. 1595–1644', Oxford D.Phil. thesis, 1994, pp. 227–63.

33. *The Countesse of Mountgomeries Urania* (London, 1621), p. 418.

4
The Voices of Anne Cooke, Lady Anne and Lady Bacon[1]

Alan Stewart

The twentieth century's reclamation of Renaissance women's writing in English Studies has been paralleled by Social History's exploration of the same women's social roles. It is an uneasy alliance. While literary critics search for an authentic continuous individual voice, historians stress the radically discontinuous lives of Renaissance women, cast successively as daughters, wives, mothers and widows, often with major financial and domestic realignments accompanying each shift in their social state. In this essay, I argue that early modern English readers were sensitive to the ramifications of this latter, discontinuous model when responding to texts attributed to women. Far from recognizing a 'women's literature' or even a 'woman's voice', they heard a number of different women's voices – the maiden, the wife, the mother, the widow – and it was to these differentiated voices that they responded. These were voices that were at once tacitly doubled by the man who defined that woman's social role (the father, the husband, the son), and yet clearly heard as the voices of women. It was only when the silent 'double voice' of the man was absent – for example, when the woman became a widow – that the woman's voice was heard 'single' for the first time.

I take as my test case one of the century's most prominent Englishwomen, Anne Cooke Bacon (1528–1610). The voices we hear today of Lady Anne Bacon, *née* Cooke, are many and various. She is the 'wel occupied Ientelwoman, and verteouse meyden' who englishes the sermons of the Siennese reformer Bernardino Ochino during the reign of Edward VI; she is the 'good wyfe' who nurses her husband Nicholas Bacon back to health during the Marian years; she is 'the right honorable learned and vertuous Ladie A.B.' whose translation of John Jewel's *Apologia ecclesiae anglicanae* is praised and sanctioned by Elizabeth's Archbishop of Canterbury; she is 'a wise and kind mother' to her sons

Anthony and Francis Bacon. But she is also a woman of 'unquietness'; she possesses, according to her elder son, 'a sovereign desire to overrule your sons in all things how little soever you understand either the ground or the circumstances of their proceedings'; she is, according to Bishop Goodman, 'little better than frantic in her age'.[2]

This progressive deterioration of Lady Bacon is usually naturalized as the effects of old age or incipient mental illness. However, in this essay, I suggest that the virtuous pious maiden and lady who translated Ochino and Jewel, and the mad old woman decaying in her country house, are in fact two complementary pictures of the same phenomenon: the educated woman who uses her education to forward and support noncomformist religious views. I argue that Lady Bacon's reputed decline in fact begins with the death of her husband, Sir Nicholas, in 1579, when she was 51 years old. Since 1528, she had lived first as Sir Anthony Cooke's daughter, then as Sir Nicholas' wife; she had published, semi-anonymously, as the English voice of Ochino and Jewel. Now, and for the next 31 years, she lived as a widow, occupying the Bacons' Hertfordshire estate of Gorhambury as a life tenant and controlling the properties left to her elder son Anthony, perceived by many associated with him as a structural obstacle to his inheritance. I suggest that until 1579 we do not hear the voice of Anne Cooke Bacon, but the doubled voice of Anne and whatever man she was translating socially or textually at the time. From 1579 Anne Cooke Bacon's voice is heard, independent, for the first time, and it is heard as mad.[3]

The natural starting point for this study must be the printed texts known to be the work of Anne Cooke Bacon: English translations of various *Sermons* by the Reformist Siennese preacher Bernardino Ochino (from the Italian), and of John Jewel's *Apologia ecclesiae anglicanae* (from the Latin). However, these were not primarily regarded, at the time of publication, as her own literary output: Ochino was firmly billed on the title-page of the former, and the latter was seen as a quasi-official publication (Jewel was not credited in print). The translator is not identified directly in either case. The attempt to detect the voice of Anne Cooke Bacon in these writings, as it might have been heard by contemporaries, is therefore misplaced. That is not to say, however, that her voice is not present, nor that it was unheard.

The publication history of the Ochino sermons is complex and telling.[4] Anne Cooke's translation first came into print in a January 1548 publication, *Sermons of Barnardine Ochine of Sena*, printed by R. Car for W. Reddell.[5] At around the same time, Anthony Scholoker printed in Ipswich six *Sermons of the ryght famous and excellent clerke master B. Ochine*, translated by the local physician and schoolmaster Richard Argentyne,[6] who also published, within the same month, translations of Zwingli and Luther. By the end of the year, however, Scholoker had moved from Ipswich to London, where he worked closely with two other printers, John Day and William Seres. It was Day and Seres who published 14 more of Anne Cooke's translations as *Fourtene sermons … concernynge the predestinacion and eleccion of god. Tr. out of Italian in to oure natyve tounge by A. C.*, probably in 1551.[7] In the same year, Day took all of Cooke's and Argentyne's englishings, now 25 in total, and published them together as *Certayne sermons of the ryghte famous and excellente clerk*.[8] Day was later to reissue this collection in 1570 as *Sermons of Barnardine Ochyne, (to the number of .25.) concerning the predestynation and election of God. Tr. AC*. It appears then that the Schokoler–Seres–Day team already had in progress a translation of Ochino, by Richard Argentyne, before they became aware of Anne Cooke's work. However, ultimately, it was A.C.'s initials that remained on the title-page, and her dedicatory epistle which was used to preface the joint project, while Argentyne's contribution fell into obscurity. All the Ochino sermon translations, including those by Argentyne, were therefore issued to the English reading public as translations *by a woman*.

The gendered nature of sixteenth-century English translations was noted both at the time, and more recently in feminist criticism. John Florio's dictum that 'all translations are reputed femalls' has been taken as the premise to argue that translation, as a 'secondary', imitative, lesser literary activity, was effectively gendered as female, and therefore was an area where female endeavour might be permitted. The objection to such an argument, however, is clear: translations by women were far out-numbered by translations by men during the period. I want to suggest that, while the gendering of certain printed translations cannot be doubted, the gendering lies not necessarily in the act of translation, nor in any specifically female angle in the translation itself. As Suzanne Trill has noted, 'a sizable proportion of the texts translated by women … were also *dedicated* to women', and it is, I believe, to this area – the directions for reading given by the paratextual elements (the dedicatory epistle, the directions 'to the reader', the eulogies and tributes that preface so many sixteenth-century texts) – that we need to turn to appreciate how Anne Cooke's translation of Ochino's sermons might have been understood by contemporaries.[9]

Although Anne Cooke is only identified by the initials 'A.C.', her gender, familial and social status is clearly identified and exploited in the paratextual materials. In her own dedicatory epistle, she identifies herself as a daughter to her titled 'mother' ('the Lady F.'), and in the dedicatory epistle 'To the Christen Reader', 'G.B.' identifies her as a gentlewoman, and a maiden still in the household of her father. When the collection was republished by John Day in 1570, these prefatory materials were retained, although Anne had been wife of Nicholas Bacon for the past 18 years, and had given birth four times. The importance of 'A.C.', therefore, lay not in Anne's fabled family setting, as one of Sir Anthony Cooke's learned daughters, but in the more generalized connotations of her status as an unmarried gentlewoman.

In the prefatory epistle 'G.B.' writes of how 'thorow the honest travel of a wel occupied Ientelwoman, and verteouse meyden' the sermons now 'speake in Englyshe.' The maiden gentlewoman's 'shamfastnes would rather have supprest theym, had not I to whose handes they were commytted halfe agaynst hyr wyll put them fourth.' The sermons are thus mediated by a pure, elaborately unworldly and recalcitrant maiden who has no pretensions to publication. This allows G.B. both to raise the spectre of criticism on the grounds of the maiden's involvement ('if any prety pryckemydantes shal happen to spy a mote in thys godly labour (as I doughte not but the nisytes wyl) seynge it is meeter for Docters of divinitye to meddle wyth such matters then Meydens') and to answer that criticism through the same device:

> let them remember howe womanly they wast their tyme the one part in pryckeynge and trymmynge to vayne hethennyshe ostentacion, and in devisyng newe fashyons of apparel, to whome if in their glasse appered the fowle fautes of their fylthy condicions as playnely as the defautes of theyr forsayde faces, I doubt much whether thei wold delight to roote therin so often as thei do. (sig. A.ii.r–v)

The anti-woman prejudice that might be activated by critics against A.C.'s translation is neatly turned into a misogynistic attack on the same critics. In a similar manner, the idleness of most women is used as a counterpoint to A.C.'s portryal as a learned maiden, thus safeguarding the integrity of the translation: 'If oughte be erred in the translacion, remember it is a womans yea, a Ientyl womans, who commenly are wonted to lyve Idelly, a maidens that never gaddid farder then hir fathers house to learne the language.'

We should not, however, fall into the trap of seeing Anne Cooke's literary endeavour as being passively moulded by male paratextual manipulation. She draws on much the same rhetoric in her own dedication, to 'Lady F.', now thought to be Lady Fitzwilliam, born Jane Ormond, third wife of Anne's maternal grandfather William Fitzwilliam[10] (once again, the precise identification is beside the point in considering the impact of the dedication). Anne's linguistic virtuosity is set in relief by Lady F.'s opposition to the learning of this vernacular language, and Lady F.'s piety. Lady F. is presented as having criticized Anne's Italian studies: 'it hath pleased you, often, to reprove my vaine studye in the Italyan tonge, accompting the sede thereof, to have bene sowen in barayne, unfruitful grounde (syns God thereby is no whytte magnifyed)' (sigs. A.iii.v–A.iv.r). Now, by translating Ochino, argues Anne, the language is of spiritual use:

> I have taken in hande to dedicate unto your Ladyship this smale number of Sermons (for the excelent fruit sake in them conteined) proceding from the happy spirit of the santified Barnardyne, which treat of the election and predestinacion of God, wyth the rest (although not of the selfe title) a perteyni[n]g to the same effect to the end it might appere, that your so many worthy sentences touching the same, haue not vtterly ben without some note in my weake memory. (sig. A.ivr)

A.C.'s unworthiness is used to bolster Ochino's worthiness: 'al be it, they be not done in such perfection, as the dignitie of the matter doth requyre: yet I trust & know, ye wil accept the humble wil of the presenter, not weghing so much the excelnecy [*sic*] of the translacion, althoughe of ryghte it oughte to be such as should not by the grosnes therof depriue the aucthor of his worthynes. But not meanynge to take vpon me the reache, to his hygh style of thealogie, and fearyng also, lest in enterprisynge to sette forth the bryghtnes of hys eloquence, I shuld manyfest my selfe vnapte, to attaine vnto the lowest degre therof. I descend therefore, to the vnderstanding of myne own debilitye' (sig. A ivr–v). The unworthiness of the female translator vouchsafes the superiority of the male author; the inability of the translation to convey all the bright eloquence of the original ironically vouchsafes the unimpeachable quality of that original. Throughout this elaborate paratextual presentation, 'A.C.' has been portrayed in such a way that Ochino's sermons are made palatable to the most doctrinally conservative reader while (it is hinted) they contain material and meanings way beyond the grasp of their present translator. The function of 'A.C.' is thus simultaneously to sanitize and to render intriguing Ochino's sermons.

When Anne Cooke Bacon came to translate Jewel's *Apologia* in 1564, however, a different persona emerged. Here she is 'the right honorable learned and vertuous Ladie A.B.', to whom the Archbishop of Canterbury, Matthew Parker, pays his respects in a dedicatory epistle. Whereas usually the translator would dedicate the work to a putative patron in order to associate the patron with the translated text, its author and translator, here the process is inverted. Instead, Parker effectively dedicates Anne's work back to her: 'where your Ladishippe hathe sent me your boke writen, I haue with most hearty thankes returned it to you (as you see) printed.' Once again, as with the Ochino translation, 'Lady A.B.' is functioning as much more than the translator.

That this is the case is suggested by other factors. The *Apologia* had already been rendered into English and published two years earlier. Now, however, Parker claims that the first englishing was 'not truely and wel translated.' He tells Lady A.B. of how 'According to your request I haue perused your studious labour of translation profitably imploied in a right commendable work.' He expresses his gratitude for the work, but 'far aboue these priuate respectes, I am by greater causes enforced, not onely to shewe my reioyse of this your doinge, but also to testifye the same by this my writing prefixed before the work, to the commoditie of others, and good incouragement of your selfe.' His prefixed writing also ensures that this is seen as an officially sanctioned publication: 'And whereas bothe the chiefe author of the Latine worke and I, seuerallye perusinge and conferringe youre whole translation, haue without alteration, allowed of it, I must bothe desire youre Ladiship, and aduertise the readers, to thinke that wee haue not therein giuen any thinge to any dissemblinge affection towards you, as beinge contented to winke at faultes to please you, or to make you without cause to please your selfe.'

These are far from being conventional niceties: Parker's letter is blatantly disingenuous. He alleges that Lady Anne has, unsolicited, forwarded to him a translation of a work already available in translation, and that he has taken this up because the first translation has proved inadequate. But none of this rings true: the first translation bears traces of revisions and corrections that must have been officially authorized (i.e. by Parker) and which, in any case, remain in Bacon's rendering. The entire project was from the start co-ordinated at the highest level: Jewel's work was one of two pieces commissioned by William Cecil (Lady Anne's brother-in-law) in Latin, and translated into English apparently at the request of Parker; both Jewel and Parker authorize Lady Anne's translation. In other words, far from being a spontaneous englishing by a pious and leisured lady, this translation has all the trademarks of an official, commissioned work.

Heard in this context, Lady A.B.'s voice is markedly different. It is here invoked to give the text a certain tone, a certain gloss or context, effectively to disguise a text which ran the risk of being seen solely as politically motivated intervention in church affairs. The usual tropes of female modesty are invoked: 'You have vsed your accustomed modestie in submittinge it to iudgement, but therin is your prayse doubled, sith it hath passed iudgement without reproche.' In addition to the benefits of having this work in a decent English translation ('ye have done pleasure to the Author of the Latine boke, in deliueringe him by your cleare translation from the perrils of ambiguous and doubtful constructions: and in makinge his good woorke more publikely beneficiall') Parker cites 'the honour ye haue done to the kinde of women and to the degree of Ladies.' This work will encourage 'noble youth in their good education, and to spend their time and knowledge in godly exercise, hauinge delivered them by you so singular a president', a phenomenon which 'youre and ours moste vertuous and learned soveraigne Ladie and Mastres shal see good cause to commende: and all noble gentlewomen shall (I trust) hereby be alured from vain delights to doinges of more perfect glory.' Parker thus makes explicit the strategic use of a female translator to present the case of a female monarch to other women.

As Suzanne Trill has shown, women served to authorize such texts as, in Thomas Bentley's words, 'woorthie patternes of all pietie, godlinesse, and religion' who had given 'their time, their wits, their substance, and also their bodies, in the studies of noble and approoved sciences, and in compiling and translating of sundrie most christian and godlie bookes.'[11] The voices of A.C. and Lady A.B. are strategically used by these publications in order to establish a tone and a frame for reading that would have been quite detectable to a contemporary reading audience trained in picking up just such voices. It is our loss that in the intervening four centuries we have buried this sensitivity, and in so doing, have radically rewritten the specific roles of Anne Cooke Bacon in the ecclesiastical history of her times.

Anne Cooke Bacon developed, through these publications, an iconographic significance that was to be exploited by her elder son Anthony, who spent over twelve years on the Continent (1579–92), often trading on his mother's Protestant credentials. In 1581 the great Reformist theologian Theodore de Bèze, in whose arms Jean Calvin had died, dedicated the French publication of his meditations on the Penitential Psalms to the now widowed Lady Bacon. In the dedicatory epistle he cites Lady Bacon's worthy familial connections – primarily her father Sir Anthony Cooke: 'this constancie and Christian patience wherewith God hath so beautified you, that in you is verily acknowledged that Christianly high minded courage which I sawe in these partes shining in the deceased of very happy memorie, Syr Anthony Cooke Knight, during those great calamities publique to the realme, and particular to him & his whole familie'. But these qualities are also testified to by her pious learning. He cites Lady Bacon's 'reading of those great and holy doctors Greeke and Latine so familiar to you' and how he knew 'by the latin letters wherewith it hath liked you to honour me, the great and singular, yea extraordinarie graces wherwith God hath indewed you'. The picture of a pan-European learned Protestant community was carefully painted, and received as true back home: the nonconformist preacher Thomas Wilcox reminded Lady Bacon in 1589 of how 'you are made truely famous abroad in forraine Churches and countries, & highly reuerenced of many worthie men there, indued doubtles with singular graces for Gods glory, and the building up of the bodie of the fellowship of Saincts.'[12]

Anthony Bacon, however, claimed the credit for this dedication which he said was negotiated while he was staying with the Bezas in Geneva: 'going to Geneva and being lodged with late father Beza it pleased him to dedicate his meditations to my Mother, *for my sake*.'[13] Beza himself states that the *Meditations* had lain forgotten in a drawer: 'I reserued them among my papers as things of no great price: where they had lyen still, had not bene the coming of master Anthony Bacon your sonne, into these partes.' Anthony is able to use Lady Bacon as a icon to authorize the dedication, as the printers of Ochino and Jewel had done years before.[14]

To read off the representations of Anne Cooke Bacon as merely male manipulations of the possibilities of female learned piety, however, is to forestall any attempt to assess Lady Bacon's own contribution to political and spiritual concerns in real terms. Here the situation becomes complicated, because while the invocation of Lady Bacon is well recorded, her own activities have been systematically written out. Twelve years later, when Beza was seeking external funds, he wrote to Jean Castol, the minister of the French Huguenot Church in London, asking him to induce Lady Bacon to write to him. Castol paid a visit to Anthony Bacon, now back in England, who relayed the message to his mother, but Lady Bacon not only failed to comply with Beza's request, but failed to answer at all. It was left to Anthony to send a gift of 20 marks to Geneva, which was duly acknowledged as the gift of Lady Bacon. However, Lady Bacon was perfectly able to make a contribution to Geneva affairs without the mediation of her elder son. In the summer of 1590, when Anthony was still in Bordeaux, she used the services of Castol, and Monsieur Lect, visiting from Geneva, to make a gift of 100 marks for the cause in Geneva, of which one third she specified was to go to Beza directly, and the remainder to necessitous ministers.[15]

The contribution of such a woman as Anne Cooke Bacon to political and ecclesiastical affairs when she was not doubling the voice of a man, whether as translator or wife or daughter or mother, still needs to be recovered and unpicked from the biased and insulting ways in which that contribution was recorded by contemporaries. Throughout the reign of Mary Tudor, for example, the influence of those women intimate to Mary, including Anne Cooke Bacon, was greatly enhanced. It was Anne Bacon who obtained a pardon for William Cecil, the future Lord Burghley, when he fell out of favour through his allegiance to John Dudley, Duke of Northumberland.[16] On Elizabeth's accession in 1558, when Charles V's ambassador Count de Feria reported the new appointments, he explained Nicholas Bacon with reference to Anne Bacon: 'they have given the seals to guard to Mr. Bacon who is married to a sister of the wife of secretary Cecil, a tiresome prude, who belonged to the Bedchamber of the late Queen who is in heaven. He is a man who is not worth much.' The insult of 'prude' mocks Lady Anne's learning and piety, but the form of the report shows that she was the better-known of the couple to an informed foreign observer in 1558.[17] In 1572, Anne united with her sisters to work on a set of verses as part of a campaign to help the preacher Edward Dering, who had insulted the queen in a sermon two years earlier, and subsequently lost his licence. Her contribution is obscured, however, by her husband's prosecution of Dering in the Star Chamber.[18] When John Walsall published his 5 October 1578 sermon at Paul's Cross, it was to Lady Bacon that he dedicated it, although he was dependent on both the Bacons for his employment as tutor to their sons, and for the living to which he was later presented.[19] Although these differences are evident, Lady Bacon's voice was often heard as the echo of her husband's: when Matthew Parker, Archbishop of Canterbury, had a disagreement with Sir Nicholas, it was to Lady Anne that he turned to remedy the situation, 'because you be *alter ipse* to him, *unus spiritus una caro.'*[20]

In February 1579, Sir Nicholas Bacon died. Lady Bacon's ecclesiastical involvement continued, but her voice was now heard differently. For example, she intervened in the Lambeth Conference controversy. When John Whitgift, Archbishop of Canterbury, gave his answer to the Commons' petition on 25 February 1585, to widespread dissent within the House, Lady Bacon was present, extraordinarily admitted through the offices of her brother-in-law Burghley. Like many of the Commons, she was incensed, but 'fearing to stay too long, I could not so plainly speak' to Burghley 'nor so well perceive your answer thereto as I would truly and gladly in that matter.' She therefore wrote to him at length the following day: 'The report of the late conference at Lambeth,' she wrote, 'hath been so handled to the discrediting of those learned that labour for right reformation in the ministry of the Gospel, that it is no small grief of mind to the faithful preachers, because the matter is thus by the other side carried away as though their cause could not sufficiently be warranted by the Word of God', calling for Elizabeth to receive the preachers, and for them to be allowed to consult together without fear. For her own part, she has heard their sermons for the past seven or eight years and 'profited more in the inward feeling knowledge of God his holy will, though but in a small measure, by such sincere and sound opening of the Scriptures by an ordinary preaching' than 'by hearing odd sermons' at Paul's Cross for 'well nigh twenty year together.' She softened her involvement somewhat: 'And indeed, though I hear them, yet I see them very seldom.' She hears the preachers, and writes, 'in their public exercises as a chief duty commanded by God to widows'.[21]

Lady Bacon's self-identification as a widow is significant. The widow came with her own set of popular stereotypes and assumptions. Now defined in relation to men only by the man's absence, she was simultaneously non-existent and absolutely existent in her own right. As the anonymous 1632 *The Lawes Resolutions of Women's Rights* puts it: 'when she hath lost her husband, her head is cut off, her intellectual part is gone, the verie faculties of her soule are, I will not say, cleane taken away, but they are all benummed, dimmed and dazled.' On the other hand, 'Why mourne you so, you that be widdowes? Consider how long you have been in subiection vnder the predominance of parents, of your husbands, now you may be free in libertie, and free *proprii iuris* at your owne Law.'[22] As long ago as 1955, Patrick Collinson noted, in respect to the rôle of women in the English Reformation, that 'there are special factors which obscure the female contribution to history, the legal disabilities of the sex, which so often hide the married woman and allow us to catch glimpses only of the widow, a "person" in law.'[23] With the double voice of parents and husbands now silent, the single voice of the widow, recognized in law, might be heard.[24]

It is indeed after her husband's death that we catch glimpses of Lady Bacon acting in her own right, becoming known as a fervent sympathizer and patron of Puritan preachers. Percival Wyborne, the nonconformist prebend of Westminster, was her chaplain at her Hertfordshire estate of Gorhambury; William Dyke was succeeded in the living of the parish church of St. Michael's (where both she and her son Francis were buried) by Humphrey Wylblud, who had served at Redbourn, location of another Bacon house. Richard Gawton and Thomas Wilcox were placed at nearby Hemel Hempstead and Bovingdon, respectively. It is possible that Lady Bacon was not only the dedicatee of the Puritan apology, *A Parte of a Register*, which featured contributions by Wyborne, Gawton and Wilcox, but that she financed the project and that it came together under her roof. When Thomas Wilcox published his *A Short, Yet sound Commentarie; written on that woorthie worke called; The Prouerbes of Salomon* in 1589, he turned to Lady Bacon to countenance his book.[25] Elsewhere there is further testimony of Lady Bacon's financial support for these ministers. The parishioners of St. Michael's claimed that their minister had been appointed by her means: 'through the godly endeavours of our very good patroness, Lady Bacon, *at her special and almost only charge,* we enjoyed one Mr. Dyke.'[26] Dyke was ejected from his preaching curacy in St. Michael's, but in 1591 became the preacher over the boundary of the Lincoln diocese at Hemel Hempstead, where Richard Gawton was vicar. Lady Bacon used the influence of her son Anthony on the Earl of Essex to transfer the vicarage to Dyke, and to obtain for him a licence allowing him to minister sacraments, although he was only in deacon's orders.

The importance of what he termed 'household religion' for recusants has been forcefully argued by John Bossy, and his findings taken up on the Puritan side by Lawrence Stone and Patrick Collinson. According to Bossy, the Catholic gentleman with a household might well consider his religious belief and practice to be his own business, conducted within the confines of his own household. When Lord Vaux, for example, was presented for failing to attend the parish church in 1581 together with 'his household and familiar and divers servants,' he countered that he 'did claim his house to be a parish by itself.' A similar situation might prevail in a noble or gentle Puritan household, where the family, servants and guests assembled for prayers, and a sermon would be provided by a local minister or chaplain.[27] Anxieties about the widowed Lady Bacon are rooted in her household at Gorhambury. Sir Nicholas had left

Gorhambury to their elder son Anthony, but Lady Bacon was a life tenant. She could be seen, therefore, as a dowager obstacle to his inheritance. The battles between mother and sons, documented in a mass of letters during the 1580s and 1590s, can all be traced to questions of money. Her letters characteristically attack what she sees as her sons' profligacy; their letters hit out at her prolonged control over their lives. Her periodic insinuations of recusancy, bastardy and sodomy against her sons are met with counter-accusations of her encroaching insanity from the sons' servants and friends. Lady Bacon is not only speaking here without the proper authorization of translation or dedication; she is spending her sons' money. It is in Lady Bacon's independent financial support of her religious beliefs that we may find the root of her alleged 'frantic'-ness.

Anthony's servant, Edward Spencer, spent time at Gorhambury during the summer of 1594, and relayed to his master some distressing anecdotes about 'how unquiet my Lady is with all her household.' He told of how Lady Bacon ordered him to hang a dog that he was keeping: when he followed orders, 'she was very angry, and said I was fransey [frenzied, frantic], and bade me go home to my master and make him a fool, I should make none of her.' On a second occasion, she took a disliking to a hawk kept by Spencer, and therefore 'she would let me have no supper. So truly I went to bed without my supper. There is not one man in the house but she fall out withal' – with the notable exception of a single constituency – 'priests, which will undo her. There is one Page which had six pound on her. Mr. Willcockes [Thomas Wilcox] had a paper with a good deal of gold in it. Willblud [Humphrey Wylblud] had two quarterns of wheat. Dicke [William Dyke] had something the other day; what I know not.'[28] The slippage in Spencer's account is very clear. Spencer is worried about her attitude to the various constituent elements of her household – her hostility to those elements that are supported by her absent son Anthony, and her amiability towards those elements that are only authorized by herself, her coterie of nonconformist ministers, which is clearly using Gorhambury as, in William Urwick's words, 'the rendezvous of the silenced Puritan minsters of [the] day'.[29] Spencer's concern is that the household's finances are being spent on the latter at the expense of the former. This situation is read off as 'unquietness'.

The voices of Anne Cooke, Lady Anne and Lady Bacon which reach us are confused and contradictory. They present us not with a single woman but with a trio of states – daughter, wife, widow – the effects of which are discrete and distinctive both when using and used by the medium of print, the first two doubling for father or husband, the last more problematically speaking for the woman herself. But this is not to suggest that Anne Cooke Bacon was either circumscribed by, or even *seen* as circumscribed by her various social roles in relation to men and property. Rather, it is to point to the productive opacity of print in relation to women in the early modern period, an opacity that could both obscure the 'real life' of women, and make possible another, equally 'real life' in print.

Notes

1. This article draws on materials and ideas generated by the research for *Hostage to Fortune: The Troubled Life of Francis Bacon 1561–1626* (London: Victor Gollancz, 1998), co-authored with Lisa Jardine. I am grateful to the College Research Committee of Birkbeck College, for their generous funding of this research.
2. The epithets are taken from G.B., 'To the Christen Reader', in A[nne] C[ooke] trans., *Fouretene Sermons of Barnardine Ochyne* (London: John Day and William Sers, 1551?), sig. A2r; Sir Nicholas Bacon, *The Recreations of his Age* (Oxford: Leslie Chaundy, 1919), p. 28; M[atthew Parker] C[antuariensis], dedicatory epistle to Lady A.B. in *An Apologie or answere in defence of the Churche of Englande* (London: Reginald Wolfe, 1564), 2nd unpaginated leaf, recto; Anthony Bacon to Lady Bacon, 16 April 1593, Lambeth Palace Library [LPL], MS 649 f. 103a (art.67); Edward Spencer to Anthony Bacon, 16 August 1594, LPL m649 fo.221a; Anthony Bacon to Lady Bacon, 12 July 1594, LPL MS 650, f. 228 (art. 150); Godfrey Goodman, The *Court of King James The First*, ed. John S. Brewer, 2 vols (London: Richard Bentley, 1839), vol. 1, p. 285.
3. A full-length study of Anne Cooke Bacon is still needed. The standard accounts are: A.B. Grosart, 'Bacon, Lady Anne (1528–1610)', *Dictionary of National Biography* vol. 2, pp. 323–4; Mary Bradford Whiting, 'The learned and virtuous Lady Bacon', *The Hibbert Journal* 29 (1930–31): 270–83; M. St. Clare Byrne, 'The Mother of Francis Bacon', *Blackwood's Magazine* 234 (1934): 758–71; Ruth Hughey, 'Lady Anne Bacon's translations', *RES* 10 (1934), p. 211; Robert Tittler, *Nicholas Bacon: the Making of a Tudor Statesman* (London: Jonathan Cape, 1976); Mary Ellen Lamb, 'The Cooke sisters: attitudes toward learned women in the Renaissance', in *Silent but for the Word: Tudor Women as Patrons, Translators, and Writers of Religious Works*, ed. Margaret P. Hannay (Kent, Ohio: Kent State University Press, 1985): 107–25; Elaine V. Beilin, *Redeeming Eve: Women Writers of the English Renaissance* (Princeton: Princeton University Press, 1987), pp. 55–61; Louise Schleiner, *Tudor and Stuart Women Writers* (Bloomington: Indiana University Press, 1994), pp. 30–51; Lisa Jardine and Alan Stewart, *Hostage to Fortune: the Troubled Life of Francis Bacon 1561–1626* (London: Gollancz, 1998).
4. See *STC* 3, pp. 51–2, 150–1, 151–2; Janet Ing Freeman, 'Anthony Scholoker, the *"Just Reckoning* Printer"', and the earliest Ipswich printing', *Transactions of the Cambridge Bibliographical Society* 9 (1990): 476–96.

5. *Sermons of Barnardine Ochino of Sena*, trans. A.C. (London: R. Car for W. Reddell, 1548).

6. *Sermons of the ryght famous and excellent clerke master B. Ochine*, trans. Richard Argentyne (Ipswich: Anthony Scholoker, 1548).

7. Ochino, *Fourtene sermons…concernynge the predestinacion and eleccion of god. Tr. out of Italian in to oure natyve tounge by A.C.* (London: John Day and William Seres, 1551?).

8. Ochino, *Certayne sermons of the ryghte famous and excellente clerk*, trans. Anne Cooke and Richard Argentyne (London: John Day, 1551).

9. Michel de Montaigne, *The essayes or morrall, politke and militarie discources* trans. John Florio (London: E. Blount, 1603), sig. A2r, cited by Suzanne Trill, 'Sixteenth-century women's writing: Mary Sidney's *Psalmes* and the "femininity" of translation', in *Writing and the English Renaissance*, ed. William Zunder and Suzanne Trill (London: Longman, 1996): 140–58, p. 145.

10. Identified by Roland H. Bainton in *Bernardino Ochino: esule e riformatore senese del cinquecento 1481–1563*, ed. and trans. Elio Gianturco (Florence: G.C. Sansoni, 1940), pp. 88–9, n.3. Franklin B. Williams Jr, in *Index of dedications and commendatory verses in English books before 1641* (London: The Bibliographical Society, 1962), p. 64, tentatively suggests an alternative reading that 'Lady F.' is a 'maiden-name maske' for Anne's actual 'mother', Anne Cooke, *née* Fitzwilliam, a hypothesis supported by Beilin, Schleiner and Trill.

11. Thomas Bentley, *The Monument of Matrones* 3 vols (London: H. Denham, 1582), vol. 1 sig. B1r; cited by Trill, p. 146.

12. Théodore de Bèze to Lady Bacon, 1 November 1581, Geneva, in de Bèze, Chrestiennes *Méditations sur huict Pseaumes du prophète David* ([Geneva:] Jacques Berjon, 1582). This translation is by John Stubbs: *Christian meditation vpon eight Psalmes of the Prophet Dauid* (London: Christopher Barker, 1582), A.v.r-v, A.v.r. Thomas Wilcox, *A Short, Yet sound Commentarie; written on that woorthie worke called; The Proverbes of Salomon* (London: Thomas Man, 1589), sig. A3v.

13. Anthony Bacon to the Earl of Essex, September 1595. LPL MS. 659, f. 24a.

14. Anthony Bacon to Lady Bacon, 2 June 1593. LPL MS. 649 f.190a (art. 123).

15. See Jean Castol to Theodore de Bèze, 22 July 1590 in Le Baron Fernand de Schickler, *Les Églises du refuge en Angleterre*, vol. 3 (Paris, 1892), pp. 141–5, p. 144. Schickler misreads 'Bacon' as 'Baron'. See also *Registres de la Compagnie des Pasteurs de Genève* (1598–94), vol. 6, ed. Sabine Citron and Marie-Claude Junod (Geneva: Droz, 1980), pp. 63, 64.

16. John Strype, *Annals of the Reformation*, 4 vols (Oxford: Clarendon Press 1824), 4: 485–9, p. 489.

17. Count de Feria to Philip II, 29 December 1558, *Calendar of Letters and State Papers, relating to English affairs, preserved principally in the Archives of Simancas, Elizabeth 1558–1567*, vol. 1, ed. Martin A.S. Hume (London: HMSO, 1892), no. 6, p. 18.

18. A manuscript copy of Bartholo Sylva of Turin's *Giardino cosmografico coltivato* was appended with dedicatory verses by the Cooke sisters, CUL MS. Ii.5.37, discussed by Schleiner, pp. 39–42.

19. John Walsall, *A Sermon Preached at Pauls Crosse … 5. October. 1578* (London: G. Byshop, 1578), sigs. Aiir-Aviiv.

20. Matthew Parker to Lady Anne Bacon, 6 February 1567/8, *Correspondence of Matthew Parker*, ed. John Bruce and Thomas T. Perowne (Cambridge: Parker Society, 1853), pp. 309–16.

21. Lady Anne Bacon to Burghley, 26 February 1584/5, BL MS. Lansdowne 43, ff. 119–20 (art. 48); James Spedding, ed. *Letters and Life of Francis Bacon*, 7 vols (London: Longman *et al.*, 1861–74), 1:40–2.

22. *The Lawes Resolution of Womens Rights* (London: John More, 1632), sig. Q4v cited by Amy Louise Erickson, *Women and Property in Early Modern England* (London: Routledge, 1993), p. 153.

23. 'The role of women in the English Reformation illustrated by the life and friendships of Anne Locke', in *Studies in Social History: A Tribute to G.M. Trevelyan*, ed. J.H. Plumb (London: Longman, 1955), repr. in Collinson, *Godly People: Essays on English Protestantism and Puritanism* (London: Hambledon Press, 1983), pp. 273–89, p. 273.

24. On widows and the law, see Erickson, part IV.

25. Wilcox, sigs. A2r–A4v.

26. The parishioners of St. Michael's to Burghley, 7 November 1589, William Unwick, *Nonconformity in Herts* (London: Hazell, Watson and Viney, 1884), pp. 110–12, at p. 111.

27. John Bossy, 'The character of Elizabethan Catholicism' *Past and Present* (1962); Lawrence Stone, *The Crisis of the Aristocracy 1558–1641* (Oxford Clarendon Press, 1965), p. 735; Collinson, *The Elizabethan Puritan Movement* (London, 1967), pp. 372–82; Patrick McGrath, *Papists and Puritans under Elizabeth I* (London: Blandford Press, 1967), p. 380.

28. Edward Spencer to Anthony Bacon, 16 August 1594, LPL MS. 649, f.221a.

29. *Nonconformity in Herts*, p. 110.

5
Old Wives' Tales Retold: the mutations of the Fairy Queen

Diane Purkiss

A recent paper on Elizabeth I was entitled 'From Fairy Queen to Drag Queen'. Without noticing much else about it, the mistakenness of the title caught my eye because it summarized two ignorances about the so-called 'cult' of Elizabeth. The implicit opposition between terms offers 'fairy queen' as the respectable, anodyne obverse of the excitingly transgressive 'drag queen'. The assumption that calling Elizabeth the fairy queen is an unproblematic compliment is widespread even in criticisms which seek in other ways to interrogate the 'cult' and show the ambivalence of male courtiers, emasculated by a female ruler. Lack of interest in such stories arises partly from our belief that fairies are cute, twee and embarrassing. Even relatively rebellious spirits like Puck conjure up awkwardly childish visions of little winged things fluttering about in an apotheosis of fake childhood innocence. A dim sense that this view is anachronistic has not prevented critics from ignoring the gender politics of fairies, seeing Spenser's *Faerie Queene* and Shakespeare's Titania alike as malleable repositories of (male) political fantasy.[1] And yet the fairy queen is the protagonist of a number of stories which deal precisely with the theme of men's endless and helpless desire for a powerful, inaccessible woman, and the danger her desires pose to them. She also comes to signify the aspect of the maternal which must be transcended for subjectivity to flourish. The fairy queen *is* a drag queen: she is always already marked by deceptiveness, disguise and imposture, and her ontological evasiveness is what allows her to represent and generate desires for sex, for money and for political power. The fairy queen does not exist except as a drag queen, yet her drag act is there not to problematize identity but to generate desire for an absolutely authentic and real presence, a presence signified not merely by sex, but also by money. These unarguably solid goods are what the queen of the fairies exists to provide. The queen of the fairies is itself a rewriting of a range of stories, probably women's stories or old wives' tales, which survive only in fragmentary form, but which gesture at women's investment in the idea of a powerful and eroticized matriarchy which is not an object of desire but a possible fantasy self. What is interesting about these stories for the purposes of this essay is not merely their flexibility but the way they are told by men and women, and also told by women to men and by men to women – to one woman in particular, Elizabeth I. I will explore these topics by telling three related fairy stories which will also begin the process of building up a picture of the forms the fairy queen could take. I want to begin with a story that is not a story, a story that is never really told. It comes from Isobel Gowdie, a woman accused of witchcraft, whose confession was given to John Gilbert on 13 April 1662:

> I was in the Deunie-Hills, and got meat there from the QWEIN of FEARIE, mor then I could eat, the Qwein of Fearie is brawlie clothed in whyte linens, and in whyt and brown cloathes, & c; and the KING OF FEARIE is a braw man, weill favoured, and broad-faced, & c.; There were elfbullis rutting and skeyling up and downe thair, and affrighted me.[2]

'& c'. A whole story might have been glimpsed in that '& c', yet because it lacked evidential value in a witchcraft case, it is not recorded. That part of Isobel Gowdie's story is lost to us; all we have is the knowledge that there was such a story, and a few slight indications of what it was about. Isobel Gowdie managed to tell that the queen of the fairies nourished her, giving her meat, but the silence surrounding this leaves us uncertain of how to interpret the information. Given Gowdie's stress on the queen's fine clothes, and the king's, we might see this as a fantasy of dining with the great, or perhaps as a traditional piece of hospitality extended to a poor woman by a rich family.[3] This would not be incompatible with seeing the story as a fantasy version of such hospitality, in which the social barriers of class are broken by the anomalousness of the supernatural, so that Gowdie can dine with the fairy king and queen almost as their friend as well as their dependant; certainly, her attempt to describe their accoutrements in detail implies an identification with their elevated social station. Is she a kind of enchanted Christopher Sly, and is this what the fairies offer? It is suggestive that the fairies give Gowdie meat, for meat suggests upper-class and celebratory meals. However, Gowdie may simply be using the term as a synonym for food in general. If so, this is indeed a fairy tale, for English folklore is full of stories about peasants who gain advancement in great or little ways by association with the fairies.

Can we also see the queen as a quasi-maternal figure, offering great – even excessive – nurturance to Isobel Gowdie, saving her from work and toil, returning her to the safety of childhood? (Another Scottish suspected witch, Bessie Dunlop, was visited by the queen of the fairies during her childbed lying-in; the queen appeared merely as 'ane stout woman' who asked for a drink, and being given one then foretold that the baby would die; here the queen assumes the surrogate-mother role of the gossip.)[4] But is this in conflict with the story's buried letter? Is there also a deleted element of sexuality in the well-favoured king, about whom no more is to be said – or, at any rate, recorded? As we shall see, the fairy queen is characterized by unruly or illicit sexuality, and men who accept her gifts are usually pay for them with sexual favours. Is Gowdie doing the same with the king of the fairies? Bessie Dunlop had an entirely asexual and much more personal relationship with Thom Reid, the fairy who acts as her spiritual adviser and who prophesizes her family tragedy, so we should not assume that because men's relationships with the fairy queen were sexual that women's with fairy men were too. Finally, there are the bulls, those mysterious bulls running about that so frighten Isobel. Are they phallic? Are they yet another sign of the nobility of fairies, that they have many cattle? Are they simply a test of Gowdie's nerve; is this one of those stories in which the heroine has to prove her worth to the fairies in order to enter their good graces? We can speculate and speculate, but the fact remains that on its own, this story is too fragmentary to be read definitively. As readers will have noticed, it has ceased to be a story Isobel Gowdie is telling, and has become a story I am telling about or for her.[5]

Folklore, including the works of early modern folklorists like John Aubrey and Robert Kirk, figures the fairies as always already departing, or 'flitting'; fairy beliefs, too, are always already on their way out, always already a matter for half-forgotten tales told by grandmothers or nurse-maids to forgetful children.[6] Certainly, as Isobel Gowdie's story shows, it can seem that it is always too late to know them. The fairies are evanescent to us. Despite the labours of eager Victorian folklorists, whose prime interest was in fairies, early modern people were on the whole reticent about fairy beliefs. There is a lot of evidence, but not of the 'authentic', unquestionably uncontaminated and 'popular' sort longed for by folklorists and other scholars. Whereas with witchcraft the statute book provided occasions on which stories of witchcraft would be told (however haltingly) and recorded (however incompletely), fairy stories were never important evidentially, and when fairy stories are told in cases of witch-craft or sorcery, they are sometimes halted by judges who are not interested.[7] The endless transformativity of the fairy becomes its hallmark. This evanescence is also complicated both by the way beliefs were changing in the sixteenth century, with new stories being added and old ones rewritten under the pressures of Reformation, print culture and the regulation of conduct and manners. These pressures ensured that the fairy when it appeared would be used to signify a range of different things, while adding new interpretative strategies to old tales, such as the godly notion that all fairies were demons. There is no simple double or forked tongue of gender difference here; rather, fairies figure in a range of differences of which gender is only one.

For whereas the queen of the fairies is characteristically seen in a personal relationship with the gallant and heroic cunning man or woman who meets her, there may have been another, less private way of understanding her. My second fairy story is also a story of fleeting impressions, flitting and transformation, a story of disguise, masquer-ade and deceptiveness. And yet here that deceptiveness is linked with the politicized usage of disguise, ritual and symbolic disorder familiar to us from other early modern political contexts.[8] In a theatrical use of the symbolic figure of the fairy queen as a signifier of rebellion, a band of Kentish protesters stole deer from the deer park of the Duke of Buckingham at Penshurst. They were a diverse group, containing some yeomen, husbandmen, various tradesmen including the local butcher, and some labourers. They

> with others unknown to the number of one hundred men, in riotous manner and arrayed for war, viz. with jakkes, salades, bry-gantes, breastplates, hauberks, cuirasses, lances, bows and arrows, and covered with long beards and painted on their faces with black charcoal, calling themselves servants of the queen of the fairies, intending that their names should not be known ... broke into a park of Humphrey Duke of Buckingham called Redleff [Redleaf] at Penshurst and chased, killed and took away from the said park 10 bucks, 12 soses and 80 does belonging to the said duke, against the king's peace.[9]

The name 'servants of the Queen of the Fairies' had been used in January 1450 by the leader of another conspiracy, and the later servants of the queen were in turn carrying on from the rising of

April 1451, which may have been caused by the threat of further repressive measures in the wake of Cade's rising.[10] These servants of the fairy queen, perhaps fairy queens in drag, signifiers of political unrest and disorder, might also signify much else. Occult knowledge? Jack Cade was supposed to have raised the Devil and used magical books to bring about his rebellion.[11] Subjects of another monarch, hence protesters against the existing order? Does allegiance to the queen of the fairies signify being outside; outside the law, for instance? Does 'servant of the queen of the fairies' mean 'no-man', nonexistent, catch-me-if-you-can? Almost certainly all these rebels gave the answer in response to a question about whom they served; the queen of the fairies is another form of disguise, of face-blacking. Inversion of the social order? Or does the fairy queen stand simply for undeserved wealth, a kind of early modern answer to the National Lottery, and hence for poaching, for rebellion, for social inversion? We shall see that she represents something of the kind to others.

Gender and gender roles are crucial to the third fairy story I want to tell, a story which itself pre-dates Elizabeth I, yet acts as a blueprint for later storytellers, who voice it, but otherwise. This is a male story, yet some of these later storytellers are women who weave enchanted skeins of narrative in order to use male desire for gold and sex to gratify their own. In two late medieval ballads and a fifteenth-century romance, the fairy queen offers extraordinary opportunities to young men, but also poses a threat to them. The ballads 'Thomas the Rhymer', 'Tam Lin' and the romance 'Thomas of Ercledoune' tell substantially the same story, ordered and arranged differently.[12] A young man is alone in the country-side when he sees a beautiful lady, who turns out to be the queen of the fairies. Addressing her, he finds himself her (sexual) prisoner and must go to fairyland with her to 'serve' her for seven years. At the end of that time, in 'Tam Lin', he is in acute danger because that is when the fairies pay 'the tiend' or tithe to hell, and he is the likely candidate.[13] This makes explicit the story's link with a number of others, in which a lover falls into the power of his or her dead beloved and makes the mistake of kissing or addressing him, thus condemning him or herself to death.[14] The fairies of 'Thomas the Rhymer' are explicitly associated with death and violence: 'It was mirk, mirk night and there was nae stern light / And they waded through red blude to the knee: / For a' the blude that's shed on earth / Runs thro the springs of that countrie'.[15] The blackness and the blood make up an alternative space of formlessness, terror, entrapment, and yet blood and darkness are also associated with sexuality, with carnality. Is fairyland hungry for human blood, vampiric?

And does this hunger for blood symbolize a hunger for blood products, for male seed, for male flesh? Is the blood the grisly symbol of the tiend to hell, and are both signifiers of female desire and its insatiability? Is fairyland – or the way to it, at least – a kind of womb as imagined by a terrified male, a maternal body which does not nurture, but rather terrifies by its formlessness, its entrapping disorder that threatens to engulf all order? Is the maternality and carnality of the fairy queen on display in this darkness flowing with blood? If so, it is significant that the escaping man characteristically receives a gift, the gift of prophecy, often associated with the maternal and the semiotic by virtue of its ambiguity and amphibology. Julia Kristeva's work shows the need to expel the fantasy mother in order to achieve mastery of the self, control over the self; by passing through fairyland, are these men born again from the mother in such a way as to give them mastery of the mother-tongue?[16] At this point, however, we might want to recall that Bessie Dunlop also encountered the queen of the fairies in the context of a birth passage, though in her case the labouring female body was her own. Perhaps the queen of the fairies can represent that dark and feminine space which both men and women have to escape and repress in order to become articulate subjects.

Occult gifts are a characteristic result of contact with the fairies, and this belief persisted firmly in early modern England, where there are numerous cases of cunning men and women claiming that they gained knowledge of the future or of current events from contact with the fairies; others claimed to have gained healing powers.[17] Such occult powers were by no means confined to young men like Thomas the Rhymer: Joan Tyrrye was on her way home from Taunton market when she met 'one of the fayre vayres, being a man, in the market of Taunton, having a white rod in his hand, and she came to him, thinking to make an acquaintance of him, and then her sight was clean taken away for a time, and yet hath lost the sight of one of her eyes'. Note that Joan loses actual sight in exchange for her occult sight; again the danger the fairies posed is figured through the threat of a dark passage, the passage of blindness. And yet the fairies 'taught such knowledge that she getteth her living by it' and that her doings 'in healing of man and beast, by the power of God taught to her by the fairies be both godly and good'.[18] Agnes Clark's daughter Mariona Clark was given a holly stick by the fairies in 1499, and her mother eagerly brought it to the curate of Ashfield, Suffolk, asking him to bless it to help her find hidden treasure.[19] In both cases, the result of contact with the fairies was occult knowledge, as early moderns understood that; not necessarily great spiritual insight, but the ability to find hidden treasure. If we read these stories as tales of the infant's transcendence of and escape from the maternal into precarious subjectivity, we can understand the ambivalence with which these cunning men and women speak of their mistress the queen of the fairies.

Sexual enslavement, vision, prophecy and death are powerfully linked in an image which to us is given its resonance of decadence by its reuse in many Romantic and post-Romantic poems and works of art. These echoes, though present in the medieval texts, should not blind us to a key feature of the queen which would not have appealed to Keats or Rossetti; the queen gains power over these young men when they mistakenly speak to her. Just as it was sometimes vital not to speak to a witch, so addressing the queen of the fairies opened the person to her, perhaps simply drew him to her attention.[20] Yet the young men do not intend to speak to the queen of the fairies; both of them mistakenly believe her to be the Virgin Mary. This mistake leads them to address her in language fraught with the rhetoric of courtly, and even amorous submission, and it is perhaps this rhetoric which both seduces and condemns them to sexual enslavement and its outcome, the threat of death and of hellfire. Thomas the Rhymer, for instance, enacts a fatal submissiveness: 'True Thomas he took off his hat / And bowed him low down till his knee: / All hail, thou mighty Queen of Heaven / For your peer on earth I never did see'.[21] Perhaps there is even a kind of discomfort with the representation of the Virgin as a beloved female ruler, a discomfort that emerges much more clearly in post-Reformation connections between the Catholic Church and the fairies.

In a Renaissance context, however, what we might notice is the extent to which the fairy queen's power over the young men depends on a kind of unconscious masquerade and transformation. Thomas's entrapment is a consequence of a trick of the light, an imperception, a failure to grasp essences through appearances; we shall see that he is not the last to be so entrapped. We still think of fairies – fairy godmothers, in particular – as those who wave their magic wands in pantomime transformation scenes, and in this respect we are for once true to early modern belief. For even in this early version of the myth, the misperception of the queen of the fairies as the virtuous Virgin Mary draws attention not only to her power to transform herself, but also to her extraordinary ontological fluidity. The fairies do not really have true, single, stable natures. The term 'fairy' is used problematically to mean a diversity of different beings from demons to household brownies to grand and courtly personages six feet high to a specific set of diseases and their symptoms. Some later, proto-Enlightenment fairies are able to alter their size from small to large. Yet this very lability associates itself with the dubious signification of the queen of the fairies, her role as representation of the chaotic and engulfing femininity that lurks beneath a deceptively lovely appearance. The historical alteration of fairies, the shifting signification of the euphemistic names they are given, their elusiveness, their ability to make themselves invisible and to blind or deceive the eyes of mortals are the principal tropes of fairy tales. That transformativity, that ontological instability, lies behind representations which might seem much more simple, even comic, and it continues to carry its charge of misogyny. As we shall see, that charge increases when the queen of the fairies comes to symbolize the excesses of transformation of the self, or self-fashioning, and the extent to which these might exceed rather than express humanist and godly notions of self-government.

Thomas the Rhymer might seem passé in the early modern period, but at least one cunning man seems deliberately to have taken him as a model. Andro Man, giving an account of his encounters with the queen of the fairies, said that 'among her company were sundry "deid men"', including 'The kyng that deit in Flowdoun and Thomas Rymour', and he affirmed that 'the quene is verray plesand, and wilbe old and young quhen scho pleissis; scho mackis any kyng quhom scho pleisis, and lyis with any scho lykis'.[22] The queen's sexual unruliness is a signifier both of her otherness and her power. In Andro Man's account, the fairy kingdom is a matriarchy. The queen is also deceptive; Man dwells on the frangibility of fairy benefits, for what seems a fair chamber disintegrates into a mossy bank in the morning. That this is a male fantasy is attested by others. Andro Man had hoped for something better than moss; he had hoped for wealth, obtained directly or indirectly. William Lilly, the astrologer and cunning man,

> As it happened not many years since with us, a very sober discreet person, of vertous life and conversation, was beyond measure desirous to see something of this nature; he went with a Friend into my *Hurst wood*, the Queen of Fairies was invocated, a gentle murmuring Wind came first; after that, amongst the hedges, a smart Whirlwind; by and by a strong Blast of wind blew upon the Face of the Friend, – and the Queen appearing in a most illustrious Glory. No more, I beseech you, (quoth the Friend) my Heart fails; I am not able to endure longer, nor was he; his black curling hair rose up, and I believe a bullrush would have beat him to the ground.[23]

Desiring the queen of the fairies is accompanied by terror of her. Here, she presents herself almost as God did to Moses, preceded by a roaring wind. But the queen's glory, too, seems apotropaic, Medusan, reflected in the upstanding, (consolingly phallic?) hair of Lilly's client.[24] What kind of incapacity is he confessing? An inability to look, to see, undoubtedly, but perhaps another incapacity also, an incapacity in meeting the demands of the queen. For another aspect of the fairy queen's disorderliness, her lack of control or containment, is her figurative sexual licence.

Thomas the Rhymer's story is also the basis, and rather an odd basis, for a series of early modern reinventions which transform it completely from lingering romanticism into a carnivalesque joke. Transformativity becomes theatricality, 'accidental' misperception becomes deliberate deception, alteration becomes comic inversion, and the queen of the fairies is less a mysteriously sexualized corpse than a common whore. Sexual licence allowed some women to tell a very simple version of this story to men and women with great effect. The story goes like this: in exchange for sex, the king/queen of the fairies will transform your goods into gold. Two such tellers of tales were Judith Phillips and Alice West, both of whom impersonated and spoke for the queen of the fairies.[25] One of many cases in which Alice West was involved was simple: West persuades a goldsmith's apprentice that 'had charge of more wealth than wit' that 'the queene of the fayries did most ardently doat upon him'. Telling the usual story, West persuades him to bring his master's silver plate to be turned into gold while 'thou shalt confer with the amorous queene of fayries'. However, what awaits him is not sexual exhaustion, but a beating:

> The young man next morning got up early according to his hour, went to the close, and placed the plate in the four corners, still expecting the queen of fayries, and then this Alice West had plast in a ditch foure of her consorts, who came forth, and with stones and brickbats, so beat the poore prentice, that he ran home, and forgot to take his plate with him. His corage was cold for meeting the Q. of fayries.[26]

In the fantasy Alice West offers, the alchemy of sex, translating blood into seed, is mimicked in the fairy queen's alchemical translation of silver or base metal into gold, also a process of making the sterile into the fertile. At the same time, both sex and transformativity are seen simply as commodities, to be exchanged profitably. What is transgressive about this, as about alchemy, is that this way of making money – literally making money, making it breed and grow from nothing – is the antithesis of the humanist and godly notion of prudent profitability, whereby money and goods could not be 'made', but only gathered and stored. Whereas the mainstream notion of enterprise involved a virtuous storing up of the fruits of labour, the fairy queen offered a way to short-circuit all that, a chance for a miraculous and meteoric rise that was intrinsically undeserved. As such, she could not help but symbolize both the transgressive pleasures and the instability of enterprise culture, and because the queen was a woman, that instability became linked with female rule through her. This has stark implications for the representation of Elizabeth as the fairy queen. Besides, the entire fantasy is so evidently based on a system of government where bribes and gifts function as ways to ingratiate oneself with the powerful that its constant denunciation as trickery and theft might itself make uneasy reading for the ruling classes. As Linda Levy Peck has shown, the practice of gift-giving became less a taken-for-granted way of doing business and more a sign of corruption as the seventeenth century wore on; here, the notion of buying favour is shown to be a cruel delusion.[27] What, after all, is the difference between the queen of England and the queen of the fairies? Ordinary people never meet either, but have unsustainable hopes of both.

'Having drained him completely dry', Alice West leaves one of her victims; the text refers to his loss of money to her, but might equally mean his loss of fluids, his loss of masculine potency. The witch in *Macbeth* threatens to drain her victim 'dry as hay' in similar fashion. Another of the queen of the fairies' eager votaries was Goodwin Wharton, the younger son of a prominent gentry family. Like Lilly's friend, Wharton was both dazzled and terrified when the cunning woman he had encountered, Mary Parish, introduced him to the amorous queen of the fairies. Wharton was acutely anxious about his ability to meet the sexual demands of the queen and Mary. He began to suffer from a backache which he thought was due to a riding accident, but which turned out to have another cause. He also thought that his back seemed worse after sex with Mary, feeling half-dead afterwards. Thinking it over, he remembered Mary's story that the king of the fairies had once told her that he could make himself invisible and enjoy her whenever he liked; Wharton began to think that a female fairy was using him similarly. It turned out to be the queen herself, whose passion for him was so great that she had taken to consorting with him several times a night. Once she had had intercourse with him three times in a row, and had then 'sucked up her breath' at the moment of climax, so that she had drawn 'the very substance of the marrow' out of his bones.[28] She had almost killed him. We might read this as a naturalization of the fears evoked by the rivers of blood and the tiend to hell in the ballads, fears of engulfment, exhaustion, female sexual excess. Yet Goodwin Wharton is also frustrated, for he never sees the queen who desires him so much.

If ever there were stories of deferral, dilation and delay, these are such stories.[29] The story Mary tells Goodwin Wharton cunningly involves Mary in the same quest for the nonexistent in which she seeks to trap Goodwin; it constructs her as his partner in pursuit of the same goals. From these beginnings, she entangles Goodwin Wharton in a rich and elaborate web of narrative, narrative which stretches onward into a glittering future of money and prestige, a future which can be told but cannot ever quite be reached. That future is symbolized by the queen of the fairies. In all these tales of cozenage, the fairy queen can appear only as a non-appearance. Her presence in narrative generates a desire without an object, or with an object that can exist only as further narrative. What if the fairy queen's excessive and unruly desires are simply reflections, mirror-images of the insatiable desires she generates by her perpetual absence? What if her lust for man's seed, for men's bodies and blood, is a reflection of their desire for gold? for in these stories it is only the queen who is driven by lust. The men are driven by a longing to make money from their royal paramour, and from another motive too: a wish to be somebody, to be elevated into the world of nobility and royal supremacy. The stories of Thomas the Rhymer and of Thomas of Ercledoune, also stories of young men becoming important, act as models for the self-fashioning which can be glimpsed not only in the activities of cunning folk and their businesses, but also in the dubious energies of courtiers on the make, courtiers like Sir Walter Ralegh, and jobbing poets eager to get into society, like Edmund Spenser. And yet for the three Thomases, getting on paradoxically involves overcoming or coming close to a horrendous threat to masculinity, a devouring femininity which might well 'drain' the victim.

And yet when the fairy queen does surface as part of the 'cult' of Elizabeth, her appearance seems blandly benign. At Woodstock in 1575, 'her majesty thus in the middest of this mirth might espy the queen of the fairies drawn with six children in a wagon of state'.[30] The fairy queen presented Elizabeth and her ladies with gifts of gowns, verses and nosegays. At first glance, this delicate and pastoral scene seems incompatible with the deceptive seductress of Thomas the

Rhymer, light years from the theatrical deceptions of Phillips and West. And yet it is not so very remote from the fantasies of (of all people) Isobel Gowdie. For Elizabeth's relation with the queen of the fairies here is precisely the one that all the gulls seek, that of favoured client. The queen gives Elizabeth elaborate gifts, including a gown, not merely as signs of her favour, figurations of Elizabeth's special status, but as a means of conveying those gifts delicately to the queen. There is also a kind of built-in pun here; two queens on a state visit, an event that, outside the realms of fantasy, would have been accompanied by a great deal of gift-giving designed to display the wealth and wisdom of the givers. To Elizabeth, too, the fairy queen was a figure for hospitality, generosity, gift-exchange. But are those gifts, for all the apparent squeaky-cleanness of the occasion, tinged with dubiety? Do they have an ambitious quality, either implying that Elizabeth herself is an upstart, or casting her as the queen of the fairies who will by alchemy turn brass into gold? Whatever the truth of this, there is no doubt that the gifts work to cast the queen in a role as giver and receiver of commodities. The drama also casts Elizabeth in the role of favourite of the fairy queen, the fairy queen's chosen knight, like Thomas the Rhymer. This is odd from numerous viewpoints, but especially because of Elizabeth's sex and the eroticism of the original story.

Thomas Churchyard's entertainments for Elizabeth in Suffolk and Norfolk in 1578 included a scene where seven boys were dressed 'like Nymphs of the water' and they played 'by a device and degrees like fairies, and to dance (as near as could be imagined) like the fairies'. The queen of the fairies drew attention to the unusual publicity of their appearance: 'Though clean against the fairies' kind, we come in open view, / And that the queen of fairies here presents herself to you.'[31] Here, the assumption is that Elizabeth is the sole authentic recipient of a favour merely promised deceitfully to others. And yet this is a theatrical performance, so as often what presents itself as authentic is most flagrantly inauthentic. Elizabeth as hapless gull again? At Elvetham in 1591 the fairy queen, named as Aureola, appeared again, dancing with her maids, and presented Elizabeth with a garland of flowers given 'by Auberon the fairy king'. Yet the fairy queen here also has some real connections with folklore; she comes from under the ground ('I that abide in places underground'), like the queen of tradition. but there is something odd about this when the tradition had been so evidently eroticized. None the less, this fairy queen so delighted Elizabeth that she asked for this part of the drama to be rerun three times, calling 'for divers' Lords and Ladies to behold it'.[32]

Apparently Elizabeth enjoyed the idea of being the fairy queen's knight and votary, of partaking in the fantasy and drama of the fairy queen's dubious magic.

Many of the same themes were re-used at Ditchley, where Elizabeth was greeted at the banquet by 'the Queen of the Fayry'; the fairy queen Eamblina also featured in a second day entertainment in which Eamblina persuades a daughter to return home with her father to make a suitable match. Here, for the first time in drama, is a fairy queen who is plainly intended to represent Elizabeth, who was of course responsible for agreeing to and to some extent arranging the marriages of her ladies-in-waiting. Yet this fairy queen is also represented as cruel: justly she makes an unfaithful knight sleep a 'deadlie' sleep. This theme of cruelty, together with the identification of Elizabeth and the fairy queen, were of course greatly extended by Spenser. The vision of Gloriana experienced by Arthur looks far less straightforwardly complimentary to Elizabeth in the light of the fairy queen's associations with masquerade, evanescence; deceptiveness into deliberate deception; with the semiotic confusion of the maternal, from which comes speech and prophecy; with death; with rebellion and the disorder of social climbing; female misrule; with sexual exhaustion; above all, with ontological nullity, for Arthur never meets the fairy queen in the version of the poem we have, and his quest, like Goodwin's, is subject to constant deferral, delay, and even the impossibility that generates narratives about the fairy queen.

Moreover, Spenser's narrative of Arthur's encounter with the queen replicates consciously and precisely the ballad narratives I have been discussing, though probably mediated through high-culture's romances and consciously shorn of its most disturbing features.[33] The encounter remains sexualized, however highmindedly, when 'her dainty limbes full softly downe did lay ... Most goodly glee and lovely blandishment / She to me made, and bad me love her deare / For dearely sure her love was to me bent' (I.ix.13.8–14.3).[34] Even the impress of the queen's body on the grass as the trace of her presence has a faint whiff of sexuality, figuring the queen as fully incarnate (as opposed to a mere vision). Arthur's misery at Gloriana's departure, a misery which leads him to embark on a quest to rediscover her, casts him as another of the fairy queen's votaries, gifted perhaps, but gifted by virtue of having encountered femininity at its most other, most alien. That encounter shapes his giftedness. Like Thomas the Rhymer's, it is manifested as solitariness; Arthur is a drifting signifier who is not fully integrated into society or family, but remains aloof from them. Aloof, or cut off? If the latter, Arthur's plight is truly Virgilian in its sadness, for his position as Gloriana's favourite seems by no means secure; rather it seems to imply an act of faith on his part.[35] Has he sacrificed love, even pleasure, for an empty vision? His isolated masculinity, surviving the fairy queen, has great power, but little pleasure. If this is one possible strand of feeling in this endlessly complex text, then Arthur also represents Elizabeth's courtiers, men who were forced to pursue her favour endlessly, often at the expense of forming more reliable ties, without ever securely grasping it. Walter Ralegh was, after all, closely concerned with the poem's development and one of its dedicatees.

Here, then is an aspect of *A Midsummer Night's Dream* overlooked by recent combatants disputing whether the poem rebukes Elizabeth's power or her sex.[36] It matters that Titania is not just any queen, but the fairy queen. As he was to do in *The Merry Wives of Windsor*, Shakespeare was indulging Elizabeth's enthusiasm for the role of the queen of the fairies or her votary, while critiquing her through the same figure.[37] All the discourses we have been discussing are caught up and reworked in this play. The similarity of Titania's love for Bottom to the narratives in which the fairy queen elevates a mortal are evident. Here, the queen's choice is desperately inappropriate, of course: Bottom is not capable of elevation. That inappropriateness casts doubt on both female rule and male attempts at social advancement. There is also a sense in which both Bottom and Titania are victims of deception, trickery and masquerade, but with a difference. Whereas both the authentic and the trickster fairy queens were firmly in control over their own impersonations, this fairy queen is the butt of the joke. Removing from femininity its power to deceive and rendering it as deceived is a very effective disarming of an otherwise terrifyingly unstable power. However, Titania retains the trace of maternal chaos which was figured in those deceptions in her speech to Oberon about the disharmony of nature resulting from their quarrel; in particular, her use of the imagery of overflow, flood, contagion, all uncontrolled movements, is reminiscent of the deadly rivers of blood which swamp the riders in 'Thomas the Rhymer' (2.1. 90, 92ff). It is these forces of chaos which Oberon is able to subdue, crucially by exposing Titania through masquerade; he thereby becomes the authentic and reassuring vision of masculinity offered by the ballads and not attained by the ever-deceived Goodwin Wharton and other gulls. Titania also retains her sexual threat. She does not want Bottom solely for the beauty of his singing, and his terror when confronted with Titania's sexual demands is very reminiscent of the reactions of Wharton and of William Lilly's client. Whereas in *The Merry Wives of Windsor* the queen's difference from Mistress Quickly is safeguarded by the protocols of class, here those protocols are allowed to collapse under the pressure of masquerade and carnival, here viewed less as licensed pleasures than as naked threats created by female lust, and by female rule. This is not, then, just about the taming of a queen. It is about the taming of a fairy queen, and hence about subduing the very dark anxieties generated for masculinity by a female ruler.

I want to return briefly to Mary Parish's stories to Goodwin Wharton in order to look at how popular and high culture were intertwined at this point. Whereas most histories of fairies by folklorists argue that an unchanging popular culture was corrupted by input from the learned, I want to claim here that Mary Parish's stories reflect and re-use materials created for the elite in order to create a plausible fantasy of social advancement for her own pleasure and profit. Mary's fairies had their principal colony between Hounslow and Colnbrooke. Passing through a door in the earth, Mary found herself looking at a fairy palace with marble courts. These fairies were not merely rich; they were also laden with political and religious symbolism. They were Catholics; indeed, they were more Catholic than the Pope by virtue of their adherence to Mosaic law and their eager adherence to the old calendar. Wharton gets his first chance to see them at home when they are celebrating St George's Day – these fairies have their own Pope. They maintain an absolutist monarchy, with descent through both male and female lines.

In comparison with the exciting radicalism of the queen of the fairies in the fifteenth century, the impact of courtly fairy representation and of French *préciosité* and its aristocratic *contes des fées* is clear.[38] The queen of the fairies who so tired Goodwin Wharton was named Penelope La Gard, a name both exotic and aristocratic, and, like the wife of Charles II, she was Portuguese, the sister of the reigning fairy king of Portugal. After her husband's death she becomes the ruler of the kingdom, and it is not long before she declares her intention of marrying Goodwin and making him the new king of the fairies. Meanwhile, the queen's sister, Princess Ursula La Perle, the most beautiful woman in the world, came to be attracted to him too and made even more lavish promises than had the queen; she offered to make him rich beyond his wildest dreams, agreed to live above ground with him, or in Italy if he preferred. Snobbish though all this sounds, it stands in direct contradiction to Wharton's desperate efforts to transcend his own position as an impoverished younger son through spectacular deployment of occult resources. He was not content to accept his place, but sought to improve it, and politically he was an ardent Whig, keen to restrain the power of the monarch, and in trouble himself for having so many family members connected with the Meal Tub Plot. In inventing fairies to suit Goodwin Wharton's needs and desires, Mary seems to have consciously evoked them as the moneyed privileged goal that he was pursuing, while using their by-now-built-in conservatism to reassure him about his own daring in challenging the social order.

In this context, is it significant that Goodwin Wharton's fairies are *small*? Though able to assume normal size if they chose, they were naturally 'not above a Yard in height' and they rode horses the size of 'masty dogs'.[39] As miniature people, they can more perfectly represent their large counterparts; indeed, they can act as commodities who literally summarize in miniature form the status, wealth and spiritual insight of society's elite. They are not yet dollhouses, tiny and labour-intensive signifiers of long and arduous craftsmanship devoted to making small that which is only usable when big, but they are clearly moving in that direction, moving, that is, in the direction of Flower Fairies and the like. Yet their size is also rationally explicable; they are human beings who simply happen to possess some magical skills which humans have unaccountably lost. Clearer still is an advertisement illustrating the way in which otherness, maternity and sexual strangeness could be commodified in a new kind of figuration of the fairy queen:

The Lest Man and Horse in the World

The First being a little Black-Man, being but 3 foot high, who is distinguished by the name of the Black Prince, and has been shown to most Kings and Princes in Christendom. The next being his wife, the little woman, not 3 foot high ... straight and proportionable as any Woman in the Land, which is comonly called the Fary Queen, she gives a general satisfaction to all that sees her, by diverting them with dancing.[40]

By now, the fairy queen is an object, even a commodity, nothing but a spectacle that can be commanded for money. Occult knowledge, desirability, even money, are no longer necessary. She has been divested of all her threatening power not only by her commodification, but by her link with race. Her otherness now reduced to blackness, the fairy queen is no longer an ontological problem, since she can be seen, bought, exploited, owned at any time. Any oddities of behaviour become explicable through the lens of anthropology. She is simply and solely a show. Such was the fate of Gloriana.

Notes

1. There have been three substantial studies of early modern fairy beliefs and texts this century: Minor Latham, *The Elizabethan Fairies* (New York: Scribner, 1930); Katherine Briggs, *The Anatomy of Puck* (London: Routledge and Kegan Paul, 1959), and Keith Thomas, *Religion and the Decline of Magic* (London: Penguin, 1971), pp. 724–34. It goes without saying that none looks at the question of gender.
2. *Ancient Criminal Trials in Scotland*, ed. Robert Pitcairn, vol. 3, pt 2 (Edinburgh, 1833), p. 604. The rest of the Gowdie trial is on pp. 602–16.
3. On the centrality of hospitality to relations between classes, see Felicity Heal, *Hospitality in Early Modern England* (Oxford: Clarendon, 1990).
4. Pitcairn, *Criminal Trials* vol. 1, pt 2, pp. 51–8.
5. Like Isobel Gowdie, many of the surviving fairy stoires I am telling here are Scottish. Yet their influence on and relation to English stories is clear, and it may simply be that Scottish inquisitorial witchcraft investigations gave an opportunity for these stories to emerge.
6. For fairies always presented as a past belief, see Reginald Scot, *Discoverie of Witchcraft* (1584), 8.15, and John Aubrey, *Remaines of Gentilisme and Judaisme*, in *Three Prose Works*, ed. John Buchanan-Brown, (Fontwell: Centaur, 1972), p. 203. See also Robert Kirk, *The Secret Commonwealth of Elves and Fairies*, from a 1691 manuscript, printed 1815. Kirk's work is very unlike other early modern musings on the subject, with a heavy injection of neoplatonism.
7. For witch trials involving references to fairies, see Annabel Gregory, 'Witchcraft, Politics and "Good Neighbourhood" in Seventeenth-Century Rye', *Past and Present* 133 (1991), 31–66; *Depositions from York Castle*, ed. James Raine, Surtees Society, vol. 40 (1860), p. 93; *The most wonderful and true story of a certain witch* (1597), p. 1; 'The Wonderfull Discoverie of the Witchcrafts of Margaret and Philippa Flower' (1619), in *Witchcraft in England 1558–1618*, ed. Barbara Rosen (Amherst: University of Massachusetts Press, 1991), p. 377.
8. See Natalie Zemon Davis, 'Women on Top', in *Society and Culture in Early Modern France* (Oxford: Polity, 1987, 1st edn 1965), pp. 189–226.
9. 29 June 1451, at Tonbridge. The jury found a true bill, but the fate of the prisoners is uncertain; *Documents Illustrative of Medieval Kentish Society*, ed. F.R.H. du Boulay (Kent Archaeology Society, 1964), pp. 254–5.
10. All this agitation took place in the aftermath of Jack Cade's rebellion, which led to savage repression. See *Six Town Chronicles* ed. R. Flenley, p. 127.

11. *Historical Manuscripts Commission* 5, p. 455.

12. F.J. Child, *The English and Scottish Popular Ballads*. 5 vols (New York: Folklore Press, 1956), nos. 35, 37A, 37 Appendix, 39.

13. On the tiend, see also James I, *Daemonologie* (Edinburgh, 1597), pp. 73–4, and the trial of Alisoun Peirson, 1688, in Pitcairn, *Criminal Trials*, vol. 1, pt 2. p. 163.

14. One of the best-known of these is the early modern ballad known as 'The Suffolk Miracle', Child, *Ballads*, 272, vol. 5. p. 58.

15. Child, *Ballads*, 37 C. The association of the fairy queen in particular with death is evident in medieval romances; in Chaucer's *Merchant's Tale*, and in *Sir Orfeo*, for instance, she is equated with the queen of the underworld, Proserpina. This equation may be based on the fact that both figures are queens who live underground. However, there are many stories which equate fairies and the dead: see L. C. Wimberly, *Death and Burial Lore in English and Scottish Popular Ballads* (Lincoln, Neb., 1927), and Lewis Spence, *The Fairy Tradition in Britain* (London: Routledge and Kegan Paul, 1948).

16. On prophecy and semiosis, see my 'Producing the Voice, Consuming the Body: Seventeenth-century Women Prophets', in *Women/Writing/History*. ed. Isobel Grundy and Susan Wiseman (London: Batsford, 1992), pp. 139–58; Julia Kristeva, *Powers of Horror*, trans. Leon S. Roudiez (New York: Columbia University Press, 1982), esp. p. 71.

17. Cf., for instance, John Walsh, *The Examination of John Walsh* (1566); spells for conjuring Oberon into a crystal stone are found in Reginald Scot (*Discoverie*, 15. 10). See also Bodleian Library MS e. Mus 173 f 72 v–r. Similarly, William Stapleton tried to conjure Oberion, among other spirits, but Oberion 'would in no wise speak to him'; this was part of one of the searches for buried treasure dear to early modern hearts, *Norfolk Archaeology or Miscellaneous Tracts Relating to the Antiquities of the County of Norfolk*, vol. 1 (Norwich, 1847), pp. 57ff.

18. Somerset Record Office, Wells Diocesan Records, D/D/CA, Act Books 21 and 22.

19. R. Seton Watson, *Tudor Studies* (London: Routledge and Kegan Paul, 1924), p. 73; see Latham, *Fairies*, pp. 137–41.

20. Falstaff in *The Merry Wives of Windsor*, 5. 5. 47, says 'They are fairies, he that speaks to them shall die'. On the inadvisability of speaking to a witch, see Diane Purkiss, *The Witch in History: Early Modern and Twentieth-century Representations* (London and New York: Routledge, 1996), p. 129, and see also Jeanne Favret-Saada, *Deadly Words; Witchcraft in the Bocage* (Cambridge, Cambridge University Press, 1980).

21. Child, *Ballads*, 37A, vol. 1, p. 323.

22. *Spalding Club Miscellanies*, vol. 1, pp. 119, 121–3.

23. *Mr William Lilly's History of his Life and Times from the Year 1602 to 1681*. ed. Elias Ashmole (1715), pp. 102–3.

24. I am of course referring to Sigmund Freud, 'Medusa's Head', in *The Standard Edition of the Complete Psychological Works of Sigmund Freud*. ed. and trans. James Strachey *et al.*, 24 vols (London: Hogarth, 1953–74), vol. xviii (1955), pp. 273–4.

25. *The Bridling, Saddling and Riding of a Rich Churl in Hampshire, by the subtle practice of one Judith Phillips, a professed cunning woman or fortune teller* (1595). On Phillips, see also *Historical Manuscripts Commission* Hatfield House, vol. v (1894), pp. 81–3; *The Several Notorious and Lewd Cozenages of John West and Alice West, falsely called the king and queen of fairies* (1613). For another similar case in a Chancery court, see C.J. Sisson, 'A Topical Reference in *The Alchemist*', in *Joseph Quincy Adams Memorial Studies*. ed. J.G. McManaway (Washington: Washington State University Press, 1948).

26. *The Several Notorious and Lewd Cozenages*, p. 10. West's tricks were not confined to men; women too were offered the oportunity to get money from the queen or king of fairies, but they were not said to be beloved or favoured.

27. *Court Patronage and Corruption in Early Stuart England* (London: Unwin Hyman, 1990).

28. British Library, MSS Add. 20006, f. 41V. This is Goodwin Wharton's autobiography, and the story told here is his account of what Mary told him. On Wharton, see also J. Kent Clark, *Goodwin Wharton* (Oxford: Oxford University Press, 1984).

29. The phrase 'deferral, dilation and delay' is Patricia Parker's, in *Literary Fat Ladies* (London: Methuen, 1988).

30. *The Queen's Majesty's Entertainment at Woodstock* (1575) ed. A. W. Pollard (Oxford, 1903).

31. Thomas Churchyard, *The Queen's Maiesties Entertainment in Suffolk and Norfolk* (1578), sig. G2v.

32. Jean Wilson, *Entertainments for Elizabeth I* (London: Brewer, 1980), pp. 115–16.

33. Spenser's immediate source was probably Chaucer's burlesque of such desires in *The Tale of Sir Thopas*, ll.778–96, where the knight dreams that 'an elf-queene shall my lemman be' and vows to forsake all other women for her.

34. All quotations are taken from *The Faerie Queene*, ed. A.C. Hamilton (London: Longman, 1977).

35. For Virgilian themes in Spenser, see Patricia Parker, *Inescapable Romance: Studies in the Poetics of a Mode* (Princeton: Princeton University Press, 1979), p. 88.

36. I refer to the notorious debate between Louis Montrose's supporters and Lisa Jardine at the Berlin Shakespeare conference in 1986; traces of the debate and starting positions can be seen in Louis Montrose, '"Shaping Fantasies": Figurations of Gender and Power in Elizabethan Culture', *Representations* 2 (1983): 61–94, and Lisa Jardine, 'Why Should He Call Her Whore? Defamation and Desdemona's case,' in *Reading Shakespeare Historically* (London: Routledge, 1996), pp. 19–34.

37. On *Merry Wives* and Mistress Quickly as 'quean' of the fairies, see my *The Witch in History*, pp. 193–5.

38. Anne Jefferies, the Civil War prophet who saw the fairies and was informed by them about the probable course of the war, reported that they supported the king and traditional religion. See *The Witch in History* for more on Jefferies, pp. 161ff.

39. BL, MSS Add. 20006, f. 32r. For the fairies' ability to enlarge themselves, see f. 100v.

40. British Library, N. Tab 2026/25, 19. Date uncertain, but after the accession of William and Mary, *c.* 1690. This is, of course, a rehearsal of cultures in Steven Mullaney's sense, but here the 'culture' is that of the fairies as well as of pygmies: 'Strange Things, Gross Terms, Curious Customs: The Rehearsal of Cultures in the Late Renaissance', in *Representing the English Renaissance.* ed. Stephen Greenblatt (Berkeley: University of California Press, 1988), pp. 65–92. Folklore and early anthropology were mutually constitutive in the early modern period; both Aubrey and Goodwin Wharton are beginning to approach the fairies as a race or ethnic group.

6
Giving Time to Women: the Eternizing Project in Early Modern England

Amy Boesky

> What can time have to do with the gift? ... what would there be
> to see in that? ... Time, in any case, gives nothing to see. It is at
> the very least the element of invisibility itself.
>
> <div align="right">Jacques Derrida, <i>Given Time</i>[1]</div>

The gift of time

In the 1570s, during a decade of heightened interest in the queen's age
as she approached menopause, Elizabeth began receiving a new kind of
gift: ornamental timepieces intended to be worn on her body. In 1571,
the Earl of Leicester gave her 'one armlet or shakell of golde, all over
fairely garnished with rubyes and dyamondes, haveing in the closing
thereof a clocke'. In 1578 and again in 1580, Leicester gave the Queen
pendants containing watches, while from the Earl of Russell she
received a 'diall' set in a ring of golde. Elizabeth received half a dozen
such timepieces in the 1570s, most ornately decorated with female
figures or with popular feminine symbols, such as flowers. From the
inventory at the queen's death come descriptions of a 'clock of gold
curiously wrought with flowers and beasts, with a queene on the top of
th'one side'; 'one clocke of golde wrought like deyses and paunseyues,
garnished with little sparks of diamonds, rubies, and emerodes'; a 'little
watch of christall ... with her Ma'ties picture in it'; several watches
fashioned like flowers, and one decorated with three antique women.
Many of the queen's watches contained chiming mechanisms or
alarms to make time audible, as well as visible. One unusual alarm-ring
contained a small prong which 'gently' scratched the queen's finger to
alert her to the passage of time.[2]

It is not surprising that these ornamental timepieces would have been seen as appropriate gifts for a queen with a penchant for extravagant novelties. But the rapid succession of watches given to Elizabeth needs to be considered within the context of her ageing and the anxieties it elicited, as well as alongside the corresponding outpouring of songs and sonnets dedicated to the eternizing theme in the 1580s and 1590s. In eternizing verse, the poet extends to his beloved images of her youthful beauty, its susceptibility to time's ravages, and his own power (through his poetry) to preserve her idealized image. Eternizing depends on positioning the beloved in a temporal realm distinct from that inhabited by the poet. Johannes Fabian has argued that the category of otherness is often secured through the construction of separate (and hierarchized) temporal spheres. Denied 'coeval time' with the writing subject, the anthropological subject is constituted as different through what Fabian calls 'allachronic discourse'.[3] Eternizing, itself a kind of allachronic discourse, worked in the early modern period to split (and to gender) temporal categories.

The project of eternizing, like the gift timepieces, carries within its ornamental rhetoric an embedded alarm. The beloved's youthful image must be preserved precisely because the threat of time's ravages is so imminent and the cost of her ageing so extreme. In the last decades of Elizabeth's reign, masques, processions and portraits testified to the queen's longevity, her miraculous preservation from time's ravages and the exquisite prolongation of her youthful visage. This 'mask of youth', to borrow Roy Strong's phrase, has been interpreted customarily in light of the queen's vanity, or of royal control over circulating images, or generalized nostalgia on the part of a populace anxious about succession. But like the gift of eternity offered to a host of mistresses in courtly sonnets, the gift to the queen of perpetual youth carried within it a countering debt or obligation. Like the queen's watches, such images worked to alarm as well as to compliment. In the last years of Elizabeth's life, a series of images was produced in which she appears as 'ever young and beautiful' or 'astoundingly rejuvenated' – Robert Peake's image of the queen painted in the so-called Procession Portrait in 1601, for example, and Nicholas Hilliard's coronation miniature of the queen, reissued in the first years of the seventeenth century, when the queen was 67 and approaching death.[4] It is instructive to compare such idealized images with the following report from a visiting French ambassador from the same period. Here we see the queen not as an icon of eternal youth, but as a death's head or *vanitas*:

She was strangely attired in a dress of silver cloth, white and crimson ... [with] slashed sleeves that hung down to the ground, which she was constantly twisting and untwisting. She kept the front of her dress open, and you could see the whole of her bosom, and passing low, and often she would open the front of her dress, as if she were too hot ... her bosom is rather wrinkled ... As for her face it is ... long and thin, and her teeth are very yellow and irregular ... on her left side less than on the right. Many of them are missing, so that you cannot understand her easily when she speaks.[5]

Countering Strong and Hilliard's preservation of the queen as eternally young was this image of the queen as *memento mori,* here vilified rather than idealized by her temporal isolation. What these opposing perspectives share is the sense of the queen positioned in time in a way that only she could occupy – a 'gift' which worked to isolate and estrange her as much as to invest her with authority.

What can the early history of ornamental timepieces teach us about the construction of hierarchized and gendered temporal spheres? It is noteworthy how little work has been done on the use of temporality in the construction of categories such as class and gender. For if personal timepieces emerged in response to crucial changes in the philosophy of time, it is also true that they in turn helped to alter ideological constructs. In the early modern period, personal timepieces rapidly became deployed in the service of constructing and deepening ideas of social difference.

Watches first began to be circulated as novelties and gifts in the early sixteenth century. Records of mechanical clocks light enough to be worn on the body date from about the year 1500; though no extant watch can be securely dated before 1540, anecdotal evidence suggests that watches were in circulation from the turn of the century.[6] Once the technology of the spring-drive was perfected in the middle of the fifteenth century it became possible to omit the weights which had previously driven clockwork, allowing timepieces to be made small enough (and light enough) to be worn or carried on the body. In 1490 there were reports from the court of Lodovico Sforza 'il Moro' of 'small chiming clocks ... attached to ball costumes', and in 1512, Johannes Cochlaus praised the locksmith Peter Heinlein for making 'from only a little bit of iron' miniature clocks which 'show and chime the hours for forty hours without any weight, *even when carried at the breast or in a purse'.*[7]

By the middle of the sixteenth century miniature clocks began to be fashioned as jewels and worn on the body, inaugurating new words highlighting their visual function ('watch' in English; 'montre' in French).[8] In England, many of the first miniature clocks were given as presents to queens. Queen Elizabeth had at least two court clockmakers late in her reign – Nicholas Urseau (d. 1590) and Bartholomew Newsam (d. 1593), and in the early seventeenth century Henrietta Maria was given an enamelled watch made by Simon Hackett, whose case included her portrait set 'within a charming floral border'.[9] Inventories reveal a table clock given as a wedding present to Anne Boleyn by Henry VIII, ten inches high and four inches square, 'richly chased, engraved, and ornamented with fleur-de-lys, little head, &c.'. F.J. Britten notes that the clock is carved with lovers' knots, with the letters H and A intertwined, 'dieu et mon droit' at the top of each side and at the bottom the phrase 'the most happye!'[10] The irony of the king's gift of a clock to the ill-fated Boleyn was evinced in the apocryphal legend that the clockwork stopped at the moment she lost her head. Time, it would seem, was the king's to give, but also his to take away.

Nearly all early watches contained an alarm, a mechanism for striking the hours, or both.[11] The word 'watch' derives from the Middle English *wacen* ('to wake'), suggesting that at least part of the function of the early timepiece was to issue warning. This embodiment of warning can be seen most explicitly in the *memento mori* or skull watches popular in the first decades of the seventeenth century. Some half a dozen of these watches have been dated between 1550 and 1650 – one of the earliest, fashioned of a crystal case with a silver dial, belonged to Henry III, made by Jacques Joly of Blois; two in the British Museum date from 1630, and another from about 1625 is comprised of a skull which opens to reveal a dial engraved with a scene from the Last Judgement.[12] These watches reified the connection between the timepiece and the arts of *memento mori,* which in Reformation Europe were collected and circulated with a passion bordering on obsession. Erasmus had a medal made for himself decorated with the god Terminus, the 'end of all things'. Luther wore a gold ring in the shape of a death's head engraved with the injunction to 'think often of death'. Rings, cups, silver plate and tiles were circulated with inscriptions admonishing that life is fleeting, and blockbooks called *ars moriendi* offered instructions on how to behave in the moments just before death.[13] Transi tombs also popularized the disjunction between the idealized image of the deceased and its contrasting image in vivid decay.[14] The skull, a metonymic symbol of the *memento mori* tradition, showed up in scores of vanitas paintings, as did more subtle, though equally pervasive symbols of fleeting life, such as bubbles, *putti,* flowers, overripe fruit, and spilled or broken vessels. By the seventeenth century the merest shadow in a still life painting or deep creases in the gathered folds of a table cloth could be imbued with melancholy meaning by the well-schooled Reformation viewer. The *memento mori* tradition was a vigorous exercise in decoding what Panofsky has called 'disguised symbolism'.[15] To the trained eye, objects of earthly existence, such as books, scientific instruments, shells, money, jewels, weapon, armour, food, paintings, busts, musical instruments, silver and the like, all hinted at mortality; skulls, bones, candles (sometimes still glowing), bubbles and timepieces all represented the fleetingness of life, whereas wheat, laurel or ivy might symbolize the resurrection.[16]

One of the most elaborate of *memento mori* skull watches is purported to have been given to Mary Queen of Scots. The skull is made of silver, engraved on the forehead with an iconographical image of Death as a skeleton, holding an hourglass in one hand, a scythe in the other, situated midway between a cottage and a palace. Carved around this scene in miniature is a Latin line from one of Horace's Odes: *'Pallida mors aequo pulsat pede pauperum tabernas regumque turris.'* On the opposite side of the skull, the figure of Time stands beside a serpent also framed by a line from Horace: *'Tempus edas rerum tuque invidiosa vetustas.'*[17] On the face quadrant of the skull is a scene from Genesis. Adam is seated in profile, hand under his chin, contemplative. Eve, naked, stands at the centre in a full frontal position, one arm extended upward holding the apple. To her right sits the serpent, waiting and admiring. The motto under this scene bears this reminder: 'By sin they brought eternal misery and destruction on their posterity.' On the skull's other side, Christ is represented on the crucifix, between the two thieves, framed by this motto in Latin: 'Thus was Justice satisfied, Death overcome, and salvation obtained.' The body of Christ, centred in this quadrant, is apparently intended to redeem the fallen Eve.[18]

But iconographically, Eve in this image is more closely allied with Death, who like her stands in full frontal position, feet and arms pointing outward, at once a centre and a mediator: her naked flesh, like his skeleton, signalling death. The centrality of Eve in this iconographic representation of mortality and suffering throws off centre the watch's careful juxtapositions and balances: death balanced by time, the fall of man by his salvation, the rich balanced by the poor, palace by cottage, text by image. Like all *memento mori,* this watch was intended to warn and to remind. But it also implied an accusation. For the skull watch's trope of devouring, borne out on its innermost dial, where Saturn is pictured consuming his children, originates in Eve's crime of intemperance, her greed, her insatiability. Eve, the watch reminds its recipient, was to blame for Time.

Watches permanently altered the relationship between time and the body. However suggestive a metaphor for the body the hourglass was and would remain for early modern writers, it was a 'moveable', a prop, whereas the watch literally pinned time to the body. Interestingly enough, almost from their invention watches were worn differently by women than by men. For women, the breast was often the place where such watches were displayed. Well into the eighteenth century women wore watches hanging from chatelaines – richly jewelled ribbons decorated with enamelled brooches – customarily pinned over one breast. This fashion must have made telling time difficult for the women who wore them. While watches set in rings or bracelets or hung at the waist on long chains might have divulged the hour to those who wore them, chatelaines did not allow for such legibility. Nor did those watches described admiringly in the middle of the seventeenth century in *The History of Most Manual Arts*, praised for being 'so small and light, that Ladies hang them at their ears like pendants and jewels'.[19] Presumably these watches were intended to be read not by the women who wore them, but by their companions. Women were thus not encouraged to read time, but to tell it, to be the bearers and not the interpreters of signification.

G.H. Baillie, noting that the weight of early watches must have made this practice uncomfortable, observes that several engravings reveal 'seventeenth-century ladies' wearing egg-shaped watches dangling from chains at their girdles.[20] In a semiotic of fashion in which certain parts of women's bodies (such as breasts) were exposed while almost every other part was concealed, such 'dangling' emphasized sexual difference: breasts, waists, 'purses' and genitals. In the early seventeenth century, the elaborately ornamented chatelaine was part of a larger fashion emphasizing (and eroticizing) the female breast. Geoffrey Squire points out that in the Stuart period the androgynous, flattened-out bodice of the Elizabethan period gave way to a new fashion:

> The neckline of the shorter, less deforming bodices, was cut often quite alarmingly low. High and close to the nape behind, it was scooped down in front into a deep round décolletage leaving the breasts almost completely exposed. Freed from suppression the

bosom bulged sensuously in natural softness. The pneumatic model-
ling which was captivating architects, sculptors and painters was
here exploited spontaneously by fashion ... Fully rounded forms
were emphasized throughout the composition: in the ruff, in the
dressing of the hair, the bared breasts, the line of the décolletage,
the padded hips, and the deep funnel shaped cuffs, which, retreating up the arm, revealed yet more softly rounded flesh.[21]

In this period, as décolletage became fashionable for unmarried
women and 'the ideal breast became larger, rounder, altogether more
emphatic in the seventeenth century',[22] the shape for watches (often
rectangular or egg-shaped in the sixteenth century) settled into the
now-conventional circle or oval. Stuart Sherman has suggested that the
most important function of early watches was display:

> the elaboration of ornament, the open display, and the utter lack of
> technical advance in the interior suggest that the privilege of time
> keeping was construed as secondary to the pleasure of display. By
> numerous decorative contrivances clock makers contrived to beguile
> the observing eye, and (at the same time) to keep it distracted from
> the moving hand, to take the mind off the patently erratic motions;
> even the interior movements were often elaborately engraved and
> bejewelled, meant to be seen.[23]

Indeed, these rounded watch cases offered a whole new field for
miniature display. Popular methods of ornamentation for watch cases
and exposed dials included engraved scenes or landscapes; piercing,
chiselling or engraving; 'chased' or repoussé work; inlay (which was
relatively rare); lapidary work (inset stones); and enamel or painted
enamel. At Blois, watchmakers' apprentices were instructed by painters
or engravers for as long as two hours a day to learn 'portraiture'; some
were required to work with engravers for a period of one to two years
before taking up their trade.[24] Yet little attention has been paid to this
watch display. Collectors often remark in passing that early watches were
popularly decorated with human figures, none mentioning that such
figures were almost always female, in many instances eroticized nudes.
Favourite subjects for European enamelled watch cases in the sixteenth
and seventeenth centuries included Eve, Mary, Esther and Susannah
from the Bible; classical figures, such as Diana, Danae and Venus; and
allegorical figures such as Vanitas, Fortitude and Prudence. Even watches
that eschewed explicit female figures might be ornately decorated with

feminized symbols, such as shells or invaginated petals of flowers – carnations, lilies, roses and tulips – flowers strongly associated with the *memento mori* tradition, further connecting the female figure to the threat of imminent death. The very intricacy and preciousness of watch display worked to advertise the status of 'private time', a concept which paradoxically found its meaning only in public show.[25] Moreover, it strengthened the connection between time and ornament, suggesting that time's passage (as the new word 'watch' so richly suggested) took place in the realm of the visual.

As fashions for women emphasized the display of watches, men's fashions altered to conceal them. Pockets began to appear in men's clothing in the first decades of the seventeenth century, almost in concert with the invention of the pocket-watch.[26] Even prior to the invention of fob pockets (from the German *fuppe*, for pocket), men began to conceal watches, carrying them in inner recesses or folds of their garments as if to accentuate the moment of their withdrawal.[27] The drama of such disclosures is frequently described in the literature of the period. In *As You Like It*, for example, Jacques meets a fool coming out of the forest who withdraws a 'diall' from his 'poke'.[28] In Dekker's *Gull's Hornbook* of 1609 the fop is advised to time the resetting of his watch for a moment of public display: 'you may here have fit occasion to discover your watch by taking it forth, and setting the wheels to the time of Paul's ... the benefit that will arise from hence is this, that you publish your charge in maintaining a gilded clock; and withal the world shall know that you are a timepleaser.'[29] The popularity of the practice is borne out by admonitions against it: later, Lord Chesterfield would advise his son: 'Wear your learning, like your watch, in a private pocket; and do not ... pull it out and strike it merely to show that you have one.'[30] The pleasure of the concealed timepiece lay partly in the potency of what Sherman has called 'chronometric autonomy'. Watches modelled 'self-containment by design', and part of their pleasure derived from the multiple layers of opening they required. (Sherman notes, for example, the invention of the English 'pair case' around mid-century, in which a second or even a third hinged lid was added, supposedly to protect the interior movement, but instead to allow for 'a sequence of layered secrets' in which the owner 'could, at need or pleasure, lay some of its secrets bare, and find a different source of satisfaction in each subsequent revelation, passing from the adornments of the outer case to the simple sheen of the inner, and from there, by opening yet another hinged compartment, to the imposing intricacies, the partly visible wheels, shafts, and springs, of the movement itself'.[31] Before the invention of the repeater in the late seventeenth century, some watches were equipped with 'feeling knobs' positioned at each hour, so the owner could discern the time without being detected. As the following excerpt from a mid-seventeenth century French conduct manual makes evident, by this concealment the polite visitor could position himself temporally without betraying his knowledge:

> Those who wear a watch showing the hours, half-hours, and quarters can sometimes use it to time the length of their visit. But it smacks too much of the business man to look at your watch in company; it is impolite to your guests because it looks as if you had another engagement and were in a hurry to keep it. As for striking watches, they are very tiresome, because they interrupt conversation. That is why one should adopt the new kind of watch in which the hour and half-hour marks are raised enough to enable one to feel them with the finger and so tell the time without having to take out the watch and look at it.[32]

Already in this conduct manual it is possible to discern two separate and competing temporal spheres. The social world, the world of the visit and the engagement, dilates time by making it invisible. The 'business world', which must be kept hidden, keeps its internal pressures closest to the bearer's body. The aspiring gentleman reading this manual would learn not only to read time secretly, but to conduct a visit to (and then escape from) a temporal world marked by dilation and delay – a world which would become increasingly familiar, and increasingly feminized, to readers of Cavalier poetry. Eventually, the 'social', the ornamental and the dilatory would become firmly associated with the feminine, whereas business, haste and pressure – as well as the secret ownership of time – would become one of the standard ways of characterizing masculinity. By the early twentieth century, Simone de Beauvoir would angrily lament the temporal gulf between the sexes:

> This inequality will be especially brought out in the fact that the time [men and women] spend together – which fallaciously seems to be the same time – does not have the same quality for both partners. During the evening the lover spends with his mistress he could be doing something of advantage to his career, seeing friends, cultivating business relationships, seeking recreation; for a man normally integrated in society, time is a positive value; money, reputation,

pleasure. For the idle, bored woman, on the contrary, it is a burden she wishes to get rid of ... He always has 'other things to do' with his time; whereas she has time to burn; and he considers much of the time she gives him not as a gift but as a burden.[33]

De Beauvoir eloquently picks up here on the way gift and burden become elided. For de Beauvoir's 'bored, idle woman', for whom the gift of time has become its own threat, the logic of *carpe diem* has closed in on itself; she is determined by a temporal sphere from which everyone (herself included) longs to escape.

My point here is not to declare the early modern period the source or origin of the gendered temporal division de Beauvoir deplores. Rather, I want to suggest that the use of time as a crucial marker in talking about gender has a history, and that the early modern period, when temporal discourses and technologies were rapidly changing, is an important place to see such differences in the process of being instantiated. The early history of personal timepieces worked both to install and to reinforce ideas of difference – difference in class, in social status and in gender. Historians of time have tended to over-emphasize the continuities that enabled 'church time' to give way to 'merchant time' in the fifteenth and sixteenth centuries. It is certainly true that humanist emphasis on time-thrift continually emphasized the need to control time, to use it, spend it and save it.[34] But more rigorous analysis of such discourse may reveal the extent to which temporality could be used to fracture and isolate further categories of class and gender. Historians have usefully elaborated the ways in which such discourses helped to shape ideas of mercantilism and business. But how did such discourse simultaneously work to produce its domestic corollary? how did time – its use, its fashion, its debt – become deployed as a way of shaping ideas of what constituted the feminine and masculine spheres?[35]

The new 'chronometric autonomy' offered by personal timepieces had its costs. One of its most insidious consequences was a new emphasis on temporal visualism. Fabian has argued that 'visualism', the privileging of visual effects, is a crucial tool in the instantiation of 'schizogenic' divisions of time.[36] Timepieces in the early seventeenth century were one of a host of connected temporal arts which emphasized the feminine as the object of the masculine gaze. While men's watches by the mid-seventeenth century came not only to eschew ornamentation but to conceal themselves – within 'plain-style' cases, and further, within folds of clothing, watches for women were all the more emphatically designed for show. Sherman admits that women's watches remained ornaments 'a good while longer' than they did for men. How much longer? In America, etiquette books and fashion guides still maintain that it is déclassé for a woman to wear a watch on a formal occasion. For such events, something else (the woman's obliviousness to time?) is on display. As twentieth-century advertising has taught us, the visible conse-quences of time for Western women are to be dreaded and resisted; however, age might be argued to dignify men – or more likely, to remain merely invisible. Judith Butler has argued that 'the ground of gender identity is the stylized repetition of acts through time.'[37] I would add that it is partly time (and its measurement) that enforces such stylized repeti-tions. Timepieces, in their exchange, ornamentation and display, helped to shape distinct histories for men and women in early modern Europe – histories connected to the most deeply held ideas (and anxieties) about gender in all its complex relations to corporeality and to power. The early history of timepieces taught men to carry time, in other words, and women to wear it.

Biological clocks

> The discourse of the sciences of man constructs the object as female and the female as object. That, I suggest, is its rhetoric of violence, even when the discourse presents itself as humanistic, benevolent, or well-intentioned.
>
> Teresa De Lauretis, *Technologies of Gender*[38]

Separate traditions of wearing and ornamenting timepieces contributed to the sense that women and watches were somehow conjoined, a belief which concretized extant ideas about the relationship between the feminine and the temporal. In Act III of *Love's Labours Lost,* Berowne plays on the multiple meanings of the word 'watch' to advance an uneasy joke about female constancy: 'What! ... I seek a wife / A woman, that is, like a German clock, / Still a-repairing, ever out of frame / And never going aright, being a watch / But being watched that it may still go right!' (III.i.191–5) The metaphor of woman as timepiece was not uncommon in Renaissance literature; the lover in Donne's 'Elegy 19', for example, describes his mistress chiming like an alarm-clock to signal her desire for bed, and in Donne's 'Epithalamion' for the Princess Elizabeth and the Elector Palantine in 1611, the speaker imagines the bride's attendants undressing her before the long-awaited wedding night as if they were 'taking a clock in pieces'.[39] Women were understood to embody time in ways that distinguished them from normative (masculinized) conceptions of the human figure. The idea of the 'biological clock', a metaphor now generally applied to women, already finds antecedents in late medieval and early modern discourse. In the fifteenth century, Christine de Pisan remarked that the properly governed body resembled a mechanical clock: 'because our human body is made up of many parts and should be regulated by reason, it may be represented as a clock in which there are several wheels and measures. And just as the clock is worth nothing unless it is regulated, so our human body does not work unless Temperance orders it.'[40] Implicit in Pisan's description of the body as clock is a warning, for if Temperance was required to make the body's mechanism run properly, surely its malfunctions could be linked to intemperance, to Berowne's charge of 'never going aright'.

By the time de Pisan was writing, there were already strong associations between timepieces and women's bodies. In the earliest known representation of an hourglass, for example, painted on the fresco of 'Good Government' in the Palazza Pubblico in Siena (1337?), the hourglass is held by a woman: Temperance, or Temperentia, one of the four cardinal virtues in the Middle Ages. In Lorrenzetti's fresco, Temperance holds the hourglass aloft in her right hand, lifted so that the upper half of the glass is level with her own face, which inclines gently towards the hourglass. The triangular composition of Temperentia's neck and visage and the dark border of her bodice strengthen the fresco's connection between the glass and the woman that holds it. Woman and hourglass are conjoined in their mutual tasks: each containing and measuring out the temporal limits of the active (and masculine) world around them. Once again, the woman's body, allied with the timepiece, suggests a warning: *Measure yourself: time is passing.*[41]

Given this link between temperance and temporality, it is striking how rapidly female excesses came to serve as ornament for mechanical timepieces. The hourglass figure is a hyper-woman, excessively feminine. Such figures, with ample bellies, breasts or buttocks coy, plump arms and pouting lips, often came to decorate watches and domestic clocks, as if the connection between the temporal and the temperate became elided with temptation. In an elaborate table clock by the eighteenth century artisan Etienne Falconet, for example, three Rubenesque Graces avert their eyes while one reaches an outstretched arm to point, like a dial hand, to the hour. What has her nudity to do with the passage of time? As Carol Armstrong has suggested, the female nude in painting works to aestheticize 'the gaze and the object of delectation', displaying 'as much while meaning as little as possible'. Part of what the nude aestheticizes is the 'erotic possession of the female body'.[42] In clocks and timepieces, that possessing gaze is heightened by the intertwining of erotic urge and temporal urgency.

Women in early modern Europe were understood to occupy, to record and to experience time differently from men. Because Eve had caused mortal time and mortality by taking the forbidden fruit, it would seem apt that her punishment was to be situated in her body, and moreover that her generative power should be instantiated as punishment ('in sorrow shall ye bring forth children'). Early modern medicine understood women to be materially connected to time in ways that made the feminine more variable than the masculine, and less knowable. Women's bodies swelled and altered in mysterious association with time – through menstruation, childbirth and menopause. Female humoral fluctuations and excesses, as Gail Kern Paster's research has evinced, proved women to be dangerously mutable. There were, in reality, very real risks faced by women in this period before the advent of hygienic practices associated with childbirth, antibiotics or reliable birth control. Less than half of women lived past the age of 50 in early modern England, many of them dying in childbirth. But the idea of the young woman cut down in the prime of life seems to have elicited far less anxiety in this period than the anticipated ravages of female age. Paster remarks that the withered hag was the most dreaded and contemptible of early modern characters.[43] Scorning desire in the aged, Burton's Democritus declares 'worse it is in women than in men ... she doth very unseemly seek to marry; yet whilst she is so old, a crone, a beldam, she can neither see nor hear, go nor stand, a mere carcass, a witch, and scare feel, she caterwauls and must have a stallion, a champion, she must and will marry again, and betroth herself to some young man that hates to look on her but for her goods'.[44] Old women's bodies were especially reviled in those places which, in young mistresses, were so idealized: the breast, for example, everywhere touted as firm, pink, round and luscious in young women, was loathed in the aged, as in Dürer's allegory of Avarice or Spenser's disrobed Duessa, whose 'dried dugs' hung down like 'bladders lacking wind'.[45] Philippa Berry has observed that Lyly's *Endymion*, whose 'faire Cynthia' is held (alone of all women) to be above 'inurious time', was published in the same year (1580) as Reginald Scot's *Discoverie of Witchcraft*, where Scot charged that old women were particularly prone to being witches: 'The most of such as are said to be witches, are women which be commonly old, lame, blear-eyed, pale, fowle, and full of wrinkles'.[46] Old women, Deborah Willis observes, were believed to retain excess blood in postmenopausal bodies, blood which could be used to nourish imps and create magical retaliations.[47] The aged crone emblematized the body clock gone wrong: disordered, intemperate, injuring man rather than proving his 'measure'.

In the 1580s and 1590s in England, the decrepit hags of Elizabethan romance were countered by that other side of the diptych: the young idealized mistress of scores of sonnet sequences, golden-haired and ivory-skinned, her perfection embalmed in the potent fluid of the poet's verse – just as Elizabeth I, having moved beyond the age of childbearing, was coming under new scrutiny as an 'ageing virgin'.[48] In Samuel Daniel's sonnet sequence *Delia* (1592), for example, the spurned lover imagines a time when his unresponsive mistress will be avenged by time. In sonnet XXX's opening octet, the mistress ages in the lover's angry imagination:

> I once may see when yeeres shall wrecke my wronge,
> When golden haires shall chaunge to silver wyer:
> And those bright rayes, that kindle all this fyer,
> Shall faile in force, their working not so strong.
> Then beautie (now the burthen of my song),
> Whose glorious blaze the world dooth so admire,
> Must yeelde up all to tyrant Times desire;
> Then fade those flowres which deckt her pride so long.[49]

In the closing sextet of the sonnet, the speaker offers the consoling *topoi* of the eternizing theme: his verse will remind her of her prior perfection, reminding the woman what she was in her youth and thus substituting for the 'winter-withered hew' reflected back to her in her 'glasse':

> When, if she grieve to gaze her in her glas,
> Which then presents her winter-withered hew,
> Goe you my verse, goe tell her what she was;
> For what she was, she best shall finde in you.
> Your firy heate lets not her glorie passe
> But Phenix-like shall make her live anew.

The lover's poem as 'glasse' is problematic on a number of levels, especially in its assumption that it is in him – in his desire and representation – that she could best discover 'what she was'. And of course, as this sonnet makes clear, the lover's poetry does not offer an image of Delia as idealized and young at all – she is hard, cold, resistant; to the extent that she becomes visible at all in the sequence, it is only to represent her corporeality ('golden haires', 'bright raies,' etc.) as it suffers a reverse alchemy through Time. So if his verse is to 'tell her what she was', she will be twice revenged: once by tyrant Time, and once again by the poet's representation – not of her beauty, but of its going. For as the chime of verbs reminds her here – chaunge, kindle, faile, yeeld, fade, grieve, passes – no sooner is 'beauty' named than it is become a shadow.

Delia is organized around the trope of wasting. In the first part of the sequence, the speaker rails against his mistress for wasting his time: she has spent 'the deere expences of [his] youth' (I); for her, he has sacrificed 'my youth, and blooming years' (XXI); he has spent the 'Aprill of [his] yeers in wayling'. But from Sonnet XXX on, the speaker inverts this trope to imagine his lover wasted. In the most famous sonnet of the sequence, XXXI, the speaker uses the familiar image of the flower to urge his mistress not to 'waste in vain' her riches. Like the half-blowne rose esteemed for its 'inclosed' beauty, Delia's perfection will decline as soon as it is 'ful-blowne':

> No Aprill can revive thy withred flowers,
> Whoose blooming grace adornes thy glorie now:
> Swift speedy Time, feathered with flying howers,
> Dissolves the beautie of the fairest brow.
>> O let not then such riches waste in vaine;
>> But love whilst that thou maist be lov'd againe.

In the concluding sonnets of the sequence, the speaker avers that the eternity he offers inheres in his love: 'The world shall find this miracle in mee' (XXXIII). The 'lasting monument' and 'marble grave' of his sonnets will allow her to live 'unburied'. But the speaker presents Delia in diptych, at once lamenting her ephemeral beauty and imagining her face in age – her face bending 'thy wrinkles homeward to the earth' (XLII), her beauty closed up, faded, spent. It is Delia's brow, face and eyes which register this divided experience of time; her value as ornament is, like an aristocratic watch, to measure his time and mark its value. The gift of time dislocates Delia, shutting off her access to the present. As Derrida points out, it is no coincidence that the word 'present' should signify a gift as well as a temporal category. The eternizing project forfeits the present in the interest of promoting its own discursive potency. It offers, inside the jewelled case of its compliment, a figuration of the feminine always already known: the death's head, the materialization of alarm.

Notes

1. Jacques Derrida, *Counterfeit Money*, tr. Peggy Kamuf (Chicago: University of Chicago Press, 1993), p. 6.
2. David Landes, *Revolution in Time: Clocks and the Making of the Modern World* (Cambridge, Mass: Harvard University Press, 1983), p. 87.
3. Johannes Fabian, *Time and the Other: How Anthropology Makes Its Object* (New York: Columbia University Press, 1983).
4. Roy Strong, *The Cult of Elizabeth: Elizabethan Portraiture and Pageantry* (London, 1977), pp. 47–54.
5. Quoted in Christopher Hibbert, *The Virgin Queen: Elizabeth I, Genius of the Golden Age* (Harlow: Addison Wesley Longman, 1991), p. 253.
6. G.H. Baillie, *Watches: Their History, Decoration, and Mechanism* (London: Metheun, 1929), p. 49.
7. Gerhard Dohrn-van Rossum, *The History of the Hour* (Chicago: University of Chicago Press, 1996), p. 122; p. 121.
8. The first known use of the word 'montre' is found in the inventories of the Florimond Robertet, a French treasurer of finance, who left at his death in 1532 twelve watches, seven striking and five silent. See Baillie, *Watches*, p. 64. According to the OED, the word 'watch' first began to be used in England to designate a portable timepiece in the middle of the sixteenth century. Between 1570 and 1600 the words 'watch' and 'clock' seemed to have been used interchangeably. The OED lists more than 35 meanings for the word 'watch', which derives from the Old English *wacen* (to wake). Many of these meanings are associated with watchfulness or guard; vigil; watching or observing.
9. The Duchesse de Bourgogne had her 'chamber clock' repaired in 1389, and a very early spring-driven clock may have been part of the wedding treasure of Maria of Burgundy in the early fifteenth century. See Baillie, *Watches*, p. 50; p. 45.
10. F.J. Britten, *Old Clocks and Watches and Their Makers*, 3rd edn (Suffolk: Antique Collectors' Club Ltd, 1977), p. 60.
11. Baillie, *Watches*, p. 55.
12. Britten, *Old Clocks and Watches*, pp. 109, 111.
13. Kristine Koozin, *The Vanitas Still-Lifes of Harmen Steenwyck: Metamorphic Realism* (Lewiston: Edward Mellon Press, 1990), pp. 15–16.
14. In transi tombs, the image of the decaying figure was superimposed over an idealized image of the deceased. See Philippe Ariès, *The Hour of our Death*, tr. Helen Weaven (Oxford: Oxford University Press, 1991), pp. 252–3.

15. Quoted in Koozin, p. v.
16. See Koozin, pp. 8–9. Reformation sermons and devotional verses had ample sources from the Bible to support the representation of life as shadowy, insubstantial and perpetually fading away. The most important source was Ecclesiastes: 'Vanity of vanities, saith the Preacher, vanity of vanities; all is Vanity.' From the Book of Job came the lament: 'My days are swifter than a weaver's shuttle, and are spent without hope' (7:6); 'my life is wind' (7:7); 'our days upon earth are a shadow' (8:9); 'He cometh forth like a flower, and is cut down: he fleeth also, like a shadow, and continueth not' (14:2). From the Psalms, 'Lord let me know mine end, And the measure of my days, what it is; That I may know how frail I am' (39:4); 'verily every man at his best state is altogether vanity' (39:5); 'For my days are consumed like smoke, and my bones are burned as on a hearth' (102:3); 'My days are like a shadow that declineth; and I am withered like grass' (102:11); 'Man is like to vanity; his days are as a shadow that passeth away' (144:4); and from Isaiah, 'All flesh is grass, and all the godliness thereof is as the flower of the field' (40:6); 'The grass withereth, the flower fadeth; because the spirit of the Lord bloweth upon them: surely the people is grass' (40:7).
17. Quoted in Britten, *Old Clocks and Watches*, p. 109, who translates them as 'Pale Death visits with impartial foot the cottages of the poor and the palaces of the rich'; 'Time, and thou too, envious Old Age, devours all things'.
18. Britten, *Old Clocks and Watches*, pp. 109–11.
19. Cited by Samuel L. Macey, *Clocks and the Cosmos: Time in Western Life and Thought* (Hamden, Connecticut: Archon Books, 1980), p. 99.
20. Baillie, *Watches*, p. 60.
21. Geoffrey Squire, *Dress and Society, 1560–1970* (New York: Viking, 1974), p. 84. See also Graham Reynolds, *Costume of the Western World: Elizabethan and Jacobean, 1558–1625* (London: George G. Harrap and Co, Ltd, 1951), p. 10, and C. Willett and Phillis Cunnington, *Handbook of English Costume in the Seventeenth Century* (London: Faber and Faber, 1955), p. 82.
22. Gail Kern Paster, *The Body Embarrassed: Drama and the Disciplines of Shame in Early Modern England* (Ithaca: Cornell University Press, 1993), p. 205.
23. Stuart Sherman, *Telling Time: Clocks, Diaries, and English Diurnal Form, 1660–1785* (Chicago: University of Chicago Press, 1996), p. 84.
24. Baillie, *Watches*, pp. 91–3.
25. See Susan Stewart on the relationship between the miniature and private time. *On Longing: Narratives of the Miniature, the Gigantic, the Souvenir, the Collection* (Durham, NC and London: Duke University Press, 1993), p. 66.
26. *Handbook of English Costume*, pp. 49–51.
27. Cunnington discusses interior 'slit pockets', often used by thieves to conceal stolen goods in the sixteenth century. See *The Handbook of English Costume*, p. 45.
28. Quoted from *The Riverside Shakespeare* (Boston: Houghton Mifflin, 1974), p. 380: II.vii.20.
29. Cited by Lawrence Wright, *Clockwork Man: The Story of Time, Its Origins, Its Uses, Its Tyranny* (New York: Horizon Press, 1968), p. 78.

30. Quoted in Samuel L. Macey, *Clocks and the Cosmos: Time in Western Life and Thought* (Hamden: Archon Books, 1980), pp. 33–4.
31. Sherman, *Telling Time*, pp. 84–6.
32. From *Les Lois de la galanterie*, cited by Baillie, *Watches*, pp. 59–60.
33. Simone de Beauvoir, *The Second Sex* (New York: Vintage Books, 1974), pp. 803–4.
34. See, for example, Jacques Le Goff, *Time, Work and Culture in the Middle Ages*, trans. Arthur Goldhammer (Chicago: University of Chicago Press, 1980).
35. It is in fact in the *carpe diem* tradition, where women are urged to 'spend' time rather than to allow it to slip by or languish, that it becomes most clear that this tradition asks women not to spend, but to be spent. Virginity may not protect them from death, but neither will its loss.
36. Fabian, *Time and the Other*, pp. 31, 21; on visualism, see pp. 106–7.
37. Judith Butler, *Gender Trouble: Feminism and the Subversion of Identity* (New York and London: Routledge, 1990), p. 141.
38. Teresa de Lauretis, *Essays on Theory, Film and Fiction* (Bloomington: Indiana University Press, 1987), p. 45.
39. *John Donne, Poetry and Prose*, ed. Frank K. Warneke (New York: Modern Library, 1967), p. 94.
40. Cited by Helen F. North, *From Myth to Icon: Reflections of Greek Ethical Doctrine in Literature and Art* (Ithaca, NY: Cornell University Press, 1979).
41. Temperance had long been associated with iconographic symbols of taming unruly beasts, such as the bridle. North discusses the emergence of the clock in such symbolism in association with Temperance in *From Myth to Icon*, pp. 31–3: 'To the obvious implications of the hourglass as an attribute of temperance (embodying a visual pun on the presence of *tempus* in temperentia) the mechanical clock, developed in the second quarter of the fourteenth century, added still more complex connotations, suggesting especially the harmony achieved when many moving parts work smoothly together' (233).
42. Carol Armstrong, 'Edgar Degas and the Representation of the Female Body,' in *The Female Body in Western Culture*, ed. Susan Suleiman (Cambridge, Mass: Harvard University Press, 1986), p. 223.
43. Paster, *The Body Embarrassed*, p. 45.
44. *The Anatomy of Melancholy*, ed. Holbrook Jackson, (Vintage Books, 1977), p. 56: III,2.
45. For the Elizabethans, heightened interest in the subject of female age may have been tied to the particular circumstances surrounding the queen. Certainly Elizabeth's youth, middle and old age, fertility, lack of fertility and longevity were subjects of pronounced interest as well as deep concern, but whether this is a cause or a result of widespread cultural attitudes towards women and age remains in question. Often critics, such as Roy Strong, have explained that the 'revival' of images of Elizabeth's youthful image in the years just before her death as strategic on the part of artists such as Hilliard and Peake. My sense, to the contrary, is that such 'revived portraits' were, like Bruyn's portraits, implied diptychs, in this instance supposing that the withered queen be contrasted with the idealized portrait from her youth.

46. Philippa Berry, *Of Chastity and Power: Elizabethan Literature and the Unmarried Queen* (London: Routledge, 1989), p. 130.

47. Deborah Willis, *Malevolent Nurture: Witch-hunting and Maternal Power in Early Modern England* (Ithaca, NY: Cornell University Press, 1995), p. 75.

48. See Helen Hackett, *Virgin Mother, Maiden Queen* (New York: St. Martin's Press, 1995), p. 176 and following on the Queen's 'immunity' to old age.

49. Samuel Daniel, *Poems and A Defense of Ryme,* ed. Arthur Colby Sprague (Chicago: University of Chicago Press, 1930), p. 25.

7

The 'Double Voice' of Renaissance Equity and the Literary Voices of Women[1]

Lorna Hutson

When Stephen Greenblatt redescribed the professional, critical reading of early modern texts as motivated by a desire to hear the voices of the past, to 'speak with the dead', he also acknowledged the force of a paradox in his contention that the voices of the dead are more audible to us from the texts of fiction than from 'any other textual traces'. The legacy of this statement for feminist criticism is distinctly double-edged. The full impact of the paradox in Greenblatt's formulation reveals itself only with his admission of just how selective he was prepared to be in his choice of suitable interlocutors. What qualifies the textual traces of the past for dialogue with the present, he went on to explain, is 'life' and 'intensity'. And, 'conventional in my tastes', he concluded, 'I found the most satisfying intensity of all in Shakespeare'.[2]

Shakespeare's once celebrated 'universality' here translates easily into a guarantor of historical authenticity, the vitality of the Shakespearean text offering a way into the understanding of a vanished culture. The most pressing question raised by the Shakespearean artefact thus became, according to Greenblatt, 'how did so much life get into the textual traces?'[3] But to equate the question of the source of vitality in Shakespeare's text with the project of entering into dialogue with a vanished culture is to ignore the most obvious fact about the selection of Shakespeare as a representative creator of 'voices': the fact that the voices of Shakespeare's *dramatis personae*, far more than those of any contemporary dramatist, give the impression of coming from *characters*, from distinctly individual beings, rather than being accessible to us in terms of what we know of early modern social codes as the 'point of intersection of a range of discourses' within their own culture.[4] The fact that we unthinkingly equate literary intensity with the capacity to produce the illusion of authentic, individual being – the dramatic 'character' that we identify as the hallmark of 'Shakespearean' drama[5] – poses particular problems for feminist criticism. As Elizabeth Harvey has pointed out, feminist criticism has found practically irresistible the tendency to conflate the voice of the female author with the voices of brilliantly achieved characters of women composed by men.[6] The common-sense response to this problem is one which simply acknowledges that men have long been better equipped by education and culture to compose strong characterological voices (that is, voices which sound as if they are emanating from individuated beings, rather than from a set of social codes or stereotypes) than have women. Yet such an acknowledgement, holding in place as it does the assumption that revelation of 'character' is the supreme achievement of first-person poetic speech, does nothing to enable us to distinguish what women who wrote in the early modern period might have brought to the established literary forms of female utterance, how they might have understood them differently from men. Another way of considering the problem, therefore, might be by offering a challenge to our assumption of the inherent superiority or even the necessary presence of characterological effects in first-person poetic speech. The pressing question for a feminist criticism which wants to investigate the relationship between male and female fictions of femininity would then shift from the usual 'What does it mean to write like a woman?' or 'What is it that constitutes the authentic voice of female experience?' to 'How can we prevent ourselves from assuming that certain conditions of first-person speech which we associate with women must be identified as expressive of the experience, and therefore of the moral qualities of an individual woman?'

I want, then, to question the extent to which it is appropriate to approach fictive first-person speech in women's poetry of the sixteenth and seventeenth centuries as if it were primarily concerned with the revelation of character. The poetry with which I shall be concerned belongs to a highly specific genre – the epistle of the abandoned woman to her lover, modelled on Ovid's *Heroides* – whence it has infused the more complex genres of dramatic and prose fiction, and conditioned our expectations of female character. Not that feminist studies of the influence of Ovid's *Heroides* on later literature have a simplistic approach to the question of character. Indeed, the most recent work has tended (having recourse to Howard Jacobson's rich and detailed study of the sources of Ovid's first 15 letters) to emphasize the extent to which Ovid's reworking of Virgilian and Homeric ideals of womanhood (Dido, Penelope) anticipates a similar process of sub-version in certain kinds of writing by women. Linda Kauffman, for example, writes, alluding to Howard Jacobson's commentary on the Ovidian Dido:

> in his portrait of Dido, Ovid is not striving to represent the central core of woman's self, or 'woman's essence', for he is sceptical about the very idea of a center, a self, an essence, and about language's representation of such concepts. Instead, Ovid's portrait is a critique of a previous representation of Dido: Virgil's.[7]

As Ovid's Dido comes to stand, in Kauffman's analysis, for 'a conscious critique of Augustan Rome, of Virgilian values, and of epic itself', so Ovidian epistolary fiction anticipates the 'quiet, stealthy work of under-mining' by means of which women's writing will, in later periods, seek to '"deflower myths" of woman by undermining mimesis'.[8] The danger, however, of this Bahktinian reading of Ovid as dialogically or novel-istically engaging with the value systems of epic, is that it is so easily assimilated to a notion of character realism. If Ovid's subversion of epic values is achieved by imagining a Dido and a Penelope who insist on speaking up for 'the private life, the life of the feelings',[9] then this sub-version offers a hardly novel precedent for identifying women with the process of revealing emotions from a scene of privacy and marginality, as if Heroidean poetry were nineteenth-century dramatic monologue. What tends to happen, in fact, is that Ovid's unidealized women are read as the precursors of a new verisimilitude in first-person speech, the very dialogism of which becomes identified with psychological realism. Thus Florence Verducci, who particularly admires Howard Jacobson's analysis of Ovid's subversion of the Homeric Penelope, writes:

> Perhaps the greatest, and surely the most original, achievement of Ovid's letters is the impression they create of psychological authenticity, of convincing fidelity to the private perspective of a speaker caught in a double process of intentional persuasion and unintentionally revealing self-expression.[10]

The supreme accomplishment of the poetry – psychological verisimilitude – is thus identified with the very ways in which Ovidian heroines puncture their own idealization in other genres. Ovid's epistolary fictions move us, some critics say, because they enable us to witness, behind the explicit protestations of the heroine, the revelation of less exalted feelings of which 'she' is barely conscious. Thus W.S. Anderson, challenging the view that Ovid's Dido is inferior to Virgil's, argues that our sense of the rhetorical contrivance with which Ovid's Dido speaks does not prevent us from imagining her to be *real*: 'as we start to respond with the pity she demands, we are stopped by our awareness that she is exploiting that pity, and we end up, I think, being charmed by the tension this one woman produces in us.' This tension then bespeaks a certain kind of female character, a character which seems the more accessible for being unidealized: 'Ovid seems intent on showing us a familiar feminine personality, warm, articulate, *self-conscious and self-deceiving at the same time*' (my italics).[11] Jonathan Bate, also alluding to Howard Jacobson's analysis of Ovid's Dido as a reworking of Virgil's, finds in her a convincing model for Shakespeare's characterisation of Cleopatra: 'This Dido has a Cleopatra-like ability to blaze with love one moment and be manipulative the next.'[12]

The popular mediation of Ovid's *Heroides* through modern translation reinforces such assumptions. Harold Isbell's introduction to his Penguin translation of the *Heroides* acknowledges the extent of his debt to Howard Jacobson, whose source study lends itself to appreciation of Ovid's mastery of pyschological realism. Jacobson observes, for example, of the letter of Phyllis to Demophoon (a poem which renders a story of great popularity in antiquity, although earlier treatments appear to have been lost[13]) that 'the poem revolves around the co-existence of apparently incompatible and (logically) mutually exclusive emotions: sincere love/genuine anger; hope/despair'.[14] This apparent incoherence is, however, resolved by an appeal to the distinction between conscious and unconscious emotion; Phyllis has decided that Demophoon is never coming back, but like any lover, she can't quite give up hope. Jacobson writes: The despondency of 11–26 is at two points brilliantly contradicted by unconscious flashes of hope ... we detect, beneath the surface of her professed despair, a faint persistence of hope in Demophoon's good faith' (p. 66). Here, then, is what Verducci called the 'double process' of the *Heroides*; the tension between the conscious rhetorical *presentation* of the self, and the inadvertent self-*revelation* that results. Our job in reading becomes the discovery of how the women's speech is belied by the revelation of unconscious motives and feelings. Isbell's Penguin introduction to individual translations accordingly invites us to pronounce judgement on the moral characters of the heroines as they unconsciously reveal themselves in their true colours.

My interest lies in the facility with which discontinuities and incoherences within the first-person speech of these fictive epistles are assimilated to a governing notion of the conscious or unconscious duplicity – what we might call the 'double voice' – of the female speaker. This tendency extends, I think, to criticism of Renaissance imitations of the *Heroides*. John Kerrigan's anthology of the genre, *Motives of Woe*, makes some of the same moves. Kerrigan is aware that the lack of credibility allocated to female speech is in part an effect of social construction, and hesitates to translate this lack into a judgement of female character. The phrase 'doble voyce', which introduces the speech of the abandoned woman in the first verse of Shakespeare's 'A Louers Complaint' indicates, Kerrigan suggests, a knowing allusion to the tendency of male listeners to dismiss or 'hystericise' the voice of the woman even before it is heard. The poem begins thus:

> From off a hill whose concaue womb reworded
> A plaintfull story from a sistring vale
> My spirits t'attend this doble voyce accorded ...[15]

Subsequently, however, Kerrigan's reading of the same phrase seems to creep back into the realm of character criticism. He makes a brilliantly suggestive connection between the woman's 'doble voyce' echoing off the hill and the 'double ... Voice and Eccho' of Rumour in Shakespeare's *2 Henry IV*. Yet he leaves the connection in the form of a question, hanging in the air, returning after all to the previously eschewed issue of the female speaker's trustworthiness:

> When Warwick assures Henry IV that the number of the rebels is exaggerated, he quibblingly says: 'Rumor doth double, like the Voice, and Eccho, / The numbers of the feared.' Where does this leave the 'doble voyce' heard in Shakespeare's printed 'quire of echoes', the quarto of 1609? ... it is important to recognise the subtlety of the possible falsehood ... Even if the 'fickle maid' reports truth, she might not report 'the whole truth' (whatever that means), or the circumstances which make it so. We should resist the promptings of 'doble' either wholly to credit what she says, or to judge her account mendacious.[16]

I want to challenge the tendency to read the influence of Ovid's *Heroides* in the sixteenth and seventeenth centuries purely in terms of an advance in the effects of character realism. I want to reverse the approach that would place the burden of intention upon the moral character of the woman speaking – 'what does her rhetoric intend?'; 'what do her words inadvertently reveal about her deeper intentions?' – suggesting, rather, that as far as early modern readers were concerned, more pressing ethical questions of intention and liability were raised in relation to the interlocutor who remained absent. I am proposing that sixteenth-century readers of Ovid's *Heroides* were more inclined than we are to read them in relation to the problem that Isabella Whitney sets out in her Heroidean *Copy of a Letter* (1567), when she challenges her 'unconstant Lover': If you 'take me to your wife', she says, '*So shall the promises be kept, / That you so firmly made*' (my italics).[17] The allegation of breach of promise at the heart of so many of the epistles of the heroines makes it possible that sixteenth-century readers of the poems perceived their affinity with *specific* developments in legal thought and practice which were then transforming attitudes to intention and liability in relation to verbal promises. These developments were part of the larger contribution of a theory of equity to the sixteenth-century English common law, a contribution which Luke Wilson has characterized in terms of a general 'increase in the sophistication of legal conceptions of intention'.[18] Equity succeeded, as J.H. Baker explains, in enabling a medieval legal system which was largely hampered by 'the persistence of archaic methods of proof designed to settle general issues', but incapable of allocating guilt or liability in relation to specific cases which did not conform to an existing common law action.[19] If we accept Luke Wilson's proposition that 'intention is that aspect of action traditionally understood as internal and subjective' (p. 22), then it is not hard to concede that a legal system that begins to pay increasing amounts of attention to the question of the relation of intention to criminal or civil liability in court is one which will have an impact on the way in which the 'internal and subjective' aspects of action are represented in other kinds of discourse. And it is thanks to the introduction of an Aristotelian theory of equity that something like this kind of attention was beginning to be paid to questions of intention in the Courts of the King's Bench and of the Common Pleas in sixteenth-century London.[20]

Aristotelian equity, or *epieikeia* was, in essence, the means whereby the inevitable discrepancy between the letter of the positive law and the exceptional circumstances of a particular case might be adjusted by forging a relationship between the two in the form of a hypothesis of the legislator's intention in making the law, and of the intentions of individual parties to the case in 'transgressing' it.[21] Recent articles by

Renaissance literary critics such as Luke Wilson and Katherine Eisaman Maus follow up the implications of earlier work on the relation of equity to the representation of intention in Greek and Renaissance drama with analyses that suggest a relationship between what Wilson calls the 'modularisation of intention' in sixteenth-century legal discourse.[22] 'In order for intentions to enter into circulation as tokens of a general symbolic economy of liability', writes Wilson, 'they must be conceptualised as detachable or modular' ('Hysterisis', p. 31). The area of the English common law in which such a 'modularisation of intention' was most in need of development was that of promissory liability. It was impossible, in sixteenth-century common law, to bring an action on a debt that rested on a mere promise to pay; the only available approximation to such an action was that known as the 'wager of law' which simply obliged the accused debtor to defend himself by finding eleven men ready to swear that he owed nothing. Gradually, however, an equitable alternative to the wager of law emerged in the form of an action on the case known as 'assumpsit'.[23] This led in a more or less direct line to the modern law of contract, according to which mutual promises are held to be binding, and actionable in law.[24] I have argued elsewhere that the disappearance of the spiritual courts' hold over the action of promises between 1500 and 1550, together with the perception of the inadequacy of the common law action of debt, focused legally-minded attention on questions of promissory liability in the 1560s and 1570s in ways which are discernible in the poetry and plays written in that period.[25] Ovid's *Heroides* – concerned as they are with women protesting the faithlessness of lovers who apparently promised to marry them – would seem to invite reading in the context of this sort of legal development, not least because (as classical scholars have noted) Ovid's poetry deploys a vocabulary which, while, 'mixed and inexact ... is real legal terminology', deriving from his experience in the centumviral court.[26] The *Heroides* are particularly rich in this technical language; the pair of letters between Acontius and Cydippe, for example, explicitly turn on the question of whether a promise or an oath made unintentionally is valid in law. Here Ovid exploits the well-known legal topic of the conflict between the spirit and the letter of the law, in other words, the conflict between the strict law and its equitable intention.

Fictions of equity in Renaissance Europe manifest an awareness of the problematic nature of a justice which is empowered to take into account the question of intention.[27] In certain fictions – particularly fictions in which what is at stake is the distinction between matrimony and illicit sex – the heroine who pleads to the impartial judge on behalf of her lover's honourable intentions towards her can come to bear the burden – at the level of 'character' – of the problematic nature of equity.[28] The heroine, in other words, embodies the temporal distortion of the legal taking of intention into account, a distortion whereby it becomes possible to re-open past events, to change the way in which they tell the story that will affect a future which still hangs in the balance. This sense of distortion is, I suggest, precisely what characterizes the peculiar temporal space opened by Ovid's *Heroides*. As we have seen, critics are inclined to read the poems as ineffectual acts of persuasion which inadvertently reveal unconscious truths, and thereby invite us to judge the culpability of the speakers. But we might, rather than seeing self-revelation as the accidental effect of incompetence in persuasion, consider the possibility that the poems offer simultaneous but incompatible motives for utterance by a woman who, at the moment of composition, knows that the circulation of her account will compound the dishonour consequent upon her loss. One motive is, indeed, persuasive; if she acts fast, she might still be able to get him to change his mind and come back, restoring love and honour. Thus Oenone's letter to Paris ends with the plea that he return, and transform her future: *tua sum tecumque fui puerilibus annis / et tua, quod superest temporis, esse precor!* ('I am yours, and I was your mate in childhood years, and yours through all time to come I pray to be!').[29] At the same time, however, another motive, which doesn't cancel out the first, is that of despair; there is no longer any point – whether or not any hope of his return remains – in preserving silence on the question of the dishonour that his failure to return constitutes for her. So Dido's complaint begins by disavowing any persuasive motive: 'Not because I hope you may be moved by prayer of mine do I address you ... but because, after wretched losing of desert, of reputation, of purity of body and soul (*merita et famam corpusque animumque pudicum*), the losing of words is a matter slight indeed' (VII, l.5, pp. 82–3). These incompatible motives are harmonized in relation to the present moment of composition by the writer's uncertainty about the absent lover's intentions, but they also necessarily offer, in the course of a single poem, competing fictions of those intentions. Thus, for example, while the poem *Phyllis to Demophoon* begins like a legal action against the violation of a contract: 'I, Phyllis, who welcomed you to Rhodope complain (*queror*) that the promised day is past, and you not here', it continues, after alleging evidence of violated oaths and broken contracts, with a readiness to believe in the very same vows, handfastings and pledges as reasons to plead the provisionality of the wrong, its recuperability under the sign of thwarted intentions: 'return only, though late, to her who loves you, and prove your promise false only for the time you delay!' (II.ll.28–9, pp. 101–2).[30] George Turberville's much-reprinted translation of 1567 stresses the suggestion of legal redress for damages. Turberville begins:

> I, that thine hostesse, Phyllis, was
> a Rhodopeian mayde:
> Mislike that thou my guest, beyond
> thy fixed time hath stayde.
> Thy plighted promise was with shippe
> here to arryve againe
> Before or neere about the time
> The waxed Moone should waine ...
>
> And yet I can but long to see
> thy comming, though be long:
> Though fixed day be past, revert
> and quite some part of wrong.[31]

Affectless as Turberville's translation might seem to us, it inflects the original in ways to which contemporaries could respond. In this version of *Phyllis to Demophoon,* Turberville's use of the term 'fixed day' evokes contemporary debates about usury, and about the difficulties of establishing a common law remedy for 'nonfeasance', or failure to act by a certain time in fulfilment of a promise or a contract.[32]

In the account I am trying to develop, then, what Howard Jacobson called the 'apparently incompatible' and 'mutually exclusive' emotional positions occupied by the speaker of *Phyllis to Demophoon* cease to be readable in terms of a contrast between surface and depth (the 'deeper' unconscious emotion breaking out to contradict the contrived emotion of the rhetorical surface). They become, rather, both effects of the speaker's obligation to render intelligible the uncertainty that surrounds the intention of the absent lover in the past moment when he promised to return, and in the present moment of writing, when the promise appears to be void. The imperative to render this uncertainty intelligible in terms of one or other fiction of intention (the fiction that matrimonial intentions informed the original vows, which in turn implies the fiction that lover still intends to return and make all good) is, of course, identical to the speaker's obligation to preserve her own good name. Phyllis both condemns Demophoon for promising without having any intention to fulfil his promise ('Demophoon to the windes ingagde / his promise with his sail' [Turberville, f.6v]), and continues to believe in the potential of his intention to prove her judgement against him wrong.

I suggest, then, that the figure of the abandoned woman may have been, in this period, associated with the new possibilities that equity was opening up in legal practice. As equity seeks to establish guilt or liability by hypothesizing a probable intention to make sense of a series of actions, so it requires a lack, an absence of certain knowledge with which to work. An unfulfilled promise creates just such a lack, and is the precondition for female speech in the *Heroides*, and its imitations. Thus, in the printed text of the 'casket sonnets' attributed to Mary Queen of Scots, the Heroidean sequence concludes with a coda in which the speaker gives, as the origin of her writing, an absence resulting from an unfulfilled promise:

> Ne vous voyons selon qu'avez promis
> I'ay mis la main au papier pour escrire
> D'un different que ie voulu transcrire.
> Ie ne scay pas quel sera vostre advis
> Mais te scay bien qui meiux aymer scaura.
> Vous diriez bien que plus y gaignera.

> (Not seing you as you had promisit,
> I put my hand to the paper to write,
> Of ane differens that I haue willit copye.
> I can not tell what shalbe your iugement,
> But I knawe well qhuo can best loue.
> You may tell who shall winne maist.)[33]

The incriminatory quality of these poems as they are presented to the reader in George Buchanan's *Detection of the duinges of Marie Quene of Scottes* is, of course, their function, identifiable as it is with the self-incriminatory tendency of a genre which necessarily confesses the loss of *merita et famam corpusque animumque pudicum*. What is new, however, is the inclusion of such poetry as part of a probable discourse ostensibly made possible by the 'equitie' of the English queen, who, according to Buchanan, requires that the evidence against her kinswoman be 'by necessarie argumentis playnly provit', rather than remaining the subject of wild rumours (Buchanan, sig. A2r; F4v).

In Buchanan's text the femininity of the speaker's voice is associated with self-incrimination, and with the capacity of the equitable judge to ascertain motive and intention from uncertain evidence. If the precondition for female speech/writing is the unfulfilled promise that requires the generation of hypotheses of intention by the writer/ speaker, it bears a strong resemblance to the precondition of the equitable action for promissory words which was being established in the latter half the sixteenth century. In the wake of what P.S. Atiyah has called 'the rise and fall of freedom of contract', we tend to assume that promises are automatically legally binding, and that intentions are anterior to promises. For freedom of contract, the cornerstone of nineteenth-century legal thinking in the West, rests on the principle that promises *per se* are morally binding.[34] This principle, as Atiyah writes, tends to be thought of as universal, but was in fact a consequence of the transformation of English legal attitudes to the actionability of promises between 1600 and 1800. In so far as we live in the wake of the idea of freedom of contract, we will tend to read the *Heroides* in the way that J.R. Searle reads the famous case of *Bardell* v. *Pickwick* when he cites it as evidence for the philosophical proposition that promissory liability cannot exist where there was no intention to make a promise. Searle writes, in the *Philosophy of Language*:

> The essential feature of a promise is that it is an undertaking of an obligation to perform a certain act ... having this intention is the necessary condition of making a promise; for if a speaker did not have this intention in a given utterance, he can prove that the utterance was not a promise. We know, for example, that Mr. Pickwick did not promise to marry the woman because he did not have the appropriate intention.[35]

Here, of course, Searle alludes to the unfortunate Mr Pickwick's finding himself sued by his landlady for breach of promise after inadvertently raising her matrimonial expectations in an ambiguous dialogue not unreasonably construed by her as a delicate courtship and proposal:

> 'You'll think it very strange now', said the amiable Mr. Pickwick with a good humoured glance at his companion, 'that I never

consulted you about this matter, and never even mentioned it, till I sent your little boy out this morning, eh?'

Mrs. Bardell could only reply by a look. She had long worshipped Mr. Pickwick at a distance ...

'It'll save you a good deal of trouble, won't it?' said Mr. Pickwick.

'Oh, I never thought anything of the trouble, Sir,' replied Mrs. Bardell, '... but it is so kind of you, Mr. Pickwick, to have so much consideration for my loneliness.'

'Ah to be sure,' said Mr. Pickwick, 'I never thought of that. When I am in town, you'll always have someone to sit with you. To be sure, so you will.'[36]

Atiyah, who gives Searle's reading of Dickens as an example of the effects of the 'triumph of contract' on the philosophy of promise-keeping, points out that Searle here ignores the difference between novels and life. '[S]ince, in everyday life, there is no benevolent author to tell us what other people's intentions are', Atiyah remarks, 'we are, in fact, entitled to assume that their intentions are what they appear to be. The jury's verdict in *Bardell v. Pickwick* ...was thus sound in law' (*Morals*, p. 147). Mrs. Bardell, then, had a case; but Dickens's comic point, of course, depends on the extent to which our knowledge of Mr. Pickwick's innocence of any intention of marrying his landlady coincides with our sense of the capacity of her desire – *the desire of the unmarried woman* – to transform ambiguity into liability; that is, to make of the man's ambiguous words a plausible fiction of his 'honourable intentions' towards her.

The modern common-sense assumption of the dependence of promissory liability upon the intention of the promissor was not quite so securely in place during the sixteenth century, as the common law groped, via the concept of equity, towards the establishment of a remedy for the non-fulfilment of verbal contracts. Until the sixteenth century, the ecclesiastical courts had overseen the jurisdiction of the violation of sworn promises, while in the common law an archaic action of debt permitted the defendant accused of defaulting on a payment to 'wage his law' which in practice meant employing eleven other men (possibly professional compurgators) to swear he was innocent.[37] The period prior to and immediately after the introduction of the common law action known as 'assumpsit' was one in which the paramount question was, precisely, how the law could establish the actionability of intention when the law could only hypothesize about intention. In the sixteenth and seventeenth centuries, I suggest, the idea of Heroidean speech as an opportunity created by masculine elusiveness for the generation of feminine arguments was associated with the trend towards a form of legal action that sought – however crazily – to establish proof of intention as the basis of liability for verbal promises. If *2 Henry IV*, a play founded on a legal anecdote,[38] proceeds towards the establishment of good relations between the monarch and the judiciary through Falstaff's being hounded by the Lord Chief Justice, it is surely significant that the action for debt pursued against Falstaff by Mistress Quickly in Act II, scene i, is transformed, at the point at which Falstaff inquires into the extent of his debt, into an equitable action of assumpsit, turning on the question of his having promised to marry her. 'What is the gross sum that I owe thee?', Falstaff asks, and Mistress Quickly replies, with a Dido-like unstoppability:

> Marry, if thou wert an honest man, thyself and thy money too. Thou didst swear to me upon a parcel-gilt goblet, sitting in my Dolphin chamber, at the round table, by a sea-coal fire, upon Wednesday in Wheeson weeke, when the Prince broke thy head for liking his father to a singing-man of Windsor – thou didst swear to me then, as I was washing thy wound, to marry me, and make me thy lady thy wife. Canst thou deny it? Did not goodwife Keech the butchers wife come in then and call me gossip Quickly? – coming in to borow a mess of vinegar, telling us she had a good dish of prawns, whereby thou didst desire to eate some, whereby I tolde thee they were ill for a green wound? And didst thou not, when she was gone downstairs, desire me, to be no more so familiar with such poor people, saying that ere long they should call me madam? And didst thou not kiss me, and bid me fetch thee thirty shillings? I put thee now to thy book oath, deny it if thou canst.[39]

There is a broad resemblance here, then, to the way in which the humour of *Bardell* v. *Pickwick* works. In both cases, the joke depends on our understanding the unmarried but unvirginal female as having a tendency to produce fictions of matrimonial intention from areas of complete uncertainty. Dickens, like Shakespeare, enjoyed the notion of there being a resemblance between the law's ability to generate proofs from circumstantial evidence, and the unmarried woman's creative capacity to generate plausible fictions of marital intention where no such intention was likely to exist.[40]

If we return, at this point, to Kerrigan's reading of the words 'doble voyce' in the first quatrain of Shakespeare's 'A Lovers Complaint', we may recall how his reading tended to construct a duplicitous female character as the origin of the voice's 'doubleness', while acknowledging this move to be unsatisfactory: 'Even if the "fickle maid" reports truth', wrote Kerrigan of Shakespeare's female narrator, 'she might not report "the whole truth" (whatever that means), or the circumstances which make it so. We should resist the promptings of "doble" either wholly to credit what she says, or to judge her account mendacious' (pp. 43–4). We may also recall, however, that Kerrigan linked the use of the epithet 'double' to Shakespeare's characterization and deployment of the figure of Rumour in *2 Henry IV*: 'When Warwick assures Henry IV that the number of the rebels is exaggerated, he quibblingly says: "Rumor doth double, like the Voice, and Eccho, / The numbers of the feared." Where,' asked Kerrigan in conclusion, 'does this leave the "doble voyce" heard in Shakespeare's printed "quire of echoes", the quarto of 1609?' (ibid.). It is a good question, and one worth pursuing. What are the poetic antecedents of Shakespeare's figure of Rumour, who introduces to us the play of *2 Henry IV*? One indisputable antecedent is Virgil's description of Fame in the fourth book of the Aeneid. Shakespeare's Rumour, *'painted full of tongues'* recognizably derives from the Titan described by Virgil (I have given Ben Jonson's free translation of the passage in *Poetaster*):

> Look, how many plumes are placed
> On her huge corpse, so many waking eyes
> Stick underneath; and (which may stranger rise
> In the report) as many tongues she bears,
> As many mouths, as many listening ears.[41]

The occasion of this monster's appearance, however, is none other than that of one the fictions of matrimonial intention that we've been concerned with. Dido willingly makes love to Aeneas in the cave:

> For now, nor rumour's sound
> Nor nice respect of state moves Dido aught.
> Her love no longer now by stealth is sought:
> She calls this wedlock, and with that fair name
> Covers her fault. Forthwith the bruit and fame
> Through all the greatest Lybian towns is gone.
> Fame, a fleet evil, than which swifter none.

> (V.iii.69–75)[42]

The 'doble voyce' of Rumour in Shakespeare is already plotted within the narrative of femininity's obligation to generate fictions of honourable male intentions – intentions to marry, intentions to return after all – which rebound back on the voice of the woman by casting doubt upon her integrity, emotional, moral and sexual. Dido 'calls this wedlock', but such a name in itself presumes to speak for Aeneas's intentions, and as such is belied by Fame, who speedily proclaims the woman's fault abroad, while we, as readers, are to understand that her fault is compounded by this act of deception, this 'fair naming'.

In view of this it actually seems *not* 'appropriate' as Kerrigan suggests, but quite inappropriate for us to read sixteenth- and seventeenth-century poems modelled on Ovid's *Heroides* as exercises in judging 'how far plaintful speakers are responsible for their downfall' (Kerrigan, p. 29). More appropriate, I think, would be a kind of reading which took account of the asymmetry of the allocation of blame for sexual misdemeanour, understanding thereby that a woman's voice may well be 'doubled' by the imperative to construct a fiction of masculine matrimonial intention in order to justify, and perhaps even bring about, the marriage that would retrospectively turn her 'fault' into her 'good name'.

Did sixteenth- and seventeenth-century women show an awareness of the legal affinities of the *Heroides*? I think they did. As Laura Gowing has pointed out, the late sixteenth and early seventeenth centuries were years of unprecedented increase in numbers of women suing in the church courts against having been sexually defamed by other women – the equivalent of Virgil's 'monstrum horrendum', the rumours spread about Dido. Yet, as Gowing observes of this phenomenon, its status as a linguistic opportunity for women was distinctly ambiguous:

> In many ways ... the language of slander offered particular linguistic powers to women, through which they asserted their verbal, physical and legal agency to judge and condemn other women. But such sexually explicit speech had its risks for women. Using sexual insult to prove other women dishonest left slanderers themselves open to charges of impropriety, and the dangers of women's speech about sex were particularly apparent when women alleged seduction, assault or rape.[43]

Isabella Whitney's verse anthology, *A Sweet Nosgay* (1573), is throughout obliquely preoccupied with the dangers of allowing oneself to be spoken about. Whitney warns her sisters, serving in London, to guard against gossip, 'Yf to rehersall oft you come,' she says, 'it wyl your quiet wound.' Yet she herself cannot name the reason why: 'I cannot speake, or wryte to much', she explains, 'because I love you well.' The reason seems to lie in the power of defamatory words: 'For words they are but winde. / yet wordes may hurt you so: / As you shall never brook the same / yf that ye haue a foe' (sig. C8r). That women should urge each other to behave in such guarded ways corresponds with the conclusion of a poem in Tottel's Miscellany, entitled, 'Of the choise of a wife'. In this poem, the author's principal criterion in selection of a wife is that she should remain quite unknown to the eye and ear of fame: 'Let fame not make her knowen whom I shall know ... Sufficeth me that vertue in her grow, / Whose simple life her fathers walles do hide.'[44]

It may be that Whitney spoke from bitter experience in warning her sisters against 'all such, / as would be word or Byll. / Procure your shame' (*Nosgay*, sig. C8r). Having written her own spirited version of a Heroidean epistle in the *Copy of a Letter*, published in 1567, she went on in the *Sweet Nosgay* to arrogate to herself the position of the most desolate of Ovid's heroines, reprimanding Dido for presuming to make such a claim. 'Good DIDO stint thy teares', she begins, 'and sorrowes all resigne / To mee: that born was to augment misfortunes lucklesse line.' The Carthaginian queen, she argues, might have lived 'a happye Woman styll' in spite of Aeneas's absence. Indeed, it seems that Aeneas's absence was just what was required to restore her happiness:

> For as the man by whom,
> > thy deadly dolors bred:
> Without regard of plighted troth,
> > from CARTHAGE Citie fled.
> So might thy cares in tyme,
> > be banisht out of thought:
> His absence might well salve the sore,
> > that earst his presence wrought.
> For fyre no lenger burnes,
> then Faggots feede the flame:
> > The want of things that breede annoy,
> may soone redresse the same.

> (sig. D3v)

Whitney here draws our attention to what is wrong with trying to account for the despair of the abandoned women of Ovid's *Heroides* simply in terms of the emotional oscillations arising from abandonment in love, without any attention to the legal questions of matrimonial intention and honour, on which the material prospects of the woman's future are contingent. The delicate Virgilian and Ovidian associations of Dido with an inextinguishable, smouldering love[45] are crudely rewritten as the brisk common-sense observation that 'fyre no lenger burnes / Then Faggots feede the flame', which, along with the irreverent opening says in effect: 'Dido, forget the bastard; you are, after all, still queen of Carthage.' Whitney's point, in the context of her own narrative (which emerges through the collection of poems that make up the *Nosgay*) is that the position from which the 'abandoned woman' speaks must be understood in terms of the deprivation of agency, which makes it at least partly a socio-economic position. If we assume that the voice of inconsolable grief over abandonment in love must be female, then we make gender an effect of the extent to which the loss of love also represents the irremediable material and social loss consequent upon the loss of good name. Whitney boldly denies the assumption that loss of love is the real cause why the Ovidian heroine weeps. In the references she elsewhere makes to the defamatory 'evell words' which were spoken about her by her 'enemies tong' (sig. D7r). She echoes Dido's own admission of having lost *'famam corpusque animum pudicum'* ('the reputation of a chaste mind and body'). Whitney's claim, therefore, that her own grief and loss exceeds that of the Carthaginian queen, is a measure of the extent to which the loss of good fame is seen as a more irreparable loss than that of the lover. For Whitney the injustice she has suffered in having 'evell words' spoken about her appears to have led directly to 'the losse ... of service' for which she now 'languish[es]' (sig. C6v) in poverty. Dido's emotional loss, by comparison, can easily, as Whitney says (using the vocabulary of justice), be 'redress[ed]' by itself.

In the third book of Lady Mary Wroth's *Urania* (1621), an ingenious Heroidean poem is similarly framed by a story of the loss of good name consequent upon a sexual liaison. The poem hovers between suicide note and attempt at persuasion; as its author says:

> when I saw no merit, no love, no remembrance, nor any thing could worke against a newe choice which he had made, I framd these lines as my last peece, resolving if they prevailed not to let all goe.[46]

Wroth first introduces the author of the poem to us in such a way as to suggest that we should, indeed, read it in the fashion of modern *Heroides* criticism, as the revelation of a self torn by conflicting emotions. Yet as this woman, Dorolina, tells her tale, it becomes less and less easy to think of reading the oscillation between different kinds of subject position in her poem as symptomatic of this feminine 'diversity in disposition', or the 'double voice' of unconscious self-deception. She tells how she loved a man, 'the brother to the Dutches I serv'd'. When, after her yielding to him, he departed, she wrote and asked for what she thought was her due as 'both giver, and bringer' of love, but without success. 'I ... recover'd not so much as dammages', she complains (p. 492). In the poem itself, Dorolina exploits the contradictory positions I have identified as typical of the genre – sustaining competing fictions of the probable intentions of the addressee, her lover – by comparing her own lot to that of one Ovidian heroine after another. She thus moves through a series of Ovidian exempla towards a position of maximum rhetorical effectiveness, both likening herself to the Heroidean victim and then denying the ill-fatedness implied by the likeness. Dorolina first likens herself to Ariadne ('I *Ariadne* am alike oppress'd, Alike deserving ...') and then to Phyllis, the injustice of whose sufferings as a result of the broken faith of Demophoon is in no doubt. '[S]hee', Dorolina says of Ariadne, saved the life of Theseus, while, 'he her honor lost / Leaving her desolate, alone to prove / His love ... but given for neede.' The death of Phyllis is explicitly linked to a similar loss of honour:

> ... *Phillis* selfe, her lovely selfe did kill,
> Making a Tree her Throne, a Cord the end
> Of her affections, which his shame did send.

> (p. 493)

The grammar makes her self-inflicted end the object of a shame which is 'his' in origin, but which he 'did send' to kill her. Having thus identified herself with heroines who, in Ovid, express extreme grief in relation to the yielding of their chastity to the departed lover (Phyllis wishes she had died the night before they made love, while Ariadne wonders whether a woman so disgraced as she can be said to continue to live), Dorolina transposes the identification, via an acknowledgement of Medea's power to enchant Jason, on to the figure of the 'other woman', thereby enabling herself to take up instead the position of the 'good woman' in the Ovidian Penelope, whose known end as the wife to whom Ulysses eventually returned implicity denies the spectre of shame and 'honor lost' aroused by the evocation of a likeness to

Ariadne or Phyllis. The epistle thus changes from complaint to an empowered assurance of forgiveness:

> Come you now backe, I thus invite you home,
> And love you, as if you did never roame:
> ... Come, I say, come againe, and with *Ulisses*
> Enjoy the blessings of your best blisses;
> Happy the comfort of a chaste loves bed,
> Blessed the pillow that upholds the head
> Of loyall loving, shame's the others due ...

> (p. 495)

Shame is disowned as the end Dorolina herself is bound to face should the addressee of the letter fail to return; it becomes the penalty of the 'other', the woman who, if Dorolina's plea is fulfilled, must become the victim of the 'evil words' that otherwise define the author herself as unchaste. If the female voice of the lover's complaint is, then, always a 'double voice', then its doubleness must be the effect of sustaining competing hypotheses of the intentions of the absent lover, while attempting to anticipate and deflect the 'voice and eccho' of sexual slander. These strategies inevitably produce the effect of an inherent duplicity or capacity for self-deception in the moral character of the female narrator. We cannot begin to 'judge' the fallen woman until she herself establishes for us the hypothesis that she has not 'fallen', a hypothesis which must remain ambiguous and unprovable, since it depends on a retrospective re-opening of the already closed-off possibility that her absent lover will, in fact, return after all.

Notes

1. I would like to thank Danielle Clarke, Elizabeth Clarke, Rosalind Ballaster, Jacqueline Rose and Erica Sheen for detailed criticism. A previous version of this paper showed its indebtedness to Jacqueline Rose's 'Just, Lasting and Comprehensive', in *States of Fantasy* (Oxford: Clarendon Press, 1996); the indebtedness remains.
2. Stephen Greenblatt, *Shakespearean Negotiations* (Oxford: Clarendon Press, 1988), p. 1.
3. Greenblatt, p. 2.
4. I am quoting Catherine Belsey from Alan Sinfield's critique of poststructuralist theory's attempt to deny the power of the 'character effect' in Shakespeare. See Sinfield, *Faultlines* (Oxford: Clarendon Press, 1992), p. 58.

5. On the importance of the illusion of 'character' in Shakespearean drama, and of the failure of post-structuralism to account for its effects, see Sinfield, pp. 52–79.

6. Elizabeth Harvey, *Ventriloquized Voices: Feminist Theory and English Renaissance Texts* (London: Routledge, 1992), pp. 15–16.

7. Linda Kauffman, *Discourses of Desire: Gender, Genre and Epistolatory Fictions* (Ithaca, NY: Cornell University Press, 1986), p. 20. Kauffman refers to Howard Jacobson, *Ovid's Heroides* (Princeton, NJ: Princeton University Press, 1974), p. 90.

8. Kauffman, p. 23.

9. Kauffman, p. 49, quoting Richard Lanham.

10. Florence Verducci, *Ovid's Toyshop of the Heart: Epistulae Heroidum* (Princeton, NJ: Princeton University Press, 1985), p. 15.

11. W.S. Anderson, 'The Heroides', in J.W.Binns, ed., *Ovid* (London: Routledge and Kegan Paul, 1973), p. 55.

12. Jonathan Bate, *Shakespeare and Ovid* (Oxford: Clarendon Press, 1993), p. 212.

13. Jacobson, p. 58n.

14. Ibid., p. 66.

15. John Kerrigan, *Motives of Woe: Shakespeare and 'Female Complaint', A Critical Anthology* (Oxford: Clarendon Press, 1991), p. 209.

16. Kerrigan, pp. 43–4.

17. Isabella Whitney, *The Copy of a Letter, lately written in meeter* (London, 1567), sig. A2v.

18. Luke Wilson, '*Hamlet*, Hales v. Petit and the Hysterisis of Action', *ELH* 60 (1993): 17–55, p. 31.

19. J.H. Baker, ed., *The Reports of Sir John Selden*, 2 vols (London: Selden Society, 1978), II, p. 32.

20. I have argued this more fully in 'Not the King's Two Bodies: Reading the 'Body Politic' in Plowden and Shakespeare', *Rhetoric and Law in Early Modern Europe* eds Victoria Kahn and Lorna Hutson (Yale University Press, forthcoming).

21. Aristotle, *The Nichomachean Ethics*, trans. H. Rackham (London: Heinemann, 1932), I.13.17–18; 146–7. See also Christopher St. Germain, *Doctor and Student*, ed. T.F.T. Plucknett and J.L. Barton (London: Selden Society, 1974), pp. 95–9; John Guy, 'Law, Equity and Conscience in Henrician Jurist Thought', in *Reassessing the Henrician Age*, ed. John Guy and Alastair Fox (Oxford: Basil Blackwell, 1986); and Zofia Rueger, 'Gerson's Concept of Equity and Christopher St. Germain', *History of Political Thought* 3 (1982): 1–30.

22. See Luke Wilson, '*Hamlet*: Equity, Intention, Performance', *Studies in the Literary Imagination* (1991); Wilson, 'Hysterisis'; Katherine Eisaman Maus, 'Proof and Consequences: *Othello* and the Crime of Intention', in her *Inwardness and Theater in the English Renaissance* (Chicago: Chicago University Press, 1995), pp. 104–27; see also Kathy Eden, *Poetic and Legal Fiction in the Aristotelian Tradition* (Princeton, NJ: Princeton University Press, 1986); Joel Altman, *The Tudor Play of Mind* (Berkeley: University of California Press, 1978); and Terence Cave, *Recognitions* (Oxford: Clarendon Press, 1988).

23. J.H. Baker, *An Introduction to Legal History* (London: Butterworth, 1979); Baker, 'English Law and the Renaissance', in *The Legal Profession and the English Common Law* (London: Hambledon, 1986), p. 463; Baker, ed., *Reports of John Spelman*, II:, pp. 37–43; R.E. Helmholz, 'Assumpsit and Fidei Laesio', *Law Quarterly Review* 91 (1975): 406–32.

24. T.F.T. Plucknett, *A Concise History of the Common Law*, 5th edn (London: Butterworth, 1956), pp. 643–4; A.W.B. Simpson, *History of the Common Law of Contract: The Rise of Assumpsity* (1975); see also Luke Wilson, 'Ben Jonson and the Law of Contract', *Cardozo Studies in Law and Literature* 5 (1993): 281–306.

25. See my *The Usurer's Daughter*, pp. 140–2.

26. E.J. Kenney, 'Ovid and the Law', *Yale Classical Studies* 21 (1969): 243–63, p. 254. For Ben Jonson's knowledge of Ovid's connection with the centumviral court, see Jonson, *Poetaster*, ed. Tom Cain (Manchester: Manchester University Press, 1995), III.iv.51n, p. 142.

27. See for example, Sidney's sympathetic treatment of the clandestine marriage of Pyrocles and Philoclea in *The Old Arcadia*; the narrator's inclination to make the reader believe in the couple's good intentions toward one another contrast with their condemnation in the 'trial ... of ... equity' performed by Euarchus. In *The Old Arcadia* ed. Katherine Duncan-Jones (Oxford: Clarendon Press, 1985), pp. 212–25, 263, 305, 251.

28. Thus in Sidney's *Old Arcadia* it is Philoclea who begs Philanax to consider Pyrocles's sexual union with her as a 'virtuous marriage' (p. 263); see also the story of Epitia by Giambattista Girali Cinthio in *Gli Hecatommithi*, 2 parts (Venice, 1566), part 2, pp. 256–62. Epitia, known to English literary history as the antecedent of Shakespeare's Isabella in *Measure for Measure*, is distinguished by her pleading to judge the good intentions of the man who seduced her with the false promise that in return he would pardon her brother from death.

29. *Heroides and Amores*, trans. Grant Showerman, revised G.P. Goold (London: Heinemann, 1986), V, ll. 157–8; pp. 68–9.

30. For other examples of broken faith urged both as accusation and as evidence of good intention, see Hypsipyle to Jason, Vi. ll.41–4, pp. 72–3; Dido to Aeneas, VII, ll. 7–8, pp. 82–3.

31. *The Heroycall Epistles of the Learned Poet Publius Ovidius Naso in English Verse* (London, 1567), f. 5v–6r. See Danielle Clarke's essay, pp. 65–7 for further discussion of Turberville's translation.

32. See, for example, William Harrys, *The Market or Fayre of Usurers* (London, 1550), sigs. F7v–G8v; William Walpul, 'The Tide Tarrieth No Man' (1576), in *English Morality Plays and Moral Interludes*, ed. E.T. Schell and J.D. Schuster; J.H. Baker, 'The Establishment of Assumpsit for Nonfeasance', in *Spelman*, II, pp. 258–72.

33. George Buchanan, *Ane Detectioun of the duinges of Marie Quene of Scottes* (London, 1571), sig. O2v. I'd like to thank Rosalind Smith for drawing this text to my attention.

34. *Morals, Promises and Law* (Oxford: Clarendon Press, 1981), p. 4; see also P.S. Atiyah, *The Rise and Fall of Freedom of Contract* (Oxford: Clarendon Press, 1979).

35. J.R. Searle, 'What is a Speech Act?', in *The Philosophy of Language*, ed. J.R. Searle (Oxford: Oxford University Press, 1971), p. 50.

36. Charles Dickens, *Pickwick Papers*, ed. James Kinsley (Oxford: Oxford University Press, 1988), pp. 138–9.

37. See above, n. 23, and Helmholz, 'Assumpsit', pp. 406–32.

38. Geoffrey Bullough, *Narrative and Dramatic Sources of Shakespeare*, vol. 4, pp. 288, 299–343; see note 20 above.

39. *Henry IV, part 2*, ed. A.R. Humphreys (London: Routledge, 1966), II.i.83–101.

40. Sometimes the 'doctrine of consideration' was employed in rather eccentric ways in equitable cases of assumpsit. Baker observes that in 1566 Plowden managed to argue successfully that desire for the continuance of male heirs was 'good consideration' for there having been contractual intention in the case of Sharrington v. Strotton. See Baker's 'Origins of the "Doctrine" of Consideration 1535–1585', *Legal Profession and the Common Law*, pp. 369-91.

41. *Poetaster*, ed. Cain, V.iii.85–9.

42. See Virgil, *Aeneid*, trans. Robert Fitzgerald (Harmondsworth: Penguin, 1983), p. 101; Shakespeare, *The Second Part of Henry the Fourth, A New Variorum Edition*, ed. Matthias A. Shaaber (London and Philadelphia: J.B. Lippincott & Co., 1940).

43. *Domestic Dangers: Women, Words and Sex in Early Modern London* (Oxford: Clarendon Press, 1996), pp. 109–10.

44. *Songs and Sonettes written by the ryght honorable Lorde Henry Hawarde* (London: Scolar Press, 1970), sig. Bb2r.

45. Virgil's allusions to Dido's 'flames' are frequent; see *Eclogues, Georgics and Aeneid 1–6*, with trans. by H.R. Fairclough (London: Heinemann, 1935), IV.54, 66, 68–9, 400–1.

46. *The Countess of Montgomeries Urania*, ed. Josephine Roberts (New York: Medieval and Renaissance Texts and Studies, 1995), p. 492.

8
'For *Worth*, Not Weakness, Makes in Use but One': Literary Dialogues in an English Renaissance Family

Marion Wynne-Davies

In *A Room of One's Own* (1929) Virginia Woolf created a Renaissance woman dramatist called Judith Shakespeare, but lamented that no real counterpart existed for Judith since

> it is unthinkable that any woman in Shakespeare's day should have had Shakespeare's genius. For genius like Shakespeare's is not born among labouring, uneducated, servile people ... how, then, could it have been born among women whose work began ... almost before they were out of the nursery.[1]

Woolf was fully accurate in identifying a female author's need for security, both economic and environmental, but the seeming lack of texts led her to assume that women of the early modern period had experienced neither, instead being trapped within a domestic vortex of familial responsibilities. However, while not questioning Woolf's primary identification of a writer's essential requirements, it has become increasingly clear that early modern women were able to access a literary voice, even a 'dramatic' one. It is the purpose of this essay to explore the ways in which such cultural productivity could be achieved from *within* a familial environment, one which both liberated and constrained its female members. I will focus specifically upon the writings of Mary Wroth, one of the first English woman dramatists, and the way in which her voice is both freed by its familial Sidneian identity, and muted by her gender in comparison with the free vocalisations of her uncle, Philip Sidney, her father, Robert Sidney, and her cousin/lover, William Herbert.

It is the idea of a 'room of one's own', however, which develops the most intriguing associations in relation to early modern women's authorship, even though the constraints on privacy during the period suggest a shared space, rather than single occupancy. The large castles and houses which surrounded London and were scattered across the British Isles served to provide a secure environment in which women could nurture their creative talents, although, as with economic independence, access to these havens was mostly controlled by men. Still, it was precisely this combination of wealth, a secure space and male complicity that allowed the Sidneian women to evade the fate of Judith Shakespeare and to experience an environment suited to literary productivity. Indeed, the perfect example of the 'safe house' concept may be seen in the Sidney family and their various residences: Philip's ideal knighthood, Robert's careful neo-Platonism, Mary Sidney's pious scholasticism, Mary Wroth's innovative independence and William Herbert's worldly statecraft are set off perfectly by the lauded pastoralism of Penshurst, the learned 'academy' of Wilton and the clandestine passages of Baynard's Castle.[2] Here the social standing, wealth and cultural position of the family combine with the beautiful, gracious and protected houses, simultaneously propagating a discourse which enabled both male and female creativity.

However, while the contribution of Sir Philip Sidney (1554–86) to creative and critical writing was lauded during his lifetime, allowing his position within the canon to remain pre-eminent, the rest of his family has not been treated with equal consideration. Philip's sister, Mary Sidney/Herbert (1561–1621), while being elevated as her brother's counterpart during the early seventeenth century, was subsequently neglected; it is only recently, particularly with the recent Clarendon Press edition of her work, Margaret Hannay's biography and a flowering of other critical interpretations that her work has been given full validation. The shifts in estimation have been considerable: from Samuel Daniel's eulogy on her translation of the psalms, 'In them must rest thy ever reverent name', through to Frances Young's well-known comment on her editing of Philip Sidney's work that 'she *added* practically nothing and *left out* some things of value',[3] and finally Margaret Hannay's more recent and more measured summation:

> Mary Sidney ... by remaining within the established limits, became the most important woman writer and patron of the Elizabethan period, one who demonstrated what could and what could not be accomplished in the margins.[4]

Their brother Robert (1563–1626) also produced a collection of poems, although during his lifetime he concealed his work from all but his family and, perhaps, close friends. He is never praised as a poet in the contemporary commendatory verses which mention the skills of his siblings and daughter, but it is clear that Wroth was familiar with her father's writing since she uses them in her own poetry. Robert's work was identified in 1973 by P.J. Croft, whose edition appeared in 1984. In the subsequent generation Mary Wroth (1587?–1653?), Robert's daughter, has probably been awarded most praise, although she, like her aunt, suffered from the neglect often accorded women writers, even though her writing was acclaimed by her contemporaries. Wroth was the first English woman to write a sonnet sequence, a prose romance and a dramatic comedy. William Herbert (1580–1630) was Mary Sidney's son and Wroth's cousin, yet his writing is neither as extensive nor as interesting as theirs, perhaps because of his political responsibilities; his poems were published in 1660. Finally, a third cousin, Philip's daughter Elizabeth Manners (1584–1615) is known to have written poetry, but this has either perished or remains lost.[5]

The excavation of this primary material over the last twenty years has, to a certain extent, altered the basic structure of Sidney criticism, for instead of looking at the single and enormous edifice of Philip Sidney's canon, perhaps tinkered with by his doting sister Mary, we can now see a range of rooms with parallel forms and features, coexisting through a period of initial development and a succeeding period of expansion. Instead of reading Philip Sidney as a lone authorial presence, it is now possible to see him as a part (albeit an important one) of a familial grouping whose members functioned both as separate entities and as participants in a unique whole. Of course, I use my trope advisedly, since the image of a building evokes the necessary ingredient for a Renaissance familial discourse, the 'safe house', a place to which the writer could retreat, where he or she was free to experiment with textual production, original or translated, protected by the close fabric of kinship and social position. Moreover, such a space was particularly important for the female members of the family whose gender barred them from the public disclosure of their literary productions. The Sidneys and Herberts used their houses not only to entertain professional writers, safeguarding their endeavours within the cloak of patronage, but also as a personal refuge from the outside world – here, mutual creativity wove an even stronger protective fabric about those encased. There are well-known examples of this usage, as in Ben Jonson's panegyric 'To Penshurst' where he praises Sidneian patronage:

> But what can this (more than express their love)
> Add to thy free provisions, far above
> The need of such? whose liberal board doth flow
> With all that hospitality doth know!
> Where comes no guest but is allowed to eat
> Without his fear, and of thy lord's own meat.[6]

A parallel usage may be seen in Philip Sidney's self-imposed retreat to his sister's house, Wilton, where he composed his *Arcadia* in her presence.[7] But there are further associations evident from tracing the patterns of travelling and of composition within the family. So, for example, we know that Mary Sidney worked on two versions of her psalm translations, one which was kept at Wilton and the other at Baynard's Castle; Mary Wroth would have had the opportunity to consult her aunt's work at either place, although perhaps especially at Baynard's Castle where she wrote some of her sonnets, which often emulate the diverse and experimental structures of Mary Sidney's psalms. However, Wroth must also have had access to her father's poems, which were kept at his house, Penshurst, and, as she explicitly uses some of them in her own writing, we may assume she composed those pieces while at her childhood home. William Herbert probably worked on some of his poems at Baynard's, his primary residence, and these could well have included the key companion pieces between him and Wroth, such as their opposing defences of love and reason. Indeed, it is these dialogic pieces which will form the central focus of the essay.[8] The manuscript copies of the family's own compositions facilitated the use and revision of those works by others within the domestic coterie and so it is no surprise to discover a web of allusion and a conscious employment of echo. Thus, when examining a poem by one Sidney/Herbert it is often impossible to trace a specific referent, since the same form, tone, metaphors, classical citations and verbal structures are all present. It might be possible to trace various discourses in their poetry, such as Petrarchan, Protestant or neo-Platonic, but all answer to the deeper stratum of a familial bonding, creating a particular Sidneian discourse. And, of all the Sidneys who encapsulated this literary tradition, it is Mary Wroth who was, as the last Sidneian vocalizer, also the final inheritor of her family's specific culture. It is her work, particularly the play *Love's Victory* that I intend to explore in this essay.

The initial site of the inquiry will, however, be Penshurst, where, in August 1617, Lady Anne Clifford made several visits, all recorded in her diary. On the first of the month she visited 'Lady Wroth' and was joined there by 'Lady Rich'; on the 12th and 13th she 'spent most of the time in playing Glecko & hearing Moll Neville reading the *Arcadia*', and then on the 19th:

> I went to Penshurst on Horseback to my Lord Lisle where I found Lady Dorothy Sidney, my Lady Manners, with whom I had much talk, & my Lord Norris, she and I being very kind. There was Lady Worth who told me a great deal of news from beyond the sea, so we came home at night, my Coz. Barbara Sidney bringing me a good part of the way.[9]

The women visiting one another during this brief period were all part of the same familial grouping, although the complexity of their relationships is made clearer when using a diagrammatic presentation (see p. 69). Anne Clifford was the daughter of Margaret Russell whose sister Anne was the sister-in-law of Mary Dudley Sidney, Wroth's grandmother; moreover, Anne Clifford was to become the second wife of Wroth's first cousin and William Herbert's brother, Philip Herbert. Lady Rich, who visited Clifford and Wroth, was most probably Isabella Rich, the daughter of the infamous Penelope Rich who had been allegorised as 'Stella' by Philip Sidney in his sonnet sequence. There was also an association between two families through the marriage of Robert Dudley (Mary Dudley Sidney's brother) to Lettice Knollys, thereby linking the family to Lettice's children, Penelope Devereux Rich, her sister Dorothy Devereux Percy, and their brother, the even more infamous Robert Devereux, Earl of Essex. Moreover, despite the fact that Penelope Rich had not married Philip Sidney, she remained a good friend of the family and in 1595 she acted as the young Robert Sidney's godmother (Robert being Wroth's adored brother).

Subsequently, on 19 August, Clifford visited Penshurst, the home of Robert Sidney and his wife Barbara Gamage Sidney who had now acceded to the title of De Lisle; while there she met four of the second-generation cousins, Robert's two daughters, Mary Wroth and Barbara, and his daughter-in-law, Dorothy Percy Sidney, who was married to the younger Robert, who was herself the daughter of Dorothy Devereux Percy and so connected to the Sidneys through her mother. Finally, making up the group of cousins was Elizabeth Sidney Manners, Philip Sidney's daughter. Turning to the Norris family, I believe 'Lord Norris' does not necessarily refer to the husband, Francis Norris, alone, but also to his wife, Lady

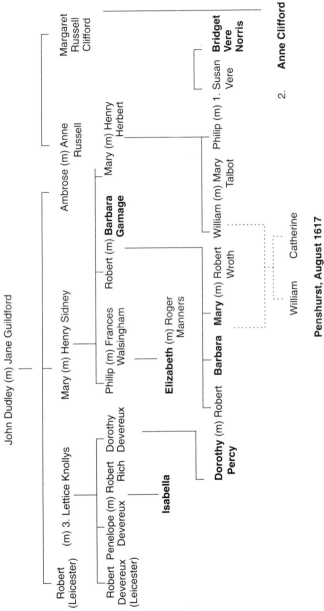

Penshurst, August 1617

Bridget Vere Norris; this interpretation would match Clifford's other gender conflations and would also make sense of her subsequent statement, *'she* and I being very kind' (italics mine). Lady Norris was, not unexpectedly, also connected to the Sidneys, since she was the sister of Susan Vere Herbert, the Countess of Montgomery, the first wife of Philip Herbert (William's brother and Mary Sidney's second son); and it was Susan to whom Wroth dedicated her prose romance, *The Countesse of Mountgomeries Urania*.[10] The Norris family had a traditional association with the Leicester faction, but the more immediate reason for their being at Penshurst was the connection through wives and sisters, not the political bonds manufactured by male courtiers thirty years earlier. On top of all this, Clifford when at home was forging another familial bond by reading the Sidney text *Arcadia*. The political factions of the country as a whole clearly thread their way through this network, the Essex faction (both generations) being an important binding force, but more overt and more prolonged are the familial ties, which were commonly manipulated by astute political players in order to underpin the more transient court alliances. However, there is yet another important element present in the gathering at Penshurst, that of gender.

Penshurst, like all familial houses, functioned as a place where noble women could find pleasure in one another's company without the darker and more dangerous intrigues of the early seventeenth-century court. The picture drawn by Clifford toys with the idea of a female 'academy': it is an image decorated with the embellishments of literary texts and toned to the liking of a companionate body of female wits; it is then an environment particularly and exclusively for women, a 'feminine' safe house.[11] One of the women present at this gathering was Lady Mary Wroth, who is described as bringing important information 'from beyond the sea', which in 1617 could have signified the continued conflicts in the Netherlands. Wroth's contribution to the gathering would, no doubt, have been considered interesting, for she was not only a member of the family group, but an accomplished author in her own right, and it is highly likely that she would have been writing in 1617, which corresponds with the period between the death of her husband (Robert Wroth died in 1614) and the aborted publication of the first part of her prose romance *Urania* in 1621. Moreover, Wroth was at the same time engaged in an adulterous affair with yet another Sidney, her cousin William Herbert, and had two illegitimate children by him during this period, possibly giving birth at Penshurst. She would have been considered a woman of notoriety and, at first, it is easy to imagine her as a marginal figure amongst her secure and sedate companions. But, surprisingly, her inclusion only compounded the network of difficulties faced by the women present at Penshurst. Anne Clifford, for example, was involved, with the strong support of her mother, in a lengthy battle to contest her father's will and win her rightful inheritance over a male relative and, despite the antagonisms of her husband and the king, she consistently refused to yield, finally triumphing by default when she inherited the titles in 1643. Indeed, almost all the other women present had, or were soon to encounter, similar difficulties. In the younger generation, Dorothy Percy Sidney had been married clandestinely the previous year, and Isabella was to be secretly married the following year. Of the older women, Bridget had frequently lived apart from her husband (who was soon to commit suicide with a cross bow), and even Barbara Gamage Sidney, the 'noble, fruitful [and] chaste' lady of Jonson's celebrated poem, had arranged a match against the queen's wishes with the now irreproachable Lord de Lisle (Jonson, p. 97). Each of the women mentioned, with the notable exception of Elizabeth Sidney Manners, were, had been or would be excluded from the court and were thus compelled to use Penshurst as a 'safe' house in a very real way. For them the refuge offered was not merely a country retreat from which they could emerge refreshed, but an absolute necessity without which they would have been ostracized and disgraced. As such, the congregation at Penshurst, with its secret alliances and clandestine affairs, offered a brief moment of security for its female participants, who were thus able to assert, however fleetingly, that while protected by these familial surroundings 'None can accuse us, none can us betray'.[12] This quotation is taken from a scene in Wroth's play, *Love's Victory*, where a group of shepherdesses decide to recount their experiences of love:

> Now we're alone let everyone confess
> Truly to other what our lucks have been,
> How often liked and loved, and so express
> Our passions past; shall we this sport begin?
> None can accuse us, none can us betray,
> Unless ourselves, our own selves will bewray.
>
> (III.ii.21–6)

What the speaker, Dalina, means when she claims that they are 'alone' is that no men are present. The women are thus able to reveal their histories to one another without the threat of patriarchal censure; their 'luck' in love and the number of men they have 'liked' may be openly

recounted rather than being concealed within a code of social expectation which allowed only for arranged marriages and a single emotional
commitment from women. Moreover, Dalina's final words echo the
need for a mutual loyalty amongst women, since the female community ('ourselves') can only be betrayed by individual women ('our own
selves'). For the women in Penshurst, with their records of illicit affairs,
sexual and economic, such a secure grouping must have proved attrac-
tive. Thus, Wroth recreated in her drama the female assemblies in
which she participated, for undoubtedly that recounted by Clifford in
her diary was a single example of a common occurrence, thereby
affirming not only the importance of the safe house, but also of the
female community within its walls.

The coterie of women sojourning that summer at Penshurst are, therefore, to a certain extent replicated in Mary Wroth's play *Love's Victory*.
There are some alterations, however: the inclusion of Susan Vere and
Mary Sidney Herbert as the two generational identities filtered through
Musella's friend Simeana being perhaps the most significant, but overall
the parallels hold true. For example, Lady Anne Clifford is probably
alluded to through Musella; although this character represents both
Wroth and Rich, she is also, through the difficulties caused by her
father's will, Lady Anne. In the play Musella is initially prohibited from
marrying Philisses because her father has contracted her to Rustic
(a character outline which is a scathing attack upon Robert Wroth) in his
will. Neither Mary Wroth nor Penelope Rich encountered such legal
difficulties, although both women were unsatisfied with their husbands
and took lovers, but Wroth did know someone who was involved in a
complex legal battle because of her father's will – Lady Anne Clifford. A
parallel to this representation occurs in *Urania I* where Wroth refers to
Clifford as 'Lucenia' and discusses the problems of female inheritance.[13]
Indeed, if we continue to extend our search for veiled figures across
Wroth's canon, Barbara Gamage and Dorothy Percy are clearly referred
to in *Urania I*, and identified as such by the late Josephine Roberts in her
edition. Wroth's parents are described in the characters of the King and
Queen of Morea, and her sister-in-law is figured as Meriana, Queen of
Macedon. There does not appear to be a named reference to Bridget Vere
Norris, but Veralinda's sisters are mentioned and, as Veralinda shadows
Susan Vere, Bridget may said to be included in this group. Similarly, it
seems likely that, as Pamphilia represents Wroth in the narrative,
Bardariana, Pamphilia's youngest sister, may be linked with Barbara,
Wroth's youngest sister.[14] This means that all the women referred to by
Clifford as being in Penshurst in August 1617 are represented in Wroth's

work, either in the play or the prose narrative. There is, however, one key exception: Elizabeth Sidney Manners. Philip Sidney's daughter is nowhere to be found, and when Wroth figures her uncle it is either as the young poet/lover, Philisses in *Love's Victory* and Sildurino in *Urania I*, or as the childless King of Pamphilia who takes the heroine Pamphilia (Wroth) as his heir. Perhaps it is this latter point which provides us with a possible reason for Elizabeth Manners' exclusion, for Wroth was not interested in seeing another woman, who was Philip Sidney's actual daughter and an accomplished poet in her own right at that, as the Sidneian 'heir'. For Wroth, the Sidneian mantle had to fall exclusively on her own shoulders, and if familial allegory has one advantage over accurate genealogies, it is that they may be remoulded, omitting those members who do not quite fit with the overall allegorical device. The final array of Sidneian female representations thus begins to shed an ambivalent light upon the familial discourses and safe houses initially evoked, for while Wroth initially appears able to trust in the bonds of family, sex and home, her veiling processes subtly rework the basic familial material to her own advantage, thereby suggesting that the actuality left something to be desired.

Indeed, Wroth's sojourn at Penshurst must have been particularly bitter, for whilst the Sidney/Herbert residences shielded her from the displeasure of king and court, William Herbert, her cousin and lover, had no need for such 'protection'. While she was banished from the hub of courtly activity and had only those 'safe houses' in which to exercise her glittering wit and sparkling intellect, Herbert was one of the most powerful nobles in the land and in the year previous to this gathering at Penshurst, 1616, had become Lord Chamberlain. The gender difference is reinforced by an interesting parallel to the seclusion of Mary Wroth within the safety of Penshurst and the careful closeting of her affair and two bastard children, for in 1601 William Herbert had entered into an affair with a court lady, Mary Fitton, but had refused to marry her when she became pregnant. Consequently Herbert was imprisoned in the Fleet; then, after the baby died at birth, he was banished from court by Queen Elizabeth, and was forced to retreat to the family home, Wilton. From the safety of this stately house Herbert fired off volleys of letters demanding freedom and a return to the court, since

I endure a very grievous imprisonment. For do you account him a free man that is restrained from coming where he most desires to be [that is, the court].[15]

William Herbert did not feel protected by Wilton, but imprisoned by it. In contrast, Wroth, in one of her many autobiographical narratives, describes the fate of Lindamira (an anagrammatized version of Ladi Mari) who is likewise banished from court by the displeasure of a queen, and whose 'honour' is 'cast downe, and laid open to all mens tongues and eares, to be used as they pleased'.[16] Neither Wroth nor Herbert pictures themselves as happy to be exiled from the court, but he is more concerned with his freedom and his self-determination, whereas she agonizes over the manner in which her reputation has suffered and the way in which her actions have allowed her to be categorized as unchaste, that is, 'laid open to all men'. As such, Wilton confines Herbert, preventing him from being a 'free man', whereas Penshurst shields Wroth from the common usage of 'tongues and eares'. More galling surely for Wroth was that when Herbert's indiscretion led to further illegitimate children, this time her own, the gender balance of the court had swayed even more in his favour, the misogynistic James promoting his noblemen regardless of sexual infidelities, and punishing the women instead. Admittedly, Elizabeth I's regular use of banishment as a form of controlling her young male courtiers revealed more about her own self-centred system of loyalties than any supposed 'feminism', but there can be no question that women's standing at court diminished rapidly and consistently throughout James's reign.

Perhaps, however, if Lady Mary Wroth was unable to compose the letters of protest undertaken by her cousin, she could recreate herself under the cover of the Sidney mantle in more ways than one; if Penshurst offered economic and locational security, then her genealogy offered a way in which she could complain against the injustices of the king and court, without endangering her 'honour'. Her uncle's sonnet sequence offered itself as a form of closeted romance, presenting himself as the spurned lover Astrophil, and Penelope Devereux Rich as his lady, Stella; her aunt's psalm translations encoded a powerful Protestant message intended to instruct as well as to please; and her father's rhymes simultaneously displayed and concealed his love for the still unidentified 'Lysa'. With this multiple inheritance of veiling devices, it is hardly surprising that in all of Mary Wroth's literary endeavours she reproduces this doubling process, this cloaking of personages and events, this familial allegory. The title-page of the first part of *Urania* leaves the reader in no doubt about her literary allegiances:

The Countesse of Mountgomeries Urania. Written by the right honorable the Lady Mary Wroath. Daughter to the right Noble Robert Earle of

Leicester. And Neece to the ever famous, and renowned Sir Phillip Sidney
knight. And to the most excelent Lady Mary Countesse of Pembroke late
deceased. (frontispiece)

Wroth's father, uncle and aunt are all brought forward to affirm her
cultural and social qualifications, while the work is dedicated to her
friend, Susan Vere, the Countess of Montgomery, who was the first wife
to Philip Herbert, brother of William (Philip's second wife was, as has
been mentioned, Anne Clifford). More particularly, Wroth reworks these
familial relationships within her texts. For example, Wroth and William
Herbert are depicted time and again: he is the fickle Amphilanthus (lover
of two) in her sonnet sequence and her prose romance, while she is the
constant Pamphilia (all-loving) in both works; subsequently in her play
Herbert becomes the true Philisses and Wroth the much admired
Musella. While the familial representations in Wroth's *Pamphilia to*
Amphilanthus and her *Urania* have been thoroughly, although perhaps
not exhaustively, analysed, her dramatic comedy, *Love's Victory*, has
remained largely unexcavated.[17] The main reason for this has been the
inaccessibility of the text, which until 1988 existed only in manuscript
form and was not edited in a complete modern edition until 1995. The
comparative neglect of the dramatic material makes it a more profitable
site of investigation, but its genre specifically endows the material with a
more direct familial identity than either the sonnet or prose romance
forms.[18] Indeed, the combination of private theatricals with familial
allegory makes *Love's Victory* the key site of the Sidneian allusions within
her canon.

The familial identifications in *Love's Victory* and Wroth's *oeuvre* as a
whole cannot be missed since the texts make direct reference to the
real lovers through the use of puns. The pun was a common Sidneian
device, practised by Philip Sidney in *Astrophil and Stella* and reactivated
by Wroth in her own works. For example, when Musella defends
herself to Silvesta, another shepherdess, against the charge that she has
been cruel to Philisses, *Will*iam Herbert is alluded to:

> Wrong me not, chaste Silvesta, 'tis my grief
> That from poor me he *will* not take relief.
>
> (III.i.41–2; italics mine)

Similarly, when Musella has convinced Silvesta of her sincerity, her
friend responds

> I do believe it, for in so much *worth*
> As lives in you, virtue must needs spring forth.
>
> (III.i.95–6; italics mine)

thereby reminding the reader/audience of the author's name as it was commonly reworked during the period; in addition to Clifford's usage in the diary extract quoted above we may add Wither's commendation of her '*Worth* and bounty' and Sylvester's designation of her as 'AL-WORTH Sidnëides' (Clifford, pp. 10–1 and Wroth [1983], p. 19). In addition to this relatively straightforward allegory, the songs in *Love's Victory* often directly evoke and answer Herbert's poems, thereby indicating a second level of interpretation, that of literary allegory, although it is still grounded in familial referents. For example, at the beginning of Act II the shepherds and shepherdesses draw fortunes from a book which are rehearsed in rhyme, at the end of which Philisses concludes:

> Love and Reason once at war,
> Jove came down to end the jar.
> 'Cupid,' said Love, 'must have place';
> Reason, that it was his grace.
> Jove then brought it to this end:
> Reason should on Love attend;
> Love takes Reason for his guide,
> Reason cannot from Love slide.
> This agreed, they pleased did part,
> Reason ruling Cupid's dart.
> So as sure Love cannot miss,
> Since that Reason ruler is.
>
> (II.i.213–24)

These lines are a direct refutation of Herbert's poetical defence of Love against Reason in 'It is enough, a Master you grant *Love*':

> It is enough, a Master you grant *Love*
> At one weapon, 'twas all I sought to prove:
> For worth, not weakness, makes him use but one;
> While that subdues all strength, all Art alone.[19]

Apart from offering a counter-argument to Wroth's uniting of Love and Reason, Herbert neatly puns upon his lady's name, so that it becomes his adoration of 'worth'/Wroth that makes him a slave to

Love and therefore able to refute her argument; in other words, Herbert suggests, she has only herself to blame. It was the dialogic mutuality of these lines in which gender and family commingled so completely that made a quotation from this poem such an apt choice for the title of this essay.

This form of textual interchange between Wroth and Herbert attains its most extreme form when she includes one of his poems within her own prose romance and attributes it to Herbert's fictional other, Amphilanthus (Wroth [1983], p. 44). However, Wroth's song in the later, more mature, *Love's Victory* moves beyond this poetic love-play with Herbert, by adding echoes of the contest between Reason and Passion in the Second Eclogues of her uncle's *Old Arcadia* where Reason argues 'that Reason govern most' and Passion replies comically that 'Passion rule the roast'.[20] This poetic allusion uncovers another identity for Philisses within the familial allegory, for the anagramatized name clearly points towards *Phili*p *Si*dney and not William Herbert. This affirms another familial identity within the play for Philisses' sister is called Simeana, a reference to *Ma*ry *Si*dney, while the name of his lover, Musella, begins to sound remarkably like *Stella*, in other words, Penelope Rich. Indeed, Wroth self-consciously alludes to this bi-play of identification when she makes Musella ask:

> And yet my true love crossed,
> Neglected for base gain, and all *worth* lost
> For *riches*?
>
> (V.i.3–5; italics mine)

Here 'riches' suggests Penelope Rich at the same time that 'worth' refers to Wroth. The familial allegory in *Love's Victory* continually functions on this double level, alluding to first and second Sidney/Herbert generations, allowing Musella to represent the author as well as Lady Rich, and linking William Herbert with Philip Sidney through the character of Philisses.

While these naming puzzles are an important aspect of Wroth's dramatic strategy (she includes an actual 'riddling' sequence in the play) the web of literary allusion extends beyond the walls of individual identification to a system of cultural, philosophical and political beliefs. The text cannot be contained within the appellative allusions since, for Wroth being a Sidney was not simply a title, a family designation, but the key to an intellectual, and moral, code which not only formulated identity via the physical surface, but also determined the complex inner convictions of the noble Sidneian edifice. Yet, with a final labyrinthine twist, the Sidneian ideology was itself framed in the locational device of pastoral, which in turn encoded the claim to a particular private familial space.

In Jan Kip's 1723 engraving of Penshurst Place the physical details of the Sidneian estate are distinct: the house, its formal gardens, the wooded mount rising behind, and the tree-lined walks are all depicted. However, I should like to add to this overall vista the information that the river Medway runs in front of the formal gardens, from which it is separated by the meadows of the Lower Land. It is this setting which recurs throughout the Sidneian canon. Each authorial voice, Philip, Mary, Robert, Wroth and Herbert, returns inevitably to the image of Penshurst with its panoply of idyllic pastoral features. While Ben Jonson might have lauded the 'Mount', the 'copse', 'the lower land, that to the river bends' and the 'high-swollen Medway' through the externalized vision of the patronage poem, these same forms were the very foundations, the very essence of Sidneian pastoral, and for the second generation the backdrop of an more intensely personal narrative (pp. 96–7). In the final pages of this essay I intend to focus upon the way in which Penshurst, both house and garden, became the site of a particularly familial discourse, which opened up the possibility of semi-autobiographical writing, the issues of gender difference and the eroticized dialogues of Mary Wroth and William Herbert.

In exploring the Sidneian estate through its material and metaphorical projections, I intend to begin with the bucolic meadows and end upon the hill, without necessarily ever entering the Great Hall. The reasons for evading the structured edifice lie in the Sidneys' own depiction of their estate, since their writing consistently evades the country house, both the actual building and the genre poem which was to be made so popular by Jonson. Indeed, perhaps it is this latter evocation of 'Penshurst', which so skilfully embraces the discourse of patronage, that allows us to excavate possible explanations for the manifest difference between the settings employed by the noble family and by the poets who depended upon their munificence. For Ben Jonson the house becomes the centre of a vibrant and bountiful community with Lord de Lisle at its heart, and he journeys from a rustic pastoralism to the ideal 'proportion' of Penshurst, weaving the panegyric message invisibly with the Edenic vision of the text. The influence of this Jonsonian map may be witnessed in several criticisms which trace the contours of the Sidneian estate along the lines set out in 'To Penshurst'.[21] Yet, the referents in the poem are clearly those of an outsider: not only was Jonson of a different class, but he was also a visitor to the estate from London, with all the country/city (not to mention court) bias implied by that divide. This was clearly not the same position adopted by the family themselves. For example, as we have seen, the women of the Sidney family were allowed far more freedom in Penshurst than they would have had in the city or court, while the male members of the family invested considerable time and effort in the development of their properties.[22] Yet, in their creative writings the Sidneys evade the house itself and turn to the encompassing lands; the Mount, woods and meadows adopt the guise of a multifaceted pastoralism, which offered to its familial body as much a freedom from their own country house as from the world at large. Through a process of successive manoeuvrings it becomes possible first to see the house at Penshurst from Jonson's point of view as an idyllic retreat from court and city, and second to perceive Penshurst's lands from the familial perspective as a personal retreat from the responsibilities of the stately home. By allowing for this change of outlook and position, Penshurst acts as a shifting signifier, 'at home' both in the discourse of patronage as well as in the more personalized form of familial allegory.

The conjunction of a semi-autobiographical voice with a recognition of instability and change occurs most frequently in the descriptions of the meadows, the Lower Lands and the Medway. This region of the Penshurst estate becomes the site of the lover's complaint in Philip Sidney's work, where he envisages his poetic second-self in this role:

> The ladd *Philisides*
> Lay by a river's side,
> In flowry field a gladder eye to please.

To this conventional evocation of a melancholic lover, he adds the recognition of fickleness in love, here combined in metaphor with the Medway's preponderance to flooding: 'you wanton brooke, / So may your sliding race / Shunn lothed-loving bankes' (*Old Arcadia*, pp. 256–9). Yet this same image is echoed in very different poetic situations by the other Sidneys: by Robert in his pastoral on unrequited love and the cruelty of women, 'To drown the fields the angry brooks do move / Their streams';[23] by Mary in her psalm translations evoking the instability of the material world, 'For all the floods';[24] by Wroth in her representation of abandonment, 'Dangerous fluds your sweetest banks t'orerunn' (Wroth [1983] p. 113); and by Herbert in a witty depiction of his own lack of steadfastness, 'this wandring *will*/ ... from the natural course stand still' (p. 41). The Sidneian canon also reverberates with similar images of the lower lands, the woods, the walks and the mount are made, which culminate in a string of pastoral figures: 'Rocks, woods, hills, caves, dales, meads, brooks, answer me';[25] 'Meadows, fields, forests, hills' (Robert Sidney, p. 153); 'The woods, the hills, the rivers shall resound / The mournful accent of my sorrowes ground' (Mary Sidney, p. 176); 'Meadows, paths, grass, flowers, / Walks, birds, brook: truly find / All prove but as vain showers' (Wroth, *Love's Victory*, p. 98); and 'Looking on the Mead and Grove' (Herbert, p. 40).

Yet perhaps the most potent of the pastoral images derived from the scenery of Penshurst is the Mount, and it is on this particular site that the second generation Sidneys locate their most intensely personal verse. In *Urania I* Wroth makes a clear reference to the Mount in her description of the island Ciprus. Here the hill is surrounded on three sides by gardens and an orchard, while on its fourth aspect there grows 'a fine and stately Wood', and finally, 'at the foote of this Hill ranne a pleasant and sweetly passing river, over which was a bridge' (*Urania*, pp. 47–8). A reference to Penshurst Mount is also made when it figures as the site where Amphilanthus (William Herbert) sits alone writing a love poem to Pamphilia (Mary Wroth), 'in the mid'st of the Wood was a Mount cast up by nature, and more delicate then Art could have fram'd it'. Not unexpectedly, one of William Herbert's poems carries an answering report:

> ... Let me call t'account
> Thy pleasant Garden, and that leavy Mount,
> Whose top is with an open Arbour crown'd.

> (pp. 10–19, ll.7–9)

Yet, in Herbert's version the lover is not sitting alone writing melancholy verses to his mistress, but rather asks her,

> Dost thou remember (O securest beauty)
> Where of thy own free motion (more then duty)
> And unrequir'd, thou solemnly did swear,
> (Of which avenging heav'n can witness bear)
> That from the time thou gav'st thy spoils to me,
> Thou wouldst maintain a spotless chastity,
> And unprophan'd by any second hand,
> From sport and Loves delight removed stand,
> Till I (whose absence seemingly was mourn'd)
> Should from a foreign Kingdom be return'd.

> (ll.56–7)[26]

William Herbert's poetic second-self forges a narrative in which the Mount becomes the site of an amorous encounter, where Wroth has given herself to him of her 'own free motion' and promises to remain faithful, even though in the poem she subsequently chooses a different lover (perhaps an allusion to Robert Wroth). The sexual character of their meeting may be uncovered through the term 'spoils' with its sexual overtones, and through the phrase '*unprophan'd* by any *second* hand', implying that Wroth's 'spotless chastity' has certainly been profaned by a first hand. Penshurst Mount becomes, for Herbert, an erotic location in which the pastoral setting evokes a succinctly postlapsarian Eden, an image hardly recognizable from the chaste melancholy encoded in his lady's verse. The difference is, of course, perfectly explicable in gender terms, since Herbert was heir to a male literary discourse which revelled in sexual allusion; indeed, Ben Jonson appears to invoke a similar characterization for the Mount, although for him it is only a prelude to the restraints imposed by the house and lord:

> Thou hast thy walks for health as well as sport:
> Thy Mount, to which the Dryads do resort,
> Where Pan and Bacchus their high feasts have made,
> Beneath the broad beech, and the chesnut shade.

> (Herbert, pp. 9–12, ll. 56–7)

Such licence was simply not an option for a noble lady, or any woman wishing to retain her reputation in the early modern period, and, as we have seen, Wroth was made to suffer for her sexual indiscretion. Thus, Wroth's depiction of Herbert (in the guise of Amphilanthus) alone on Penshurst Mount writing forlorn love poems to her was a far more desirable form of female self-presentation. On the other hand, it is enticing to imagine that Herbert's more explicit interpretation of familial pastoralism allows us to discover exactly when and where the cousins consummated their sexual passion for one another; although, of course, we inevitably remain frustrated in such an act. Finally, however, both lovers display a virtuoso skill at manipulating the pastoral language to uncover an intimate identity, thereby setting up a personalized reading of the lyric poems. Simultaneously, however, they engage in a more covert process of familial appropriation, by transplanting the very form of the pastoral into the Sidneian family estate. For, as Wroth and Herbert appear in the pastoral, so the pastoral becomes absorbed by and appears in the lands of Penshurst Place.

As Wroth's and Herbert's dextrous manoeuvrings through the undergrowth of pastoralism suggest, the Sidney family had become adept at the process of acquiring, reworking and personalizing the literary and philosophical ideologies of their day and to a certain extent this privileged the women writing within that specific familial discourse. The secure space and economic security foregrounded by Woolf allowed the Sidneian women to cultivate their literary skills, producing the translations of Mary Sidney, the diary of Anne Clifford, the lost canon of Elizabeth Manners and the pre-eminent *oeuvre* of Lady Mary Wroth. Yet, even though combined within a family, the gender differences are mutinously apparent, especially when excavating the works of Mary Wroth and William Herbert. While these first cousins may have united in love, their treatment by contemporary society and their evocation of sexual passion show them to be deeply divided. What was acceptable for a man, both in material and literary terms, was simply forbidden for a woman, whatever her familial connections. Still, the very shifting nature of the gendered discourses offers a way in which the whole notion of a 'safe house' may be questioned, for male and female versions of familial allegory may be seen to jostle with the discourse of patronage in the presentation of the Sidneian estate. Penshurst, therefore, becomes a site of shifting signification, where, for example, the externalized vision of Ben Jonson is metamorphosed into the inward interpretation of the Sidney family. Yet, by eschewing the house in favour of the fields and Mount, the Sidneian pastoral transcends the traditional city(court)/country divide in order to infuse the conventional genre with a surprisingly intimate and triumphantly personalized interpretation. In so doing, the gendered divisions are subsumed in the assertion of an expressly familial identity. The Sidneian voices, split along gendered lines, in the final summation become a doubled assertion of kindred singularity and mutual cultural productivity. Thus, as familial discourse allows itself to be overtaken by various other literary forms such as pastoral, it simultaneously incorporated those alternative genres into the overwhelming presence of a multiple, yet harmonious family voice. Moreover, while the female Sidneys appear to be less authorized than their male counterparts by this familial discourse, the very presence of a male/female merging of cultural activity liberated them in ways unknown for women writing without such support, and their mutual endeavour served to liberate both sexes in their claim for an independent self. As such, the complex negotiation between an externalized adventurism, in which modes, genres and styles were conquered by the explicit personal allegory of the individual, and a colonial retrenchment which harnessed all cultural productivity for their own benefit, embraced by Mary Wroth and William Herbert, was ultimately to secure a specifically Sidneian discourse within the categorically Sidneian location of Penshurst.

Notes

1. *A Room of One's Own* (St Albans: Triad Paperbacks, 1977), pp. 47–8.
2. Gary Waller, *The Sidney Family Romance: Mary Wroth, William Herbert, and the Early Modern Construction of Gender* (Detroit: Wayne State University Press, 1993), pp. 49ff and 108–21.
3. Samuel Daniel, *Delia and Rosamund Augmented. Cleopatra* (London, 1594), sig. H6v; Frances Young, *Mary Sidney, Countess of Pembroke* (London: David Nott, 1912), p. 147.
4. Margaret Hannay, *Philip's Phoenix: Mary Sidney, Countess of Pembroke* (New York: Oxford University Press, 1990), p. x.
5. *Ben Jonson: The Complete Poems*, ed. George Parfitt (Harmondsworth: Penguin, 1975), p. 466.
6. *Jonson*, ed. Parfitt, pp. 96–7.
7. Hannay, pp. 47–50.
8. Waller, pp. 108–21, 142.
9. *The Diaries of Lady Anne Clifford*, ed. D.J.H. Clifford (Stroud: Alan Sutton, 1990), pp. 60–1.
10. Indeed, Philip Herbert had been betrothed to Bridget before Susan. The connection between the sisters was affirmed by the fact that Bridget's daughter was placed in Susan's household to be brought up.
11. See Mary Ellen Lamb, *Gender and Authority in the Sidney Circle* (Madison: University of Wisconsin Press, 1990), p. 215; Louise Schleiner, *Tudor and Stuart Women Writers* (Bloomington: Indiana University Press, 1994), pp. 15–23; and Waller, pp. 102–4, 277.
12. Wroth, *Love's Victory* in *Renaissance Drama by Women: Texts and Documents*, ed. S.P. Cerasano and Marion Wynne-Davies (London: Routledge, 1995), pp. 90–126. The citation is from III.ii.25. All subsequent citations will be made within the text.
13. *The First Part of the Countess of Montgomery's Urania*, ed. Josephine A. Roberts (New York: Medieval and Renaissance Texts and Studies, 1995), pp. 422, 144.
14. For the first two identifications I am indebted to Josephine Roberts; for the two latter characters I have used my own reading of Roberts' edition. See Roberts, *Urania*, pp. xcii–iii, 107, 190 and 804.
15. Quoted in Waller, p. 79.
16. *The Poems of Lady Mary Wroth*, ed. Josephine A. Roberts (Baton Rouge: Louisiana State University Press, 1983), p. 31.
17. In my identification of the familial allegory in Wroth's works the following have been the most helpful: Tina Krontiris, *Oppositional Voices: Women as Writers and Translators of Literature in the English Renaissance* (London: Routledge, 1992); Lamb; Barbara K. Lewalski, *Writing Women in Jacobean England* (Cambridge, Mass: Harvard University Press, 1993); Roberts (1983); Schleiner; and Waller.

18. To date the following critical essays are the only ones that appear to be available on *Love's Victory*: Barbara K. Lewalski, 'Mary Wroth's *Love's Victory* and Pastoral Tragicomedy', in *Reading Mary Wroth: Representing Alternatives in Early Modern England*, ed. Naomi J. Miller and Gary Waller (Knoxville: University of Tennessee Press, 1991), pp. 88–108; Margaret Anne McLaren, 'An Unknown Continent: Lady Mary Wroth's Forgotten Pastoral Drama, *Love's Victory*', in *The Renaissance Englishwoman in Print: Counterbalancing the Canon*, ed. Anne M. Haselkorn and Betty S. Travitsky (Amherst: University of Massachusetts Press, 1990), pp. 276–94; Carolyn Ruth Swift, 'Feminine Self-Definition in Lady Mary Wroth's *Love's Victory* (c. 1621)', *English Literary Renaissance* 19 (1989), pp. 171–88; Roberts (1983), pp. 156–74; and Waller, pp. 220–45.

19. William Herbert, *Poems Written by the Right Honourable William Earl of Pembroke* (London, 1660), ed. Gaby Onderwyzer (Los Angeles: Augustan Reprint Society, 1959), p. 7.

20. Sir Philip Sidney, *The Old Arcadia*, ed. Katherine Duncan-Jones (Oxford: Oxford University Press, 1985), p. 119.

21. Don Wayne, *Penshurst: The Semiotics of Place and the Poetics of History* (London: Methuen, 1984), p. 85; and Alastair Fowler, *The Country House Poem: A Cabinet of Seventeenth-Century Estate Poems and Related Items* (Edinburgh: Edinburgh University Press, 1994), pp. 53–62.

22. The development of the buildings at Penshurst is discussed by Wayne, pp. 81–105.

23. *The Poems of Robert Sidney*, ed. P.J. Croft (Oxford: Clarendon Press, 1973), p. 209.

24. *The Triumph of Death and Other Unpublished and Uncollected Poems By Mary Sidney, Countess of Pembroke (1561–1621)*, ed. G.F. Waller (Salzburg: Institüt für Englische Spraeke und Literatur, 1977), p. 106.

25. *Selected Poems*, ed. Katherine Duncan-Jones (Oxford: Clarendon Press, 1973), p. 101.

26· Roberts also quotes this poem in relation to Wroth's description, but her transcription appears to be different from my own; Wroth, *Urania*, 1995, 731.

9
'Whom the Lord with love affecteth': Gender and the Religious Poet, 1590–1633

Helen Wilcox

I

This essay is concerned with the work of four English poets from the late sixteenth and early seventeenth centuries – Mary Sidney (the Countess of Pembroke), John Donne, Aemilia Lanyer and George Herbert – who, despite their differences of class, gender and chosen literary form, shared a common inspiration, the profound sense that they were among those 'whom the Lord with love affecteth'.[1] The impact and expression of religious experience took a variety of poetic shapes in the work of the four writers. Mary Sidney produced a verse translation of the psalms, revising the text of the first 43 psalms drafted by her brother before his death, and single-handedly translating the remaining 107 psalms into increasingly sophisticated lyric verse forms. John Donne wrote occasional religious verse and dramatic meditative sonnets, while Aemilia Lanyer's *Salve Deus Rex Judaeorum* is an extended verse narrative of the Passion, and George Herbert's *The Temple* includes a sequence of over 150 devotional lyrics. Their work reached the reading public by a variety of routes over four centuries. Sidney's psalms, completed around 1599, and Donne's religious verse, written in the first three decades of the seventeenth century, are known to have circulated in manuscript, reflecting the courtly tradition of coterie writing which eschewed the public mode of print.[2] Lanyer, a middle-class woman on the margins of court society, took the bold step of publishing her own small book in 1611.[3] Herbert's *The Temple* came out in printed form immediately after his death in 1633, the same year as the belated posthumous publication of Donne's poems. The complete text of the Sidney Psalm translation was not published until 1823.[4]

In spite of their contrasting poetic modes and publication histories, the poets were working in a tradition of certain shared and fundamental principles. Their poetry, for example, betrays a common aesthetic of dependence which is typical of religious writing, recognizing that devotional creativity must always be a reworking or copying of a preceding divine text, the scriptural and incarnate 'Word'. This spiritual intertextuality is not only discernible in the more obvious rewritings of biblical sources – the Old Testament sacred songs of Sidney's psalms, the New Testament narrative of Lanyer's *Salve Deus* – but also in the biblical phrases interwoven within Herbert's lyrics and the redramatizing of scriptural scenes in Donne's Holy Sonnets.[5] All four poets were engaged in the process of seeking 'quaint words' with which to 'copie out' divine love, that deceptively simple task of the religious poet recounted in Herbert's 'Jordan' (II).[6] The 'readie penn'd' biblical text, with which all four poets were dealing, also laid down some dominant metaphors for the relationship of the soul to God, ranging from the Old Testament concept of the elect, to the assertion of the freedom to be 'sons' not 'slaves' in the New.[7] Perhaps the most prevalent biblical metaphor for the intimacy of the dialogue between God and the human soul was that of marriage. The partnership of the female church, and within it, individual souls, with a male God – earthly brides with a heavenly bridegroom – is a fundamental trope of Christian devotional thinking, deriving in biblical terms from allegorical readings of the Song of Songs.[8] This is a patriarchal marriage between the virginal soul and the sacred lord, who is at once both husband and divine father.

My concern in this essay is to explore some of the ways in which (Mary) Sidney, Lanyer, Donne and Herbert worked within, and beyond, the inherited gendered framework of devotional thought and writing. How did these poets depict themselves in their religious texts, and with what materials did they envisage and construct their relationship with God? Are there significant differences between male and female poets: did they, perhaps, create God to some extent in their own (gendered) image? Can the new canon of religious poetry, now including the work of women writers, bring about changes in the way we interpret the familiar texts of devotion?[9] Or is there a sense in which the distinctions of gender cease to be of any significance in the sphere of the spiritual?

II

Given the nature of the perceived distance between the human being and God, it is not surprising that all four poets embark on their poetic approach to Him from a position of utmost humility. Herbert, echoing the biblical idea of the 'first fruits' of the harvest as an obligatory offering to God,[10] begins *The Temple* with a 'Dedication':

> *Lord, my first fruits present themselves to thee;*
> *Yet not mine neither: for from thee they came,*
> *And must return. Accept of them and me.*

(p. 32)

The poet's modesty is intensified by the syntax here, in which the 'first fruits', the poems of *The Temple*, are active; they 'present themselves'. The poet's involvement is reduced to the personal pronoun of owner-ship ('my'), which is then immediately negated ('Yet not mine'). The poet's first presence in the text is, in fact, more predominantly an absence. Lanyer also uses the metaphor of 'first fruits' in dedicating her volume of poems, but the dedicatee in this case is not God but the 'Lady Elizabeth', daughter of James I and Queen Anne:

> Even you faire Princesse next our famous Queene,
> I doe invite unto this wholesome feast,
> Whose goodly wisedome, though your yeares be greene,
> By such good workes may daily be increast,
> Though your faire eyes farre better Bookes have seene;
> > Yet being the first fruits of a womans wit,
> > Vouchsafe you favour in accepting it.

(p. 11)

Lanyer invites the Princess to the 'feast' of her book, and the speaker is not afraid to play an active part in the syntax of the stanza. However, the one whose 'favour' she is initially seeking is not divine, and not male, both of which factors inevitably affect the tone here; Lanyer is addressing a royal woman, to whom she can readily confess that her poems are the 'first fruits of a woman's wit'.

It is revealing of their situation as women writers that neither Sidney nor Lanyer present their poems directly to God, but through human intermediaries. Although the women writers' protestations recall many written by their male contemporaries when facing the divine, Lanyer and Sidney's texts demonstrate an additional dimension of humility; they not only dedicate and present their work indirectly, but also express an intensely gendered sense of sinfulness which initially increases their distance from God. Disclaiming any education in the art of poetry, Lanyer, for example, asserts her humility before male poets as well as God:

> Not that I Learning to my selfe assume,
> Or that I would compare with any man:
>> But as they are Scholers, and by Art do write,
>> So Nature yeelds my Soule a sad delight.

(pp. 9–10)

The woman poet's access to God is not, she suggests, via the masculine scholar's art, but through an untutored femininity graced by 'Nature' (p. 10). Later in *Salve Deus*, Lanyer addresses her own muse on the paradox that greater weakness can lead to more intensely religious verse:

> But yet the Weaker thou doest seeme to be
> In Sexe, or Sence, the more his Glory shines,
> That doth infuze such powerfull Grace in thee,
> To shew thy Love in these few humble Lines.

(p. 63)

To be the weaker in gender and in art can be, in the world of Christian paradoxes where the 'last shall be first', ultimately the greater strength.[11]

On the one hand, then, the woman poet is conscious of her 'presumption bold' (Sidney, p. xxxvi) and the disadvantage of her additional 'defects' before God (Lanyer, p. 10). On the other hand, her professed lack of art and skill takes her into the realm of nature, truth and grace, clearly an advantage in the complex world of divine poetry. As Donne noted, in his enthusiastic poem on the Sidneian Psalter, the writer who attempts to find 'new expressions' for God faces an impossible task, confining in 'strait corners of poor wit' that which is 'cornerless and infinite'.[12] In his 'Litany' Donne himself asks for deliverance from the temptation to 'seem religious / Only to vent wit', and in 'The Cross' he recognizes the need to 'cross and correct concupiscence of wit'. (pp. 167, 144). Both male poets were university men, Donne with a legal bent and Herbert with an orator's skill; they knew 'the wayes of learning', 'reason', 'laws and policie', as Herbert wrote in 'The Pearl' (p. 103), and their task was to resign this knowledge, skill and eloquence to the cause of religious experience and expression. The male poets approach God with their hands full, as Herbert subsequently makes clear in 'The Pearl':

> I know all these, and have them in my hand:
> Therefore not sealed, but with open eyes
> I flie to thee, and fully understand
> Both the main sale, and the commodities;
> And at what rate and price I have thy love.

(p. 104)

Donne and Herbert consciously make an offering of themselves and their skills, which they are obliged to 'resign' to God, as Donne observes in his first Holy Sonnet (p. 173). They know all along that what they are giving is not theirs even to offer, in practice or in poetry, so their full hands turn out to be empty.[13] Lanyer and Sidney, reversing the conventional mix of presentation and humility, approach God conscious of their lowly status. Their empty hands turn out, paradoxically, to signify what Sidney calls a 'full soule':

> I render here: these wounding lynes of smart
>   sadd Characters indeed of simple love
>   not Art nor skill which abler wits doe prove,
> Of my full soule receive the meanest part.[14]

III

If devotional writing is a process of reworking and rewriting, the next stage after the poet's self-presentation is the challenge of self-*re*presentation. The religious poet, taking on the impossible but unavoidable task of giving linguistic expression to spiritual experience, has to discover a personal voice, a subject position for the self from whose perspective the divine is viewed. The idea of self-representation as 'discovery' is important, since all four poets were aware that their task was to find themselves in pre-existent texts rather than to invent an appropriate new language; as Herbert wrote, 'Thy word is all, if we could spell'.[15] Of the four poets with whom this essay is concerned, Mary Sidney worked most closely with this given scriptural word, playing the role of translator to the divine muse of the Psalms. Although the subservient role of translator was thought to be well suited to women, we should not forget that a modern synonym for translator is interpreter, and, as one of her twentieth-century editors

has pointed out, Sidney's poems are certainly 'more than translations'.[16] One of the most significant ways in which Sidney's psalms are
a development of their biblical originals is in respect of the voice of the
speaker. In her dedication Sidney writes of her poems being the
'dearest offrings of my hart / dissolv'd to Inke' (p. xxxviii), a striking
image which personalizes the perspective of the translation. As she
puts it in individualized terms in the opening of Psalm 45:

> My harte endites an argument of worth,
> > The praise of him that doth the Scepter swaie:
> My tongue the pen to paynt his praises forth,
> > Shall write as swift as swiftest writer maie.

> (p. 107)

The comparison with other writers – the wish to point out that her
writing is 'as swift' as that of any other (presumably male) writer – is a
personal twist not found in the biblical original. By identifying the
poetic persona of her translation with her own 'hart' and an eagerly individual 'pen', Sidney not only inserts herself into the psalm texts but
shifts their perspective, ultimately dissolving the gendered position of
the original Davidic voice. Significantly, as Margaret Hannay has noted,
Sidney never uses the male personal pronoun for the singer, thus
opening up the Old Testament verse for the seventeenth-century woman
who articulates the psalms in reading, speaking or singing.[17] Despite the
often overtly masculine world depicted by the psalms, Sidney manages
to make her voice join in the 'tryumphant song' of a 'virgin army',
finding a place in the psalms for the experiences of those who 'weake in
howse did ly' (Psalm 68, p. 154). One of the most revealing moments of
self-inscription is to be found in Psalm 104, where she seeks acceptance
for her song despite the presence of 'my self, my seely self' within
the text (p. 244). Her additional interpretive task in Christianizing the
psalms is overtly declared in Psalm 132, where Sidney meditates on
the (female) city of Sion, the type of the church:

> O how in her shall sprowt and spring
> > The scepter Davids hand did beare!
> How I my Christ, my sacred king,
> > As light in lantern placed there
> > > With beames devine,
> > > Will make abroad to shine!

> (p. 309)

The fertile city, and the church which it anticipates, are the means by which the gospel of Christ will be spread. The parallel between these feminized vessels (the city, the lantern) and the proclaiming female voice of the psalm translator is unmistakable.

Like Mary Sidney, Aemilia Lanyer took the scriptures as the immediate starting point for her religious poetry. This similarity between the two women poets in their overt dependence on large tracts of the Bible is perhaps not coincidental, since the closer their work was to an identifiably biblical source, the more easily women writers could justify their disobedience to another biblical text which insists that women should not be allowed to 'teach, nor to usurp authority over the man, but to be in silence'.[18] If 'silence' could be interpreted as uniting their voices with God's through the scriptures, then women might be able to get away with the temporary assumption of the authority of the pen.[19] Biblical influence can, however, be highly selective, and in Lanyer's case it leads to a firmly feminine perspective for the speaker in *Salve Deus Rex Judaeorum*. As the 1611 title-page announces, Lanyer's narrative recounts the events of the first Good Friday with an accompanying cast of biblical women: the poem's four sections are 'The Passion of Christ', 'Eves Apologie in defence of Women', 'The Teares of the Daughters of Jerusalem' and 'The Salutation and Sorrow of the Virgine Marie'.[20] Amidst this strongly feminine entourage, Lanyer also represents her own self throughout the poem unequivocally as a daughter of Eve, voicing the often unheard defence of 'us Women' (p. 84) who have been wrongly denied 'our Libertie' (p. 87). Lanyer gives a similarly representative function to Pilate's wife, asserting that she spoke on behalf of all women in refusing to give consent to Christ's crucifixion (p. 87). The individual woman poet and the biblical women whose roles she highlights become identified with their gender as a whole, just as Lanyer's female reader is addressed as part of the group of 'all vertuous Ladies in generall' (p. 2). It is not only the female speaker – the poet and her soul – who will be the bride of Christ, but the readers, too:

> Put on your wedding garments every one,
> The Bridegroome stayes to entertaine you all.

> (p. 12)

In this thoroughly female company – the wise virgins keeping their lamps burning in preparation for the marriage feast, the poet addressing them, the feminized 'Virtue' guiding them – the reader progresses through Lanyer's *Salve Deus* and its praise of Christ the Bridegroom.[21]

Sidney and Lanyer, then, intensify their womanly identity in their self-representation before God. What happens when the poet who must identify with the bride of Christ is, in fact, male? In the case of Donne, the metaphors of spiritual marriage employed in his poetry have achieved a certain notoriety which can create a misleading impression of the poet's self-representation in the religious context. In his Holy Sonnet 'Batter my heart', Donne evokes the metaphor of the bride of Christ only in order to show his perversity as one who is, instead, 'betrothed unto your enemy'; he famously concludes that he will never be 'chaste' unless ravished by God (pp. 177–8). This is by no means a straightforward adoption of the biblical trope, since the sinful speaker is a decidedly unwise virgin who has to be rescued from a mistaken partnership and then violently purified. The metaphor is one of a series which express the speaker's vulnerability – metal being melted and battered into shape, the 'usurped town' in war, a prisoner, a slave. The context is startlingly different from that of the devotion and willing sensuality found in the Song of Songs. Donne's deliberate use of paradox is also found in Holy Sonnet 18, 'Show me dear Christ', in which the spousal image of the church is again deliberately cast in a framework of adultery and prostitution:

> Betray kind husband thy spouse to our sights,
> And let mine amorous soul court thy mild dove,
> Who is most true, and pleasing to thee, then
> When she is embraced and open to most men.

> (p. 88)

The bride of Christ here recalls the paradoxically chaste yet ravished soul of 'Batter my heart'. The speaker's perspective in 'Show me dear Christ', however, is that of a suitor of the true church; his 'amorous soul', in the poem's metaphoric scheme, is a male rival to Christ, and not Christ's own partner. While using the marriage trope, Donne maintains a male poetic voice and stance.

The feminized perspective of the speaker in 'Batter my heart' is the exception and not the norm for Donne's religious poetry. As he writes in Holy Sonnet 1, 'As due by many titles',

> I am thy son, made with thyself to shine,
> Thy servant, whose pains thou hast still repaid,
> Thy sheep, thine image, and, till I betrayed
> Myself, a temple of thy Spirit divine.

> (p. 174)

These alternative biblical versions of the relationship of the human to the divine – son, servant, sheep, image, temple – are at least as popular with Donne as the marriage metaphor. And when Donne adopts the convention of identifying his soul as female, he often speaks of the soul in the third person, as feminine but other than his bodily and speaking self. In his poem 'Upon the Annunciation and Passion falling upon one day. 1608', for example, Donne takes witty delight in the clash of two days in the church calendar which commemorate such opposite events – Christ's conception and death – and explores the paradoxes with the repeated use of 'she' for his observing soul (p. 155). In the much later 'Hymn to God my God, in my Sickness', he adopts a similar distance and distinction from his soul, this time in order to preach to her.[22] The parallel with the secular Donne's willingness to give his female lover a 'lecture' on 'love's philosophy' is very striking.[23]

It would seem logical that, since both Donne and Herbert were ordained into the exclusively male priesthood of the Church of England, they should represent their speaking selves in an ecclesiastical context as male. This is clearly true of Donne's imaginary sermon to the congregation of his soul, but the situation is far more complex in his poem 'To Mr Tilman after he had taken orders', where he likens priests not to Christ, the great 'high priest' of Hebrews 8.1, but to Christ's mother (p. 287). As vessels to carry the Word, preachers have an affinity with the Virgin Mary and are feminized. By the end of the poem, Donne has wittily combined the maleness of priesthood with the female capacity to bear offspring:

> the heavens which beget all things here,
> And the earth our mother, which these things doth bear,
> Both these in thee, are in thy calling knit,
> And make thee now a blessed hermaphrodite.

> (p. 288)

It is clearly a mistake to assume that there is no place for gender in spiritual experience or in devotional wit, but its possibilities are extremely flexible in Donne's religious imagination. The self in the poems can certainly adopt the role of a woman, but is more frequently divided between a male body and a receptive female soul. Though the preaching voice – often to be heard in both the secular and the sacred poems of Donne – is consciously male, the priestly function as conveyor of Christ can be seen as female, or is merged, as in the case of Mr Tilman, into a 'blessed hermaphrodite'.

Herbert's self-representation in his devotional lyrics, though intensely witty, plays less openly with gender and sexuality. His sense of himself in relation to God follows familiar biblical tracks: he is the loving servant at God's court but is, even at his lowest moments, conscious of having been called to be a child of God.[24] Most commonly, he depicts himself through metaphor, as a passive musical instrument, for instance, on which God plays – or which, as in 'Deniall', lies 'out of sight, / Untun'd, unstrung' in God's apparent absence (p. 96). Herbert grants his speaker a more active role in the devotional process when he places the emphasis on his vocation as a poet, and then the gendered echoes from secular love poetry (and music) come into play, as in 'Dulnesse':

> The wanton lover in a curious strain
> > Can praise his fairest fair;
> And with quaint metaphors her curled hair
> > Curl o're again.
> ...
> Where are my lines then? my approaches? views?
> > Where are my window-songs?
> Lovers are still pretending, & ev'n wrongs
> > Sharpen their Muse.
>
> > > > (p. 128)

The devotional poet is working within a highly gendered tradition in which poetic creativity is a male skill. This masculine poetic perspective is strengthened in 'The Forerunners', in which it is not God whom the poet is wooing, but fallen language itself – or herself, since the gendered opposition here is between the male poet-priest baptizing (with his tears of repentance) a female discourse which was formerly prostituted to worldly love:

> Farewell sweet phrases, lovely metaphors.
> But will ye leave me thus? when ye before
> Of stews and brothels onely knew the doores,
> Then did I wash you with my tears, and more,
> > > Brought you to Church well drest and clad.
>
> > > > (p. 181)

The evocation of language as the rescued fallen woman – reminiscent of Mary Magdalen in her relationship to Christ – suggests a devotional realm of masculine friendship in which the poet offers his 'best', feminized, gift to God. In the subsequent stanzas the 'lovely enchanting language' threatens to leave the church again, enticed by 'some fond lover', intensifying the rivalry of secular and sacred poets for the control of language. The religious poet here is certainly not the bride of Christ; he is, if not the bridegroom himself, the father and priestly counsellor who attempts to bring the bride to church.

Herbert's lyric on 'The British Church' addresses that undoubtedly gendered establishment as 'deare Mother' (p. 122), implying that the marriage of Christ and his church has produced the speaker as offspring. Once again, Herbert's devotional position is that of the child, which he clearly considered a more appropriate role than that of a feminized soul. In 'H. Baptisme' (II), Herbert asserts that 'Childhood is health', (p. 65), whereas in 'Home' he brags to himself (and to his Lord) of his indifference to the world in damningly gendered terms:

> What is this weary world; this meat and drink,
>   That chains us by the teeth so fast?
> What is this woman-kinde, which I can wink
>   Into a blacknesse and distaste?

> (p. 121)

Once more, the poet's spiritual world is an all-male affair, and the 'weary world' of sin which enslaves others is embodied in the distasteful 'woman-kinde'. This is a very different spiritual environment from that created by the outspoken daughter of Eve, Aemilia Lanyer.

Gender plays a significant role in the devotional poet's self-representation, largely determined by the actual sex of the poet, though capable of subtle variations. There is perhaps greater freedom in the use of biblical stereotypes than we might have expected, if we recall Sidney's de-masculinized psalmist's voice, or Donne's male soul wooing Christ's spouse, the church. As religious poets, the authors cast themselves in roles which make dramatic use of gender for solidarity as well as difference, as in Lanyer's identification with the prophetic wife of Pilate, or Herbert's Christ-like role in saving the fallen woman, language. Those 'whom the Lord with love affecteth' were not only picked out or favoured by God's attentions; Sidney's phrase also suggests that they were 'affected' in the more modern sense – changed or altered – by his love. The language and traditions of gender, also, could not remain unaffected by this experience.

IV

In the complex interaction of gender, love and religion, the most intriguing element is that of an ostensibly male God. To what extent can an explicitly patriarchal Godhead be subject to shifting gender perspectives? Once again, the extent to which Mary Sidney introduced flexibility into the given psalm text is surprising. In her detailed rendering in Psalm 139 of the miraculous 'hidden workings' of creation, (p. 321) she expands the original biblical reference to a human body 'fashioned' by God 'beneath in the earth' (v.14) to an intimate account of the embryo in the womb:

> Each inmost peece in me is thine:
> While yet I in my mother dwelt,
> > All that me cladd
> > From thee I hadd.
> Thou in my frame hast strangly delt:
> Needes in my praise thy workes must shine
> So inly them in my thoughts have felt.
>
> Thou, how my back was beam-wise laid,
> And raftring of my ribbs, dost know:
> > Know'st ev'ry point
> > Of bone and joynt,
> How to this whole these partes did grow,
> In brave embrod'ry faire araid,
> Though wrought in shopp both dark and low.

> (p. 320)

The biblical source suggests a link with the creation of Adam from the dust of the earth as recounted in Genesis, but Sidney's verse shakes off those associations and specifically feminizes God's creativity by transferring the focus of the account to the workshop of the womb. This is not only further evidence of the incorporation of Sidney's own female perspective into the Psalm text – she knows all this creativity from the 'thoughts' of her formation as a child of God, and in her own capacity as a mother – but the passage also indicates how, as a consequence of this feminine angle of poetic vision, the God whom she depicts is newly gendered, too. The work of this divine parent is associated with the maternal knowledge of the growing foetus developing into a whole within the womb, 'inly' felt and depicted; the skill of God's design is likened to the traditionally feminine art of 'brave embrod'ry faire araid'.

There is thus a tendency for devotional poets to make God in their own image, an observation which should not be surprising since the aim of spiritual discipline and expression is to enable the Christian to become more like Christ, and in the process it is perhaps natural that the object of devotion is increasingly constructed in the image of the devotee. We have only to think of the frequent references made by the poets to God as the author and creator of texts – as Sidney writes in Psalm 139, God shaped her in 'the booke / Of thy foresight' (p. 321) – to be reminded of the function of devotion as a 'thankfull glasse' in which soul and saviour can together be mirrored.[25] Herbert's verse in particular is full of mutual reflections of the poet and his God. He locates Christ, for example, among the poor in 'Unkindness' and 'Redemption', and at the end of 'Lent' the speaker finds himself 'banquetting the poore, / And among those his soul' (p. 102). The poor, a 'blessed' group uniting the speaker and his lord, is a genderless category, but Herbert's frequent references to Christ as his 'friend' suggest a male bonding between speaker and God which we have already seen present in 'The Forerunners' and 'Home'.[26]

All four poets betray a longing to experience the physical company of their God, in a (necessarily gendered) body. Herbert, for example, opens his poem 'Decay' with a nostalgic reference to the good old days when God was ordinarily present among his faithful:

> Sweet were the dayes, when thou didst lodge with Lot,
> Struggle with Jacob, sit with Gideon,
> Advise with Abraham ...
> One might have sought and found thee presently
> At some fair oak, or bush, or cave, or well.

> (pp. 113–14)

The everyday immediacy of this recreation of God's tangible presence is paralleled in the imagined spiritual encounters with Christ and other biblical figures described by Aemilia Lanyer. In her wistful poem 'The Description of Cooke-ham' appended to *Salve Deus Rex Judaeorum*, Lanyer addresses the Countess of Cumberland with memories of their experiences at the country estate:

> In these sweet woods how often did you walke,
> With Christ and his Apostles there to talke;
> Placing his holy Writ in some faire tree,
> To meditate what you therein did see:
> With *Moyses* you did mount his holy Hill,
> To know his pleasure, and performe his Will.
> With lovely *David* you did often sing,
> His holy Hymnes to Heavens Eternall King.
>
> (p. 133)

The recollection of spiritual proximity is depicted in physical terms – 'walke', 'talke', 'see', 'mount', 'performe' – and is set topographically in a biblical landscape which is translated into the pastoral of rural England. There is a strong sense of the maleness of the biblical characters, intensified by the fact that Christ, his Apostles, Moses and David are the only men to appear in 'Cooke-ham'. These biblical males are the 'other' – spiritual as opposed to earthly, male as opposed to female – with whom the poet and her countess contentedly interact in a specifically localized environment, not far removed from Herbert's 'fair oak, or bush, or cave, or well'. But in Lanyer's lines, the need for an imagined physical presence expressing God's 'Will' and 'pleasure' is cast in terms of gender difference, a feature which is all the more noticeable in the absence of earthly males from the poem.

In the main body of her poem *Salve Deus Rex Judaeorum*, Lanyer first introduces Christ through a conscious reference to his gendered distinction from herself and her patron, the Countess of Cumberland. After an extensive preamble addressed to the Countess, Lanyer turns to the subject of her narrative, the Passion of Christ, and intriguingly approaches Christ by means of the 'Heavenly grace' (p. 61) to be seen in her female patron:

> This Grace great Lady, doth possesse thy Soule,
> And makes thee pleasing in thy Makers sight;
> This Grace doth all imperfect Thoughts controule,
> Directing thee to serve thy God aright;
> Still reckoning him, the Husband of thy Soule,
> Which is most pretious in his glorious sight:
>> Because the Worlds delights shee doth denie
>> For him, who for her sake vouchsaf'd to die.
>
> (p. 62)

Although the basis for this poetic manoeuvre from earthly patron to heavenly lord is the trope of the marriage of Christ and the soul, the impact is considerably changed by the reversed perspective. In place of the conventional stress on the humility and timidity of the blushing bride, the passage depicts a soul which is already 'pleasing' and 'pretious' and which, though possessed by grace in the theological sense, also conveys an impression of confident female gracefulness.[27] From this angle, seeing the soul (which is both metaphorically female and in a real female body) before we meet her 'Husband', the patriarchal priority of male to female, bridegroom to bride, is – temporarily – destabilized.

When Lanyer's 'lowely Muse' (p. 62) eventually comes to focus on Christ, she is all too conscious of the dangerous eagerness of her 'forward Mind', which Icarus-like seeks to 'flie, / Above the pitch of thy appointed straine' (p. 63). The solution to this classic devotional poet's crisis is, of course, to seek heavenly aid (p. 65). Although all devotional poets seek divine inspiration in some form or another, it seems to me that this invocation introduces a new element in the depiction of the 'pure unspotted Lambe'. For a female poet who reminds the reader on almost every page that the poem is the product of her 'womans wit' (p. 11), the partnership with a divine muse is another meeting of gendered opposites, and a precise reversal of the conventional relationship of the male poet inspired by a female muse. Lanyer's muse is not the Holy Spirit, the least masculine member of the Trinity and traditionally associated with the ghostly breath of inspiration; in her lines it is the incarnate Christ who will guide her 'Hand and Quill'.[28] Once again, the introduction of a self-consciously feminine aesthetic into the devotional equation has altered the balance of a metaphorically heterosexual partnership, that of writer and muse. When the woman is the writer, the parallel with the marriage trope is unsettled; the 'bride' – church, soul, woman – has become the scribe, too.

What are the consequences of the principle of gendered opposition for the depiction of God by male poets? We have already seen that a stress on difference can lead to a feminizing of the male poet's soul, as in the work of Donne, though in several instances this leads to a three-way relationship between patriarchal God, male speaker and third-person female soul. In Herbert's transformation of secular love literature, the lover-poet takes on an overtly male role, wooing

God with his verse. The impact that this has on the gendering of the divine is to feminize God as the 'bitter-sweet' beloved of the 'complaining' poet.[29] The concluding lyric of *The Temple*, 'Love (III)', evokes a God in the general spiritual tradition of the forgiving father welcoming home his prodigal son, but this compassionate principle is specifically personified as a gentle female lover:

> Love bade me welcome: yet my soul drew back,
> > Guiltie of dust and sinne.
> But quick-ey'd Love, observing me grow slack
> > From my first entrance in,
> Drew nearer to me, sweetly questioning
> > If I lack'd any thing.

> (p. 192)

Though the soul, as we have observed, is feminized in biblical tradition, Herbert's text endows the soul instead with the physical attributes of an uncertain and impotent male.[30] As a consequence, the depiction of the divine figure of Love assumes conventionally female characteristics: 'sweet', 'quick-ey'd', awaiting the 'entrance' of the male. This welcoming God takes more initiatives than would have been expected of a modest woman – thus suggesting the daring overtones of prostitution also found in Donne's 'true' church in Holy Sonnet 18, which is best when 'embrac'd and open to most men'. To the very end of Herbert's lyric, even though the personified 'Love' is clearly the crucified and risen Lord, the metaphors of feminine physicality and domestic provision prevail:

> You must sit down, sayes Love, and taste my meat:
> > So I did sit and eat.

> (p. 192)

The last lyric of Herbert's sequence is not the only moment when an evident shifting of gender may be observed in the depiction of the divine by these four poets. We have already witnessed the convergence of speaker and creator in Mary Sidney's translation of Psalm 139, among others, and there is a notable instance in Donne's Holy Sonnet 9, 'What if this present', where the sight of the crucified Christ is compared as a sign of 'pity' with the female beauty of the speaker's former 'profane mistresses':

> but as in my idolatry
> I said to all my profane mistresses,
> Beauty, of pity, foulness only is
> A sign of rigour: so I say to thee,
> To wicked spirits are horrid shapes assigned,
> This beauteous form assures a piteous mind.

(p. 177)

In this play of gendered opposites the male speaker once again preaches to his female soul, and openly draws the parallel between the explanation he gave in the past to his (plural) 'mistresses' and the reassurance he is now offering his timid soul. The effect of this conversational dynamic on the depiction of Christ is to render him doubly feminine. First, his 'beauteous form' is under discussion in the same way as the beauty of the mistresses had been in the past, to be interpreted by the male observer as a hopeful sign of 'pity'. Second, the setting in which the 'picture' of Christ is to be carefully scrutinized is within the speaker's heart, which is exactly the place where the image of the female beloved was supposed to reside in the secular (Petrarchan) love tradition.[31] The image of Christ is thus part of a passive femininity as constructed by the poem: the picture, as of a mistress, is housed within the male lover-speaker, and reassuringly interpreted by him for the benefit of a female audience.

Donne's reworking of the Petrarchan mistress into the role of Christ recalls a similar framing of the image of the redeemer in Lanyer's *Salve Deus*. Having completed her poetic 'Storie; that whole Worlds with Bookes would fill' (p. 65), she turns to address the Countess of Cumberland, whose soul she had described as partnered by Christ in the preamble to the poem. At its conclusion she writes:

> Ah! give me leave (good Lady) now to leave
> This taske of Beauty which I tooke in hand,
> I cannot wade so deepe, I may deceave
> My selfe, before I can attaine the land;
> Therefore (good Madame) in your heart I leave
> His perfect picture, where it still shall stand,
> > Deepely engraved in that holy shrine,
> > Environed with Love and Thoughts divine.

(p. 108)

In the sometimes tense encounter of poet and patron – in this case, both female – the portrait of the male redeemer, inscribed in the poet's verse but also metaphorically 'engraved' in the patron's heart, is offered as a memento and token of goodwill. This situation is a re-gendered and differently slanted variant of the scene in Herbert's 'The Forerunners' in which the male poet offered a reformed female, language, as his best gift to his male saviour. The interaction of language and status, gender and spiritual honour, human and divine, is fundamental to the functioning of devotional poetry and occurs in a fascinating range of relationships.

The seeds of the complexity of gender and spiritual love are sown in the Bible, and particularly in the Song of Songs, where the sensuous beauty of both bride and bridegroom is equally richly suggested, and the charm of the male contains features which later came to be associated with female beauty. In the description of the risen Christ which immediately precedes Lanyer's presentation of his 'perfect picture' to the Countess, the saviour is shown as the bridegroom cared for by 'his faithfull Wife / The holy Church' (p. 106) and

> So sweet, so lovely in his Spouses sight,
> That unto Snowe we may his face compare,
> His cheeks like skarlet, and his eyes so bright
> As purest Doves that in the rivers are,
> Washed with milke, to give the more delight;
>> His head is likened to the finest gold
>> His curled lockes so beauteous to behold.

> (p. 107)

As Lanyer notes in the margin, this description is 'upon the Canticles', that is, based on the Song of Songs. We see in it some elements of the apparently feminine 'Love' in Herbert's 'Love' (III), such as sweetness and bright eyes, which are indeed features of the bridegroom's attractiveness in the biblical original. However, what is curious about Lanyer's account of Christ's perfection is that she also includes elements of beauty which in the Song of Songs are reserved for the bride, such as the lips 'like skarlet threeds'.[32] Herbert also echoes the combination of snow-white purity and blood-red passion idealized in the Song of Songs when he describes Christ in 'Dulnesse' as

> my lovelinesse, my life, my light,
> Beautie alone to me:
> Thy bloudy death and undeserv'd, makes thee
> Pure red and white.

(p. 128)

The witty turn on the idea of innocent whiteness stained by the blood shed in the crucifixion makes the beauty a theological as well as physical epitome, but the impact is just as uncertain in terms of gender as in Lanyer's blurring of boundaries. In the surrounding stanzas, Herbert likens himself to the secular poet who 'in a curious strain / Can praise his fairest fair', and the object of his adoration is clearly identified as female. Is Herbert implying not only a parallel but also a shift of direction, away from the idealized woman to the ideal lord who is beyond gender distinctions? Whether gender is to be noted or transcended, it plays a major and often perpexing role in the construction of the divine image.

V

A comparative reading of Sidney, Donne, Lanyer and Herbert not only opens up new perspectives in our understanding of the role of gender in religious verse. It should also help us to develop a more accurate sense of the interdependence of these writers, and to modify the conventional canonical ordering of devotional writing from this period. The poets do not simply share a crucial common source text, the Bible; three of the four were also significantly influenced by the first. The translation of the Psalms, begun by Sir Philip Sidney but substantially the work of his sister Mary, was fulsomely praised by Donne; addressing God, he explains

> That, as thy blessed spirit fell upon
> These Psalms' first author in a cloven tongue;
> (For 'twas a double power by which he sung
> The highest matter in the noblest form;)
> So thou hast cleft that spirit, to perform
> That work again, and shed it, here, upon
> Two, by their bloods, and by thy spirit one;
> A brother and a sister, made by thee
> The organ, where thou art the harmony.

(pp. 303–4)

In the elaborate conceit of a positive 'cloven tongue', Donne honours the double nobility of form and matter in the biblical text of the psalms, but also praises the poetic duo of Philip and Mary, 'this Moses and this Miriam', in 'their sweet learned labours' together (pp. 304, 305). Here, indeed, is an image of the 'double voice' with which this collection of essays is concerned. The 'cloven tongue' represented by the work of Mary Sidney and her brother, and, further, to be seen in the gendering of the ensuing tradition of devotional poetry in the early seventeenth century, has been seriously underestimated in critical histories of the period and the genre. In place of the all-male 'school of Donne' which has shaped official accounts until now, we need to recognize the significance of the Sidneian influence which preceded it – not forgetting that Mary Sidney was responsible for over two-thirds of their translation. And by tracing the role of Mary Sidney in parti- cular as a model for other women writers of devotional verse, we may begin to understand the 'cloven' tongues in the tradition of religious poetry. For Donne was not alone in his view of the importance of the Sidney psalm translation. The longest of the dedicatory poems preced- ing Lanyer's narrative of the Passion in *Salve Deus Rex Judaeorum* is 'The Authors Dreame to the Ladie *Marie*, the Countesse Dowager of *Pembrooke*'. Mary Sidney is acclaimed as the singer of 'holy Sonnets' which are the 'rare sweet songs' of David 'written newly by the Countesse' (p. 27); her Psalm translation is the only poetic precedent, apart from the Bible itself, named by Lanyer in her book. And although there is no surviving poem by Herbert to complete a trio in praise of the Sidney psalms, there is, in his case, no need for one, since it is clear from his family connection with the Sidneys that he would have known the translation in manuscript, and the evidence of his poetic style speaks louder than any eulogy. The inventive lyric forms and expressive devotional voice of the Sidney Psalms are undoubtedly the most important forerunner of *The Temple*.[33]

Thus we may suggest, with considerable justification, that the group of poets whose work has been the subject of this essay should be referred to as the school of Sidney, or perhaps, even, the tribe of Mary. These phrases, parodies of the more familiar labels for early seventeenth-century English poetry, may jolt us into a re-vision of the literary landscape of the period. Critical history has hitherto tended to be blind to the interactions of the work of familiar male authors with the texts by their female contemporaries whose work has recently, and belatedly, come under scrutiny. This essay has attempted to challenge the assumptions which guide and circumscribe our reading, both by offering these new perceptions of the sequence of influence and authority and, in the main body of the discussion, opening up fundamental questions concerning the role of gender in religious poetry. The effort of listening to the 'double voice' will, I trust, change not only what we read but, perhaps more fundamentally, how we do so.

Notes

1. *The Psalms of Sir Philip Sidney and the Countess of Pembroke*, ed. J.C.A. Rathmell (New York: Anchor Books, 1963), Psalm 149, p. 340. All subsequent references will be to this edition, which prints the first 43 psalms (originally translated by Sir Philip Sidney) in the revised form completed by his sister, followed by Mary's own rendering of Psalms 44–150.
2. See G.F. Waller, 'The Text and Manuscript Variants of the Countess of Pembroke's Psalms', *RES* 26 (1975), pp. 1–18; and Arthur F. Marotti, *John Donne, Coterie Poet* (Madison: University of Wisconsin Press, 1986). For a fuller account of the manuscript culture of the late sixteenth and early seventeenth centuries, see Arthur F. Marotti, *Manuscript, Print, and the English Renaissance Lyric* (Ithaca, NY: Cornell University Press, 1995).
3. For what is known of the biography of Lanyer, see the introduction to Susanne Woods' edition of *The Poems of Aemilia Lanyer: Salve Deus Rex Judaeorum* (Oxford: Oxford University Press, 1993), pp. xv–xxx. All references to Lanyer's text are to this edition.
4. For the publication history of the Sidney Psalms, see Sidney, op.cit., pp. xxix–xxx.
5. See, for example, Herbert's 'Colossians 3.3' and Donne's Holy Sonnets 'At the round earth's imagined corners' and 'Spit in my face you Jews'.
6. *The English Poems of George Herbert*, ed. C.A. Patrides (London: Dent, 1974), pp. 116–17. All subsequent references are to this edition.
7. Psalm 33.12; Galatians 4.7.
8. See Song of Songs, especially 4.8–5.1; Isaiah 61.10 and 62.5; Ephesians 5.25–32; Revelation 19.7. For a fuller discussion of the Song of Songs, see Elizabeth Clarke's essay later in this volume, pp. 216–17.
9. The change in the canon has been brought about by pioneering anthologies such as *The Paradise of Women: Writings by Englishwomen of the Renaissance*, ed. Betty Travitsky (Westport, Conn.: Greenwood Press, 1980, rpt. 1989), *Her Own Life: Autobiographical Writings by Seventeenth-Century Englishwomen* ed. Elspeth Graham et al. (London: Routledge, 1989), and *Kissing the Rod: an Anthology of Seventeenth-Century Women's Verse*, ed. Germaine Greer et al. (London: Virago, 1988). An anthology of English seventeenth-century women's devotional verse is currently in preparation by Elizabeth Clarke and Helen Wilcox, and the work of individual women poets is being brought out, as in Susanne Woods' edition of Lanyer (op. cit.) and Sidney Gottlieb's recent edition of An Collins' *Divine Songs and Meditacions* (Tempe, Arizona: Medieval and Renaissance Texts and Studies, 1996). The critical discussion of the expanding canon of religious

texts was initiated by *Silent but for the Word: Tudor Women as Patrons, Translators of Religious Works*, ed. Margaret Patterson Hannay (Kent, Ohio: Kent State University Press, 1985).

10. Exodus 22.29; Deuteronomy 26.10. In the New Testament (1 Corinthians 15.20; James 1.18) the 'first fruits' become a metaphor for the self-offering of Christ and his followers.

11. Mark 9.35.

12. *The Oxford Authors: John Donne*, ed. John Carey (Oxford: Oxford University Press, 1990), p. 303. All further references are to this edition.

13. See, for example, Herbert, 'The Holdfast' and Donne, Holy Sonnet 1.

14. Mary Sidney, 'To the Angell spirit', p. xxxviii.

15. 'The Flower', p. 172. As Herbert noted in the sonnet reprinted in Walton's *Life of Mr. George Herbert*, divine 'beautie lies in the discoverie', Herbert, op. cit., p. 206.

16. As John Florio notoriously commented, translation is always second best, never the perfect original but 'defective' and therefore 'reputed femalls' (Florio's translation of Montaigne's *Essayes*, London 1603, A2r). See Suzanne Trill, 'Sixteenth-century Women's Writing: Mary Sidney's *Psalmes* and the 'femininity' of translation', in *Writing and the English Renaissance*, ed. William Zunder and Suzanne Trill (London: Longamn, 1996), pp. 140–58. See also Tina Krontiris, *Oppositional Voices: Women as Writers and Translators of Literature in the English Renaissance* (London: Routledge, 1992), and the introduction to *Silent but for the Word*. Sidney, op. cit., p. xi.

17. Margaret P. Hannay, '"House-confinéd Maids": The Presentation of Woman's Role in the *Psalmes* of the Countess of Pembroke', *ELR* 24.1 (1994), pp. 44–71.

18. I Timothy 2.12.

19. Lady Mary Wroth, Sidney's niece, was severely criticized by Lord Denny for *not* limiting her writing to a scriptural basis; see *The Poems of Lady Wary Wroth*, ed. Josephine A. Roberts (Baton Rouge: Louisiana State University Press, 1983), pp. 237–41. For a discussion of literary women in the English Renaissance religious context, see Suzanne Trill, 'Religion and the Construction of Femininity', in *Women and Literature in Britain, 1500–1700*, ed. Helen Wilcox (Cambridge: Cambridge University Press, 1996), pp. 30–55. For an account of seventeenth-century radical women and their relation to Scripture, see also Hilary Hinds, *God's Englishwomen: Seventeenth-century Radical Sectarian Writing and Feminist Criticism* (Manchester: Manchester University Press, 1996).

20. In addition to accounts of Lanyer's work offered by Barbara K. Lewalski, in *Writing Women in Jacobean England* (Cambridge, Mass.: Harvard University Press, 1993), and Elaine V. Beilin, in *Redeeming Eve: Women Writers of the English Renaissance* (Princeton, NJ: Princeton University Press, 1987), see also Achsah Guibbory, 'The Gospel According to Aemilia', in *Sacred and Profane: Secular and Devotional Interplay in Early Modern British Literature*, ed. Helen Wilcox *et al.* (Amsterdam: Free University Press, 1996), pp. 105–26.

21. See the parable of the ten virgins, Matthew 25.1–13. This passage presumably also lies behind Sidney's reference to the 'lantern' of her verse. Of the ten virgins, five were foolish, failing to keep their lamps burning (to be alert and ready) for the arrival of the bridegroom.

22. 'And as to others' souls I preached thy word/Be this my text, my sermon to mine own / Therefore that he may raise the Lord throws down' (p. 333).

23. Donne, 'A Lecture upon the Shadow', from the *Songs and Sonnets*.

24. Herbert, 'Man', and 'The Collar'.

25. Herbert, 'The H. Scriptures I'.

26. See Matthew 5.3, and 2 Corinthians 8.9. See 'Jordan' (II), and 'Unkindnesse'.

27. See, for example, Donne's Holy Sonnet 2, in which his soul 'blushes'.

28. Compare Milton's account of the Holy Spirit as muse in *Paradise Lost* I, 17–23, and Herbert's 'Easter', in which the 'blessed spirit' completes his verse.

29. Herbert, 'Bitter-Sweet'.

30. For fuller discussion of this point, see Michael Schoenfeldt, *Prayer and Power: George Herbert and Renaissance Courtship* (Chicago: Chicago University Press, 1991), especially chapter 6; for a comparative reading of gender in Herbert's 'Love' (III) and Eliza's 'The Lover', see Helen Wilcox, 'Where is Feminist Criticism Taking Us in Our Reading of Traditional Religious Literature?', in *Literature and Theology at Century's End*, ed. Gregory Salyer and Robert Detweiler (Atlanta, Ga: Scholars Press, 1995), pp. 249–61.

31. See, for example, Shakespeare's Sonnet 24.

32. Song of Songs 4.3.

33. See, for example, Louis L. Martz, *The Poetry of Meditation* (New Haven, Conn.: Yale University Press, 1962), p. 278.

10

Ejaculation or Virgin Birth? The Gendering of the Religious Lyric in the Interregnum

Elizabeth Clarke

The titles of male-authored lyric collections during the period of the Civil Wars and Interregnum indicate a privileged method of poetic composition: ejaculation. The first of many editions of Christopher Harvey's *The Synagogue: or Sacred Poems and Private Ejaculations* appeared in 1640. Cardell Goodman's 'Sacred Meditations and Private Ejaculations, digested into Verse' was composed in manuscript sometime before 1648. The alternative title to Jeremiah Rich's 1650 volume *Mellificium Musarum* is *An Epitome of Divine Poetrie, Distilled into Pious Ejaculations and Solemne Soliloquies*. Francis Quarles' son John annexed *Divine Ejaculations* to his *Gods Love and Mans Unworthiness* of 1651. Henry Vaughan in the 1650 *Silex Scintillans* made clear the model for his *Sacred Poems and Private Ejaculations* by using the same sub-title as his hero, George Herbert, a connection which he expounded in the Preface to the 1655 edition.[1] The ubiquity of this title is partly accounted for by the popularity and perceived sanctity of Herbert's volume *The Temple: Sacred Poems and Private Ejaculations*, which was reprinted several times in this period. Stanley Stewart christened these poets the 'School of Herbert'.[2] However, several of these collections have nothing in common with Herbert's volume other than the title. For example, John Quarles' 149 *Ejaculations* are composed in strict iambic tetrameter, a metre whose plodding insistence is far from the subtle rhythms and metrical variety of Herbert's collection. The apotheosis of ejaculatory poetry is perhaps Nicholas Billingsley's *A Treasure of Divine Raptures*, promising *Serious Observations, Pious Ejaculations and Select Epigrams* in 1667. These alphabetical Raptures, composed by a self-styled 'chaplain to the illustrious and renowned Lady URANIA' work methodically through from Abba to Axel tree, Babel to Byway and Cabinet to Cynosure. There is no record of a subsequent volume of

Raptures from D to Z despite promises to produce one if there were to be a demand: Billingsley's readers did not apparently share his optimism about their origin.

Titles were clearly perceived to be important in seventeenth-century responses to poetry. A wide readership thought that Herbert and Harvey's ejaculations were of the same ilk: the joint issue of *The Temple* and *The Synagogue* went into 13 editions between 1640 and 1700. Harvey was sometimes quoted by mistake for Herbert, an understandable error in view of the close association of the two volumes.[3] The phenomenon of titular ejaculations is particular to a very specific period within the seventeenth century, and coincides with the relaxation, in the Interregnum, of strict legal and social restrictions on publication, allowing women poets to appear in print. Helen Wilcox has noted that these women – An Collins, 'Eliza', Elizabeth Major and Margaret Cavendish, for example – see their literary production in terms of 'offspring'. Is it a coincidence, she asks, that male poets of the same period often describe their work in terms of 'ejaculation'?[4] If the sexual sense of 'ejaculation' circulates in the Civil War period, it is tempting to assume a simple answer to Wilcox's question: women don't write *Ejaculations* because they don't ejaculate. However, this is to assume an exclusively gendered referent for both terms.

Thomas Laqueur's aggressively constructionist account of sexuality, *Making Sex*, insists that in the seventeenth century ejaculation was not exclusively a masculine phenomenon. According to classical theories of conception women did ejaculate physically, a medical detail necessarily implied in the 'one-sex' model offered by both Aristotle and Galen, whereby a woman is simply an inferior version of a man. The one-sex theory, however, is not as hegemonic as Laqueur claims. One of the first and most controversial English anatomies of the seventeenth century, Helkiah Crooke's *Microcosmographia* of 1618, disputes the Aristotelian model, using Laurentius to argue for real sexual differentiation in the bodies of men and women.[5] Jonathan Sawday locates the cause of controversy over this volume in the assertion of sexual difference.[6] It is tempting to posit women's rejection of the title *Ejaculations* as a rejection of the one-sex model, and therefore as an assertion of their own sense of sexual difference, but there is a lack of evidence about seventeenth-century women's sexual experience, as even Laqueur admits.

However, there was a heated controversy on the Milton-List in the spring of 1996 over the question of whether Herbert's *Ejaculations* have any sexual referent at all. The apparent precedence of the sexual definition of the term in the OED was cited as evidence on one side of the argument: the first quoted use of 'ejaculate' in this context, in 1578, pre-dates by nearly 50 years the first citation of its spiritual use in 1624. In fact, a wider sample reveals that the priority of the sexual meaning of the term is by no means certain in 1633. Widely reprinted classical discourses about the emission of semen offer no specialist vocabulary different from that used to describe the emission of urine.[7] This is true for the two great medical authorities of the early modern period, Aristotle and Galen. The specific term 'ejaculation' became familiar only during the seventeenth century, and then only in English. John Banister was the first anatomist to use the term 'ejaculate' in his *The Historie of Man, sucked from the sappe of the most approved Anathomistes, in this present age* (London, 1578). In this particular case his 'approved Anathomiste' is Renaldus Columbus, for the passage in which Banister uses the word 'ejaculate' is a straight translation of *De Re Anatomica Libri XV*, where Columbus employs an unusual verb for the emission of semen ('emittere', also used for urine, was the norm):

> neque enim lotii unius emittendi, sed seminis quoque in uterum sobolis gratia eiaculandi natura penem effinxit.

> For it was not onely done for the emission of Urine, but to eiaculate seede in to the matrix.[8]

Thereafter, the OED suggests that the verb 'ejaculate' became available as another term for the emission of all kinds of bodily fluids. The noun, 'ejaculation', by contrast, seems to have been used more specifically in the seventeenth century for male orgasm: Philemon Holland used it in his 1603 translation of Plutarch's *Moralia*. It may be that the word was in common use at this time, as Holland does not list it among the glossary of 'certeine obscure words' at the end of his translation. At any rate, it seems that the term was coined before 1603, and it sounds as if it is a translation from the Latin 'ejaculatio'. The OED suggests that the English word is an invented Latinism, as 'ejaculatio' does not exist at this date. In fact, 'ejaculationem' does appear in the 1594 Latin edition of Ambroise Paré's *Opera Chirurgica*, despite the lack of an equivalent in the original French. Not surprisingly, Thomas Johnson's 1634 English translation from the Latin edition of Paré has the English word 'ejaculation' here: but it is still rather rare.[9]

There are obvious difficulties in locating any conscious appeal for seventeenth-century religious poets of the title *Ejaculations* in sexual terminology of the most explicit kind: and in the decades immediately before and after the publication of *The Temple* it is clear that 'ejaculation' in the spiritual sense is more familiar than its equivalent in medical discourses. In 1633 when *The Temple* appeared with its subtitle *Sacred Poems and Private Ejaculations*, the word was new as a title for any kind of literary work, and was part of an Augustinian discourse associated with Puritan teaching on prayer. Elnathan Parr in his 1618 treatise *Abba Father* had felt the need to define 'the Prayers called Eiaculations': they are not necessarily verbal, but a 'sudden lifting up of the heart to God, from manifold occasions occuring every day'.[10] In 1619 Francis Rous assumed knowledge of this type of prayer when he advised the use of 'short eiaculations' if answer to prayer were delayed, a suggestion he repeated sixteen years later in *The Misticall Marriage*.[11] Thomas Gokins' 'Meditation on the Lord's Prayer' of 1624 suggested that ejaculatory prayer is particularly valued by God: 'he taketh recreation in ... one eiaculation.'[12] All these authors are drawing on Augustine's use of the word *jaculatas*, 'darted', to describe the prayer style of the desert fathers when they had no time to use formal set prayers: very brief, very sudden.[13] As Augustine conceived it, the intensity of mental effort, the expression of love kindled in the heart, is what is important in ejaculatory prayer: too many words can defuse the emotion, and blunt the force of the prayer, which is seen as a weapon. The power of an ejaculation is in the spiritual 'motion' which gives rise to it, as Thomas Gokins makes clear, situating his praise of ejaculatory prayer within a bleak Calvinist view of the total depravity of man:

> But we have nothing good: no, not a motion;
> Nor one poor drop of grace but from thine ocean.
> And all our store is but meere poverty
> Except thine all sufficient grace supply;
> But so supplied, thou takest recreation
> In one good thought, or one ejaculation.

All the Calvinist dichotomies are on display here. Heavenly plenitude is opposed to earthly aporia: in this analysis, the only hope is to eliminate the earthly and the 'carnal', so that the Christian becomes entirely spiritual, heavenly-minded. Just as 'good works' cannot signify within the Calvinist scheme unless they are prompted by God, and carried out through the agency of his Spirit, so the *copia* of human rhetoric has no power: God hears only the ejaculation, inspired by the motion of His own grace. Minimizing verbal utterance, the 'ejaculation' is the distillation of rhetoric into the purest form of words: 'Brief spiritual, sublime *ejaculation*', as the poet Robert Aylett put it in 1654.[14]

It is unlikely that George Herbert himself coined the subtitle for *The Temple*, as he would have been painfully aware of the incongruity of bestowing on a volume of complex verbal artefacts a title with non-verbal connotations. *Ejaculations* do not have to be articulated in words. This is Jane Cavendish dying an exemplary death:

> her Speech Fail'd her: upon the Loss of which she had no other means of Expressing those pious *Ejaculations* she in her last Sickness incessantly poured forth, but by Sighs, and Eyes and Hands lifted up to Heaven.[15]

Herbert himself used the word in the classic Augustinian sense, although he was prepared to bestow the title 'Sighes and Grones' on several stanzas of highly complex rhetoric.[16] The dilemmas of the Christian poet in pursuit of the purity which only silence or spontaneous ejaculation is perceived to bestow, are made explicit in some of Herbert's more famous poems: 'Jordan (i)' & '(ii)', 'A true Hymne', 'Grief', 'The Forerunners'. It seems likely that Nicholas Ferrar of Little Gidding, who oversaw its publication, gave *The Temple* its subtitle. If so, the source Louis Martz postulates for it, François de Sales' term 'jaculatory prayer', may have some basis.[17]

An Introduction to the Devoute Life was one of the books copied and bound at Little Gidding, as Isaac Basire notes in a letter of 1636, and it seems plausible that Herbert's lyrics reminded Ferrar of de Sales' definition of ejaculatory prayer:

> there are certain words, which have a particular force of efficacie to content and satisfie the heart in this behalf: such are the daintie sighes, and passionate complaints, and loving exclamations, that are sowed so thick in the Psalms of David; the often invocations of the sweet & delightfull name of IESUS; the lovely passages which be expressed in the Canticle of Canticles; and spirituall songs also do serve for this ende, when they be song with attention.[18]

The link between 'oraison jaculatoire' and the English 'ejaculation' was well established by 1633. St. François' *Traité de l'amour de Dieu* had been translated by Miles Car, priest of the English College at Douai, in 1630, as *A Treatise of the Love of God*, when the French edition of this work, published in 1616, had already gone into 18 editions. Miles Car frequently employs the noun 'ejaculation', although there is no direct equivalent in French beyond 'oraison jaculatoire'. It is clearly natural to him to use the word wherever there is a sense of short, emotional prayer directed at God.[19] The distribution of Continental devotional treatises in England, which, as Danielle Clarke has pointed out, reached its peak between 1611 and 1615, makes it extremely unlikely that the concept of 'jaculatory prayer' was unknown before the coining of the English term by John Yatesley, François de Sales' translator.[20]

Such a context makes the unproblematic use of the OED entry on 'ejaculation' a nonsense. The increasing number of popular manuals of medicine do not, on the whole, use the term 'ejaculation' for male orgasm.[21] In 1684, *Aristotle's Master-Piece: or, the Secrets of Generation*, written specifically for a female audience, uses the term 'ejaculatory vessels' for what appear to be the fallopian tubes: 'the Deferent, or Ejaculatory Vessels, are two obscure Passages, one on either side, nothing differing from the Spermatick Veins in substance'. This is the terminology of the 1634 edition of Paré, who had used the phrase *vasa ejaculatoria* to describe the vessels in both men and women assumed to have the function of distributing seed.[22] However, the term 'ejection' is used for male orgasm in *Aristotle's Master-Piece*, whilst Albertus Magnus' *Secreta mulierum et virorum*, reprinted frequently until the nineteenth century, uses no form of 'ejaculor' to describe sexual processes.

Given the relative rarity of the medical term, it is probable that outside of élite medical discourses the term 'ejaculation' has spiritual rather than sexual connotations in the mid-seventeenth century. 'W.S.' in his 1656 edition of Bullokar's dictionary, 'Newly Revised, Corrected, and with the addition of above a thousand words enlarged', offers as one of these thousand, 'ejaculation', with a specifically spiritual definition, and no sexual referent. It is in this spiritual sense of 'a short fervent prayer' that the appeal of the common title of the 'ejaculatory' school of poetry can be found. Whilst not using the title for her own poems, Elizabeth, Viscountess Mordaunt expressed the longing for divine utterance to replace human words:

> How dare I aproch thee with words of my owne, Silanc best becomes my vilnes, when I apear befor thy throne, exsept thou inspir me from above.[23]

The appeal of Augustinian ejaculation is that it offers the cessation of sinful human rhetoric, and its replacement with divine utterance. This enables the Christian poet to claim a kind of holy silence, much as George Herbert would ejaculate, mid-sermon, 'Oh my Master, on whose errand I come, let me hold thy peace, and doe thou speak thy selfe' and then continue to preach.[24] The widespread perception of Herbert's poetry as divinely inspired was partly a function of the theological context evoked by the subtitle. An ejaculation is the most likely form of words to be inspired by God as an answer to the prayer for aid from a religious poet: it is the least indebted to human effort, and the most characteristic of the operation of the Holy Spirit in human utterance. However incongruously, all the poets who write *Ejaculations* make explicit their invocation of a divine Muse. To call his poems *Ejaculations* was the ultimate validating strategy of the religious poet who still, in the mid-seventeenth century, felt the need to offer some justification for his poetic activity in the face of Puritan attacks on all rhetorical constructs.

Many of the women beginning to publish their poetry in this period show themselves engaged in a search for just such validating strategies. Most of them are writing religious poetry, the particular referent of 'ejaculations' in the discourse I have described, and most of them share with the male poets I have mentioned an élite royalist culture. Yet the literary 'ejaculations' all-pervasive in manuscript and printed works by men of the mid-century are almost unknown in women's writing. Anna Cromwell, who despite her relationship to the Lord Protector was a keen Royalist (her family changed their name to 'Williams' at the Restoration), includes an ejaculation in her commonplace-book, entitled 'A Booke of Severall devotions collected from good men by the worst of siners'. In fact, the volume also contains several original pieces, some explicitly by women, and some probably by herself: a 'Divine Fancy' (one of Cromwell's heroes was Francis Quarles) and prose 'Ejaculations'.[25] Clearly Anna Cromwell, who is by no means a confident author, is eager to share in an authorized ejaculatory discourse, but this single example highlights an overwhelming absence in mid-century women's writing.

Part of the explanation for this is the radical background of many women writers of this period: ejaculatory terminology belongs to the Reformed heritage of the 1620s and 1630s common to Anglicans and Presbyterians, but rejected by religious radicals, to whom rhetorical ejaculation such as that of the lyric collections, or the set prayers recommended in Jeremy Taylor's *Holy Living* and Richard Allestree's *The Whole Duty of Man*, seemed like a contradiction in terms. Mary Pennington notes that her radical congregation in the 1640s 'scrupled' the use of the Psalms, that holiest of ejaculatory discourses, because they did not have their origin in spontaneous prayer.[26] However, the women writing lyric poetry do not come from a radical context, where such rhetorical exercises are suspect. Anglican women such as Elizabeth Brackley, Countess of Bridgewater, do use the term ejaculation in its classic Augustinian sense. Other women use the discourse of exemplary biography, where 'ejaculation' plays an important role. Ursula Quarles, one of the earliest writers of either sex to use this discourse in 1645, has her husband Francis utter holy ejaculations on his deathbed as proof of his elect status.[27] Alice Thornton describes her mother uttering deathbed ejaculations, as well as composing them for use during the taking of the Sacrament, a practice which had become familiar by the late seventeenth century.[28] 'Ejaculation' as prayer is widely practised by women: it is all the more strange, then, that poetic ejaculation in women's writing is entirely unknown.

The emerging female religious poets of the mid-century, moving onto classic ejaculatory territory, prefer the vocabulary of childbirth for poetic composition, most famously, 'Eliza', in *Eliza's Babes*. An Collins extols the merit of classic Augustinian 'ejacculacions' in her lyrics, but calls her poems her 'offspring'. Elisabeth Major names her volume her 'babe'.[29] As we have seen, it is unlikely that this is an assertion by women writers of their differently gendered bodies. In 1624 Thomas Goad, introducing one of the earliest seventeenth-century women's texts, Elizabeth Joceline's *The Mother's Legacie to her unborne Child*, represented her writing as that child's sibling.[30] From long before that, men had been using the birth topos for literary production: even Bullokar claims paternity for his dictionary 'lest like an unknowne Infant, it should be exposed to over hard usage'.[31] Scholars of the early modern period contest the significance of this topos. Katharine Eisaman Maus identifies the womb image as used by male poets as a site of gender disorientation, arguing that 'the womb is another of those small enclosed spaces in which so many seventeenth century poets discover their poetic identity and freedom'.[32] In this volume Diane Purkiss reminds us of Kristeva's positing of the womb as 'a dark and feminine space which both men and women have to escape and repress in order to become articulate subjects'. Jonathan Sawday disputes Charlotte Otten's claim that that use of female reproductive metaphors by the woman writer 'establishes her female identity' and he is right to assert that the discourse of female reproduction is certainly not 'an area free from male mediation'.[33] However, the repressive Pauline texts quoted by Sawday are ignored by female lyric poets, who use a different and highly creative biblical context for their claims to authorship as motherhood – the biblical poem that is The Song of Songs.

An Collins' volume, *Divine Songs and Meditacions* (London, 1653) begins, as well it might given the novelty of this kind of publishing enterprise for a woman, with a careful account of how she came to compose poetry. She situates herself firmly within the home, restricted by illness, temperament and ultimately God himself. In the Calvinist paradox exploited by so many prison writers in this period such confinement offers an 'inlargedness of mind, and activity of spirit' which expresses itself in poetry. Her first poem, 'The Preface', repeats this account of how she came to compose holy poetry, but situates her writing in a larger narrative of the unfolding revelation of Christ to the Church. It is in this context that she calls her poems 'the offspring of my mind', apologizing for her lyrics as Elisabeth Major and 'Eliza' do: 'they here appear in homly dress' (p. 5). An Collins' poems often begin in a garden, either the garden of England, or the garden of the mind, or simply the natural world. However, these gardens are not sufficiently protected from 'evil mocions', either the 'commocion' which is Civil War, or the violent movement of the storm, or the psychological 'mocions' of fear. In order for her mental conceptions not to prove 'abortive' the scene has to shift to a more inward garden, a spiritual one. It is in this location that she can bear 'mentall fruit'. The horticultural sense of 'fruit' might have overwhelmed the suggestion of human reproduction to produce the strictly vegetable 'firstfruits' which are George Herbert's lyrics, but for the fact that this garden is explicitly the 'enclosed garden' of The Song of Songs, the body of the Bride of Christ. Elisabeth Major also represents herself in this way.[34] A narrative of union with Christ, expressed in the erotic terms of the Song of Songs, follows (p. 30). Sexual interpretation of the biblical text is firmly ruled out along with all other sins subsumed under the heading the Flesh. The conditions of spiritual inspiration are spelt out: spiritual virginity and marriage to Christ. The poem ends with those 'motions' 'darted' from the face of Christ which are to bring 'perfection' and, presumably, authorship. Collins spells out the implications for authorship in a later poem, in which she views her life as a series of rather unsatisfactory seasons: the winter of infancy, the stormy spring of youth:

> Yet as a garden is my mind enclosed fast
> Being to safety so confind from storm and blast
> Apt to produce a fruit most rare,
> That is not common with every woman
> That fruitfull are.

> (pp. 55–6)

The contrast of this spiritual fruitfulness with the natural conception of ordinary women is important, and we shall come back to this later.

If An Collins silently assumes the role of Bride through her identification with the female speaker in The Song of Songs, 'Eliza' is not so hesitant. Her bid for spiritual freedom and authorship is played out on the battlefield of marriage, both human and divine. Whereas many emerging women authors of the seventeenth century stress their submission to their husbands to justify their freedom in authorship, 'Eliza' is quite definite that human marriage is 'mortals thraldom'. For her the biblical figure of the Bride offers a subject position which is authorized by a higher obligation: she is 'onely bound' by her marriage to Christ. So confident is 'Eliza' in this union that she does not need to offer the conventional excuse that her poems are written for the glory of God alone: 'And if any unlike a Christian shall say; I wrote them, for mine own glory. I like a Christian, will tell them; I therefore sent them abroad; for such a strict union is there betwixt my deare God and mee, that his glory is mine, and mine is his'. Of course, although submission to God is her only restriction, it is an absolute one, and she has to come to terms, in her poem 'On marriage', with the fact that her divine husband might insist on an earthly wedding. With the prospect of real children in the air, 'Eliza's' confident rhetoric falters. She turns back with relief to her spiritual Babes, her poems, which offer no such dilemmas. The literal implications of the discourse of divine birth are too difficult to handle: it works as a trope only for aggressively non-sexual activities such as authorship. The very subtitle of *Elizas Babes*, *A Virgins Offering*, dispels any suggestion of physical conception, whilst the first page of *Eliza's Babes* insists on the divine origin of the poems in a kind of parthenogenesis.

To My Sisters

Looke on these Babes as none of mine,
For they were but brought forth by me;
But look on them, as they are Divine,
Proceeding from Divinity.[35]

Pondering in Anne Clifford's funeral sermon the reason why women's lives are often exemplary, Edward Rainbowe concludes that women are often used by Him as instruments, such as when Mary bore Jesus.[36] It is exactly this instrumentality that 'Eliza' is claiming here, as her insistence on her virginity throughout the volume makes clear. As in An Collins' writing, the discursive context of the birth trope is a sacred one, the referent of which is the Annunciation to the Virgin Mary. This literary production is a virgin birth: 'ejaculation' is therefore irrelevant, as is all human sexuality. Phyllis Mack notes that in using birth imagery female prophets drew less attention to female bodies than men: the weakness and imperfection associated with the female body was a symbolic state assumed by men in the prayer for spiritual strength, whereas for women it was a concrete reality, the physical aspects of which were unhelpful to their spiritual project.[37] It is striking that both An Collins and 'Eliza' place their literary offspring in opposition to the products of bodily conception, most obviously in 'Eliza's 'To a Lady that bragg'd of her children'. These women are not 'writing their bodies'. They are engaging in authorship in conscious resistance to the cultural construct of femininity in the seventeenth century.

The politicizing of ejaculatory poetry, and the adoption of Herbert's holiness in vindication of the Royalist cause, is apparent from the political affiliations of the authors who chose the title *Ejaculations* for their deeply conservative writing projects. Herbert's rhetorical ejaculations offered an alternative model of divine inspiration to the extemporary prayer of anti-liturgical Puritans or the disturbing spontaneity of radical 'inspired' discourse in the 1630s and 1640s. Jeremy Taylor in his extremely influential *Rules for Holy Living* of 1650 effectively completed the process, removing the term from its origins in spontaneous prayer by writing 'Acts of love by way of praier and ejaculation, to be used in private': set, rhetorical, ejaculations.[38] *Ros Coeli*, an anonymous volume subtitled *A Miscellany of Ejaculations, Divine, Morall & Politicall*, a highly rhetorical Royalist prose work, was published in 1640 and went into several editions. Christopher Harvey and Henry Vaughan's *Ejaculations* are explicitly Royalist and Anglican in affiliation. The association of the Herbertian poetic of ejaculation with a Royalist politics is seen most graphically in the early work of Payne Fisher, who later became Cromwell's poet laureate in a completely different style. His manuscript poetry, written before he deserted the Royalist cause after the battle of Marston Moor, consists of English lyrics in ejaculatory mode, much like Herbert's, beginning with a classic 'ejaculation, In sense of my present condition': his later Republican poetry was to be public, celebratory and in Latin. Other Royalist poets who wrote ejaculations include Robert Herrick and James Howell, and the savagely anti-nonconformist R. Fletcher.[39] The choice of the title 'Ejaculation' for a poem has less to do with its origins in religious discourse than with its symbolic function in enlisting the contents in a sanctified tradition of holy poetry. This attempt to sanctify political discourses in the mid-seventeenth century by using the title *ejaculation* indicates, I believe, that its sexual connotation is not current in popular discourse.

Potentially, the 'birth' topos could be used in the same sanctification project, and more effectively. The products of divine conception are more various than those dictated by the logic of ejaculation. The ejaculatory rhetoric requires emotional, prayerful and ideally brief utterances, and restricts the uses for which ejaculation may be employed. Women give birth, by divine inspiration, to all kinds of discourses, even overtly political ones. The clear sense of the prompting of God seems to have emboldened 'Eliza' in some daring authorial enterprises. She sent her 'babes' to Charles I, in 1644, with some very specific and timely political advice:

> Do not with war my Babes affright,
> In smiling peace is their delight,
> My Prince by yeelding won the field,
> Be not too rigid, dear King yeeld.
>
> (7–10)

'Eliza' was clearly in the forefront of Royalist agitation for a ceasefire in 1644, the period of one of Charles' flirtations with peace, after the disaster of Marston Moor at the beginning of July. In the 1652 printed edition, 'Eliza's' poem to Cromwell also shows an awareness of political issues (p. 54). The compilers of *Kissing the Rod* took their title from this poem, quoting lines 3–6 as an epigraph to the volume:

> But why do I complain of thee?
> 'Cause thou'rt the rod that scourgeth mee?
> But if a good child I will bee,
> I'll kiss the Rod, and honour thee.

This reads like an archetypal text of female submission. In the context of an address to Cromwell, however, 'Eliza''s poem appears as an entirely different kind of text. The first two lines of the poem which immediately precede the *Kissing the Rod* epigraph make clear that the rod in question is Cromwell himself:

> The Sword of God doth ever well
> I'th hand of vertue! O Cromwel.
> But why doe I, complain of thee?

The obedience vowed to it is conditional, to say the least:

> And if thou'rt vertuous as 'tis sed,
> Thou'lt have the glory when thou'rt dead.

The intention to 'kiss the Rod', in this context, seems to refer to Cromwell's increasingly obvious intentions to assume the trappings of monarchy, including the sceptre and the rod. The poem as a whole is a rather subtle expression of political negotiation rather than the abject surrender suggested in the extract. The posture of humble obedience described here is a safe position from which to utter the demands about keeping lawyers in order in stanza 2:

> Sith Kings and Princes scourged be,
> Whip thou the Lawyer from his fee.

In the year after the publication of 'Eliza's' volume, the Nominated Parliament voted to abolish Star Chamber in just this spirit, accusing the lawyers of 'Delatories, Chargeablenesse and a facultie of letting Bloud the people in the purse-veine, even to their utter perishing and undoing.'[40] The final lines of the poem include an implicit accusation of tyranny, a gesture of resistance to the rod of the first stanza:

> If then from Tyrants you'l us free,
> Free us from their Laws Tyranny.
> If not! wee'l say the head is pale,
> But still the sting lives in the tail.[41]

This sting in the tail of her own poem is a kind of threat, a stance far removed from the abject submission which the quotation of lines 3–7 out of context seems to indicate.

The visionary and even prophetic insight bestowed by An Collins' privileged position in the enclosed garden is expressed in poems such as 'A Song composed in time of the Civil war, when the wicked did much insult over the godly'. In the first stanza she disparages the 'Poems neat' of classical authorship in a move which seems to echo her rejection of ancient liturgy elsewhere in the volume as 'frozen Forms long since compos'd'.[42] She presents her poetry as a discourse of spiritual liberty, so much so that it resists liberary structures:

> Such mentall mocions which are free
>   Concepcions of the mind,
> Which notwithstanding will not be
>   To thoughts alone confind.

(5–8)

Her preferred model for authorship is represented in stanza 2 of 'A Song composed in time of the Civil war': she is a Biblical woman prophet manqué, a Deborah without a victory to celebrate. The military progress of the Civil War is not alluded to here: conflict is primarily conducted through the various discourses mentioned in stanzas 3, 4, 5 and 6. The 'Foes of Truth' use slander against their opponents, and false application of Scripture: they subject the conquered to binding with oaths. Collins' own poems, represented as non-rhetorical and therefore 'truthful', play an active part in the struggle, speaking out 'betimes in Truth defence'. The following poem, the last 'Song' in her volume, seems to speak from a more recent, and more positive, standpoint.

> But from those storms hath God preserved
> A people to record his praise
> Who sith they were therefore reserved
> Must to the height their Spirits raise
> To magnify his lenity,
> Who safely brought them through the fire
> To let them see their hearts desire.

This sentiment, if recorded near to the publication date of 1653, can only refer to the triumph of Independency, and of toleration. Her particular nuanced position is marked in the elaboration of her 'heart's desire':

> Which many faithfull ones deceased
> With teares desire to behold,
> Which is the Light of Truth professed
> Without obscuring shaddowes old,
> When spirits free, not tyed shall be
> To frozen Forms long since compos'd.[43]

Her dual claim both to an authentic and 'inner light' and to the heritage of Reformed Protestantism places her as an Independent, as does her carefully delineated moderate Calvinist theology and range of metaphor: but her theology and spirituality as expressed here is irenic. It is an intriguing possibility that this is a Government-sponsored volume designed to unite those who thought of themselves as 'the godly' behind the new Protector of the Commonwealth.[44]

The context for poetry both as ejaculation and birth is primarily a discursive one, and I would suggest that these *topoi* serve a similar function. Both ways of describing authorship are associated with discourses which stress the agency of God and the passivity of the human author in composition. An Collins is unusual in claiming, in the final stanza of her preface, only divine assistance. The more usual formulation is a denial of any human ownership of the poems. 'Not mine neither', says George Herbert, 'for from thee they came'. Vaughan's 'Dedication' goes like this:

> Nor can I say this is all mine,
> For, dearest Jesus, 'tis all thine.[45]

The 'mine/thine' rhyme which encapsulates this exchange is daringly modified to 'mine/Divine' in 'Eliza's' Dedication, which serves the same function (sig. A1v). The basis for this exchange is embedded in the Calvinist doctrine discussed at the start of this essay. Only that which is prompted by God, and in effect carried out by Him through His Holy Spirit, is worth publishing. Publication, still an ambivalent enterprise in this period both for men and women, seems to require such justificatory strategies.

However, there is a difference between the way ejaculation functions for male poets and birth functions for women. 'Ejaculation', with its presumption of silence on the part of the poet, or at least lack of art, functions as a disabling trope: what Caroline Walker Bynum calls, tracing the familiar pattern of strength through weakness in male-authored medieval writing, 'inversion' imagery.[46] Statements of disablement are commonplace in seventeenth-century spiritual autobiography and biography. Herbert's first biographer, Barnabas Oley, records one such statement of specifically intellectual impairment as proof of the inspired nature of his lyrics: 'God hath broken into my study and taken off my Chariot-wheels, I have nothing worthy of God.'[47] The discursive context of male experiences of weakness and illness, although never framed in gender terms, casts light on the frequently noted claims of women in this period to these same authorship conditions. Helen Wilcox identifies the aesthetic of the religious lyric in the mid-century as 'feminized', whether authored by men or women: and one reason may be that, as Diane Purkiss notes in her essay, physical impairment itself is feminized in this period.[48] In an even more tangible sense, religious authorship moves into a female realm in this period: its location is in private, often in the 'closet', which has been the physical space to which women have been assigned by conduct books in the late sixteenth and early seventeenth centuries.[49] Thus religious discourses have made authorship available to women, who are seen to 'qualify' more obviously than men for the condition of inspiration. However, sexual difference is acknowledged by the female author only as a stage in the transcending shift to spiritualised tropes of femininity. Caroline Walker Bynum suggests that in spiritual writing of the Middle Ages men choose images of inversion to construct their spiritual subjectivity, whilst women affirm their everyday experiences of illness, confinement and childbirth. In women's writing of the Reformation, however, female experience is troped as an escape from its literal and physical reality, which necessarily subordinates women to men. Women apparently speak from an authorized submissive female position, but the Husband to whom they submit is divine. As 'Eliza' put it, rejecting all merely human authority:

> My boundlesse spirits, bounded bee in thee:
> For bounded by no other can they be.

(p. 36)

Discourse composed under these circumstances is perceived to be every bit as authoritative as male *Ejaculations*.

It may be, however, that the reason for the choice of the 'offspring' image is rhetorical rather than spiritual: it is a happier trope for literary production than ejaculation, because it has far more scope. Female reproduction is unproblematically connected with a spiritualization of sexual union in a way that 'ejaculation' is not, nor can be: the biblical text of The Song of Songs, usually allegorized as a version of the relationship between Christ and the Church, authorizes the tropological link between female sexuality and a state of holiness, and the dominant speaking voice is female. The confidence which such a discourse gives the woman author is displayed in the second paragraph of 'Eliza's' address to the reader:

> and I will tell them too, I am not asham'd of their birth; for before I knew it, the Prince of eternall glory had affianced mee to himselfe; and that is my glory.[50]

This passage has its validation in a range of biblical texts throughout the Old and New Testaments. The terminology of ejaculation, by contrast, is unbiblical and comparatively limited in application. In particular, it does not translate into any representation of the relationship between Christ and the Chuch. Proof of this, I think, is found in the visual representations accompanying Francis Quarles' *Emblemes*. As the engravings were originally from a secular, erotic context, arrows, darts and Cupids abound throughout the volume: Cupid is usually associated with Love, who in the context of Quarles' religious discourse is Christ. The 'Entertainment' to the third book of the *Emblemes* shows the arrows going in a different direction, from the believer to God. These are explicitly 'ejaculations': they are given verbal content. However, the visual representation with the arrows apparently emerging from the believer's chest is at odds with any human bodily function. As often in Quarles' engravings, the imagination at work is abstract and rhetorical, and the attempt to incarnate spiritual truth in the visual representation of human bodies is not entirely successful. The phenomenon of spiritual 'ejaculation' has little to do with bodies, either male or female. By contrast, the 'birth' topos had already been extensively exploited by Calvinist theologians developing the biblical text. The spirituality of Calvinism is conducted in terms of 'motions'; the evil motions of the flesh of which An Collins is very aware, and the 'good motions' of the Spirit which Thomas Cranmer's Collect urged parishioners to obey on the first Sunday in every Lent.[51] 'Motions' in fact become the guarantee of election and perseverance in the Catechism sandwiched between Old and New Testaments of the Quarto Bible so popular in the second half of the seventeenth century: these inner sensations signify the irreversible indwelling of the Holy Spirit in the Calvinist scheme. Since discernment of these inner motions was so crucial to the believer's state of mind, it was not long before they were compared to the movement of a child in its mother's womb, the movement that in a Renaissance physiology signified the coming of human life to a foetus. This is from Anne Lok's translation of Jean Taffin's *Of the Markes of the Children of God*, where the inspired prayer elsewhere labelled 'ejaculation' is associated with the womb:

> these holie prayers, being the motions of the holie Ghost in us, are testimonies of our Faith, although they seem to us small & weake. As the woman that feeleth the moving of a childe in her wombe, though verie weake, beleeveth and assureth herself ... that she goieth with a

live childe: so if we have these motions, these holie affections and desires before mentioned, let us not doubt, but that wee have the holie Ghost (who is the author of them) dwelling in us.[52]

William Perkins too offered the experience of pregnancy and motherhood as a trope for the 'new birth'.[53] A conflation of the secular 'birth' topos for authorship and the imagery for spiritual experience is an obvious move for those involved in spiritual authorship, but no male author performed it. The term for verbal articulation of a divine 'motion' became, instead, 'ejaculation'.

Caroline Walker Bynum argues that for medieval men, the invocation of the reproductive power of the womb was a claim to divine creativity. In the spiritual economy which I have argued is its authentic context, however, ejaculation is part of a disempowering trope, an 'inversion' trope. The rejection of the secular birth topos for sacred male-authored writing is partly an index of how far it is implicated in discursive traditions of rhetorical artifice. Women's claim to literary 'children' probably begins as a nod in the direction of conventional prefatory strategies: but in the case of writers such as An Collins and 'Eliza', the pretext of The Songs of Songs authorizes the extension of the metaphor into a justificatory framework for many kinds of writing. The gendered subject position of the Bride allows women poets to mobilize more effectively the vocabulary of 'motions' so close to the heart of Calvinist doctrine. The 'motion' to speak, envisaged by both men and women as divine impulse, is incarnated in the rhetorical image of the female body adopted by these women writers, authorizing them to give birth to discourse at will: the men writing *Ejaculations* pursue the fiction of replicating the inspired utterance, expelling it in a form which is as faithful to the original silent 'motion' as possible. Given the theological resonance of the birth trope it is surprising that male authors did not pursue the 'offspring' metaphor, sanctifying what was already a secular trope, especially given that works such as Henry Finch's 1613 commentary offered 'the Christian man' a spiritual identification with the Bride of The Song of Songs. However, literary birth, whether spiritual or rhetorical, to some extent sexualizes and feminizes an authorship role. For men writing spiritual discourses in this period, tropes of the feminine are not invoked even as part of an 'inversion' strategy. For women, the initial affirmation of their femininity in the choice of authorial persona offers access to powerful textual strategies troped as feminine, but producing transcendent words: the archetypal Virgin gave birth to the Word made (male) flesh. To answer Helen Wilcox's question, the difference between the titles of male- and female-authored volumes in the mid-seventeenth century is no coincidence. The authorial decision to write *Ejaculations* explicitly enacts a rejection of rhetoric and 'the flesh'. Implicitly, it rejects a feminized version of spiritual authorship which women are happy to claim for their own.

Notes

1. Henry Vaughan, *The Complete Poems*, ed. Alan Rudrum (Harmondsworth: Penguin, 1976), p. 142.
2. See Stanley Stewart, *George Herbert* (Boston, 1986), pp. 128–56, for details of his 'School of Herbert'.
3. John Flavel, *Husbandry Spiritualized: Or, The Heavenly Use of Earthly Things* (London, 1669), p. 264.
4. Helen Wilcox, 'Exploring the Language of Devotion in the English Revolution', in *Literature and the English Civil War*, ed. Tom Healy and Jonathan Sawday (Cambridge: Cambridge University Press, 1990), p. 86.
5. Helkiah Crooke, *Microcosmographia. A Description of the Body of Man* (London, 1618), p. 249.
6. Jonathan Sawday, *The Body Emblazoned: Dissection and the Human Body in Renaissance Culture* (London: Routledge, 1995), p. 226.
7. See the section on 'urinate' and expressions for 'ejaculate' in J.N. Adams, *The Latin Sexual Vocabulary* (London: Duckworth, 1982), pp. 142–4.
8. Renaldus Columbus, *De Re Anatomica Libri XV* (Venice, 1559), p. 239: John Banister, *The Historie of Man, sucked from the sappe of the most approved Anathomistes, in this present age* (London, 1578), p. 88.
9. Ambroise Paré, *Opera Chirurgica* (Frankfurt, 1594), p. 96: *The Workes of that famous Chirurgion Ambrose Parey, translated out of the Latin and compared with the French*, trans. Thomas Johnson (London, 1634), p. 121.
10. Elnathan Parr, *Abba Father: or a Plaine and Short Direction Concerning Private Prayer* (London, 1618), p. 9.
11. Francis Rous, *The Arte of Happiness* (London, 1619), p. 327: *The Misticall Marriage, Or, Experimentall Discourse of the heavenly Marriage betweene a Soule and her Saviour* (London, 1635), p. 161.
12. Thomas Gokins, 'Meditations on the Lord's Prayer, the Key of Heavenly and Earthly Paradise' (London, 1624), in Edward Farr, *Select Poetry chiefly Sacred of the Reign of King James the First* (Cambridge: Cambridge University Press, 1847), p. 325.
13. St. Augustine, *Opera* (Paris, 1688) Vol. II, 389ff. 'Dicuntur fratres in Ægypta crebras quidem habere orationes, sed eas tamen brevissimas, & raptim quodam modo jaculatas, ne illa vigilanter erecta, quae oranti plurimum necessaria est, per productiores moras evanescat atque hebetetur intentio. Ac per hoc etiam ipsi satis ostendunt, hanc intentionem, sicut non est

obtundenda, si perdurare non potest, ita si perduravit, non cito esse rumpendam. Absit enim ab oratione multa loquutio, sed non desit multa precatio, si fervens perseverat intentio. Nam multum loqui, est in orando rem necessarium superfluis agere verbis. Multum autem precari, est ad eum, quem precamur, diuturna & pia cordis excitatione pulsare. Nam plerumque hoc negotium plus gemitibus quam sermonibus agitur, plus fletu quam affatu. Ponit autem lacrymas nostras in conspectu suo, & gemitus noster non est absconditus ab eo, qui omnia per Verbum condidit, & humana verba non quaerit.'

14. Robert Aylett, *Divine and Moral Speculations in Metrical Numbers Upon Various Subjects* (London, 1654), p. 241.

15. Adam Littleton, *A Sermon at the Funeral of the Right Honourable the Lady Jane Eldest Daughter to his Grace William, Duke of Newcastle, and Wife to the Honourable Charles Cheyne, Esq. at Chelsey* (London, 1669), p. 55.

16. 'The country parson ever begins the reading of Scripture with some short inward ejaculation, as *Lord, open my eyes, that I may see the wondrous things of thy Law*', George Herbert, *The Works of George Herbert*, ed. F.E. Hutchinson (Oxford: Oxford University Press, 1945), p. 229.

17. Louis L. Martz, *The Poetry of Meditation: A Study in English Literature of the Seventeenth Century* (New Haven: Yale University Press, 1954), p. 254.

18. Isaac Basire, *The Correspondence of Isaac Basire DD*, ed. W. N. Darnell (London, 1831), p. 22. François de Sales, *An Introduction to the Devoute Life* (Rouen, 1613), p. 170.

19. François de Sales, *A Treatise of the Love of God*, tr. Miles Car (Douai, 1630), p. 429.

20. Danielle Clarke, 'Translation, Interpretation and Gender: Women's Writing 1595–1644' (unpublished DPhil thesis, Oxford 1995), appendix.

21. Helkiah Crooke's *Microcosmographia* of 1618 does use the English word 'ejaculation' for male orgasm. Helkiah Crooke, *Microcosmographia. A Description of the Body of Man* (London, 1618), p. 214. Crooke seems to be an independent thinker on these issues, rejecting the term *vasa ejaculatoria* common to other textbooks as inappropriate (he prefers *vasa deferentia*) and arguing against the one-sex model (see p. 249).

22. *Aristotles Master-Piece: or the Secrets of Generation. Very necessary for all Midwives, Nurses, and Young-Married Women* (London, 1684), p. 107; *The Workes of that famous Chirurgion Ambrose Parey*, p. 126. For an extended account of this 'one-sex' model in seventeenth-century England, see Thomas Laqueur, *Making Sex: Body and Gender from the Greeks to Freud* (Boston, Mass.: Harvard University Press, 1990).

23. Elizabeth Mordaunt, *The Private Diarie of Elizabeth, Viscountess Mordaunt* (Duncairn, 1856), p. 201.

24. Herbert, *Works*, p. 233.

25. BL MS Harl. 2311, f. 42r, ff. 49v–52r.

26. Mary Pennington, *Some Account of Circumstances in the Life of Mary Pennington from the Manuscript left for her Family* (London, 1821), p. 12.

27. In Frances Quarles, *Solomons Recantation, entituled Ecclesiastes, paraphrased With a Soliloquie or Meditation upon every Chapter* (London, 1645), sig. A4r.

28. *The Autobiography of Mrs Alice Thornton*, Publications of the Surtees Society, 62 (1873), pp. 109, 117.

29. An Collins, *Divine Songs and Meditacions*, ed. Sidney Gottlieb (Tempe, Arizona: Medieval & Renaissance Texts & Studies, 1996), pp. 24–5. Subsequent quotations from Collins are from this edition.
30. Elizabeth Jocelin, *The Mothers Legacie to her unborne Child* (London, 1624), sig. A10r.
31. John Bullokar, *An English Expositor* (London, 1616), sig. A2r.
32. Katharine Eisaman Maus, 'A Womb of His Own: Male Renaissance Poets in the Female Body', in James Grantham Turner, ed., *Sexuality and Gender in Early Modern Europe: Institutions, texts, images* (Cambridge: Cambridge University Press 1993), pp. 273–5.
33. Sawday, p. 228.
34. Elisabeth Major, *Honey on the Rod* (London, 1656), p. 160.
35. *Eliza's Babes, or, The Virgins-Offering* (London, 1652), sig. A1v.
36. Edward Rainbowe, *A Sermon preached at the funeral of the Right Honourable Anne, Countess of Pembroke, Dorset and Montgomery* (London, 1677), p. 7.
37. Phyllis Mack, *Visionary Women: Ecstatic Prophecy in Seventeenth-Century England* (Berkeley: University of California Press, 1992), pp. 114–15.
38. Jeremy Taylor, *Holy Living* (London, 1650), p. 292.
39. *Ex otio negotium*, a 1656 volume from the pen of one R. Fletcher, combines Royalist and savagely anti-nonconformist satire with religious poetry in a Herbertian strain that includes an 'Ejaculation'.
40. L.D., *An Exact Relation of the Proceedings and Transactions of the Late Parliament* (London, 1654), pp. 12, 15.
41. *Elizas Babes*, p. 54.
42. Collins, *Divine Songs and Meditacions*, p. 63.
43. Collins, *Divine Songs and Meditacions*, p. 65.
44. Note the discussion of inner Light in 'The Preface', 5, and the nuanced theological position elaborated in 'The Discourse', 8–30. The eclectic nature of her spiritual vocabulary perhaps explains why critics have had so much difficulty deciding on her politico-religious affiliations: these are summarised by Sidney Gottlieb in his edition. He is inclined to link her with Quakerism: *Divine Songs and Meditacions*, p. xvii.
45. Vaughan, *The Complete Poems*, p. 145 (ll. 21–2).
46. Caroline Walker Bynum, *Fragmentation and Redemption: Essays on Gender and the Human Body in Medieval Religion* (New York, 1991), p. 33.
47. *Herberts Remains, or, Sundry Pieces of that Sweet Singer of the Temple, Mr. G.H., sometime Orator of the University of Cambridge, Now exposed to Public Light*, ed. Barnabas Oley (London, 1652), sig. C6r.
48. Wilcox, p. 86. Diane Purkiss, 'Producing the Voice, Consuming the Body: Women Prophets of the Seventeenth Century', in *Women, Writing, History 1640–1740*, ed. Isobel Grundy and Susan Wiseman (London: Batsford, 1992).
49. Hilary Hinds has recently shown how these sites of limitation function for women as conditions for inspiration, and An Collins' poetic activity is a classic example of this. Physical restraint leads to spiritual enlargement: in the words of Luke 12, 'that which ye have spoken in the ear in closets shall be proclaimed upon the house-tops'. See Hilary Hinds, *God's Englishwomen: Seventeenth-century Radical Sectarian Writing and Feminist Criticism* (Manchester: Manchester University Press, 1996), p. 101.

50. *Eliza's Babes*, sig. A2r.
51. *The Booke of Common Prayer* (London, 1619), sig. D5r.
52. Jean Taffin, *Of the Markes of the Children of God, and of their comforts in Afflictions*, tr. Anne Lok (Paris, 1609), p. 27. On Lok's texts, and her Calvinism, see Rosalind Smith's essay, pp. 41–60.
53. William Perkins, *The Works of that famous and worthie Minister of Christ in the Universitie of Cambridge* (Cambridge, 1603), p. 437.

11

Unfettered Organs: the Polemical Voices of Katherine Philips

James Loxley

I

Introducing the poetry of Katherine Philips more than 90 years ago, her first modern editor found his attention diverted by the engraved frontispiece to the posthumously published *Poems* of 1667. 'It is an obvious fancy,' he wrote:

> but neither too obvious nor too fanciful, to compare the attraction of her verse to that of the large portrait-bust which serves as frontispiece to the folio edition of her poems ... In this portrait the features are too much accentuated and the expression hardened and vulgarized a little by adherence to fashion, and supposed proportion, and the like: but there is still an *aura* of possible charm about it.[1]

There are several different processes at work here. On one level, George Saintsbury's 'fancy' furnishes him with a comment on the stylistic features both of the engraving and of Philips's own verse: mediate convention and immediate truth are located in both, and a description of their interplay provides the basis for a critical evaluation. But even a casual reader can discern another evaluative process at work in Saintsbury's assessment of the 'possible charm' and 'attraction' of both poetry and portrait, one which comes rather suddenly to the fore in the editor's subsequent assertion that Philips's husband 'was by more than convention a fortunate man in his marriage, and an unlucky one in his widower-hood.'[2] As such a statement demonstrates, the reference to Philips's likeness – a move initially bracketed as a digressive lapse into fancy – actually enables a redirection of the evaluative process away from the texts which are its proper object. The features of Philips's poetry give way to the features of her face, and the encounter of reader and text is reimagined as an encounter between husband and wife. At the heart of these moves is the critical subject itself, a judge of 'possible charm' whose gaze effects an imagined or fanciful transformation of its textual object into a corporeal entity.

These slippages, and the bracketing which seems designed to forestall them, are indicative of an awareness disruptive of the usual process of critical reading. Saintsbury's essay is struggling to incorporate what seems to be the unavoidable mark of gender borne by Philips's poetry, a mark not carried by the male poets whose works populate the rest of Saintsbury's collection of Caroline verse. The engraving on which he comments makes its subject's partially revealed breasts, as markers of her biological sex, a prominent feature: Saintsbury is obliged to acknowledge this inscription of a gendered authorship, yet attempts to exclude it from his critical endeavour. Once admitted, though, it cannot be contained. The feigned immediacy presupposed by the shift in focus from text to author overwhelms the apparently genderless, disinterested and unfanciful encounter of critic and text.

Saintsbury's essay, though, is far from unique in demonstrating this cluster of difficulties. Indeed, it repeats a manoeuvre familiar not only from the frontispiece to Philips's poems but also from the written accounts of her work given by many contemporaries. In its regress from considering a body of work to assuming the availability to the senses – and therefore to an evaluative process – of the author's body, it echoes the kind of anxious moment to be found in a commendatory ode by Abraham Cowley. His 'On *Orinda's* Poems' is unable to consider those poems without an insistent emphasis on the poet's sex.[3] Like Saintsbury's essay, Cowley's ode moves swiftly from praise of Philips's 'numbers gentle, and thy Fancies high' (48) to an equivalent appreciation of her 'fore-head smooth' and 'sparkling ... eye' (49). The topos of poetic birth provides a figural means for the tracing of Philips's works back to their point of origin. Here, Cowley's fundamental contrast is between his subject's poetic fecundity and the reproductive activity of other women, those who:

> as if the Body were there [*sic*] whole
> Did that, and not the Soul
> Transmit to their Posterity.

> (18–20)

Yet the ode's use of this topos, and the unrelenting focus on Philips's biological sex it involves, undermines the claims of the contrast. Cowley's poem ensures that her body, designated the site of sexual difference and the mother of invention, remains as unavoidably visible as Saintsbury was subsequently to find it.

Not that contemporary criticism would necessarily want to eschew such a focus. For one thing, the rise of a 'new somatics' has left 'more bodies in literary criticism than on the fields of Waterloo,' as Terry Eagleton has put it.[4] These bodies, though, have most often been encountered as subjected, written on, as signs or as the media of signification. The body in question for this essay is rather that of the author, apparently located outside and prior to signification, a corporeality which enables a particular means of gendering texts. This focus, of course, could simply repeat the emphases of Cowley or Saintsbury, but it can also carry a thoroughly different political resonance. The enormously valuable project of recovering and reading the neglected works of women writers, for example, insists in some of its forms on the significance of the connection between texts and their authors' sex. In its encounter with Philips's work this essay, too, finds itself attendant on what might be a matter, or the matter, of gender. It is an attempt to work through the figure of the author, to explore the ways in which the language of sexual difference plays across the variously modelled articulation of writer and written. In doing so it seeks to avoid the conflations and slippages of earlier readers, elaborating an alternative critical perspective – one which does not presume, furthermore, to gaze ultimately on the body of Katherine Philips.

II

At an unknown point during the 1650s, the moderately successful administrative career of James Philips of Cardigan was suddenly endangered. Jenkin Jones, one of his radical opponents, sought to undermine Philips's position by exposing the potentially embarrassing activities of his wife to public view. Some of Katherine Philips's verse had fallen into Jones's possession, and he was now threatening to publish it.

This contextual narrative (minus the more recently excavated detail of Jones's first name) is the burden borne by the title of one of the few poems Katherine Philips ever addressed to her husband.[5] Though encountered in different forms and greater or lesser detail, this title (given as 'To Antenor, on a paper of mine wch J. Jones threatens to publish to his prejudice' in the most recent edition of Philips's works) encourages its readers to see the poem it names as the remnant of a particular social moment involving an author, an addressee, and the defining threat of Jones. We are asked to reconstruct this latter's strategy, one which depended on the fundamental assumption – what we might term more strongly the fundamental social reality – that Philips's questionable 'paper' would reflect as badly upon her husband as upon herself. Jones's threat takes its force from the fact that readers of Katherine's text would understand James, as husband, to have been as much responsible for it as his wife. In other words, the contextual narrative presented in the poem's title provides us with two models of authorship, one tracing her works to Katherine, and the other tracing them back to James.

The contradiction between these models furnishes the poem with its structural dynamic. While 'To Antenor' contains a few muted notes of apology, its central argument – as Elaine Hobby notes, 'a quietly radical statement' – is set squarely against Jones's patriarchal assumption.[6] Indeed, he is characterized as a 'magazine of hell' (13) and a 'mint of slander' (25), the implicit addressee of a work which strives to refute the suggestion that Orinda's 'follies' should 'blast Antenor's name' (18). As she points out to her husband:

> this is mad designe; for who before
> Lost his repute upon anothers score?
> My love and life I must confesse are thine,
> But not my errours, they are only mine.
>
> (5–8)

Distinguishing clearly between husband and wife, Philips takes full responsibility for the 'crimes' and 'faults' represented by her earlier work. As the last couplet quoted makes clear, however, these loyal and protective gestures – the necessary signs of the good wife – enable a move beyond their confines, a barely concealed progression from the rhetoric of self-sacrificing service which dominates the poem's first few lines. Through such strategies Philips is able to stake a claim to the position of author: although a woman and a wife, and therefore not overly encumbered with property, the writings for which her husband is presumed to be responsible are in fact 'only mine'. Furthermore, towards its conclusion the poem explicitly insists on the *value* of the very work that it has previously described only in derogatory terms, declaring that such writing can only 'through malice ... prov[e] a staine' (23). If her poetry is not after all to be characterized as folly, as such a declaration suggests, then an attempt to claim authorship takes on a different complexion altogether. Far from taking the blame, this good wife is taking the credit.

Behind the fig-leaf of an apologetic address to her husband we find a trenchant articulation of some of the concerns fundamental to the whole corpus of Philips's writing. 'To Antenor' is a text preoccupied with authorship, striving to establish a clear and unbreakable line between writing and its point of origin, and demanding that the nature and identity of that origin should be allowed to determine the meanings which can subsequently be located in the text. It is in this sense a critical account of another, prior, poem, a reading which attempts to define the boundaries and goals of legitimate interpretation. It marks an absent text with a defining context, locating it in an occasion or moment of a social structure which governs its meaning. Yet it also defines a poetry thus characterized as an action upon, or intervention into, that social structure, a series of occasions or moments in its own right. A poetry of this kind is necessarily more than text. In embracing context, in appropriating agency and situating itself in a social moment, poetry traces itself back to its author through the figure of voice. 'To Antenor', for example, insists that Philips's earlier 'paper' speaks in the female voice of Katherine, rather than the male register of James which Jenkin Jones would like the public world to hear.

This is not necessarily or immediately the Derridean *phonè*, an illusion of presence or moment of critical naivety.[7] It is a voice written rather as a figuration of political agency, the trope of engagement and resistance. In feminist writing, Elizabeth Harvey has suggested, 'voice is often used as a powerful metaphor for the rebirth of what has been suppressed by patriarchal culture. As women struggle to repossess a power taken from them, as they challenge patriarchal institutions that have deformed them and limited their potential, the synecdochic expression of that liberation is often localized in the voice.'[8] There is, though, a problem here. If voice is metaphor, it is placed at one end of a relation between the figural and the literal. Here, it is plainly in a dynamic of substitution with the agents it seeks to name. As synecdoche, however, it occupies a different role – one, indeed, which requires it to be other than figural and to reach beyond the literal. The synecdochal voice marks text as necessarily bound to the speaker or agent of which voice is merely a part. It is the apparent means of effecting a metaphysics of substance, an articulation of being and attribute, speaker and spoken, which invests the former term with a reality independent of – indeed, prior to – that of the latter.

The voice of Philips's poems can be read as synecdochal, striving to make the corporeality of the author the necessary pre-text of the poetry, to mark it as a gesture out and back to a defining origin.

Indeed, a poem such as 'To my Lady Elizabeth Boyle, Singing' insists on the phenomenal reality of this authorial voice, further distancing it from the perception of synecdoche as a rhetorical figure. Appropriating the figurative resources of the love lyric to enact an aesthetic encounter between listener and singer, the poem is organized around the singular experience of hearing:

> Your voice, which can in moving strains
> Teach beauty to the blind,
> Confines me yet in Stronger chains,
> By being soft and kind.

> (13–16)

The voice which is here identified as agency is a literal, phenomenal voice, one rendered present to the senses. It is, however, not authorial. Indeed, the poem allows the aesthetic experience to be complicated by its acknowledgement that Boyle is merely performing a song written by Philips herself, almost as if it were seeking to destabilize the synecdochal articulation of authorship. But instead of permitting such destabilization, this detail actually enables the reaffirmation of the necessary vocal relation between author and poem. Boyle's performance is described as the Aristotelian form which gives full materiality to the potential of the text:

> Whilst you my trivial Fancy sing,
> You it to wit refine,
> As Leather once stamp'd by a King,
> Became a currant coyne.

> By this my verse is sure to gain
> Eternity with Men,
> Which by your voice it may obtein,
> Though never by my Pen.

> (17–24)

Within this actualization two differently constituted voices are fused, as the phenomenal voice around which the poem is centred becomes the voice of authorship itself. It gives that voice the presence of a phenomenon, and in so doing ensures the move out of the merely textual which the synecdochal voice promises to perform.

The political resonance of this manoeuvre is clear enough, shared and elaborated in the enacted moments of 'To Antenor' and the poem which it set out to read. 'On the Double Murther of K. Charles' is, as its subtitle declares, an 'answer to a libellous rime' penned by a radical preacher named Vavasor Powell. In this it is as much a critical account of a text as 'To Antenor', but it also prefaces this reading with an account of its own coming into being:

> I thinke not on the state, nor am concern'd
> Which way soever that great Helme is turn'd,
> But as that sonne whose father's danger nigh
> Did force his native dumbnesse, and untye
> The fettred organs: so here is a cause
> That will excuse the breach of nature's lawes.
> Silence were now a Sin ...
>
> (1–7)

Voice here is a means of marking the text, of gendering it, and also of making its meaning. Like 'To Antenor', this poem enacts – indeed, *is* – the emergence into visibility and audibility of a gendered agency occluded by patriarchal culture. This is of course a political act, but it is overlaid here by an imperative of a politically different kind. Indeed, it is the undesired death of the patriarch which enables the emergence of the repressed, and the female voice is manifested in lamenting his loss. In this it is doubly voiced: a poem which marks itself as the work of a woman simultaneously claims the political identity of royalism.

In doing so, it aligns itself with the huge body of polemical verse occasioned by the civil conflicts of the 1640s. In many of the crucial royalist texts of the period – Cowley's 'Civil War', the widely read epideictic of John Cleveland, collectively authored volumes by the 'Doctors Militant' of royalist Oxford, the coopted populism of John Taylor – verse functions as a means of fulfilling the fundamental obligation of service on which the King grounded his demands for support.[9] The commonplace comparison between writing and fighting is settled with new urgency into a homology: verse polemic accounts itself not just the sign but the substance of commitment, overlaying its textuality with the image of political agency, and as such it continually elides and evokes the scenes of authorship and utterance which most clearly give agency a form. Indeed, in predicating itself on the synecdochal voice which admits writing to the extra-discursive world of military conflict, it shares in the metaphysics of substance which underlies the forging of political agency in Philips's poems. Cleveland's satires appropriate the performative identity of Archilochean iambics, while Lovelace's lyrics join innumerable ballads and drinking songs in positing a poetry indistinguishable from the deeds which can be understood as the attributes of a material agent.[10] In 'The Grasse-hopper', 'show'rs of old Greeke' (31) – both wine and the Anacreontics which accompany it – constitute the restoration of Christmas festivities, while 'To Althea, From Prison', dramatizes the circumvention of defeat and inaction by a resort to verse:

> When (like committed Linnets) I
> With shriller throat shall sing
> The sweetnes, Mercy, Majesty,
> And glories of my KING;
> When I shall voyce aloud, how Good
> He is, how Great should be;
> Inlarged Winds that curle the Flood,
> Know no such Liberty.
>
> (17–24)[11]

When, in Marvell's 'Tom May's Death', the resurrected Ben Jonson presents the singing voice of the royalist poet as the synecdoche of resistance, he echoes the polemical self-definition which had been loudly elaborated for the previous decade:

> When the sword glitters ore the Judges head,
> And fear has Coward Churchman silenced,
> Then is the Poets time, 'tis then he drawes,
> And single fights forsaken Vertues cause.
> He when the wheel of Empire, whirleth back,
> And though the World's disjointed Axel crack,
> Sings still of ancient Rights and better Times,
> Seeks wretched good, arraigns successful Crimes.
>
> (63–70)[12]

Voice here, as for Philips, offers the means of subsuming textuality under the figure of an agent, a singer, who personifies in a strong sense the opening of writing onto a world beyond or prior to discourse. Yet in its resort to voice, the royalist polemic to which 'On the Double Murther' and 'To Antenor' declare a generic affiliation threatens to cancel the female voice through which those poems are marked and defined.

III

In its attempts to elide poetry with loyal service, royalist polemic overlaid *its* resort to voice with another discourse of the body, the rhetoric of action and idleness to which early modern writing returned again and again. The recovery of classical texts necessarily revived the polarities which had marked those texts, foremost among which was the opposition of the life of public service to an *otium* variously conceived as virtuous contemplation, harmless pleasure, or pernicious sloth.[13] Early modern reworkings of this topos drew on the figurative resources of gender in that the conflict over the moral value of the active life and its opposite was often located in prosopopeia ascribed to gendered bodies. The familiar Ovidian epyllion of Salmacis and Hermaphroditus, for example, offered a gendered allegory of the dangers attendant on a man's falling away from the life of action which was often rehearsed in the decades prior to the civil war. Francis Beaumont's version, published in 1602 and reprinted in his *Poems* of 1640, identified in Salmacis a personification of morally questionable leisure, a 'lazie idlenesse' ([1640] sig. C2v).[14] The subsequent transformation of Hermaphroditus becomes a myth of surrender to wanton indolence, a loss of manhood, rather than anything else: the androgyne defines not a third sex but a grotesquely imperfect male. An earlier translation by Thomas Peend described the young man's immersion in Salmacis's fountain:[15]

> He entred lyke a man therin,
> > and shulde come foorth agayne
> But halfe a man.

> (sig. A4v)

George Sandys' rendering also conventionally emphasizes Salmacis's 'sloth' (p. 120), and reads the transformation of her beloved as a lessening: to be 'halfe-woman' is to be 'infeebled' (p. 122).[16] In the commentary which he appends to his translation Sandys glosses the text with a rendering of a passage from another of Ovid's works, the *Remedia Amoris*, a juxtaposition which fixes the story of Hermaphroditus as a warning against the dangers of an idle life.[17]

The generic form in which these narratives are couched further prescribes this kind of reading, 'a reduction from masculine fullness' being written into 'the style and substance of the epyllion,' as Thomas Healy has pointed out.[18] And other reworkings of myth shared its emphases. *The Brazen Age*, by Thomas Heywood, displayed a Hercules bewitched and enslaved by Omphale, 'attired like a woman, with a distaffe and a spindle' (sig. K1r) and unrecognizable to his companions.[19] Jason views this departure from the heroic as a surrender of maleness:

> This is some base effeminate groome, not hee
> That with his puissance frighted all the earth:
> This is some woman, some *Hermophrodite*.
>
> (sig. K1v)

Hercules's attempt to reverse this movement, to 'shake off this effeminacy', requires him to re-enter the life of action. 'By our deeds', he declares, he will 'repurchase our renowne' (sig. K3r). Similarly, the first of George Wither's *Epithalamia* for the wedding of Frederick of the Palatinate and Princess Elizabeth contrasts the 'dangers, deaths, and wounds' suffered by a real soldier with the merely dramatic and less than manly 'Chamber-combatants' to be found at the pacific English court.[20] Where the former deserves the name of man, the latter is simply a 'Twelfth Night': Viola initially opts for the disguise of a eunuch, then takes a name which is itself redolent of castration, as Stephen Orgel has recently noted.[21] Though the identity of eunuch soon drops out of view, its trace – Cesario – remains to name the riddling androgyny of 'I am all the daughters of my father's house, / And all the brothers too' (II.iv.121–2), and to underpin the comic duel with Sir Andrew in Act III scene iv. Shortly before drawing his sword, Cesario confides to the audience that only 'A little thing would make me tell them how much I lack of a man' (III.iv.307–8), an emphasis on imperfect maleness that replaces the narrative of disguised womanhood actually underlying Viola's sexual ambiguity with an imaginary origin in castration. And the aside makes clear that Cesario's inaptitude for martial heroics can be understood in the context of this trope of emasculation.

It is this constellation of homologous oppositions which shapes the images of self and other central to royalist polemic. The corporeal agency such poetry demands is marked as biologically male, defined against a particularly physical lack. Thus the 'neuter' who seeks to play 'fast and loose' – in Robert Heath's words – with both parties to the conflict was condemned as a site of the same metaphorized sexual indeterminacy on which Peend, Beaumont and Sandys focused.[22] As one brief character of 'A Newter' put it, he was 'like an Adjective, that varies case and gender with his Substantive.' Being only '*Lukewarme*', this 'spectator' lacked the heat necessary both for action and, in Galenic physiology, for the full attainment of manhood.[23] His was the grotesque indeterminacy which an Oxford celebration of the 1642 Kentish petition found in all gentlemen of quality who had failed to heed the King's call to arms.[24] They were, the poem declared, 'the female Gentry of the smocke' (f. 34r), the cross-dressed images of emasculation evoked for different ends in Wither's epithalamium. With a bitter irony, the poem recounts how, 'betwixt eating, sleeping, drinking, play / they haue not leasure for to liue a day,' before urging them to cast off idleness and 'Chide [their] dull blood to action' (f. 34r).

In claiming the male body of action as its own, royalist polemic also strove to characterize its Parliamentarian enemies as somehow unmanned. Their rebellion was the touchstone of a process of inversion which 'doth surpasse all *Ovids* Transformation', John Taylor suggested:[25] those who could be represented as exchanging an allegiance to the King for the practice of rebellion were attacked as the grotesque incarnate. Taylor contrasted George Wither's militantly anti-royalist *Campo-Musae* with the same author's much earlier praise of Charles, accusing Wither of being a 'rayling Hypocrite, *Hermophrodite*, Nor Male or Female, nor both or neither.'[26] The Oxford poet Thomas Weaver similarly condemned Archbishop John Williams – criticized for his hostility to Laud and his allegedly lukewarm support for the king's cause – as 'Nature's Master-piece of errour', '*Religions Hermophrodite*', in a polemic originally published as Cleveland's.[27] That the military leader of the revolt should be the Earl of Essex, a man famously divorced for impotence, allowed royalist satire to locate emasculation in a figure who was the iconic centre of the parliamentarian cause for most of the first civil war.[28] Cleveland's panegyric to Prince Rupert ridiculed 'Impotent *Essex*' (45), the 'Gelding-Earle' (49), and lamented:

> is it not a shame
> Our Commonwealth, like to a *Turkish Dame*,
> Should have an *Eunuch*-Guardian?

> (45–7)[29]

Rather more subtly, John Berkenhead's *Mercurius Aulicus* recounted the story of Essex's ignominious flight after his defeat at Lostwithiel in August 1644. The Lord-General made his way to Plymouth in a cock-boat, a small rowing vessel, a detail which the royalist newsbook enshrined at the centre of a narrative it then titled 'the history of the Cock-boat'.[30] *Aulicus* pointedly expressed its incredulity at finding 'his Excellency in a cock-boat',[31] partly, no doubt, because of the indignity implied – but also because 'cock-boat' was a none too opaque euphemism for the vagina.[32]

An insistent emphasis on the identity of royalist action and corporeal, substantive maleness is the necessary corollary of this satiric endeavour. Cleveland's attack on the commonwealth's '*Eunuch-Guardian*', for example, is paired with a focus on the excess of male sexual power to be found in Rupert and the King: the poem gives voice to the unpleasant hope that the female body of the state will be 'Ravish'd by Charles, rather then sav'd by [Essex]' (48), while the Prince's name is declared 'wit's Superfoetation' (56), the cause of a generative superabundance which 'Makes fancy, like eternitie's round wombe, / Unite all Valour' (57–8). The love lyric, for so long the territory of both an explicitly male desire and the figurative use of the language of war, gains new impetus. Lovelace's 'To Lucasta, Going to the Warres' furnishes the most celebrated – though far from only – example of this reinvigorated elision of male potency and political action, while what Thomas Corns has called the 'sordid carnality' of the erotic verse in *Lucasta: Posthume Poems* can perhaps more usefully be described as the reduction of textuality to a bodily maleness that assists in the production of this elision.[33] The poem 'Her Muffe', for example, follows four stanzas praising both Lucasta's hands and the muff that covers them with a fifth which self-reflexively casts this courtly idiom into doubt:

> This for Lay-Lovers, that must stand at dore,
> Salute the threshold, and admire no more:
>   But I, in my Invention tough,
>   Rate not this outward bliss enough,
> But still contemplate must the hidden Muffe.

> (17–20)

The poem's subject claims not to be standing 'at dore', his 'Invention' taking him over the threshold as the male partner in hetero-sexual intercourse. This is a contemplation where textuality somehow shades into the solipsistic reiteration of an apparently defining act of maleness.

In this gendered pattern of constitutive difference and equivalence, the figure of voice which allows polemic to claim the substance of action is itself inevitably claimed as both a sign and property of full manhood. Lovelace's account of his 'Invention tough', or the 'strong lines' with which Cleveland and others were credited, are both clear cases in point.[34] It is noticeable too, in another example, that Cowley's *The Civil War* signals Essex's emasculation by asserting his rhetorical impotence.[35] The poem imagines how, before the battle of Newbury,

> th' Essexian Rebell strove,
> His fainting Troopes with powrelesse words to move;
> His Speech was dull and taedious, for him made
> By some great Deacon of the Preaching Trade.
> Of Tyr'anny and Pop'ery much hee told;
> An hundred Declaration Lies of old;
> Unhappy man; even their ill Phrase hee tooke,
> And helpt it neither with his Toung nor Looke.
> But with long stops the livelesse sentence broke.

(III, 329–37)

By contrast, the verbally potent king has just delivered a skilful oration, the force of which is then echoed and proven by a military triumph. When voice is claimed in this way, the structure of the discourse demands that it be set in a dynamic of mutual definition with the topoi of action and manhood. It is fused in a figure of agency rampant, wielding a defining instrument which looks simultaneously like pen, sword and penis.

IV

The polemical exchange enacted in 'On the Double Murther of K. Charles' and 'To Antenor' allows Philips's work to signal its affinity with this kind of writing. It is an affinity further evidenced by the appearance of a poem by Philips in Humphrey Moseley's edition of William Cartwright's works, a piece which marks her first appearance in print and is easily assimilated into the volume's polemical strategies.[36] The edition, published in the politically tense summer of 1651, displays the marks of political censorship like battle scars, drawing attention to the absence of one political ballad and marking each excision from other poems with the space the censored lines should have occupied.[37] Its gallery of tributes to Cartwright, meanwhile, reconstitute both this Caroline paragon and the royalist Oxford he epitomized. Yet the conjunction of Philips's poetry and this royalist practice reveals its difficulties when we consider how her poetry locates in *its* voice a synecdoche of the explicitly female author. Something of this difficulty might be detected in the Cartwright volume: Philips's poem appears over the initials 'K. P.', and is in this way indistinguishable from many of the commendatory poems penned by the more than 50 male writers who also contributed to the volume, but it is placed first, ahead even of the few lines written by the Earl of Monmouth. Signed simply with initials, the poem does not mark itself as the effect of either male or female utterance (which is as much to say, in this context, that it assumes the normatively male royalist voice). Signed simply with initials, but accorded precedence over the works of noblemen, the poem is marked off from others so signed as the product of a differently gendered voice – precisely *because* it shares this signatory form.

It is possible to trace the same problematic in the opening lines of 'On the Double Murther of K. Charles'. These lines, as we have noted, enact a doubly political moment: the emergence of the woman as writer, and the supplanting of a politically disengaged subjectivity by one which, in its speaking, emerges into engagement. The story of Croesus's dumb son, borrowed from Herodotus, serves simultaneously as a particularly striking allegory of both movements.[38] Yet in its assimilation of a woman's writing to a contrarily gendered prosopopeia, this doubled allegory puts in question the apparently unproblematic corporeal origin and referent of the language of sexual difference. The synecdochal voice itself is undermined. To begin with this striking transformation of the voiceless figure is to insist that the author's social position can be read off from her sex, and that the poem's polemical strength and urgency derives from the clearly female voice which self-reflexively utters it. Yet that polemical strength is itself marked, both here and elsewhere in royalist writing, as an attribute of a male subject. The poem displays a doubleness that appears irresoluble, at least within the terms on which it is grounded.

In their very reliance on the synecdochal voice, these polemical works seem to show up the fraudulence of its claims. As we saw in 'To my Lady Elizabeth Boyle, Singing', it offers a move out of textuality into a world ontologically prior to discourse, as well as making the authorial body present as a securely unproblematic determinant of a text's identity. But the contradictorily – and impossibly – gendered origin to which 'On the Double Murther' points reveals the invalidity of that offer: sexual difference has disrupted and undone the determining body of which it ought to be simply an effect.

This is only true, however, as long as we understand the synecdochal voice simply to be making an ontological claim. In fact, any such claim is complicated by other factors. We perhaps ought to remember that the authorial body which looms large in both Philips's poems and the royalist polemic of her contemporaries is primarily a *political* body, its substance defined by an enacted cultural conflict. It is an agent constituted in a series of specific social moments, the assertions and disruptions of patriarchal relations around which 'To Antenor' and 'On the Double Murther' are organized, or the contestation in which the crucial texts of Cleveland and others took their form. As an agent it is defined precisely by attributes – the poems themselves – from which it is inseparable, which indeed may be said to constitute it *as* an agent. The body from which these poems speak is thus one which the texts themselves make necessary, and which remains necessary only within this relation. 'The body posited as prior to the sign, is always *posited* or *signified* as *prior*,' Judith Butler has written. 'This signification produces as an *effect* of its own procedure the very body that it nevertheless and simultaneously claims to discover as that which *precedes* its own action.' The synecdochal voice is precisely a strong means of positing the body, but one which continues to operate at the level of signification, as a rhetorical trope. Voice may be that which articulates text and its apparent corporeal origin, but it is also testament to the failure of the latter to subsume the former. If anything, the contrary process is at work. As Butler continues, 'If the body signified as prior to signification is an effect of signification, then the mimetic or representational status of language, which claims that signs follow bodies as their necessary mirrors, is not mimetic at all ... It is productive, constitutive, one might even argue *performative*, inasmuch as this signifying act delimits and contours the body that it then claims to find prior to any and all signification.'[39] 'To My Lady Elizabeth Boyle, Singing', we remember, is a poem organized around a performance, but a performance obscured by an insistent quest for authorial origins.

How then are we to read the interrelation between these textual processes, the political moments which enable their performance of authorship, and the language of sex and gender which the resort to the body seems always to involve? Butler's contemporary project, like much cultural theory, entails an engagement with claims of origin – not simply the determining relationship of sex to gender, but also the very meaning of a non-discursive 'sex', as the quotations above demonstrate. Thomas Laqueur argues that in the early modern period the lack of an absolute distinction between male and female in Galenic accounts of sexual difference – accounts which gave credence to the reiterated tales of sexual transformations in men and, particularly, women – made gender constitutive of sex, or at least kept differentiation from the absolutely originary position it would come to occupy in medical science.[40] 'In the imaginative world that I am describing,' he writes, 'there is no "real" sex that in principle grounds and distinguishes in a reductionist fashion two genders. Gender is part of the order of things, and sex, if not entirely conventional, is not solidly corporeal either ... What we call sex and gender are in the Renaissance bound up in a circle of meanings from which escape to a biological substratum is impossible.'[41]

It is possible to read the untying of the silent figure's 'fettred organs' in 'On the Double Murther' as an echo of those reiterated tales, the release of the apparatus of voice signifying, in Galenic terms, the sudden outward move of genitals from the confines of the body: as a metamorphosis, that is, of the female into the male. In the poem's allegorical scheme the eruption into the voice of royalist polemic becomes the emergence into manhood; read back into the poem's self-dramatization, this scheme produces a narrative diametrically opposed to that of a woman's emergence into the public sphere. Instead, the assumption of a masculine social role engenders a transformation and disappearance of the female body. Sex follows and corroborates the performance of gender, yet the body that makes such a change stands revealed as provisional, a posited origin, one which draws its authority from the occasions or moments within which it is forged. The trope of voice in this poem thus opens up a constellation of related uncertainties just as it appears complicit in attempts to close them down. As a trope, it undermines the synecdochal imperative to escape the confines of the textual. And it is also, in its varying forms, uncertain in its political resonances: most clearly a synecdoche of women's emergence from occlusion, yet also subtextually marked as a sign of a unitary maleness and masculinity. Vocality here is something of a *brisure*:[42] the articulation of text and body, gender and sex, writing and the world, and at the same time the fracture between them.

None the less, it remains both unavoidable and necessary even as its fixity is surrendered. Voice is not, after all, something extraneous to writing, something which stands apart either as origin or as illusion. As Paul de Man pointed out, it is 'a mere figure of speech or play of the letter' – but he acknowledges also that 'the principle of intelligibility, in lyric poetry, depends on the phenomenalization of the poetic voice.'[43] The readings on which the poems discussed here are built, the accounts of poetic function they mimic, are attempts to make poetry intelligible precisely in a specific pheno-menal moment. The political occasion which these texts enact is the circumstance which requires their identity with utterance, the reason for a repeated focus outwards from textuality. And despite the erosion of a secure vocality, poetry's political enactment survives – voice's very contradictions produce the meanings and politics of its occasions. Challenging the claims on which its own readability depends, the woman's voice puts in question the very means by which 'woman' is defined.

Notes

1. George Saintsbury, *Minor Poets of the Caroline Period*, 3 vols (Oxford: Oxford University Press, 1905, reprinted 1968), I, 486–7.
2. Ibid., p. 487.
3. Cowley's poem is included in the most recent edition of Philips's works: Patrick Thomas, Germaine Greer and R. Little, eds, *The Collected Works of Katherine Philips, The Matchless Orinda*, 3 vols (Stump Cross: Stump Cross Books, 1990–3), III, 191–5. Line references are included parenthetically in the text.
4. Terry Eagleton, *The Illusions of Postmodernism* (Oxford: Blackwell, 1996), p. 17.
5. See Philips, *Collected Works*, I, 346.
6. Elaine Hobby, *Virtue of Necessity: English Women's Writing, 1649–1688* (London: Virago Press, 1988), p. 133.
7. See, particularly, Jacques Derrida, *Of Grammatology*, trans. Gayatri Chakravorty Spivak (Baltimore: Johns Hopkins University Press, 1976). For a paradigmatic reading of mid-seventeenth century verse through the *phonè* and its erasure, see Jonathan Goldberg, *Voice Terminal Echo: Postmodernism and English Renaissance Texts* (New York and London: Methuen, 1986).
8. Elizabeth Harvey, *Ventriloquized Voices: Feminist Theory and English Renaissance Texts* (New York and London: Routledge, 1992), p. 5. For a survey of the uses of 'voice' in feminist writing, see Susan Gal, 'Between Speech and Silence: The Problematics of Research on Language and Gender', in Micaela di Leonardo, ed., *Gender at the Crossroads of Knowledge: Feminist Anthropology in the Postmodern Era* (Berkeley and Los Angeles: University of California Press, 1991), pp. 175–203. See also Leslie Dunn and Nancy Jones, eds, *Embodied Voices: Representing Female Vocality in Western Culture* (Cambridge: Cambridge University Press, 1994).

9. See James Loxley, *Royalism and Poetry in the English Civil Wars* (London: Macmillan, 1997). For a broad analysis of the place of poetry within the conflicts of the civil war period, see Nigel Smith, *Literature and Revolution in England, 1640–1660* (New Haven, Conn.: Yale University Press, 1994), particularly pp. 203–356. The phrase 'Doctors Militant' was coined by John Cleveland in his panegyric 'To P. Rupert', l. 3.

10. Smith, *Literature and Revolution*, pp. 253–5, pp. 306–9, and Lois Potter, *Secret Rites and Secret Writing: Royalist Literature, 1641–1660* (Cambridge: Cambridge University Press, 1989), pp. 140–8.

11. Quoted from C. H. Wilkinson, ed., *The Poems of Richard Lovelace* (Oxford: Oxford University Press, 1930). Line references are included in the text.

12. H. M. Margoliouth, ed., *The Poems and Letters of Andrew Marvell*, 3rd edn 2 vols (Oxford: Oxford University Press, 1971), I, 94–7.

13. See Brian Vickers, 'Leisure and Idleness in the Renaissance: the Ambivalence of Otium', *Renaissance Studies*, 4 (1990), pp. 1–37, 107–54; Markku Peltonen, *Classical Humanism and Republicanism in English Political Thought, 1570–1640* (Cambridge: Cambridge University Press, 1995), esp. pp. 18–53, 119–89, 271–307.

14. [Francis Beaumont], *Salmacis and Hermaphroditus* (London, 1602); reprinted in his *Poems* (London, 1640).

15. T[homas] Peend, *The Pleasant Fable of Hermaphroditus and Salmacis … with a morall in English Verse* (London, 1565). For a brief discussion of this translation see James H. Runsdorf, 'Transforming Ovid in the 1560s: Thomas Peend's Pleasant Fable', *ANQ*, 5 (1992), pp. 124–7.

16. G[eorge] S[andys], *Ovid's Metamorphosis English'd, Mythologiz'd and Represented in Figures* (Oxford, 1632).

17. Ibid., p. 159.

18. Thomas Healy, *New Latitudes: Theory and English Renaissance Literature* (London: Edward Arnold, 1992), p. 163.

19. Thomas Heywood, *The Brazen Age* (London, 1613).

20. George Wither, *Epithalamia: or nuptiall poems upon the mariage betweene prince Frederick the fifth, and the princesse, Elizabeth* (London, 1612).

21. Stephen Orgel, *Impersonations: The performance of gender in Shakespeare's England* (Cambridge: Cambridge University Press, 1996), pp. 53–4. See also, and with a different emphasis, Keir Elam, 'The Fertile Eunuch: *Twelfth Night*, Early Modern Intercourse, and the Fruits of Castration', *Shakespeare Quarterly*, 47 (1996), pp. 1–36.

22. Robert Heath, 'Epitaph on *John Newter'*, in *Clarastella* (London, 1650), 'Epigrams', 36.

23. T. F[ord], *The Times Anatomiz'd, in Severall Characters* (London, 1647), sig. [c10r-v]. For Galen's influence on early modern constructions of sexual difference, see Thomas Laqueur, *Making Sex: Body and Gender from the Greeks to Freud* (Cambridge, Mass.: Harvard University Press, 1990).

24. 'Kents Invitation to take Arms', in BL MS Harley 6918, f34r-v. The poem is attributed to a William Taylor in Bodl. MS Rawl. poet. 65, f. 55.

25. John Taylor, *Mad Fashions, Od Fashions, All Out of Fashions* (London, 1642), sig. A2r.

26. John Taylor, *Aqua-Musae* (Oxford, 1645), p. 2.

27. 'On I. W. A. B. of York', published first in [John Cleveland], *The Character of a London-Diurnall: with severall select Poems* (London, 1647), p. 49. Printed with the rest of Weaver's work in *Songs and Poems of Love and Drollery* (1654); it also appears in Weaver's holograph collection, MS Rawl. poet. 211.

28. Essex's importance as a prosopopeia of the cause is detailed in John Adamson, 'The Baronial Context of the English Civil War', *Transactions of the Royal Historical Society*, 5th Series, 40 (1990), pp. 93–120.

29. 'To P. Rupert', in Brian Morris and Eleanor Withington, eds, *The Poems of John Cleveland* (Oxford: Oxford University Press, 1967). Line references are incorporated into the text.

30. *Mercurius Aulicus*, 1–7 September 1644, p. 1148.

31. *Mercurius Aulicus*, 25–31 August 1644, p. 1142.

32. See Gordon Williams, *A Dictionary of Sexual Language and Imagery in Shakespearean and Stuart Literature* 3 vols (London: Athlone Press, 1994), I. 263.

33. Thomas Corns, *Uncloistered Virtue: English Political Literature, 1640–1660* (Oxford: Oxford University Press, 1992), p. 247.

34. For the latter, see Gregory Dime, 'The Difference between "Strong Lines" and "Metaphysical Poetry"', *Studies in English Literature, 1500–1900*, 26 (1986), pp. 47–57.

35. Abraham Cowley, *The Civil War*, ed. Allan Pritchard (Toronto: University of Toronto Press, 1973). Line references are included in the text.

36. William Cartwright, *Comedies, Tragi-Comedies, with other Poems* (London: Humphrey Moseley, 1651). Philips's poem, 'To the Memory of the most Ingenious and Vertuous Gentleman Mr William Cartwright, my much valued Friend', appears on sig. Ia6v.

37. See G. Blakemore Evans, ed., *The Plays and Poems of William Cartwright* (Madison: University of Wisconsin Press, 1951), pp. 68–70.

38. The narrative can be found in Herodotus, *History of the Greek and Persian War*, I, §85.

39. Judith Butler, *Bodies that Matter: On the Discursive Limits of Sex* (London: Routledge, 1993), 30.

40. These narratives have been the focus of recent critical attention. See, for example, Laqueur, pp. 122–42, and the influential essay by Stephen Greenblatt, 'Fiction and Friction', in *Shakespearean Negotiations: the Circulation of Social Energy in Renaissance England* (Berkeley: University of California Press, 1988), pp. 66–93.

41. Laqueur, *Making Sex*, p. 128.

42. Derrida, *Of Grammatology*, p. 65.

43. Paul de Man, 'Lyrical Voice in Contemporary Theory: Riffaterre and Jauss', in Chauiva Hööek and Patricia Parker, eds, *Lyric Poetry: Beyond New Criticism* (Ithaca: Cornell University Press, 1985), p. 55.

12

A Voice for Hermaphroditical Education

Frances Teague

John Milton's 'Of Education' (1644) was written in reaction to a group of educators known as the Comenians, who advocated the extension of humanistic education to women (as well as to the non-élite). Milton responded by arguing for a humanist revival, heightening the 'manliness' of his style, writing as a man for a male audience. Mary Astell's *A Serious Proposal to the Ladies* (1694) reacts against both the Miltonic and the Comenian constructions of humanism for women's education: she wishes to create an educational programme which is uniquely feminine and excludes men. She too shapes her response in gendered terms, writing as a woman about feminine education for a female audience.[1]

Bathsua Makin in *An Essay to Revive the Antient Education of Gentlewomen* (1673) responds hermaphroditically.[2] I use the description 'hermaphroditically' cautiously, having considered 'androgynous', 'cross-gendered' and 'queer'. While androgynous, like hermaphrodite, points etymologically to the combination of male and female, connotatively it suggests indeterminacy. 'Cross-gendered' suggests someone of one gender posing as the other: while that may be the case in Makin's essay, I shall argue that she is also intellectually 'male' and biologically 'female'. Given the cultural disjunction between male and female homosexuality in the seventeenth century, using queer might (paradoxically) blur difference. While 'hermaphrodite' is best used to describe someone who has both male and female genitalia, I use it here to mean someone like Makin, who learned, thought and wrote as a man, while living, teaching, and bearing seven children. Makin writes in a 'double' voice that is sometimes constructed as male, sometimes female, for an audience that includes both men and women. As James Loxley suggests elsewhere in this volume, the hermaphrodite was a complex identity in early modern England. While the term could mean a surrender of maleness, it could also be defined as a celebratory union of complementary, harmonious qualities'. Yet this positive sense has little application in the context of the kind of education available to early modern women. As Margaret Ferguson remarks:

the enormous interest in writing, on the part of male humanist intellectuals, frequently went hand in hand with conceptualisations of writing as a fundamentally masculine domain. Pens were repeatedly likened to men's weapons by the international (and multilingual) set of writers who made their living by writing and teaching; and in English, the pun on 'pen' and 'penis' makes the metaphor of the pen as a weapon a particularly gendered concept.[3]

Makin was one of relatively few women with a humanist education, obtained from her schoolmaster father, Henry Reginald. As a girl she had assisted her father in his school, which was one of the humanist academies (although both her father and she had quickly changed direction when they learned of Comenian reforms, probably from their friend Samuel Hartlib).[4] One pupil, Sir Simonds D'Ewes, recounts:

He had a daughter named Bathshua, being his eldest, that had exact knowledge in the Greek, Latin, and French tongues, with some insight also into the Hebrew and Syriack; much more learning she had doubtless than her father, who was a mere pretender to it; and by the fame of her abilities, which she had acquired from others, he got many scholars, which else would neither have repaired to him, nor have long staid with him.[5]

Her early training in languages allowed her, aged sixteen, to publish *Musa Virginea*, a collection of poetry in Latin, French and Greek, with epigraphs in Spanish, German and Hebrew. In addition to her reputation as a prodigy, Makin was well known for having taught languages to Charles I's daughter, Princess Elizabeth, widely praised for her learning.[6]

A woman who received an education that allowed her to be multilingual or to use the pen was one whose gender was already complicated by intellectual accomplishments that were gendered male. When Anne Killigrew insists that she wrote her verses herself, she is complaining that she has been mistaken for a man because she has done what men do.[7] When Ben Jonson attacks Cecily Bulstrode for writing, he says she is guilty of raping the Muse, implying that she has a penis.[8] When Sir Edward Denny attacks Lady Mary Wroth for writing *Urania*, he calls her a 'Hermaphrodite in show, in deed a monster / As by thy words and works all men may conster.'[9] In Makin's case, what I am calling her hermaphroditical rhetoric is neither an assumption of a penis, a diminution of masculinity, nor a complementary union: it is instead an inclusive inconsistency that combats a cultural process that is singly gendered.

I

Scholars have sometimes commented that Makin, by coincidence, seems to respond to Milton and that Astell, even if she did not know Makin, suggested some of the same reforms. I argue that no coincidence linked Makin and Milton: Makin knew and disliked Milton's essay. I also argue that Astell knew Makin's essay, with which she largely disagreed. These linkages are not, in themselves, important: what is important is that all three essays are *reactive*. Each writer sets out ideas about education not in a vacuum, but in response to what others propose about the gendering of education. Because each writer is reactive, each voices (and genders) the particular response in the way that the writer thinks will be most convincing.

Milton's essay was composed in part as a response against the English Comenian group.[10] Following the teachings of Johan Amos Comenius, the Comenians urged a variety of social, economic, political and educational reforms. Among these ideas was universal education for all classes and both sexes, so 'that all young ones, whether males or females, none excepted, may be brought up in learning'; they also sought to initiate more efficient and pleasant pedagogical methods.[11] At their centre was Samuel Hartlib, who translated one of Comenius's works in 1642 under the title *A Reformation of Schools*. Evidently Hartlib urged this work upon Milton, among others, and asked him to set down his thoughts on education. Ernest Sirluck argues that Hartlib was dismayed by the result, 'Of Education', and returned the essay, at which point Milton published it himself in 1644 (*CPW* 2: 211).

This essay is Milton's principal statement about education, but not the only one. Milton returned to the subject by publishing one text-book on *Accedence* (1669) and another textbook on *The Art of Logic*

(1672).[12] R.C. Alston notes that the work on accidence may have been written much earlier: 'In Milton's tract *Of Education* (1644) he had suggested that in acquiring a knowledge of Latin grammar the student would be recommended to use either Lily's grammar "or any better."'[13] The work *Accedence*, Alston comments, 'is, in fact, a sort of "abridged Lily" with most of the quotations taken directly from Lily's grammar.' Donald French, who edited *Accedence* for the Yale edition of Milton (*CPW* 8: 31–128), also regards the work as one written to champion Lilian grammar over other schools of thought. In addition to the texts with which one might teach, Milton revised and republished 'Of Education' as *A Tractate of Education* for a 1673 collection of poetry.

Milton disagreed with most Comenian ideas, although he accepted the need to reform the educational system. Dismissing Comenius's *Janua Linguarum Reserata* and *The Great Didactic* he remarks that 'to search what many modern Januas and Didactics, more than ever I shall read, have projected, my inclination leads me not' (*CPW* 2: 365–6). The rest of his essay describes what he would prefer: a return to the ideals of sixteenth-century humanism. Students are to live apart from society, learning Latin and Greek, exercising themselves with 'the exact use of their weapon' and practising 'all the locks and gripes of wrestling' so that they may be 'enflam'd with the study of learning, and the admiration of vertue; stirr'd up with high hopes of living to be brave men, and worthy patriots, dear to God and famous to all ages' (409, 385). Milton thus reveals himself to be still committed to the educational program of humanism with its emphasis on a classical education that prepared male students for their public lives.[14]

Milton's return to humanism was precisely what Comenians did not want. The Comenians were interested in extending education to all classes, not simply to those whose families could afford to send them to academies; they wanted women educated as well as men, while the sort of humanism that Milton endorses is intended for male students only. Even the texts that Milton recommends are books that a Comenian would dislike: he suggests teaching Lily's *Grammar* (and his own *Accedence* would help make Lily more usable), a textbook using a system of language instruction that Comenius hoped to discard and replace with his *Janua Linguarum Reserata*. Milton's sneer at Comenius's works did not go unnoticed. G.H. Turnbull notes that one Comenian, John Dury, read Milton's pamphlet with 'no great praise, and other opinions were also mixed' among the Comenians.[15]

The position of women within humanism is tenuous as best. Hilda Smith has recently argued that '[w]hile women were a part of the intellectual and social changes tied to the spread of humanist ideas, they were always on the periphery';

> The humanist educational programme ... underlay the educational revolution of 1580–1640 that provided a classical and civic education for greater numbers of men from a wider class spectrum. ... Thus through the 1630s that tie between education and public duty favoured by the earlier humanists flourished, and women continued to be omitted.[16]

Milton's essay is part of this patriarchal humanist tradition: students will be passionate scholars, sturdy warriors and male. What is particularly interesting, however, is that because humanism did permit the education of a few women, 'on the periphery' as Hilda Smith says, it produced some women who were raised in a female culture, but educated in this 'masculine' context.

One of these was Bathsua Makin, who had rejected humanism, a system in which she was educated, for the Comenian reformers' ideas. Makin used her 'masculine' education for a masculine end: to pursue a career as an educator for over 50 years. This career culminated in 1673 when Makin published *An Essay to Revive the Antient Education of Gentlewomen* to argue that women deserved education, and to offer a catalogue of learned women as precedents for such a process. In it she attacks the sort of training that Milton had advocated, arguing for the very Comenian reforms that he had mocked:

> If any doubt how this may be done or what authors we shall use that words and things may be learned together, I answer Comenius hath prepared nomenclatures for this purpose. His *Orbis Pictus* ... may be learned by beginners in three months and is as a system of his *Janua Linguarum*. ... I do confess, to proceed in Lily's method, as is before mentioned, to commit the very accidence and grammar to memory requires three or four years, sometimes more (as many can witness by woeful experience); and when all is done, besides declining nouns and forming verbs and getting a few words, there is very little advantage to the child. This being supposed, it's not likely children of ordinary parts should in so short a time be improved in any competent measure in the Latin tongue.

For Makin the chief reform that the educational system needed is the inclusion of girls, and she would have both sexes educated in the same way. She is concerned with pedagogical method, vehemently opposed to Lily and just as vehemently favouring the works of Comenius for language study. Yet while she disagrees with Milton's methods, she does not question the humanist assumption that learning languages, especially classical ones, is the principal aim of education, and an important secondary aim is to produce good citizens. In other words, she rejects those parts of the humanist programme that would exclude her feminine body.

If Milton's essay has an unspoken purpose, 'to disassociate himself from the Comenian program' (*CPW* 2: 208), so does Makin's: to disassociate herself from Milton's humanism. Both Jean Brink and J.L. Helms have argued that Makin's essay offers a response to Milton, although both are scrupulous about arguing the works need not be causally related.[17] Yet neither Brink nor Helms notes several items that strengthen the suggestion that Makin has Milton specifically in mind: her critique of Lily, her use of a proverb, and her comments on a syntactical feature. The opposition between their ideas is seen most clearly when they discuss the textbooks suitable to teach children. She mocks Lily's method, which Milton had endorsed, complaining that 'Lily's *Grammar* hath no more respect to the English than to the Welsh or Irish.' Yet many scorned Lily; this point does not establish that Makin was thinking particularly of Milton. What does seem specific to Milton is a favorite proverb. Milton's daughter Deborah told Thomas Birch that Milton often repeated the proverb, 'One tongue was enough for a woman,' a comment that Makin mocks in her essay:

> Many say one tongue is enough for a woman: it is but a quibble upon the word. Several languages understood by a woman will do our gentlemen little hurt who have little more than their mother-wit and understand only their mother-tongue: these most usually make this objection to hide their own ignorance.[18]

I need not labour the obvious: the proverb mocks the woman's body, while Makin's rebuttal uses her masculine rhetorical training. In this case, the proverb claims that to be a learned woman is to be a grotesque figure, many-tongued like Fama; Makin's education in the humanist system allows her to recognize a quibble as a quibble, match it with a further quibble about the 'mother tongue,' and dismiss the proverb with contempt. Our knowledge of Milton's attitude toward his daughters' education is complicated by their undoubted hostility toward their father. Nevertheless, according to his nephew Edward Phillips (who praised Milton's teaching of boys) Milton cared little about his daughters' education, and Phillips even claims that they were 'condemned' to read work in various languages 'without understanding one word.'[19] Makin and Milton had mutual friends: Pell, Hartlib and Dury all knew Milton and Makin. Pell, Makin's brother-in-law, had attended Cambridge at about the same time as Milton, and was Cromwell's agent in Switzerland in the 1660s; Hartlib, dedicatee of Milton's 'Of Education' mentions Makin several times in his manuscript *Ephemerides* (now at the University of Sheffield); Dury, who had dealt with Milton when he was Secretary of State, had been placed in charge of the education of the king's children when Makin was tutor to the Princess Elizabeth. Makin was in a good position to have met Milton, and he might have repeated the proverb in her presence; if not, their mutual acquaintance could have told her about the proverb.

Even if Makin does not have Milton in mind when she writes disparagingly of the proverb, she almost certainly is alluding to his essay when she writes about the way to teach children Latin. In *Accedence*, Milton altered Lily by changing the handling of agreement and verb forms. French thinks Milton's treatment of the 'three concords or kinds of agreement: subject with verb, adjective with noun, and relative pronoun with its antecedent' is a significant improvement over Lily (*CPW* 8, 'Introduction', 58, *Accedence* pp. 113–14) and 'perhaps most important is his handling of the *As in praesenti*,' or determination of verb forms (*CPW* 8: 59, 105–10). When Makin discusses a reformed way of teaching, she focuses in particular on precisely these points, viz., the concords and the *as in praesenti*:

> There are but three general rules for that part of grammar called the 'as in praesenti'; the irregular verbs, which most frequently occur in authors, in number about five hundred, are learned as a vocabulary.
>
> As to the syntax, the two first concords only are of use; and the rules for government (eight score in Lily's *Grammar*) are competently accommodated to the signs of the cases thus:
>
> Substantives have their cases by the signs, and they are governed of the word going before on which they depend, according to the signs 'of,' 'to,' 'for,' 'with,' 'from,' 'by,' 'than,' 'in,' 'at,' 'on,' 'a,' 'the.'

Four exceptions subjoined to this rule may make the syntax complete enough for a woman that intends only a superficial knowledge
in the tongue; ten more exceptions (that concern only particular
words) will make them as profound as most men are by Lily's
rules.[20]

Accedence, Milton's improved version of Lily, uses two pages to teach
children the concords; Makin dismisses his concern for agreement
between relative pronouns and antecedents and suggests that a
teacher tell the child to look at the case of the noun to determine
agreement (nominative if the noun is a subject; genitive, dative,
accusative or ablative depending on what preposition is intended).
Milton spends five pages on his improved system for determining how
to form the various principal parts of the verb. Makin would teach
three rules for regular verbs and have the pupils simply memorize the
irregular verbs. Certainly, Milton's method is the more thorough, and
those pupils who learn it will better understand how language
operates. Makin's method, however, will indeed make her students 'as
profound as most men are by Lily's rules.' Her rejection of precisely
those improvements that Milton put forward in his *Accedence*, coupled
with her refutation of his proverb, suggests that Makin is reacting
against Milton's work on education.

One woman who read and admired Milton was Mary Astell.[21] When
she was in her late twenties, she found herself alone in London and
nearly destitute, but determined to make her way by writing rather than
by teaching.[22] Her first work, *A Serious Proposal to the Ladies* (1694),
argues for an education different from that advocated by Milton or
Makin. Ruth Perry argues that Astell wanted women to have the
opportunity to study metaphysics, not language, for she thought that
'Mastery of ancient languages and a great range of books was mere
pedantry, useful for those who cared more about worldly knowledge
than about spiritual equilibrium' (p. 87). In this essay, she clearly rejects
the formulation of humanism that Milton had proposed and the
Comenian reforms that Makin had proposed. Unlike Milton and Makin,
both of whom think that one must study the classics and that education
leads one to a fuller role in public life, Astell rejects the classics and
embraces the academic retreat as an end in itself. Astell differs from
Milton and Makin in another way: both of them had taught, while she
had not. Despite these differences, her pamphlet, urging a community of
women dedicated to philosophical learning, owes an unacknowledged
debt to the ideas of both Milton and Makin.

In composing it, she clearly read others' works about education, although she specifies only William Wotton's *Reflections upon Ancient and Modern Learning* (1694), which she names (p. 78). Whether or not she had read Milton's essay 'Of Education,' her rationale is identical to Milton's: both argue that to be educated is better to understand God. She remarks that for women a retreat for education 'will be the introducing you into such a *Paradise* as your Mother *Eve* forfeited, ... Here are no Serpents to deceive you, ... and ... Men will resent it, to have ... Women invited to tast of that Tree of Knowledge they have so long unjustly *monopoliz'd*' (pp. 67, 87). He says that education is necessary to overcome the error of humankind's first parents and to understand most fully the beneficence of God. She too imagines students spending all their time contemplating and serving God.[23]

From this common starting place, they make very different proposals for a curriculum. Milton would have students study Latin and Greek, learn something about agriculture and medicine, and take vigorous physical exercise to train themselves as soldiers. The ultimate purpose for the education he proposes is that the students will enter the public sphere as informed and worthy citizens. Astell has no interest in language learning, although she does allow that French is useful for reading Descartes and Malebranche; she would have students study philosophy and theology, while their exercise is to be in performing 'spiritual and corporal Works of Mercy' (p. 89). The students she imagines do not enter the public sphere at all, although they may leave the academy for their own households as married women. One similarity in their plans is that both include music. After the students take wrestling lessons, Milton writes, they should refresh themselves with 'the solemn and divine harmonies of music heard or learned,' especially 'religious, martial, or civil ditties'; Astell's school will 'not only permit but recommend harmless and ingenious Diversions, Musick particularly, and such as may refresh the Body, without enervating the mind' (p. 93). Even the music each recommends is gendered in these schemes: in Milton's school the music will stir male students to public achievement in their 'religious, martial, or civil' duties; in Astell's, music will refresh female students from the fatigue of private study.

The difference in the curricula set out by the authors is indicative of their diverse objectives. Astell would have women kept away from the world to contemplate religion, while they either wait for an arranged marriage or learn to accept their spinsterhood. Her community of women (including 'Heiresses and Persons of Fortune') will live dedicated to study and devotion in

> a *Monastery*, or if you will (to avoid giving offense to the scrupulous and injudicious, by names which tho innocent in themselves, have been abus'd by superstitious Practices,) we will call it a *Religious Retirement*.[24]

For Astell, marriage and learning could not be reconciled. Female education is reserved seemingly for women, not girls, who have money. Milton would also leave the city and place his students in 'a spatious house and ground about it fit for an *Academy*', away from corruption as they learn 'to perform ... all the offices both private and publike of peace and war' (*CPW* 2: 378–9). However, his system is intended for boys, not men, and he does not demand that they be from wealthy families. Whether Astell knew Milton's essay, 'Of Education', before she wrote *A Serious Proposal to the Ladies*, she would undoubedly have found much in it with which she would have agreed. Both assume that education takes place most easily when students are isolated and celibate. They share the idea of an establishment in the country far removed from the usual social round.

In their insistence on retreating from the world, both Milton and Astell are unlike Makin, whom Astell probably had read as one of the few models available to her of a woman writing about education.[25] Like Makin, Astell begins with a dedicatory letter to a Princess when she writes the second part of her essay. Both try to answer obvious scepticism about their plans, such as the objection that educating women might make them ambitious for a greater place in the church. Astell rejects this idea:

> We pretend not that Women shou'd teach in the Church, or usurp Authority where it is not allow'd them; permit us only to understand our *own* duty, and not be forc'd to take it upon trust from others; to be at least so far learned, as to form in our own minds a true Idea of Christianity, it being so very necessary to fence us against the danger of these *last* and *perilous days*, in which Deceivers, a part of whose Character is, to *lead captive silly Women*, need not *creep into Houses*, since they have Authority to proclaim their Errors on the *House top*. (pp. 84–5)

Twenty years before, Makin too had defended the education of women as 'a hedge against heresies' saying, 'Heresiarchs creep into houses and lead silly women captive,' alluding to the passage from 2 Timothy 3:6 echoed in Astell. Other phrases in *A Serious Proposal* also echo Makin, suggesting that Astell was well aware of her predecessor. Astell writes about the importance of educating women, 'to furnish our minds with a stock of solid and useful Knowledge, that the Souls of Women may no longer be the only unadorn'd and neglected things' (p. 75). Makin also regards knowledge as adornment: 'If there be any persons so vain, as are yet pleased with this apish kind of breeding now in use, that desire their daughters should be outwardly dressed like puppets, rather than inwardly adorned with knowledge, let them enjoy their humor.' Astell insists 'it is not intended she shou'd spend her hours in learning *words* but *things*' (p. 77), a clear echo of Makin's 'My opinion is, in the educating of gentle-women, greater care ought to be had to know things than to get words.' Serious study will draw women away from 'Plays and Romances' in Astell (p. 83); 'cards, dice, plays, and frothy romances' in Makin. Makin will not mention all women who 'have been smatterers in learning', and has little patience with men who fear that women ought 'not by any means to be suffered to meddle with arts and tongues, lest by intolerable pride they should run mad'. Astell would agree, arguing that 'If any object against a Learned Education, that it will make Women vain and assuming, and instead of correcting, encrease their Pride: I grant, that a smattering in Learning may; for it has this effect on the Men' (p. 153). There can be little doubt that Astell has read and thought about Makin's work, but she rejects the bulk of the reforms that Makin proposed.

Astell reacts against the linguistic training that Makin proposes, as Makin reacts against the version of humanism that Milton proposes, and Milton reacts against Comenian reforms. The common topic of gendered educational reform receives disparate treatment as each fashions a voice distinct from the opposition and true to an intellectual position.

II

If these three essays are reactive, as I have argued, then the way each author shapes the essay's voice with regard to gender is conditioned by its context, the body of thought against which each essay reacts. Some features of these gendered authorial voices are predictable, but other features are not. Astell is reacting against both Comenian reformers and the humanist educators, since both insist not only upon the primacy of the classical tradition, but also upon the utility of their systems when a student leaves school to enter the public sphere (although Comenians and humanists defined that public sphere rather differently). Despite the Comenian claim that they intended their system to include women as well as men, Astell sees no benefit to women in either the classics or in public (i.e. patriarchal) society. Her focus is on women's needs as radically unlike those of men, and the voice she constructs is intended to be female. In *Timber, or Discoveries*, Jonson comments on what he would consider a feminine style:

> Others there are that have no composition at all, but a kind of tuning and rhyming fall in what they write. It runs and slides and only makes a sound. Women's poets they are called, as you have women's tailors. (p. 541)

This description corresponds closely to the style employed in Astell's essay. Specifically, her style is informal, voluble, conversational. Ruth Perry remarks of Astell:

> She punctuates for the rhythms of speech, which are choppier and more active than the rhythms of prose. She gives end stops to incomplete phrases and runs sentences together; she uses commas and semicolons in accord with the patterns of breath rather than syntax. (p. 101)

If a seventeenth-century masculine style reveals its author's classical education, Astell's conversational style reveals the lack of pedagogical training that she writes about. She can be amusing, for example, even acerbic about her observations:

> The *Beaux* perhaps, and topping Sparks of the Town, will ridicule and laugh at it [her plan]. For Vertue her self as bright as she is, can't escape the lash of scurrilous Tongues; the comfort is, whilst they impotently endeavour to throw dirt on her, they are unable to foil her Beauty, and only render themselves the more contemptible. They may therefore if they please, hug themselves in their own dear folly, and enjoy the diversion of their own insipid Jests. She has but little Wisdom and less Vertue, who is to be frighted from what she judges reasonable by the scoffs and insignificant noises of ludicrous Wits, and pert Buffoons (pp. 161–2)

Her tone is sharp. A contraction such as 'can't' and the pert diction ('topping Sparks' or 'hug themselves') clearly indicate the rhetorical situation. She does not speak dispassionately to her audience, but assumes her readers are others like herself rather than skeptics she must persuade. When she is sharp-tongued, however, she is not inveighing against a hostile auditor, but rather sharing an amusing observation with an intimate.

Another feature of gendered prose style in the early modern period that scholars often point to is anonymous publication. They argue that men published their work openly, but women were expected to mask their identity more discreetly. In all three of these essays, however, anonymity as an index of gender is misleading since all are ostensibly anonymous.[26] Neither Milton nor Astell's anonymity is difficult to penetrate, in keeping with the transparent gendering of the voices each uses. Thus, Astell wrote as 'a Lover of her SEX', a phrase establishing her womanliness; her disguise quickly slipped away when the pamphlet became popular since her bookseller willingly identified the author. Milton too names his friend Hartlib without hesitation; no one with any curiosity would have had difficulty learning his identity.

Makin's essay is also anonymous, but while Astell's anonymity is clearly gendered as feminine, thanks to the phrase 'a lover of her sex,' and Milton's is clearly masculine, Makin uses multiple voices, implicitly claiming both masculine and feminine identities. In one prefatory letter, she writes in the first person as a man who favours women's education:

> I am a man myself that would not suggest a thing prejudicial to our sex. To propose women rivals with us to learning will make us court Minerva more heartily, lest they should be more in her favour.

Her strategy is to employ the authority of an educated man (hence the classical allusion), and this voice is the one used most often in the essay. This voice, which affiliates itself with masculine education, is as much Makin's own as it is a voice gendered female. In contrast to this sympathetic voice, Makin constructs an oppositional male voice which lists objections to women's education. The objector is a blunt-spoken and ineloquent man:

> Women do not much desire knowledge; they are of low parts, soft fickle natures; they have other things to do they will not mind if they be once bookish; the end of learning is to fit one for public

employment, which women are not capable of. Women must not speak in church; it's against custom. Solomon's good housewife is not commended for arts and tongues, but for looking after her servants. And that which is worst of all, they are of such ill natures, they will abuse their education and be so intolerably proud, there will be no living with them. If all these things could be answered, they would not have leisure.

To answer these objections the advocate first rolls out long lists of learned women, next explains in detail what women ought to study and how they should be taught, and then gives specific responses that mock the objector:

> Objection: Women do not desire learning.
> Answer: Neither do many boys, as schools are now ordered, yet I suppose you do not intend to lay fallow all children, that will not bring forth fruit of themselves, to forbear to instruct those, which at present do not thank you for it.

Makin uses a woman's voice from time to time. When she discusses the reluctance of her pupil, the Dowager Countess, to be named as a learned woman, for instance, Makin writes: 'I am forbidden to mention the Countess Dowager of Huntingdon (instructed sometimes by Mrs. Makin) how well she understands Latin, Greek, Hebrew, French and Spanish; or what a proficient she is in arts, subservient to divinity, in which (if I durst I would tell you) she excels.' She refers to herself in the third person, to be sure, but clearly she does so facetiously in the course of teasing her student: this is her own voice. The voice slips into the feminine at another point when the speaker says of an objection that 'every thick-skulled fellow that babbles this out thinks no Billingsgate woman can answer it.' The speaker immediately goes on to answer it, and the clear implication is that the speaker is a woman, while the precise and clever answer denies the perjorative epithet 'Billingsgate.' Again when the speaker argues that Solomon's virtuous woman had to have been educated, the voice suggests that the speaker has first-hand knowledge of housewifery:

> To buy wool and flax, to dye scarlet and purple requires skill in natural philosophy. To consider a field, the quantity and quality, requires knowledge in geometry. To plant a vineyard requires understanding in husbandry. She could not merchandize without

knowledge in arithmetic. She could not govern so great a family well without knowledge in politics and economics. She could not look well to the ways of her household, except she understood physic and chirurgery. She could not open her mouth with wisdom and have in her tongue the law of kindness, unless she understood grammar, rhetoric, and logic. This seems to be the description of an honest, well-bred, ingenious, industrious Dutchwoman.

The fundamental voice in this essay is that of a parent: the speaker uses 'daughter' 40 times, for example, twice as often as 'wife' or 'wives' (20 times), almost twice as often as 'husband' (23 times), and five times as often as 'son' (8 times). The shifts from masculine advocate or objector to feminine advocate to concerned parent are in keeping with Makin's cultural position: educated and working in the way an early modern man was, married and mothering as an early modern woman, teaching and writing as someone who is rhetorically hermaphroditical. Nor is the anonymity very secure.[27] As with the other essays, anyone seeking the identity of the author would be able to learn it easily. Frequent mention is made of individuals who could identify the author. In addition to the bookseller, the essay names Makin's colleague, Mark Lewis, and her students: Lucy Davies Hastings, Dowager Countess of Huntingdon; and Dr Love's daughters. Finally, the essay names Makin herself four times, a broad hint about the author.

Makin is well aware of the gender issues raised by women's education: she writes far more argumentatively than either Milton or Astell and assumes there will be greater opposition to her position. Makin is not hostile to the company of other women; her catalogues suggest she hungered for other women like herself. Her adoption of a masculine voice for her advocate shows she is no misanthrope either. Neither Milton nor Astell is willing to allow their opposition a voice, but Makin does. Because the objector as well as the advocate, the male as well as the female, has a voice in Makin's essay, she makes room, in a way that no other essayist did until this century, for the idea that learning really is for all and that it cannot be distributed by gender.

Throughout *An Essay*, she addresses the importance of having a housewife who can use her knowledge to benefit her family and children. The usual argument was that learning should be reserved for women without family responsibilities, a position that Makin certainly recognizes and partially assents to when she agrees that education best suits women of independence and means. Nevertheless, she returns to her insistence on the importance of learning in marriage, both in reference to the actions of married women during the Civil War and Commonwealth and in her doubled analysis of Solomon's housewife. With this insistence, Makin breaks from other advocates of educating women; her position is that a learned woman does not have to live homosocially within Christine de Pizan's 'city of ladies,' as one of Anna Maria van Schurman's 'learned maids,' or in Astell's 'monastery.'

Makin writes as a hermaphrodite, constructing masculine and feminine identities within herself: she had lived as an intellectual hermaphrodite because of her learning. As a girl she had wrestled with the male-gendered subjects of Latin and Greek (to say nothing of Hebrew and Syriac), but her work was invariably singled out for notice because of her feminine body.[28] As an adult, she had earned her own living like a man, but had stopped publishing while she was a married woman. As a widow in 1673, she resumes her publication and does so with a double voice. The masculine voice expresses a strong belief that although some men, like the objector, attack women, others enthusiastically defend women. The feminine voice expresses indifference toward men's attitudes and enthusiasm for other women like herself.

To argue for learning, she draws upon learning, providing an inventory culled from her reading of women who had been distinguished for their learning. This conventional practice may seem both tedious and inaccurate to a twentieth-century reader; at least I have found no one who praises it. Hobby notes that 'The text is not particularly orderly,' and Mitzi Myers calls it 'thin.'[29] Makin's catalogue simply lists with no attempt to analyse the quality of its exemplars, many of whom are inadequately described. The catalogue is put together from other catalogues rather than from primary research into the women it names. Today Makin's influence seems slight, yet she expands the lists she would have found in other catalogues to include herself and her circle. She clearly regards herself as part of the tradition, and an important part at that, because she uses her reputation as a teacher and her colleagues' and students' success to establish the need to educate women. The voice that presents the catalogues is deliberately multiple: a man who admires women, a woman who seeks models for herself, a scholar placing herself in a scholarly tradition.

If I am correct about Makin's hermaphroditical voice, several things become clear. Her use of male voices in her essay is not simply a disguise to protect her modesty, as Elaine Hobby suggests, but rather the exercise of the voice in which she had herself been trained.[30] Humanist rhetorical training often employed exercises that required students to argue a point for and against, to try out various voices in *imitatio*.[31] Moreover, humanist education is gendered male. To argue against humanism, or rather to argue for the reform of humanism, then, Makin draws on that early training, modifying it with her woman's voice from time to time.[32] What critics have sometimes seen as inconsistency may in fact be part of a rhetorical style that seems anomalous to modern readers because so few early modern Englishwomen underwent a humanist training. Furthermore, if she is consciously reacting to Milton, it is precisely the mixture of voices that she employs that corresponds to her central point about women's ability to learn. Makin argues that women are capable of learning just as men do, and she uses a male voice to make this argument; she also argues that education can include both men and women, and she uses both male and female voices in that argument. Milton and Astell, arguing for homosocial education, employ single-gender vocies.

What is at stake in this argument about education is no longer of great concern: neither classicism nor metaphysics is apt to regain the centre of our educational system. But what this analysis does offer is a new way of considering other writers who fell into that relatively small group of early modern women with a humanist education. While few were as learned as Makin, the idea of the hermaphrodite's voice that I have proposed might apply to some extent to them as well and might shed light on particular elements in their work that have been regarded as problems. One might consider, for example, Margaret More Roper's letter to Lady Alington; the dialogue includes sections in her father's voice as well as her own, and analyses have argued that 'it is not certainly knowen' whether she or her father wrote it or whether it is a 'joint effort.'[33] Possibly, however, we see here another instance of rhetorical hermaphroditism. Again, scholars have been troubled by Elizabeth Jocelyn's advice book for her unborn child, in which she outlines an educational system modelled on her own humanist training if the child is a son, but urges her husband to limit the education if the child is a daughter; again, the very training that Jocelyn received may have resulted in a male-gendered rejection of extending that education to her daughter. Another instance of a humanist-trained women is Queen Elizabeth; one might re-examine her use of the doctrine of the monarch's two bodies in light of the training that provided her with a male as well as a female voice. The multiple voices found in such women's writing are constructed from their experience: educated as men, reared as women, they can claim both male and female voices as authentic. In *The Tempest* when Stephano finds a monster of the beach, he complains that it has two voices: 'Four legs and two voices, – a most delicate monster! His forward voice, now, is to speak well of his friend; his backward voice is to utter foul speeches and to detract' (2.2.91–4). Yet both voices are the actual voice of the 'delicate monster'. So too is the male voice heard in the work of educated early modern women.

Notes

1. I shall cite these texts: for Milton, the text edited by Donald Dorian in *The Complete Prose Works of John Milton* (henceforth cited as *CPW*), Don Wolfe, general editor (New Haven, Conn.: Yale University Press, 1959), 2: pp. 357–415; for Makin, the text I have edited for *Bathsua Makin: Woman of Learning* (Lewisburg, PA: Bucknell University Press, 1999); and for Astell, the first edition of *A Serious Proposal to the Ladies, For the Advancement of Their True and Greatest Interest* (London: Richard Wilkins, 1694). (Later editions conflate Astell's original essay with her continuation in Part Two.) A useful abridged version may be found in *The First English Feminist: Reflections upon Marriage and Other Writings by Mary Astell*, ed. Bridget Hill (New York: St. Martin's Press, 1986), pp. 135–72.
2. Useful works about hermaphroditism in the seventeenth century are Marie Delcourt, *Hermaphrodite* (Paris: PGF, 1958); Mircea Eliade, *The Two and the One* (New York: Sheed and Ward, 1965); Jean Brink et al., eds, *Playing with Gender* (Urbana: University of Illinois Press, 1991); Grace Tiffany, *Erotic Beasts and Social Monsters* (Newark: University of Delaware Press, 1995). Useful for my own argument is Vincent Crapanzo, '"Self"-Centering Narratives', *Yale Journal of Criticism* 5.3 (1992), pp. 61–79.
3. Margaret Ferguson, 'Renaissance Concepts of the "Woman Writer"', in *Women and Literature in Britain 1500–1700*, ed. Helen Wilcox (Cambridge: Cambridge University Press, 1996), p. 152.
4. Information about Makin's life can be found in Jean Brink, 'Bathusa Reginald Makin: Most Learned Matron,' *Huntington Library Quarterly* 54 (1991), pp. 313–27; Frances Teague, 'The Identity of Bathsua Makin', *Biography* 16 (1993), pp. 1–17; and my biography of Makin, *Bathsua Makin, Woman of Learning*.
5. Sir Simonds D'Ewes, *The Autobiography and Correspondence of Sir Simonds D'Ewes, Bart*, ed. J.O. Halliwell (London: Richard Bentley, 1845), 1: p. 63.
6. On the 'masculinity' of learning languages, especially Latin, see Walter Ong, *Orality and Literacy: The Technologizing of the Word* (London: Methuen, 1982). For a modification of this view, see Jane Stevenson's essay in this volume. For contemporary accounts of Princess Elizabeth's learning, see the assessments in William Greenhill, *An Exposition of the First Five Chapters of Ezekiel* (London: 1645); Alexander Rowley, *The Schollers Companion* (London: 1648); Samuel Torshell, *The Womans Glorie: A Treatise, Asserting the Due Honour of that Sexe, and Directing Wherein that Honour Consists* (London: 1645); Christopher Wase, *Electra of Sophocles* (Hague: 1649).

7. Anne Killigrew, 'Upon the Saying that My Verses Were Written by Another,' in *Kissing the Rod*, ed. Germaine Greer et al. (New York: Farrar, Strauss, Giroux, 1989), pp. 303–5.

8. Ben Jonson, 'On the Court Pucelle,' in *Ben Jonson: The Complete Poems*, ed. George Parfitt (New Haven, Conn.: Yale University Press, 1982). See also my discussion of the issue of women writers and sexuality in Robert Evans and Anne Little, eds., *'The Muses Females Are'* (West Cornwall, Conn.: Locust Hill Press, 1995), pp. 173–9.

9. Quoted in *The Poetry of Lady Mary Wroth*, ed. Josephine Roberts (Baton Rouge: Louisiana State University, 1983), pp. 32–3.

10. Ernest Sirluck's account of Milton's relations with the Comenians, *CPW*, 2: 184–216, is excellent; Wolfe provides other background, *CPW*, 1: 151–66.

11. Johan Amos Comenius, *A Reformation of Schooles*, translated by Samuel Hartlib (London, 1642), p. 92.

12. Donald French provides the introduction to *Accedence Commenc't Grammar*, *CPW* 8: 31–128; Walter Ong to *A Fuller Course in the Art of Logic*, *CPW* 8: 139–407.

13. 'Preface' to *Accidence*, ed. R.C. Alston (Menston: Scolar Press, 1971). This edition is an unpaginated facsimile of Wing M2088.

14. 'The most impressive defender of the older values was, of course, John Milton, whose work subsumed the whole history of humanism in one grand restatement at the moment of its demise.' O.B. Hardison, *English Literary Criticism: The Renaissance* (New York: Appleton-Century-Crofts, 1963), p. 11.

15. G.H. Turnbull, *Hartlib, Dury and Comenius* (London: Hodder and Stoughton for the University Press of Liverpool, 1947), p. 39. Charles Webster, ed., *Samuel Hartlib and the Advancement of Learning* (Cambridge: Cambridge University Press, 1970) also discusses Milton's standing among the Hartlib circle, pp. 41–3.

16. Hilda L. Smith, 'Humanist Education and the Renaissance Concept of Women', in *Women and Literature in Britain 1500–1700*, ed. Helen Wilcox (Cambridge: Cambridge University Press, 1996): pp. 10–11. In this collection, both Smith and Margaret Ferguson address explicitly humanism as a school of thought that gestures toward including women, while ultimately excluding them. To have a thorough humanist education, as Makin has, is to be masculine intellectually, whatever one's cultural identification might be. See also Mary Ellen Lamb's interesting discussion of the misogyny to be found in humanist writing about women's education, 'The Cooke Sisters: Attitudes toward Learned Women in the Renaissance,' in *Silent but for the Word: Tudor Women as Patrons, Translators and Writers of Religious Works*, ed. Margaret Hannay (Kent, Ohio: Kent State University Press, 1985), pp. 107–25.

17. J.R. Brink, 'Bathsua Makin: Educator and Linguist,' in *Female Scholars: A Tradition of Learned Women before 1800* (Bloomington: Indiana University Press, 1980): 'Milton's neglect of women's place in the educational scheme of things, with other imponderables, in that plenum of wise and civil speech, his tractate *Of Education* was effectively answered (but probably only coincidentally) by a satiric feminist tract [by] Bathsua Reginald Makin'. J.L. Helms, 'Bathsua Makin's *An Essay to Revive the Antient Education of*

Gentlewomen in the Canon of Seventeenth-Century Educational Reform Tracts,' *Cahiers Elisabethains,* 44 (1993), pp. 45–51.

18. Helen Darbishire, *The Early Lives of Milton* (New York: Barnes and Noble, 1965), pp. lviii–li.

19. Christopher Hill points out that the saying 'One tongue is enough for any woman' is proverbial and one must be cautious about accepting what his daughters reported; he therefore doubts that Milton would have said such a thing seriously. I think he did, and that Makin is answering him here. Christopher Hill, *Milton and the English Revolution* (NewYork: Viking Press, 1977), p. 144.

20. As her essay makes clear, Makin recommends a grammar system based on Comenian principles, set down in textbooks by Mark Lewis, her partner in the school she proposed to establish for girls.

21. See Joseph Wittreich, *Feminist Milton* (Ithaca, NY: Cornell University Press, 1987), p. xvi, although elsewhere in his book he assumes Astell had reservations about Milton (pp. 52–3). Perry sees no reservations: she argues that Astell accepts Milton's ideas about the hierarchy of the sexes (p. 165).

22. Ruth Perry, *The Celebrated Mary Astell* (Chicago: University of Chicago Press, 1986), p. 64.

23. Makin certainly would agree on the connection between education and religion, although she has less to say about original sin or the pleasures of metaphysics than either Milton or Astell. On the subject of Adam and Eve, Makin refers to a dialogue by Isotta Nogarula that suggests Adam was more at fault than Eve and comments that opponents to women's education operate 'as Satan against Adam, by seducing our women, who then easily seduce their husbands.'

24. Astell, p. 61. Perry discusses the monastery idea, pp. 131–6.

25. Lady Elizabeth Hastings was Astell's patron. It is tempting to speculate that Astell read the Hastings' family copy of Makin's essay before she wrote her own essay. (Makin taught Lucy Hastings, Countess of Huntingdon, as well as two of her children, Elizabeth and Theophilus.) Since Lady Elizabeth and Mary Astell had not met (their first recorded contact is in 1714; Perry, p. 263), that possibility is remote.

26. Another womanly method was to use a pseudonym ('Eliza') or to insist that publication was done without her knowledge (Anne Bradstreet or Katherine Philips). Scribal publication, the circulation of unprinted manuscripts, also solved the need for ostensible modesty.

27. Elaine Hobby, *English Women's Writing 1649–88* (Ann Arbor: University of Michigan Press, 1988), raises the possibility that Makin did not write the essay, but that seems unlikely. As Hobby points out, the essay employs a woman's perspective throughout. The only likely male candidate for authorship, Mark Lewis, is mentioned in the closing pages and his textbooks are paraphrased in the syntax discussion. Yet Lewis never hesitated to publish under his own name, so there is no reason for him to have published this essay anonymously.

28. See, for example, the title-page for her poetry book, *Musa Virginea Graeco. Latino. Gallica* (London, 1616), or George Eglisham's poem on her as 'eruditiones eximiae virgini' (an exceptionally learned virgin), in *Duellum*

Poeticum, Contendibus G. Eglisemmio et G. Buchanano pro Dignitate Paraphraseos Psalmi (London, 1619).

29. Mitzi Myers, 'Domesticating Minerva: Bathsua Makin's "Curious" Argument for Women's Education,' *Studies in Eighteenth-Century Culture* 14 (1985), p. 174.
30. Hobby, p. 199.
31. See, for example, the comments on *imitatio* in Roger Ascham's *The Scholemaster* (1570) and the rhetorical exercises proposed by Thomas Wilson in *The Arte of Rhetorique* (1553).
32. 'By being able to present herself as an educated man, her text symbolically foreshadows its own objective: the lessening of the educational gulf between men and women. Here androgyny articulates its own sexual challenge.' Catherine Sharrock, 'De-ciphering Women and De-scribing Authority: The Writings of Mary Astell,' in Isobel Grundy and Susan Wiseman, eds, *Women, Writing, and History 1640–1740* (Athens, Ga: University of Georgia Press, 1992), p. 110.
33. See Elizabeth McCutcheon's discussion, 'Margaret More Roper', in *Women Writers of the Renaissance and Reformation*, ed. Katharina Wilson (Athens, Ga: University of Georgia Press, 1987), especially pp. 462–4, pp. 472–5.

Index